W9-CBH-462

DATE			
MAY 0 2 1990			
APR 2 4 1996			

IMPROVING PRODUCTIVITY THROUGH ADVANCED OFFICE CONTROLS

IMPROVING PRODUCTIVITY THROUGH ADVANCED OFFICE CONTROLS

Robert E. Nolan

Richard T. Young

Ben C. DiSylvester

amacom

A Division of American Management Associations

Library of Congress Cataloging in Publication Data

Nolan, Robert E

Improving productivity through advanced office controls.

Includes index.

1. Office management. I. Young, Richard T., joint
author. II. DiSylvester, Ben C., joint author.
III. Title.
HF5547.N57   651.3   80-65705
ISBN 0-8144-5617-0

First Printing

Foreword

"May you always work for a demanding boss."

AN ANCIENT EASTERN CURSE? No, a blessing for my children, and yours. May they always serve under leaders who demand the best they can give! May they—may you and I—always work for leaders who are strong. Not stern, *strong*.

Who is this strong boss? One who sets high standards, who communicates them clearly, and who administers them judiciously and fairly. One who demands the best of you, and then helps you bring it about. One who encourages you to risk and to stretch. One who has faith in your ability to surpass yourself.

Let's give this strong boss an ideal employee. Who is this perfect employee? At bottom, one who does what the job requires—but does it in a particular way. One whose competence gently deepens and broadens. One who searches, without letup, for ways to do it better. One whose drive for greater competence seems to be an inborn process. One who habitually competes against the accomplishments of the past.

Ideal bosses and perfect subordinates need not be rare creatures. Certainly there are more applicants than ever before. Our society sends forth prospective jobholders with higher aspirations and sharper mental equipment than their predecessors had. What must be done to nourish these talented people and make them into strong leaders and committed followers? To be sure, some impediments must be removed, especially preoccupation with today's hotspot problems and immediate results, and inadequate training. But what then, after the housecleaning? The unmistakable need is for attention to the basics of the job itself—a cleanly defined job with sensible performance standards and results that are accurately measured and justly rewarded.

This book, with the correct but lifeless title of *Improving Productivity Through Advanced Office Controls,* can be the wellspring for organizational life. It will show you how to create jobs that are challenging, rewarding, and nourishing. And it will portray the craft involved in aligning tasks and work standards. It will show you how to go about creating families of jobs that are intrinsically sound and thus are breeding grounds for strong leaders and energetic, committed employees. Further, it provides insight into the development of control techniques for monitoring the organization's effectiveness in providing service at a reasonable cost while providing opportunities for its employees.

Robert E. Nolan and his coauthors are supremely qualified to write this book. They have mastered the mechanics; they are craftsmen. And they know the purpose of their work. They speak from experience: Their daily work involves translating dry science into human change. They have learned what works and what doesn't, what convinces and what bothers employees. They see the interconnectedness of their domain with the rest of management. They are out to improve the world, not reform it.

Bring to this book your own inner urgings to see a better, healthier, more productive world of work. Bring to this book your own need to bestow upon your subordinates the blessing of the opportunity to work for a demanding boss.

DR. JAMES GATZA, CPCU
Director of Management Education
American Institute of Property &
Liability Underwriters
(Malvern, Pennsylvania)

Preface

THIS BOOK IS WRITTEN at a time when inflation is running rampant throughout the Western world. Our very survival will depend on how we cope with this problem. We believe that the only effective way to fight inflation is to improve productivity. To do so, however, requires good management. And that is what this book is about. Specifically, this book is about office management and how office managers can get the maximum benefit from the resources available.

The authors recently conducted a survey involving more than 200 chief executive officers of banks and insurance companies. One of the questions asked was: "Where, in your opinion, is the greatest area for cost savings in your company?" The top choice of 89 percent of those polled was "Better management of time and people."

There are two major stumbling blocks to productivity improvements in offices. First, the analysis and organization needed for productivity improvement—so commonplace in the industrial and manufacturing sectors—are noticeably lacking in the office. Second, productivity in the office is simply harder to measure, and thus harder to improve. It is estimated that by 1985, 75 percent of the U.S. economy will be service-oriented and/or involved in information processing. The rise in the number of workers in the service sector is one of the reasons why productivity gains are getting harder and harder to come by. It is also one of the major reasons we all must do what is necessary to improve the productivity of this growing segment of the work force.

Neither of these problems, however, is insurmountable. The major hurdle is convincing office managers and supervisors to think like their manufacturing counterparts—to automatically view a task in terms of the organization, incentives, technology, and skills which will improve productivity. What is needed is not more energy to perform tasks but rather more managerial imagination and innovation to make the necessary tasks easier to perform.

This book is designed to be helpful to a wide audience: executives, managers, supervisors, and work study analysts in all sectors of business, as well as anyone who takes part in the development or use of office systems. The contents will provide the reader with a thorough understanding of the various techniques and approaches that are available.

Advanced Office Controls is several things. First and foremost, it is a unique approach to presenting the concept of accountability in an acceptable way to all levels of the organization. It is an approach that has proved successful in more than 100 companies in the United States. Second, it is a proprietary standard data system, or predetermined time system, of the Robert E. Nolan Company, Inc.—and, we believe, the most advanced system available today. Third, it is a set of practical techniques enabling the modern manager to look at the people in a work situation in a realistic way and improve organizational effectiveness.

This book presents various proven techniques and approaches for improving productivity in offices. There is no singular approach or technique that is best for every type of office situation. However, we hope to have presented the alternatives in such a way that the reader can easily recognize the most practical approach for his or her situation.

The text is divided into four parts. Part I, Managing the Modern Office, develops the concept of accountability and shows that it is inherent in the very principles of management. Accountability is traced through all levels of the organization, including the worker. The major focus is on the all-important job of the supervisor and the skills and techniques necessary to get the job done well.

Part II, Techniques for Improving Office Productivity, examines many of the most accepted ways to improve work and the various approaches to setting standards. This part carries the development of the concept of accountability in Part I through to practical application based on the use of performance standards and other controls.

Part III, Designing and Implementing the Program, explains how to plan, announce, and implement a results-oriented program for productivity improvement. It shows how to evaluate and select the techniques for setting standards, announce the program, conduct a study, and develop feedback reporting systems.

Part IV, Using the Data, covers the practical part of getting results from a productivity improvement program. This section deals with the critical role of management in getting good results, how to use the data generated by the program to plan ahead, how to reward employees whose contribution warrants special recognition, and how other major functions such as cost accounting and personnel can benefit from a well-conceived and properly implemented program. The impact of new technology on the management techniques discussed is also covered.

This book is a major step in explaining to all levels of management how to improve office productivity. It tells in plain English how to determine the right program, how to present it to all levels, and how to get the best results.

ROBERT E. NOLAN
RICHARD T. YOUNG
BEN DiSYLVESTER

Contents

PART

MANAGING
THE MODERN OFFICE

1

Management and the Concept of Accountability

WHEN AN ORGANIZATION grows from a single-person entrepreneurship to two or more people, all the forces and situations that call on the principles of management are immediately set into motion. Whereas the single entrepreneur is answerable only to himself (except, perhaps, to creditors), the larger companies that we are all so familiar with must begin to divide tasks, communicate goals, and experience all the events that naturally occur when individuals and groups of workers interact.

The company that does the best job of organizing is not necessarily the one that will be the leader in its field. Rather, it is the company that gets results, measured in terms of profitability, that survives. The more a company maximizes its profitability, the more it grows. It does this by being successful in its marketing efforts, in managing its finances, and in handling customer and administrative services.

When we say a company maximizes its profitability, what we really mean is that the people who are responsible for the key areas of the company are doing their jobs successfully. It is people who make up companies, and those people performing inside the framework of the organization determine how well the company does. Since people have varying abilities and varying views on what must be done to accomplish the goals of the company, we are reminded of the familiar definition of management: "getting things done through other people." This directly determines why some companies succeed and others fail. The more skilled and successful the leaders in the company are in getting things done through other people, the more successful the company will be. Because businesses, as an aggregate, make up our

3

country's economy, and our economy determines the standard of living for our population, each supervisor and manager has an obligation to understand the role of management and carry out that role to the best of his or her ability.

ORGANIZATION

In order to make sense out of the complex structure of the larger companies, it is necessary to first examine how they are organized. Because organizations are made up of people, it is difficult to separate the two. However, we will look at the people aspects of organization once we have examined the principles which govern the concept of organization.

Principles of Organization

In the early stages of a company's evolution—that is, when only one person is involved—organizational structure is very simple: the entrepreneur does it all. Marketing, financing decisions, and servicing are accomplished by the same person. However, because time is a limiting factor, that individual can accomplish only so much, no matter how well organized and efficient he or she is. When the saturation point is reached, the only way growth can occur is to add more time by "getting help," or adding people. Once that decision is made, the next questions to be answered are, Who does what? How will people be organized? The larger the company, the more complex the organizational structure.

With the Industrial Revolution came the age of specialization through the division of labor. In other words, when work is divided, it is best to take advantage of specialized knowledge and skills by putting all similar functions together in one organizational unit. Similarity of functions is an underlying principle of all modern organizations.

There is an inverse relationship between size of a company and similarity of job functions. In smaller companies, a department or individual will have more varied tasks than in larger companies. The larger the organization, the less varied a department's or individual's job is apt to be.

For example, in a small life insurance company, there may be one customer service department that handles all types of service requests, such as paying premiums, making a policy loan, changing an address, or changing a beneficiary. In a larger life insurance company, there may be one department whose sole function is to change addresses. If you want a policy loan, the policy loan department will handle that request. Similarly, in states where branch banking is allowed by law, the main office of a bank will have a mortgage loan department and a collections department, whereas in one of the bank's smaller branches, the branch manager may perform both of those functions, plus fill in at the teller window occasionally.

Layers of Organization

The principle of similarity of function is evident throughout the organization. Beginning with the company itself—today's conglomerates notwithstanding—each corporate unit is usually organized to provide similar or related products and services. Exxon's function is to provide energy-related products and services. Prudential Insurance Company is organized to provide insurance products and services or, as some insurance companies term it, financial security. Chase Manhattan Bank provides financial services.

Within each company, the first level of organization is the division. At this level, all the major functions are divided into logical administrative units usually based on, but not limited to, product, service, customer, or geographical area. In some companies, divisions are set up for marketing, financial, customer service, legal and administrative services, or some combination of these. In larger companies, divisions are based on product lines or geographical location. General Motors is a combination of both product line divisions, such as Chevrolet, Oldsmobile, and Pontiac, and divisions based on geographical location, such as its Overseas Division.

In order to facilitate meeting the objectives of each division, it is usually necessary for companies to subdivide their divisions into departments, where specialists are gathered into similar disciplines. In a financial division, it is not unusual to find an accounting department and an investment department. In divisions based on geographical or product lines, you find personnel departments, marketing departments, accounting departments, and service departments, to name a few.

As departments grow, they too must be divided into administrative "units." Here, the specialization becomes even greater. In a personnel department you have payroll units, employment units, benefits units, and training units, as examples.

The organizational layers can be taken one step further to the employee level. Specialization is the name of the game for best effectiveness in larger companies. In our personnel department example, the sole responsibility of one particular individual in the employment unit may be to input data into the employee history file, while another individual is strictly a receptionist, and another conducts interviews. In the smaller company one individual will perform all these functions and others as well.

Division of Labor

The underlying concept of organization is division of labor. Because most companies are so complex, it is unreasonable to expect any one person to know everything about running a company. For one thing, there isn't enough time in the day. Administratively, one person could not effectively manage in an environment that is too diverse. Proper attention could not be devoted to all the different things that would need to be worked on. Therefore, to facilitate higher productivity of the organization, the tasks must be divided among many people.

Once labor is divided, however, certain "problems" arise. Communication becomes important. When a craftsperson begins to build a cabinet, he or she knows the desired end result and works toward that end result at all times. If one person works on just the doors while another works on just the drawers, they will have little knowledge of the total end product in terms of size, color, and so on, and quality problems are apt to arise. If the door specialist must wait for the hinge specialist before the assembly specialist can put it all together, everyone must know and work toward the promised date for delivering the cabinet. Productivity, sense of accomplishment, service, and quality could all be negatively affected by the division of labor. Effective management through good communication will minimize the negative effects.

Among the advantages of the division of work is the fact that skills can be developed more quickly because of the smaller range of skills needed and the shorter work cycles. As a result, it costs less to develop skills. It is easier to find people to do the work under these conditions. Another major advantage of the division of work is that the different operations necessary to achieve an objective can be performed concurrently.

One of the disadvantages of the division of labor is that the further the division goes, the less flexible the organization becomes. An interdependency among all the jobs is created, and coordination becomes difficult. Workers have difficulty recognizing the overall objective of the job, because they see only a very small part of the total.

MANAGEMENT

Organizational structure itself can do nothing. It is only the people in that structure who can accomplish things. The structure merely facilitates or hinders people from accomplishing stated objectives. (Sometimes it does both concurrently.) It becomes readily apparent that the higher up in the organization a person works, the more of a generalist he or she must be, and the less important knowledge about the day-to-day operation becomes. Therefore, the higher one progresses in the organization, the more one must depend on other people to meet the objectives or to fulfill the purpose of that organizational unit. Ultimately, it is management, good or bad, that steers the organization on its course.

Line and Staff

There is yet another type of division of work that expands the organization chart: that between line and staff. Line is usually defined as that part of the organization that is responsible for achieving the primary objectives of the organization. Staff is that part of the organization that prepares the way for the line people to accomplish their goals. Many people feel that there is always friction between line and staff, because of staff's apparent infringement on line's authority. However, we look at the line and staff functions differently.

Both line and staff should work toward achieving the objectives of the organization. In fact, no activity or organizational unit should be created unless it contributes to the achievement of the organization's primary objectives. There is no inherent friction between these two organizational structures, only the potential for friction because of lack of understanding or communication.

However, there are major differences between line and staff. The biggest difference is that of orientation. Everyone in the organization should be working toward the success of the organization. Line is trying to get the work out. It is responsible for production. Line's orientation comes from the fact that, more often than not, line people are technically more knowledgeable about their own specific area or work. Most line supervisors and managers came up through the ranks. Line is accountable to deliver the end product, whether it be a completed piece of equipment, an insurance policy, or the clearance of all the checks drawn on the bank earlier in the day.

Staff's orientation is toward cost-effectiveness, control, and good management principles. In all cases, however, staff has, or should have, no authority to direct line to do something. Rather, line people are so busy getting the work out that they need help in gathering and evaluating data and in implementing better ways to manage. Staff's contribution is to advise line about more efficient and effective ways to operate.

The problems between line and staff arise from some very identifiable sources. the feeling on line's part that staff is out to make line people look bad; staff's erroneous attitude that line doesn't know what it is doing when it comes to management; and misuse of staff by top management, which gives staff either too little backing and support or too much power.

Line is responsible for getting the work out. Staff is responsible for assisting line people to do their jobs by providing expertise in workflow, personnel practices, productivity measurement, marketing techniques, auditing procedures, or whatever specialty staff may be organized to provide. In no case should staff have authority to direct or require line to follow its recommendations. Line's function is strictly advisory. On the other side, line should be responsible to evaluate staff recommendations objectively rather than summarily reject or ignore them.

Since staff has no power to command, it should have an avenue of appeal for recommendations that are thought to be valuable to the goals of the organization. Skilled staff people and dedicated line people minimize the need to appeal to higher levels of the organization if they both keep the good of the organization in mind.

History

In the early 1900s, in the wake of the Industrial Revolution, there began to emerge the concepts of management as we know them today. Up to this time, the boss merely ordered and/or threatened the worker to produce. However, Frederick W. Taylor, after observing inefficiencies and the ineffectiveness of that style of management, formulated what he called scientific management.[1] Taylor identified four steps to scientific management.

1. Reduce knowledge of work to rules, laws, and formulas.
2. Study the workers for the purpose of selecting the right person for the job and training that person properly.
3. Bring together the science and the worker by making it worthwhile to the worker to do the job the right way.
4. Divide the work so that management has its duties, which are planning and preparing, and the workers have theirs, which is carrying out those plans.

What Taylor's principles amount to is that each worker should be given a specific job to be performed in a specific manner, with a specific time allotted to accomplish that job. Taylor spent considerable energy developing the time it should take to do the job.

At about this time, another school of management thought was being developed by Frank and Lillian Gilbreth. Their approach was to analyze the method that was used to perform each task, and to simplify the job by eliminating unnecessary or wasted motions.

While Taylor pointed out that work should be divided into those activities that the worker should perform and those activities that management should perform, Henri Fayol formulated the basic elements of management.[2] The five elements identified by Fayol are planning, organizing, commanding, coordinating, and controlling.

Although current management has made some revisions to Fayol's basic elements, they remain essentially the same today. The changes are primarily ones of emphasis or application, prompted by the fact that Fayol never considered the human element in his principles. Fayol also identified 14 principles of management:

1. *Division of work.* Fayol advocated this for purposes of increased efficiency. However, although this principle was identified by others as being important for the hourly workers, Fayol applies the principle to all levels of the organization.

---

[1]*The Principles of Scientific Management*, William E. Schlender, William G. Scott, and Alan C. Filley, reprinted in *Management in Perspective: Selected Readings*, Boston: Houghton Mifflin, 1965, pp. 19–33.

[2]*General and Industrial Management*, London: Pitman & Sons, 1949.

2. *Authority*. This principle applies to the manager's right to give orders.

3. *Discipline*. Emphasis is on fairness.

4. *Unity of command*. A subordinate should have to serve only one superior.

5. *Unity of direction*. Though similar to the fourth principle, this applies to the work rather than individuals. This principle states that the work activities of a group should have only one plan and only one leader for maximum organizational effectiveness.

6. *Subordination of the individual interest to the general interest*. This principle means that the firm comes first and the individual or smaller group within the firm comes second.

7. *Fair remuneration*. Fayol believed that remuneration should be equitable and should be satisfactory to both the company and the individual employee.

8. *Centralization of authority*. This principle was not rigidly defined by Fayol. Since centralization means a reduction of authority and responsibility of employees, the degree of centralization is dependent on the specific situation in which this principle is applied.

9. *Scalar chain*. Fayol identified this principle with lines of authority. He said that exact lines of authority should be established from bottom to top of the organization. These lines should be clearly defined between successive levels of management.

10. *Order*. This principle means that both things and people should have a specific place in the organization. It applies to people through the organization chart, which shows where each person belongs in the organization and the relative position to other employees in the organization.

11. *Equity*. To Fayol, this meant that all practices and policies would be applied equally to all individuals and groups. The two ingredients in this principle are kindliness and justice.

12. *Stability of tenure of personnel*. Fayol said this principle is desirable for all levels of the organization. The emphasis he placed on this principle is exhibited in his belief that it is better to have ineffective managers with tenure than a series of brilliant managers with high turnover.

13. *Initiative*. As viewed by Fayol, this applies to the participation in the solution of problems by all levels of the organization.

14. *Esprit de corps*. To Fayol, this means that strength of organization comes from unification of all divergent groups and individuals.

These principles were the basis for success, according to Fayol. They could be isolated and taught to others. The principles are easily identified in today's organizations that operate smoothly. Where problems exist in an organization, chances are that one or more of these fourteen principles are being violated.

It took Oliver Sheldon to introduce the human element. Sheldon identified

two social aspects of organizations, namely, service to the community and responsibility to subordinates. He also identified forces outside the organization such as
government, the public, foreign trade, and finance, which help determine the
shape of industry.

These early classical theorists of management, plus others such as Mary Parker
Follett, who stressed coordination as a key management principle, set the
foundation for the more contemporary students of management to expand and
improve upon, rather than contradict. As organizations became more complex, the
principles expounded by the classical theorists evolved into the concepts of the
behavioral school of management.

The Hawthorne Studies at Western Electric Company in the 1920s bridged the
gap between the principles of management and the human element of management. Elton Mayo led the series of research studies at the Hawthorne plant. These
studies showed that factors other than working conditions affect productivity. It
became evident that environmental factors such as illumination and rest periods did
not have as much effect on productivity as did the interest of management in the
individual worker and the chance for an employee to participate in experiments.
These studies focused attention on human relations. The disciplines of psychology,
sociology, and anthropology began to influence management thought. Scientific
research was initiated to learn more about why humans behave the way they do in
organizations.

One of the more familiar names of the behavioral school is Abraham H.
Maslow, a psychologist who identified the hierarchy of needs.[3] Maslow says that a
person's needs depend on what he or she already has. These needs are arranged in a
hierarchy, with certain needs arising only after the lower-order needs are satisfied.
Physiological needs such as hunger, thirst, and sex must be satisfied first. Next are
safety, which includes security or protection from physical harm; belongingness and
love, which include affection, acceptance, and friendship; and esteem, both from
self and from others. It is only when each of these needs is satisfied that a person can
achieve self-actualization, that is, become what he or she is capable of becoming.

Frederick Herzberg took the subject of motivation one step further. Herzberg
says that motivation comes from the work itself. Through his studies with
professional people, Herzberg found that motivators in the work environment
include self-improvement, achievement, opportunity for advancement, and recognition. Things such as salary, working conditions, company policies, and benefits do
not motivate an employee to work harder. Rather, these factors are considered
hygienic: if they are viewed by the employee as inadequate, they act as dissatisfiers.

The Essence of Management

As can be seen by studying the work of the pioneers of management thought,
the very essence of the activity we know as "management" is its recognition of both

[3]*Motivation and Personality*, New York: Harper & Row, 1954.

organizational and human factors. Management is the coordination of the organization's human resources and its goals to the ultimate benefit of both the organization and its employees. If this seems altruistic, we must be quick to note that there is no organization unless there are people. Also, there is no point in gathering or keeping people together in an organization unless the company makes a profit and is able to pay the people for their efforts. Naturally, the skills and the motivation of employees will affect the degree to which the organization (and its people) will prosper. There are many complicating factors which affect the interaction of the human and organizational aspects of a company. However, unless the organization continues to turn a profit, the human relations problems will disappear along with the company.

THE ROLE OF MANAGEMENT

Any serious discussion of management must include the concepts of responsibility and authority, which are implicit in the very role of management. Without these factors nothing could be accomplished. No man is an island. Even the president of the organization is answerable (responsible) to someone (board of directors), and the board of directors is answerable to the stockholders or owners.

In the scalar chain of command, there is a superior–subordinate relationship at each level. Every subordinate has a superior. Every superior in turn is someone's subordinate. To be effective, each level needs the power (authority) to carry out the duties for which that level is responsible. The very concepts of responsibility and authority produce an even more important concept which holds the organization together and enables top management to be so far removed from day-to-day activities. This concept is that of accountability. Without accountability, there is no organization, because each member will go his own way rather than work toward common objectives, and eventually will pull the organization apart. Without accountability, the organization will go out of control. If the situation persists, the organization will go out of existence. Responsibility, authority, and accountability are the essence of management, the essence of being able to get things done through other people. Let's explore each of these important concepts in detail.

Authority

Authority is where management starts. If management means getting things done through other people, then it is necessary that the person attempting to get things done has the authority to direct other people as to how they will spend their time on the job. Authority assumes a power base. Power is derived when you have what someone else wants. In business, an individual goes to work for a wage or salary which is needed for subsistence, security, and recreation. If we return to our example of the one-person company that must expand to two, the second person, if brought in as a subordinate, must recognize the founder as the authority in the business. The assistant will regard the head of the organization as the individual who directs his or her actions. If that authority is rejected, then the assistant will have to leave the organization.

Authority, then, implies the power to direct the actions of others. However, the real power of authority comes from the subordinate's acceptance of that direction. We need only to look at the social unrest of the 1960s to illustrate this point. Everyone generally regards our law enforcement agencies as having the authority to maintain order. When a group, such as college students, rejects this authority, the agency can be rendered powerless to enforce the law without the use of brute force.

As organizations grow, authority must be delegated to others. The concept of delegation becomes important here. Authority comes from a higher source.

Responsibility

Responsibility and authority go hand in hand. Responsibility is generally assigned from a higher level, although it is sometimes assumed by default. In any case, responsibility is useless unless the authority to carry out the assigned task is delegated with it.

When an activity is delegated to an individual and the assignment is accepted, there is an immediate obligation created by that individual to perform or to ensure that the activity is performed according to expectations. Naturally, if someone has or accepts the responsibility to perform a job but has no authority to carry out that job, he will be unable to do the work effectively.

If a manager directs a subordinate to resolve a problem with a customer who wants a cash refund, but that subordinate has no authority to grant a refund, then the problem will not be resolved. If a purchasing agent has no authority to spend company funds or to commit the company to monetary obligations, no supplier will deal with that agent. They will request to see the person in the organization who has the necessary authority. If a supervisor does not have the authority to direct the activities of his or her people, these people will take direction only from the person who has that authority.

Accountability

Accountability is created as a result of the assignment of responsibility and the delegation of authority. In complex organizations, the concept of accountability is what makes it all work. Simply, accountability means that everyone in the organization is accountable to someone else for his or her actions. The chief operating officer has the responsibility and the authority to run the business. He or she is accountable to the board of directors for the performance of that responsibility. The unique aspect is that while responsibility and authority can be delegated, accountability cannot. If a manager's subordinate is assumed to be accountable to the manager's superior for carrying out a job, then there is no need for the person in the middle—the manager.

Have you ever wondered how the president of a giant corporation can manage the operation? It can be done only because, as corporate objectives are communicated to division, department, and unit levels, each person in the chain who accepts the responsibility to carry out part of the plan and strategy, and is delegated the necessary authority, immediately becomes accountable for the performance of these duties.

If management does not demand accountability, the organization will fail. The most obvious area of accountability is finance. The company's financial officer must ensure that all funds received or spent, due or payable are accounted for and duly recorded. Financial statements must be prepared and submitted to the board of directors and the owners. If this accounting is not done, the board of directors or the stockholders have no basis for telling if the affairs of the company are being managed properly. Just as financial accounting must be made, so must accounting for all other activities. It can be safely stated that any individual in the organization who is not accountable to someone either makes no contribution toward the corporate objectives, and thus is expendable, or is the sole proprietor of a debt-free company.

To illustrate this point on the lower levels of the organizational structure, a supervisor is accountable to the manager for the completion of the work assigned to the unit. Each employee is accountable for his or her performance of each task assigned.

Accountability implies controls. And people dislike controls. So the very basis of delegation, and of the organizational process, is brought to question by the members of the organization. To the degree that management sets the climate for willing acceptance of accountability, it has a chance of success.

It is human nature to fulfill expectations. However, if nothing is expected, or accountability is not demanded, then individuals may direct their efforts to things that are not in line with corporate objectives. Only if management sets the climate for accountability, along with the assignment of responsibility and the delegation of authority, will it always know what is going on and be able to make the decisions necessary to keep efforts toward objectives on target.

Because we are dealing with human beings whose individual goals may be different, or whose perception of the objectives of the organization is different from reality, management's job is fraught with difficulties. We will explore these difficulties and their solutions in future chapters.

2

Concepts of
Modern Office Supervision

THE SUPERVISOR IS THE MEMBER of the management team who has the most direct contact with the workers actually producing the products or providing the services for which the company exists. By the very nature of the position, the supervisor has a dual responsibility: to get the work out through other people and to see that the needs of the employee are met.

In the early days of the Industrial Revolution, the emphasis was on getting the work out. Later, behavioral scientists introduced the concepts that enable management to better understand the needs of the people doing that work. As organizations, products, and services become increasingly complex and the work environment becomes more sophisticated with computers and advanced electronic communications capabilities, so the needs, desires, motivation, and education levels of the worker are changing too. Supervisory skills must keep pace with these changes if production is to remain at a high level, if employees' needs are to be fulfilled, and if the organization is to remain profitable.

There is overwhelming evidence that supervisors determine the productivity of the employees under their control by the skill with which they exercise authority. Unfortunately, the lack of development of the supervisor position within many organizations contradicts this apparent importance. This is illustrated by poor supervisor selection and training techniques and management's inability to set the proper supervisory climate. All contribute to ineffective supervisor performance. In this chapter, we will examine the meaning of supervision, how the supervisor affects

14

productivity, and why the style of the supervisor is as important as the substance of supervision.

Before going any further, however, it is important to make it clear where the supervisor fits into the organizational structure so as to understand where the supervisor's authority originates.

LAYERS OF MANAGEMENT

Management, to be effective, must have a division of work, just as the organization itself must have layers. Each management layer has specific responsibilities. As organizations grow, the number of management layers also grows to assure that each organizational unit will receive proper attention. To be most effective, each layer should do that work which the title and position call for. To do more will result in either duplication of effort or creation of an unnecessary layer. To do less will hurt the overall effectiveness of the organization.

Top Management

The upper layer of management usually includes the chairman of the board, the president, and the executive vice presidents and senior vice presidents or division heads. This layer's function is to do the long-range planning for the organization and to assure that there is an appropriate organizational structure to carry out those plans. This level of management is answerable to the company owners—usually the stockholders—through the board of directors. The emphasis is on the "bottom line," or profitability of the company.

Corporate objectives and plans are formulated by this group and communicated downward. Major decisions that affect the total organization are either initiated or approved. Managers at this level generally deal with broad issues. They assess the company's role in society, the effects of the economy on the bottom line, the major markets to exploit, and the sources of funds to carry out the plans. Once decisions are made, the organization must implement the plans or programs. This upper layer relies on reports from lower levels to discover how successfully plans and programs are progressing.

Top management's focus is always on the total organization. It formulates strategies and plans for marketing and expansion of the company's horizons. The day-to-day decisions that top management makes are usually concerned with situations that will affect the total organization rather than any one operating area of the company.

To be effective, much of the activity of the upper layer of management must take place outside the organization. This is so because the organization as a whole is affected by the business environment, economic conditions, and governmental actions. Upper management must ensure that the organization is in tune with these forces, influence these forces if necessary (especially in the case of giant conglomerates), and anticipate changes for which the organization must be prepared.

It is also a key task of top management to perpetuate the organization, not only by assuring that the company operates profitably, but also by guaranteeing that there are enough people within the organization who are sufficiently trained and developed to take over as key individuals retire or leave the company.

Although the lower organizational echelons are often heard to complain that top management "doesn't understand my problems," this is the way it ought to be. By its very essence, top management performs different functions from those of the rest of the organization. Although this layer must keep abreast of the situation, there should be very little need for involvement in the day-to-day operation of the company. The notable exception to this is if the activity is crucial to the survival of the company. Only in a company experiencing a crisis that threatens its very existence would top management be expected or required to work at the operating level of the company, taking over key functions such as financial transactions, marketing management, or administration. Otherwise, when top management involves itself in day-to-day operations, it is often at the expense of its true role, and potential growth and internal systems are weakened.

There is one intangible area for which top management is responsible: setting the style and spirit of the organization. The style of the top level, usually the very top individual, ripples throughout the organization as decisions, plans, and strategies are communicated and put into action. It is this style that will ultimately determine the total effectiveness of the organization, assuming that the normal activities are attended to. The degree of control, motivation, and dedication will be greatly influenced by the style of the top people.

Middle Management

Middle management is the group responsible for translating corporate objectives into operating plans. It must formulate departmental objectives and goals that will make possible the attainment of corporate objectives. Naturally, the scope of middle management is narrower and more technically oriented than that of the upper echelons. Decision making is done only for the specific area of responsibility and expertise. Because middle managers are closer to the point where tasks are actually performed, their skills in motivating people become even more important.

While upper management must stay abreast of the environment external to the company, the middle manager must be constantly aware of the overall internal environment of the company. Middle managers must coordinate and integrate the activities of their specific departments with the activities of other departments in the company. Changes in another department or a shift in direction by upper management must be understood, evaluated, communicated, and adjusted to by the management of a department if the total organization is to operate smoothly.

Middle managers should have direct responsibility for supervising and controlling the activities of other managers, technicians, and supervisors in the company. They are also responsible for developing people under them to assume their own or other management positions in the company. The spirit and climate of each department is set by the manager. This includes the approach by which a specific department will work toward company goals and implement company plans and strategies. A department's effectiveness reflects the individual abilities of the manager.

Controls developed and used by middle managers will usually involve more detail than required by upper management. The bottom line for middle management will be more specific than just total company profitability. Rather, the department's contribution to the total company profit will be evaluated. The more effective middle management is, the less upper management must concern itself with the internal workings of a department.

Supervisors

In the words of Peter Drucker, "supervisors are, so to speak, the ligaments, the tendons and sinews, of an organization. They provide the articulation."[1] Since organizations are composed of people, and since it is the supervisor who has direct control over the activities of the greatest number of people in the organization, the supervisor is crucial.

The supervisor must plan, organize, motivate, and control the work of others. The scope at this level is more narrow than at any other level in the organization. Planning is done only in relation to the more immediate need to get the work out accurately, economically, and on time. It is short-term planning, and generally will involve a time cycle of hours, days, weeks, months, or at most a year. Decisions are made in the narrow scope of responsibility of the organizational unit. The organizational part of the job is that of organizing work within the unit and organizing people's time to perform the work rather than deciding on the overall structure of the company. Direction is over nonmanagerial employees, and coordination is with peer levels, that is, other supervisors in the company. The objectives set by the supervisor are concerned primarily with meeting the objectives of the department or unit as set forth by middle management.

The supervisor's job is heavily people-oriented, since it is necessary for the supervisor to see that the worker's needs, as well as those of the organization, are met. The controls are on individual activities and the time of the people who are doing the jobs.

[1]*Management: Tasks, Responsibilities, Practices,* New York: Harper & Row, 1974, p. 280.

The Nature of Supervision

The supervisor is management's representative to the worker. The supervisor must put into action the objectives and plans developed by the upper levels of management. However, the supervisor is also the person who ensures that the employees' needs are attended to.

Definition of Supervision

Supervision means "overseeing." The National Labor-Management Relations Act of 1947 was more specific. That federal law defined a supervisor as:

> . . . any individual having authority, in the interest of the employer, to hire, transfer, suspend, lay off, recall, promote, discharge, assign, reward, or discipline other employees, or responsibility to direct them, or to adjust their grievances, or effectively to recommend such action, if in connection with the foregoing the exercise of such authority is not of a merely routine or clerical nature, but requires the use of independent judgment.[2]

Inherent in this definition is the fact that the nature of the work performed by the supervisor is substantially different from that of the employees being supervised—specifically, it is of a higher level.

Yet another definition is offered by Ralph C. Davis, who states that supervision is "the function of assuring that current execution is taking place in accordance with plans and instructions."[3] Davis also introduces the concept of leadership at the supervisory level. According to him, supervision involves face-to-face leadership.

Leadership

Inherent in the supervisor's job is the role of leader. A leader is one who attempts to influence the actions of others. The supervisor is in a position to influence the actions of employees for the purpose of achieving the goals of the organization. A supervisor's effectiveness as a leader depends on many things, including the supervisor's self-image, the amount of confidence the workers have in the supervisor's ability, the ability of the supervisor to motivate the workers, and, last but not least, the supervisor's style, or how he or she operates in the workplace.

Edward Gross identified the major dimensions of leadership behavior.[4] The first is goal definition. This is usually the task of the leaders at the very top of the organization. Goal clarification is the second dimension of leadership. Usually, the top management group will develop goals that are broad in scope, or expressed in general terms. The leader must clarify these goals so that the worker can carry out

---

[2]National Labor–Management Relations (Taft-Hartley) Act, 1947 (as amended), Section 101, Subsection 2 (11).

[3]*The Fundamentals of Top Management,* New York: Harper & Row, 1951, p. 407.

[4]"Dimensions of Leadership, William E. Schlender, William G. Scott, and Alan C. Filley, in *Management in Perspective: Selected Readings,* Boston: Houghton Mifflin, 1965, pp. 510–518.

the jobs necessary to achieve the goals. The next major task for the leader is to determine what means should be used to achieve the goals. For the supervisor, this means deciding on the proper use of resources, methods, and procedures, and on the schedules necessary to get the job done. If a supervisor simply lets employees devise their own means, that supervisor is not properly fulfilling his or her leadership role.

The fourth dimension of leadership is to assign the tasks and coordinate their completion with other tasks that must be accomplished. The next dimension is motivation. The individual worker's needs and goals must coincide with the needs and goals of the organization. It is the leader's job to point out to the worker why and how individual and organizational goals are compatible. Connected with this dimension is that of integration. Here the leader convinces the worker that the company or the job is a good one, and attempts to build pride in the job, the company, and the work. Gross identifies the seventh and last leader behavior dimension as the "sparking function." With respect to the supervisor, this refers to getting the action started. It is an essential function and, to be effective, must be accomplished at the right time.

QUALIFICATIONS OF THE SUPERVISOR

There are two aspects of the supervisor's qualifications that must be considered: expectations of the organization and factors that have a bearing on how employees accept the leadership of the supervisor.

One of the complexities that a supervisor must face is the dynamics of group behavior. Inherent in any group behavior are the norms that the group develops, and the group automatically develops norms concerning the individual who supervises it. Not only must the supervisor fulfill the expectations of superiors and maintain or extract good employee productivity, but there are employees' expectations concerning the supervisor that are just as critical to the supervisor's success. If the supervisor does not fulfill these expectations, employee productivity will not reach its full potential.

We'll examine the qualifications of the supervisor from the viewpoints of both employees and management.

Employees' Expectations of Supervisors

The latest research by behavioral scientists shows that when employees list the ten things they want most from the job, five of these items relate directly to the supervisor. Appreciation of work is usually listed first. Employees want supervisors to show appreciation for a job well done through recognition and rewards. The supervisor must be aware of what each employee is doing and show appreciation whenever it is merited.

Another expectation employees have is the need to feel "in on things." They want their supervisor to keep them abreast of changes and the reasons for those changes. Employees are quick to notice when "big things" appear to be happening, and they rely on the supervisor to let them know what is happening. Prudent supervisors keep the lines of communication open and not only give the employees the information they need to know but also keep them up to date on other major events that are taking place in the company. A supervisor who does not do this leaves this information to the employee rumor mill, or grapevine, and in effect tells the employee, "You are not important enough to know this."

The third most desirable behavior employees want is understanding and help with problems at work. Employees *want* to do a good job. If a supervisor believes this, he or she will naturally be more helpful to employees when problems arise and will resolve things on a more rational basis.

Another item that appears in the top ten is the fact that employees want the personal loyalty of the supervisor. They want a supervisor who will "go to bat" for them in a time of need. In that kind of environment, employees are encouraged to take on more responsibility and to develop in their jobs, knowing that, should something go wrong, their supervisor will be fair and protect rather than blame them.

The fifth item employees want is tactful discipline. They want guidance and feedback on their performance. They respect supervisors who follow up on target dates and actual performance, and they will respond with good work. Knowing that discipline will be tactfully applied, with emphasis on ways to improve and sparing feelings, employees will be encouraged to strive for further improvement.

Characteristics of a Good Supervisor

When it comes to first-line supervision, it is essential that the supervisor know the technical aspects of the jobs being performed. This does not mean that the supervisor must know how to do each job. However, the supervisor must know enough about the jobs to give guidance to employees and resolve work-related problems. It should also be pointed out that this knowledge of the job need not be a prerequisite in all situations. Rather, the new supervisor must begin acquiring this knowledge as soon as possible.

Decisiveness is another important characteristic of a good supervisor. Naturally, the quality of the decisions made is essential. However, the supervisor's ability to gather the necessary information, analyze the data, and arrive at the logical conclusion as to what action to take is just the beginning. Having done all that, the supervisor must initiate the necessary steps to put the decision into effect.

Another important attribute of the effective supervisor is good communication skills. Because the supervisor must translate plans into action, keep employees informed, discuss performance and appraisals, discipline, train, and take remedial or corrective action, communication skills are essential. How and what the supervisor communicates affects employee morale, attitude, and performance.

Another important characteristic of the good supervisor is that he or she establishes a good work climate. High performance standards are generally set, and a no-nonsense atmosphere pervades the department. Employees like working in the department, accept the standards and rules in effect, and follow them closely. Employees know that they can discuss problems with the supervisor, but also understand the limits within which they can act. There is usually good delegation in the department, and the supervisor does little or no routine work. In short, everything is under control.

In all too many companies, supervisors are appointed for their technical ability, seniority, or knowledge of the job, rather than their leadership or human relations skills. (This does not mean that these supervisors are doomed to failure; if they are open-minded and interested in people or self-development, they will seek to acquire the necessary leadership skills and will put them to use.) Many managers lament their past appointments of supervisors, yet they continue to repeat the error. This occurs for a number of reasons.

One of the reasons is that managers feel they are practicing good employee relations by promoting from within. Another is that many managers came up through the ranks and everything worked out just fine. A third reason is that lack of job knowledge on the part of the first-line supervisor is inconceivable to some managers. Another reason—and a more serious one—is that management has not properly developed the organization, with the result that no well-rounded supervisory candidate is available to fill an opening.

When managers take this approach to filling the supervisor positions under them, they are ignoring the fact that today's worker is different (see Chapter 3) and that there is more to getting the work out than just knowing how the job should be performed. In today's environment, good human relations skills are crucial to a supervisor's success. Armed only with good technical knowledge, the supervisor is exposed to pressures affecting his or her behavior and, therefore, effectiveness. These pressures and their results are covered in the next section.

All the characteristics of a good supervisor can be summed up in the word leadership. If a supervisor is a good leader of people, then employees will follow his or her direction—sometimes by faith alone. This is especially so when past performance indicates that everything always works out as the supervisor said it would. We will explore the leadership subject in more detail in Chapter 5.

Characteristics of a Poor Supervisor

It is easy to agree about the characteristics of a good supervisor. A supervisor also may agree that these are all very good characteristics to develop in oneself. Sometimes, the supervisor who lacks the needed characteristics but wants to do a good job, or would like to think he or she is doing a good job, may give himself or herself the benefit of the doubt. To properly grasp the subject, those characteristics that are found in poor supervisors should also be identified.

Naturally, the opposites of the characteristics of good supervisors will describe the poor supervisor. However, there are some other undesirable attributes that are found in the action of poor supervisors.

Defensiveness is one sign of a poor supervisor. All comments and events are quickly evaluated in light of someone or something attacking the supervisor's territory. Usually these comments or events cause the supervisor to reject the new event out of hand. This is generally evidenced by a firm and deep-seated resistance to change.

Lack of emotional stability also is evident in the poor supervisor. Events that do not advance as the supervisor intends cause obvious anger and frustration, which embarrasses employees and does nothing to solve the problem.

Poor delegation is another signpost of a poor supervisor. The supervisor is so inundated with work, there is no time for guiding employees and listening to their problems. This presents little opportunity for employee development, and there is a constant series of crises because of the lack of adequate planning.

Inflexibility is another characteristic of a poor supervisor. Everything is run strictly by the book. This causes employees to seek ways to circumvent the rules or to openly ignore them in a time of need when exceptions are necessary. An inflexible supervisor is often also a poor disciplinarian. The supervisor who insists that everything be done exactly as he or she directs is too limiting for employees. A signpost of this type of supervision is that productivity drops when the boss is not present.

The overall result of poor supervision is low morale and low productivity. It usually causes high turnover with its attendant training problems, and poor quality of work.

THE SUPERVISOR'S JOB

As we have seen, the supervisor must be concerned with both work and people. The concepts of modern supervision must therefore cover both of these subjects. Let's look a little closer at these concepts. (In Chapter 4, we will give a detailed discussion of the activities related to the supervisor's job.)

Supervising Work

As we have seen, planning, organizing, directing, and controlling are the concepts associated with supervisory work. Planning means that the supervisor understands the relationship of the company goals and plans to his or her department and is able to formulate the needs of the department in advance. This planning is usually short-term in nature. It keeps the department operating smoothly by assuring that the resources of manpower, money, materials, methods, and machines (the five M's of management) will all be accounted for and available as needed.

Organizing these resources is closely related to the planning activity. Organizing means to ensure that the resources anticipated during the planning activity will be available when and where they are needed, and in the proper amounts.

Directing the resources occurs when the work is actually being done. The supervisor must react to situations calling for unexpected changes in the use of resources and handle day-to-day problems and questions as well. The characteristic of decisiveness becomes important in the directing function.

The controlling function includes establishing performance standards, measuring performance against these standards, and taking corrective action. Again, the controlling function applies to manpower, money, materials, methods, and machines.

Supervising People

Because it is people who must do the work, the supervisor must have good human relations skills. Martin Patchen summed it up well when he said, "The supervisor must have a clear perception of his role as a leader and must make a careful determination of how closely he should follow and oversee the work of subordinates."[5] All the planning, organizing, directing, and controlling will go for naught if the supervisor does not perform the "people" part of the job properly. The first step is for the supervisor to realize that each employee must be treated as an individual. Those supervisors who treat all employees equally are really not being fair, because they ignore individual differences. Because the human relations aspect of the job is the most difficult, unskilled supervisors will hide behind numbers, production reports, target dates, and other tangible factors, to the exclusion of the individuals who must do the work.

Motivating employees means determining what they need to spur them on to do a good job. Participative decision making, where employees give input and make recommendations, may be desirable, but it requires skill to accomplish and maintain. The supervisor must be secure and knowledgeable and must believe firmly in the ability of the employee to contribute positively. The amount of autonomy allowed each employee must relate directly to the desire and commitment of the employee to operate on his own. If the employee wants close guidance, the supervisor must recognize this and act accordingly.

[5]"Supervisory Methods and Group Performance Norms," *Administrative Science Quarterly*, December 1962, pp. 275–293.

Communication skills are essential to working with people. This involves more than just talking to the worker—it also requires listening. The supervisor must understand that employees are filtering what they hear on the basis of their personal experiences and desires. There must also be an awareness of the need to "listen between the lines"—to recognize that what people say is not necessarily what they mean.

Another human relations skill needed is the ability to manage work groups effectively. In larger organizations, individual workers are part of groups that have their own norms and behavior. Everything the supervisor does in the workplace must be done with full consideration of how it will affect the group as well as the individuals within the group.

This is what is meant by leadership. How effective the supervisor is in handling the human relations part of the job will relate directly to his or her leadership abilities. *What* the supervisor does is the substance of the job and is related to the work itself. *How* the supervisor does it is the style of supervision and is people-related. There are many different leadership styles, and no one style is the best—they all must be related to the situation and the people involved. We will discuss substance and style and the different styles of leadership in Chapters 4 and 5.

CHAPTER
3

Understanding Today's Office Worker

THE STUDENT OF ORGANIZATIONAL BEHAVIOR must understand what motivates people to act as they do in work situations. Because of the dynamic environment in which these acts occur, it is a never-ending study. However, it behooves managers and supervisors to understand as much as possible about motivation if they have any desire to be successful leaders.

The leader must beware, however, for there are no easy answers. To understand the behavior of today's worker we must consider the cultural environment, the worker as an individual, and the powerful forces of the group on the individual worker's behavior.

A manager has a natural tendency to rely on past experience, which may well be out of date. A manager may have deep-seated attitudes toward employees which no amount of "enlightenment" will change. Each manager has a different style of working with subordinates. It is obvious that the path to effective leadership is littered with pitfalls that could trap an organization in a mire of ineffectiveness, low morale, high turnover, and less than satisfactory profits.

WHY PEOPLE WORK

The Cultural Environment

Prior to the Industrial Revolution, 90 percent of the American people lived on farms. The entire economy revolved around the family, which worked and received

25

its subsistence from the land it lived on. Things which could not be made by the farmer and his family were purchased with money made by selling crops. The man worked the fields, the wife took care of the household chores such as sewing, cooking, cleaning, preserving foods, and raising children. As soon as the children were able, the boys helped Dad in the fields and the girls helped Mom around the house. Ruined or poor crops brought rough times, but unemployment for the farm owner was unheard of. Sons were taught to take over the farm when Dad grew too old to continue, or to get a piece of land to develop for themselves and their families. The fruits of their efforts were very tangible. The harvested crop, the barn full of hay, the fattened calf, the warm house were the "bottom line" results of getting the job done. Satisfaction at the end of the day or the growing season was easy to experience if the farmer and his family worked hard. If the job didn't get done, the sparse dinner table, the worn-out clothing, the lack of cash to buy some luxuries or that new rifle to hunt with were immediate feedback, and the farmer could blame no one but himself.

The other 10 percent of the population consisted mainly of craftsmen, who prided themselves on making quality goods for the successful farmer. If we ignore that small percentage of the population who were the common laborers of the day, who had no profession, no craft, and no land but were just hired hands, we are dealing with people who were primarily their own bosses, or were planning to be their own bosses as soon as they served their apprenticeship.

Life was not easy in this environment. Some had it easier than others, but when the opportunity came to leave the farm and head for the urban areas that were growing as a result of the Industrial Revolution, there started a flow that has yet to stop. The grass certainly looked greener on the other side of the fence. At the dawn of the Industrial Revolution, people began to jump at the opportunity to leave the farm for work of a different nature. The age of specialization was approaching. Rather than perform a job from beginning to end, workers were assigned just one small operation to perform. They hardly ever saw the end product of their labor. The hours were still long, and the work was hard and mostly boring.

Income in most jobs was no longer tied directly to weather conditions. However, in spite of this seeming security, the worker was no longer his own boss. What he did and how he did it was dictated by someone else. Economic conditions of the country were being raised to higher levels, because there was more money being made by more people. A drought did not affect the factory worker adversely as it did the farmer. However, the worker's income was affected by the more mysterious conditions of business cycles that created alternate inflation, recession, depression, and boom.

While we were turning from an agricultural to an industrial nation, the description of the work force changed from "farmer" to "blue-collar worker." By 1979, the percentage of the American population on farms had dropped to less than

4 percent. As a result of this shift, the work environment has changed drastically. But have the employee's needs in the workplace changed? We think not. Today's workers may have lost a sense of accomplishment because they are removed from the end product; they may be bored because the work assignment has turned them into specialists, eliminating the variety or control our forefathers enjoyed in their work; but the human being must still satisfy certain basic needs. Our material needs and wants are much different, but as we attempt to satisfy them through work, the basic drives rooted in our agricultural backgrounds are still present, consciously or unconsciously. Managers and supervisors must be aware of these basic drives if they are to be successful.

The Individual

The farmer got intrinsic satisfaction from the work he did. The results of his efforts were eminently tangible. If you planted the crops, cared for them, and harvested them at the right time, you ate. The better you did these things, the more you had to eat and sell to your neighbors. Today's worker agrees to take a job for a certain salary. If you don't show up for work, maybe you won't get paid. But in most cases, even if you don't perform your job especially well, the paychecks will continue to roll in, though advancement may be limited.

So, to return to the question, "Why do people work?" the obvious answer is money. Even those who do not "need" their paychecks to live on do not offer their services to General Motors, the friendly insurance company, or the neighborhood bank for nothing. However, since the basic paycheck is seemingly so automatic, the worker has other, nonfinancial reasons for working.

No matter for what financial reasons people enter the office work force, once they do, another major force immediately acts upon them: the social aspects of working. Keith Davis calls the nonfinancial aspect a "psychological contract" an employee makes with an organization.[1] This psychological contract calls for security, treatment as a human being, rewarding relationships with people, and support in fulfilling expectations. When employees perceive that one or more of these items are missing in their job, they will become dissatisfied with the company and the work, because nonfinancial needs are not fulfilled, even if their financial needs are. The degree to which these elements are missing determines whether the employee will be happy, dissatisfied but stay on, or leave the organization to seek employment elsewhere. To the degree that "organizations help employees reach their personal goals by making resources and opportunities available to them,"[2] the morale of those employees will be directly affected.

[1]"Human Behavior at Work," in Keith Davis, ed., *Human Relations and Organizational Behavior*, 4th edition, New York: McGraw-Hill, 1972, p. 39.

[2]Ibid., p. 237.

Motivational Theory

In order to understand today's office worker, we must understand basic motivational theory. Earlier in this chapter we related work to the materialistic things one gets from it. We mentioned that there were some psychological needs of workers that must also be understood. The theory of motivation that is best known in management literature is that of Abraham H. Maslow, who identified a hierarchy of needs.[3] Specifically, he identified five basic needs, with each need emerging as the previous need is fulfilled—thus the concept of hierarchy. (Actually, he talks about seven basic needs, but the needs for knowledge and understanding and aesthetic needs are not fully substantiated in his works, nor have they any useful application in the work environment.) Figure 3-1 illustrates the order of the basic needs, from bottom to top. Because no need is fulfilled once and for all but rather comes and goes, or becomes stronger or weaker as a motivator of behavior, Figure 3-1 shows the lower-level needs still present as the higher-order needs appear.

Figure 3-I. Order of basic needs.

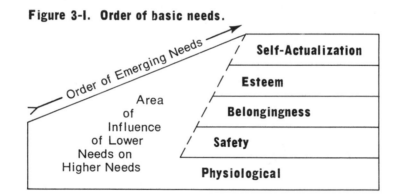

The first level of needs includes the physiological drives of hunger, thirst, and sex and other biological needs. In today's work environment these needs are generally fulfilled. However, we should point out that if none of a person's needs are being met, the strongest drives will be the physiological needs. The second-level need that emerges once the physiological needs are satisfied is safety. Generally, this level relates to security, protection from physical harm, and avoidance of the unknown. Habit-forming behavior is a result of this basic need. Among the reasons people will stay with a particular job rather than accept a promotion or seek a higher-paying job is the safety need of avoiding the unknown. Resistance to change is also rooted in this need.

[3]*Motivation and Personality,* New York: Harper & Row, 1954, Chapter 5.

When you consider that physiological needs are generally fulfilled, safety becomes the dominant motivating force for behavior. Financial income provides a degree of safety to many, and the old adage "A bird in the hand is worth two in the bush" illustrates most people's desire to avoid the less sure, the risky or unknown, for the known. Learning a new job after already having mastered the present job could be viewed as a threat to a worker's safety or security, if the threat is not removed somehow. Role-playing exercises in training sessions enable a person to practice new things in a true-to-life environment without consequences of failure. Lack of proper training of a new employee could frustrate the need for security by forcing that employee to face an unknown ("How am I supposed to do this right?"), thus threatening his or her security.

The third level of needs is belongingness and love. This level is based on the fact that humans, with rare exception, are social beings. Once the physiological and safety needs are fulfilled, the individual seeks companionship with peers, friends, colleagues, relatives, other human beings. This is often the dominant motivator that causes someone to enter the workplace. A housewife whose children are grown and on their own, a widow, a high school graduate whose friends have gone off to college or jobs—all are fulfilling their basic need to belong and associate with others when they go to work without any real financial need.

The esteem need emerges as an individual fulfills the other, lower needs. To the degree that the esteem needs are fulfilled, self-confidence, prestige, and self-esteem are enhanced. In the workplace we sometimes see an individual who wants to be important in the eyes of other workers or the supervisor. This desire relates to inviting recognition and having others show appreciation, but it must be based on the firm foundation of achievement. An employee gains self-confidence, strength, and a feeling of self-worth when recognition and appreciation, based on sound achievement, are exhibited. When an individual receives no esteem, a basic need is frustrated, and assuming the lower-level needs are fulfilled, the person will go elsewhere to get it. Sometimes, when a move due to lack of esteem is ruled out by safety needs, the individual will join groups outside of work and accept positions of responsibility for esteem. Another possibility is joining an informal group at work in a leadership capacity that is anti-company.

Self-actualization exhibits itself as a basic need after the other needs are fulfilled. Even if all the other needs are satisfied, frustration can set in if an individual perceives that his or her potential is not being fulfilled. Maslow explains this need with the sentence "What a man can be, he must be." Everyone has certain potential, and to fulfill the self-actualization need, that potential must be realized. A clerk who feels he or she has the potential to be a member of management will not be happy until that goal is fulfilled. This need is the basis for the statement that "everyone wants to do a good job." Self-actualization is doing the best job possible in what you want to do. If a manager of a processing department in a bank truly wants to operate the local hardware store, self-actualization needs will not be fulfilled until he does.

With Maslow's theory, which is easy to understand and can be confirmed through logic and common sense, we are on our way to understanding human behavior. Each worker who enters today's office environment has these basic needs, and each person is at some level of the hierarchy in terms of need fulfillment. It must be noted, however, that we are not always conscious of exactly what need we are trying to fulfill. The supervisor or manager should not attempt to play amateur psychologist and analyze the reasons why someone is doing something. There are many other complex factors that go into human behavior. Knowledge of the needs hierarchy will, however, remind us not to frustrate any of the basic needs of the worker.

Employee Wants

Much research has been done to determine what people want from their jobs. The early results of this research were surprising to supervisors, who thought that employees cared only about money. Table 3-1 shows a comparison of rankings of what employees want most from the job versus what supervisors think the employees want. Although this study was done originally in the industrial environment, the authors have continued the research in the office environment with essentially the same results.

Appreciation of work ranks number one with employees. This fits into the esteem needs. When we consider that most clerical office workers are women,

Table 3-1. What employees want most from their jobs, as viewed by supervisors and by employees themselves.

Items Ranked	Ranking by Supervisors	Ranking by Employees
Good wages	1	5
Job security	2	4
Promotion and growth	3	7
Working conditions	4	9
Interesting work	5	6
Personal loyalty of supervisors to employee	6	8
Tactful discipline	7	10
Appreciation of work	8	1
Understanding and help with problems	9	3
Feeling in on things	10	2

Source: Paul Hersey and Kenneth H. Blanchard, *Management of Organizational Behavior: Utilizing Human Resources*, Englewood Cliffs, N.J.: Prentice-Hall, 1969, p. 35.

whose salary frequently is not the sole supporting income of the family, physiological and security needs are not a major factor here. This appreciation of work can be shown through verbal praise, monetary reward, citing an employee's accomplishments in the company newspaper, delegating additional responsibilities, and promotions.

Feeling in on things is listed by employees as the second most important thing they want from the job. This is related to the security need. Having advance knowledge of a major change or participating in the development of the change eliminates the element of the unknown. It also contributes to an individual's self-esteem if the boss deems it necessary to discuss important matters with the employee before the event occurs.

The third most important thing employees want from the job is understanding and help with problems. This has to do with the fact that the worker is also a parent, a patient, a spouse, a consumer, a homeowner, or whatever. When problems come up, the worker needs to handle them, and understanding and help from the boss contribute to satisfying the individual's safety and self-esteem needs.

Job security naturally ranks high as the fourth most important attribute. The hierarchy of needs has it in the second position. The fact that it doesn't rank higher with employees may have to do with the age composition of the office population surveyed. However, the safety needs of avoiding the unknown are still strong.

Good wages ranks number five. The most obvious needs that wages fulfill are the physiological needs of food, clothing, and shelter, as well as the safety needs, since financial security is a major goal of most people. However, pay is a complex issue when it comes to satisfying needs, since it also contributes to self-esteem when used as a barometer of a person's worth to the organization or of progress relative to a peer group. Good pay could also contribute to self-actualization in that it enables a person to be what he wants to be.

Interesting or meaningful work contributes to satisfaction of both the safety and the self-esteem needs. Performing work that employees perceive as useless causes them to worry that their job is easily expendable and, therefore, that they are expendable too. Even if there is no fear that the job is going to be eliminated, the other problem of low self-esteem is still present. Performing a job that is viewed as meaningless gives the employee the feeling of not contributing to the company's end product.

The seventh most mentioned item is promotion and growth. Not all employees are interested in promotions. However, even though an employee may choose not to seek or accept a promotion, the knowledge that opportunity exists is enough to fulfill the need for self-esteem. Those who do seek promotion are motivated by security (higher pay) and esteem (appreciation of a job well done, and recognition as a valuable member of the company).

Another major want of the employee is the personal loyalty of the supervisor. This item relates to many of the needs, including security (knowing that the supervisor will protect the employee when problems arise).

Working conditions are also important to employees, especially when it comes to their safety. Beyond that, esteem becomes important in that the building, the equipment, the personal office area, and the furniture reflect prestige or status.

Tactful discipline becomes important to an employee, first of all, for security reasons. When an employee sees discipline being properly exercised, he gains a sense of security that order will be preserved and the job will continue to exist. This item also is related to esteem insofar as the person applying the discipline is recognized as a capable person who is taking an interest in the employee.

Group Behavior

When trying to understand today's worker and the reasons for behavior, it is necessary to look at group behavior as well. Since the individual in an organization is a member of both formal and informal groups in the workplace, we will examine how these groups modify individual behavior.

It has been noted by psychologists that man, being a social being, operates more effectively when a member of a group. The basic social need of belonging is very strong. As noted earlier, it is sometimes the major motivational factor that brings people to the workplace. The mere organizing of the people in a company creates groups having common goals and, often, team spirit. An individual who is put into a group will observe how that group acts, when its members take coffee breaks, how they help or avoid each other, and who talks to whom. The individual's behavior will be affected by what is apparent. The desire to belong will cause the new individual to conform to the group norms for acceptance. While we all can think of instances where certain people have decided to ignore the group and go their own way, it is unusual enough to attract attention as odd behavior. If the group takes its coffee break at 9:15 AM but one individual continues to work and takes a break at 9:45 AM, the difference becomes obvious.

These groups that form within the organizational structure are usually referred to as informal work groups. The work group fulfills many of the needs identified in the hierarchy depicted in Figure 3-1. The group provides security by protecting its members from outside forces such as demands for higher productivity or changes wanted by other areas of the company.

Especially the smaller work group provides satisfaction of social needs, as pointed out earlier. One of the authors witnessed a drastic drop in productivity of five smaller departments in one insurance company when for organizational, workflow, and communication purposes all the physical barriers were removed and the five smaller work areas were combined into one large open area. Morale also suffered. The former department groups all demanded some type of delineation, such as painting the side wall directly adjacent to their area a different color from the department next to them. There was a constant stream of suggestions such as placing signs at the location of each department or using high-standing cabinets to block off departments.

Joining a group may also fulfill the need for esteem, because some groups are held in high regard by others. There is also the possibility that an individual will receive esteem from the other members of the group.

In each work group an informal group leader will emerge. The informal group leader gives some direction to the group, based on example, statements made, or personal characteristics that are recognized as leadership qualities by the other group members. If management wishes to implement any major change, the informal group leader must be sold on the change. This seemingly more powerful position (sometimes more powerful than the formal leader) arises simply out of the fact that informal power attaches itself to a *person* while formal (and sometimes weaker) authority attaches to a *position*. The individual occupying the formal position of authority needs excellent leadership qualities to successfully overcome or avoid the resistance of the group. Informal groups are a fact of organizational life, and the appointment of the informal group leader to the formal leadership position usually results in the emergence of yet another informal group leader.

Some of the major advantages of this informal work structure are that it can assist greatly in getting the job done, it can provide a source of satisfaction and stability to the work force, and, if it is used properly, it is a useful channel of communication.

The Concept of Pride

There is no doubt in the authors' minds that employees want to do a good job. Hundreds of empirical studies confirm this. Employees want to take pride in the work they do, in terms of what is accomplished, how well it is accomplished, and the value of the end product to others.

Employees also want to have pride in the company for which they work. They want to know that their company contributes something good to the economy and to the community in general. They will come to the company's defense if necessary, and will proudly admit that they work for a company generally recognized as a "good company." Everyone wants to be part of a successful operation. Success breeds success. By having pride in their work and their company, employees have pride in themselves as well. The end result is a happy and motivated employee who enjoys going to work and putting forth the extra effort necessary to make a company successful. Morale is high in such companies. Good performance leads to a good attitude.

Today's Worker—A Final Word

Going back to the basic needs and motivational forces, as well as the modern worker's origins, one other emerging situation is becoming more evident: today's worker wants to be master of his own destiny. This is creating more pressures on management to allow employees more freedom on the job and greater participation in key decisions that affect the employee. While this seems to smack of less controls, this is not the case. The concept of accountability becomes even more critical in this environment. The freedom to act in the workplace creates the situation where the employee carries more responsibility for success and failure. It makes him more accountable. If we are to follow the recommendations of the behavioralists, we must believe that the employee wants it that way.

The Supervisor's Job

We have amply described the position of the supervisor conceptually and theoretically in Chapter 2. However, as students of management discover in today's business schools, putting these definitions and concepts into practice is far from an automatic process. In this chapter we will get down to specifics and examine what a supervisor does.

RESPONSIBILITIES OF THE SUPERVISOR

Ask any supervisor what he or she is responsible for, and the answer, eventually if not initially, will be a resounding, "Get the work out." That is it. However, unfortunately—or fortunately, depending on your viewpoint—there are certain constraints on the supervisor in his efforts to get the work out. These constraints include three factors: money, time, and usefulness of the end product.

Most supervisors do not have unlimited monetary resources available to them. Departmental functions must be funded through a budgeting process. Although exceptions can be made, generally a supervisor must live and operate by the approved budget.

Another constraint is time. By the very nature of office work, which is usually service-oriented, certain service standards must be adhered to. It would not be very long before complaints would hit the executive desk if service levels were perceived as low by the customer. Even if the service level is merely irritating rather than critically poor, a gradual loss of sales will result.

Usefulness of the end product refers to the quality of the work performed. A timely but erroneous answer to a question serves no useful purpose. It creates rework that is expensive in terms of lost productive time and materials as well as customer dissatisfaction.

A supervisor must therefore get the work out accurately, on time, and economically. To do that he or she must plan, organize, direct, motivate, and control all the resources available. These resources include manpower, methods, materials, machines, and money.

SUPERVISORY FUNCTIONS

Let's now review the primary functions of supervision. This will give the reader a general framework with which to work.

Planning

From the first-line supervisor's point of view, the planning that must be done is primarily short- to medium-range. Short-range planning is concerned with planning activities for the coming day, week, or month, whereas a medium-range time frame refers to planning a year or perhaps eighteen months to two years ahead. Short-range planning usually relates to the work and the supervisor's personal activities. Medium-range planning generally occurs in relation to annual budgets.

All too many supervisors bemoan the fact that there is too much work to do to allow them to do any planning. Lack of time is usually the primary excuse. So many unexpected things happen each day in many supervisors' work days that the tendency is not to do any planning. Since the root of many of the crises that eat up the planning time is the very fact that there is an insufficient amount of time spent planning, the all too familiar vicious circle is in motion: "There is no time to plan because I am fire-fighting. I am fire-fighting because I have no time to plan." The constant lack of attention to planning becomes the source of low productivity, misdirected effort, and waste of resources.

It can be said that any supervisor is in fact only doing part of the job if he does not allocate a percentage of his time to planning. Self-evaluation by a supervisor should include the question: "Do I not plan because I do not have time or because I do not know how to plan?" An effective supervisor will make time. (We will cover the principles of personal time management in Chapter 5.) Others welcome interruptions and seek out activities that inhibit planning because they do not know how to plan.

Organizing

Supervisors have certain resources available to them, and they must organize those resources to get the work done. How well this organizing function is performed has a direct effect on the efficiency and effectiveness of the operating unit.

Because a supervisor inherits an existing organization, this function is sometimes overlooked. This is how inefficiencies are continued for years in a company. When new products or computer systems force everyone to look at how the work is processed, the results of the lack of attention to organizing the work come to light. This also helps to explain why objective outsiders will spot so many potential improvements.

Directing

In order to get the work done through other people, it becomes necessary to direct who does what and when. This involves assigning work and making decisions as the need arises. Inherent in the function of directing is the element of leadership. How effective a supervisor is in influencing the workers to follow directions will reflect on the supervisor's leadership ability. A more complete discussion of the concept of leadership can be found in Chapter 7.

Motivating

In the preceding chapter we discussed the theories of motivation. In the next chapter we will cover the practical application of motivational techniques. The supervisory function of motivating illustrates that there is more to getting people to do things than just telling them. This is the human relations function of the supervisor.

Controlling

The supervisor cannot be everywhere at the same time. He needs controls that tell him if things are going according to plan. Controlling means more than that, however. There are three key steps to the control function:

1. Identify strategic points in the workflow where the volume or quality or the current condition of some particular aspect of the work will reflect how well things are going.
2. Set standards at these strategic points, based on what you would like to happen.
3. Set up a reporting system that will indicate where attention should be placed.

We will discuss approaches to setting standards in future chapters. Appropriate standards are most important if the proper degree of control is to be exercised. In any event, the control system set up must be a basis for action, not just a passive reporting system.

ACTIVITIES

It is always a revelation to the authors when a group of supervisors is asked to list all their regular activities at work. They generally are stumped at four or five activities before a few suggestions open up the floodgates of longer and longer lists. What are some of these major activities?

Hiring

The work cannot get done without people. Since most supervisors take over operations already in existence, the staffing function tends to get overlooked. However, it is essential. How well a supervisor selects new employees contributes greatly to that supervisor's success. It is a big decision to select a job applicant. Some supervisors call it "strictly a game of chance." But under today's constraints in dealing with an unsatisfactory employee, it is important that a supervisor set standards in terms of background, personality, skills, and knowledge, as set forth in the position description.

There hardly seems to be a supervisor who feels that the salary levels he must work with are adequate to attract employees of the right caliber. This attitude could cause the supervisor to lower the standards for hiring good employees. When this happens, it is the supervisor's ability, not the salary structure, that should be questioned, unless the salary level is far out of line. Supervisors must always strive to hire the best qualified employee possible for the job.

Training

The hallmark of an effective supervisor is well-trained employees. The effective supervisor attends to all the details involved in making sure that a new employee receives proper training. How an employee is assimilated into the working unit will affect that employee's performance in the long run. The training program sets the tone for determining the quality level and concentration that will be expected, the general level of employee expectations, and employee attitudes toward the job.

It is also important that a supervisor have an ongoing training program to ensure that even the experienced workers are properly performing the job, as well as to cross-train employees so there is sufficient backup to handle peak workloads or substitute for key workers. Any time a supervisor has a job that is known by only one employee, there is a potential problem. The unit will be inflexible and unable to react to crises. For every task there should be at least one backup person who performs that task on a regular basis to maintain proficiency. If the task is a high-volume one, there should be at least two backup employees. The smaller the unit, the greater the need to cross-train.

Cross-training is usually an excellent morale booster and encourages teamwork as well as stability of the work force. One large Midwestern company conducts regular "truck sessions." A manager and the boss discuss what would happen to the unit's effectiveness if an employee were to be hit by a truck at lunchtime. The sessions uncover lack of depth and point to areas where training and development are necessary.

Maintaining Discipline

Discipline comes in many forms and degrees. The most effective supervisors let no mistake pass without seizing the opportunity to use the incident to avoid a future mistake. The skill of the supervisor comes into play to assure that the degree of emphasis or focus is kept in direct proportion to the gravity of the error or transgression. In all cases, the discipline must remain impersonal. The emphasis should be on correcting the situation rather than criticizing the individual.

Evaluating Performance

Most supervisors say that this is the toughest part of their job. To judge a person's performance, to put that judgment into writing, and, many times, to have to defend that judgment to the employee and the boss forces the supervisor to do something he or she usually has no training to do. This causes the supervisor to fall back on impressions and personal opinions rather than facts, which often are not available anyway.

The supervisor needs some objective tools to assist him or her to do the job of performance evaluation properly. Work standards and individual production reports comparing actual versus standard performance are the foundation for a fair and objective performance appraisal. Preparation for an appraisal session should include reviewing the job or position description, adding to or subtracting from the list of duties on the basis of actual practice, and appraising how the employee performed each of the duties listed.

Distributing Work

The assignment and distribution of work is a key function for the supervisor in getting the work out. It is the supervisor's responsibility to see to it that effort is directed to the proper tasks. If work begins to backlog, or if service requirements are not met for a certain type of business, the supervisor must review the work distribution process.

Even if a supervisor does not physically hand each job to the employees, there is an inherent work distribution responsibility that must be understood. If work flows directly to a worker, the authorization to do that work comes implicitly from the supervisor. The reason the supervisor does not overtly acknowledge the work assignment or positively say, "Do this now" is that it is an understood standard procedure. Routine work assignments are generally understood, and responsible employees can take the initiative to start and process the work.

If the need does arise to assign work to employees on a daily basis, it is the supervisor who should do it, since it is such an important function. If work to be processed is centralized at a work desk or sorting station, with employees going to that station to help themselves to what they will work on next, the supervisor is abdicating a major responsibility. Some control should be set up to ensure that the work is distributed properly.

Firing

Despite the best of intentions and apparently proper steps to assimilate a worker into an organization, mistakes are sometimes made. The supervisor must be decisive in these situations where an employee is not suited for the job that must be done. The decision that, despite all efforts, an employee just cannot handle the job is not an easy one. Even tougher is taking the step to actually terminate the employee.

Government regulations protect employees from unfounded actions. Companies have developed policies that are perhaps even more stringent to ensure that all regulations are adhered to. Therefore, once a supervisor has concrete indications that an employee is unsuited for the job, the personnel department manual must be consulted to determine the proper procedures to take to ensure that the employee has been given a fair chance to perform to expectations. If all steps have been followed, the final step is the actual dismissal of the employee. Recognizing that this is a time of stress for both the employee and the supervisor, the supervisor must be factual and decisive. To do anything else is unfair to the employee and the company.

Many companies have a probationary period of 60 or 90 days. During this time the new employee is considered a trainee who is on probation. If his or her performance is satisfactory during this period, the employee becomes a "permanent" employee. If performance does not meet minimum requirements, the employee is terminated with no strings attached. This procedure prevents future problems.

Developing Employees

Because the supervisor is part of an organization that can exist only if it has people who are capable of carrying on the business as members of that organization come and go, the supervisor has a responsibility to develop employees to take on more responsibility. This is more than just training in how to process work; it also means developing an awareness of what the organization's objectives are and how those larger objectives are achieved.

A supervisor who wishes to take on more responsibility himself must be sure not to make himself indispensable in his present job by not having someone who can step into his position should the supervisor have the opportunity to move up. Although insecure supervisors often are reluctant to develop their own replacements, it actually hinders a supervisor's progress if there is no one to take over in the event of an advancement opportunity. However, there is an even better reason to develop employees: employees who are developed into potential supervisory material can be considered better employees, and better employees mean a more effective organization.

Handling Crises

No matter how well things are planned or controlled, crises inevitably will occur. Some of these crises are completely out of the control of the supervisor—complaints to the chief executive from customers who just did not like the letter written to them to explain a procedure, or a letter that fell behind the cabinet and never got answered, or the marketing department needing some key numbers by noon time to get a new campaign off the ground.

The supervisor should look at these crises as opportunities rather than problems. It is his chance to demonstrate to the immediate boss or senior management his ability to ferret out the details, put together a report, and solve the problem. To develop a defensive posture at the very best solidifies the supervisor at the level attained.

Answering Questions

Usually the supervisor is the most knowledgeable about the work, and is therefore called upon by the employees to answer questions about items with which they are not familiar. Even if the supervisor is not the most technically knowledgeable, the authority of the position enables him to decide how questionable items or exceptions should be handled.

An inordinate amount of questions may sometimes indicate inadequate training of the employees. If the questions are the result of confusing procedures, the supervisor might want to review the methods and procedures and the documentation available. If the questions result from the employees' feeling that they have no authority to act on their own, then the supervisor might review the need to delegate more or to examine the basic job design. Some continuing questioning relates to employees' social needs—using questions as a medium for interaction with others.

Preparing Reports

All supervisors are accountable for the performance of their units. Usually, the supervisor's superiors will require some reports on productivity, timeliness of service or work being processed, unusual conditions, and size of work backlog. It is important that the reports accurately reflect what is going on. A glowing report of how well things are going will not be well received if it hits the boss's desk at the same time the systems department's analysis shows a three-week backlog and the best customer has reached the end of the line waiting for a reply to a letter. Realistic and factual reports comparing results to objectives serve the purpose best and alert all interested parties to the true conditions and the actions taken if necessary.

Processing work

This activity is best kept at a minimum if the unit has six or more employees. The supervisor who spends more time processing routine work than attending to the other supervisory functions and activities is more of a head clerk than a supervisor. Usually, a supervisor feels compelled to handle the harder cases or to jump in to cover a desk when someone is absent. It is better to develop flexibility through cross-training, or to delegate effectively to avoid being a part of the routine workflow. This approach gives the supervisor time to do the planning that usually gets ignored because of lack of time. The working supervisor is neither an effective worker nor an effective leader.

Miscellaneous

There are a number of miscellaneous activities that require supervisory involvement. These include holding or attending meetings, communicating new procedures or changes, scheduling overtime, settling differences between employees or with other departments, putting together special projects as the need arises, or serving on committees that are formed to study special programs.

THE END RESULT

All the effort put into the functions and activities discussed in this chapter is best evaluated in terms of how well the areas of responsibilities of a supervisor are taken care of. The bottom line is getting the work out accurately and within budget while providing good service. This means using the correct staff and the right equipment.

In the next chapter we will discuss the leadership qualities needed to properly conduct the required activities.

5

Eight Steps
to Becoming a Better Leader

WHAT DOES IT TAKE to be a really good supervisor? There is no easy answer to this question. We know what functions a supervisor has to perform, and we have examined what activities the supervisor spends time on each day. However, the bottom line is not just knowing about it but *doing* it all effectively.

THE GOOD SUPERVISOR

In every organization, there are supervisors who are judged to be very good and are recognized as such by management, peers, and employees alike. The "good department" is usually run by the "good supervisor." What seem to be intangible characteristics of good departments and/or supervisors actually become very concrete upon closer examination.

Good service. The good supervisor is in charge of a department that provides good service. The department takes the extra step to assure that work is completed on a timely basis. Any complaints are resolved quickly and equitably. There is a true sense of urgency. Usually, teamwork abounds and a good cooperative spirit among employees exists. You never hear, "That's not my job."

Good quality. The good supervisor sets high quality standards in the department. Employees take pride in the work being accomplished and show a real concern for things being done correctly the first time. There is a fine line here between a concern for quality and a defensiveness that causes employees to

43

double-check everything because, if the boss hears about an error, "he'll get mad at us."

High productivity. The good supervisor's department is characterized as one where the employees work hard with a sense of purpose rather than a fear of punishment. If there is a question about something, it is asked and the problem is resolved. Work does not pile up; it moves. Employees are not clock-watchers. There is little or no pacing of work because the end of the day is near. Rather, there is extra effort to get that letter in the mail tonight because it really ought to go out tonight.

Good spirit. Cooperation among employees is obvious in the well-run department. The atmosphere is friendly but not lax. The supervisor is fair to all but firm when necessary. The supervisor has been known to bend a rule here or there for the department, but is considered company-oriented and loyal to company goals.

Receptivity to change. The good supervisor always is the one who is asked to try the new program first. His or her department is always going through some important, meaningful change that will benefit the company and the employees.

Willingness to develop people. The good supervisor "suffers" from fairly high turnover, because his people are good and are in demand in the organization to take on more responsibility. The good supervisor always seems to get the "good people." The main reason for the high turnover in the good department is the ability of the supervisor to develop people.

The good supervisor hires for longevity, not in his department, but rather for the company. Only an individual with self-confidence and leadership ability would do this consciously.

Action orientation. It may appear that the good supervisor never has any problems with work or people. This is not true. Three people may quit in one week due to family transfers, better offers elsewhere, or whatever. A new employee may turn out to be a bit too slow. A backlog develops in one part of the department. Perhaps a serious error was made on the president's personal account. The big difference is that the good supervisor does not just shrug and say, "Fate is against the department," or "You just can't get good people any more," or "The stupid computer burped again," or "If only the mail department would learn to read!" Rather, the situation is analyzed, and solutions are formulated and implemented to change the situation for the better. In short, things are not allowed to just happen. The supervisor feels everything is controllable, and steps are taken to change things for the better.

Good organization. The good supervisor is well organized and knows the work, the key facts, and the employees' abilities, strong points, and weaknesses. He is able to react to crises effectively because the information needed is known or can be quickly referenced.

LEADERSHIP IN THE OFFICE

The better the leadership ability, the better the supervisor. Although there is no one style of leadership that can be judged best, we do know that leadership ability has a direct bearing on employee productivity.

When we talk of leadership, we are referring to the ability to accomplish group goals by working with and through people. It is not just the ability of one person to tell another what to do. Rather, it is getting people to do what is necessary without always having to tell them.

During a discussion with one group of supervisors, the question was asked, "What objectives do you as a supervisor have?" One supervisor immediately called out, "I want to be able to do less supervision of my people." A request to clarify this seeming paradox uncovered some key points.

Essentially, this supervisor was saying, "If I hire good people, train them properly, and give them the proper leadership, these people will know what to do and when to do it. When that happens, I have time to plan and develop new programs and spend less time 'supervising' the people." In short, a good supervisor works himself out of a job.

LEADERSHIP STYLES

There are four general styles of leadership. No one style is the best to the exclusion of the others. However, better understanding of the different styles helps us select the correct one for the situation.

Autocratic

The autocratic leader is characterized as one who makes all the decisions. Power is fully centralized in the leader, who assumes full responsibility and authority.

This style of leadership has advantages when decisions must be made quickly, such as in a crisis situation or when the department staff is new and inexperienced or insecure. This style is best where positions require little education.

The effective leader will immediately revert to this style in emergencies where there is physical danger to the group and/or there just is no time to get input from other people.

The autocratic style is resented if the employees are well trained and capable of thinking for themselves. Also, if the decision to be made is trivial, employees expect that they can make the decision themselves.

Bureaucratic

This leadership style is characterized by the strict adherence to fixed rules and a hierarchy of authority. Decisions are made strictly by the book, with no exceptions. Everything must go through channels. A subordinate could not discuss a problem directly with the boss's boss.

The bureaucratic style of leadership has the advantage of having all policies and rules applied consistently. There is never any question as to where someone goes for a decision or where one fits into the organizational structure. This becomes especially important when it concerns personnel policies and practices. It characterizes the military and government agencies, as well as civilian organizations which are very large or can be considered "political" in nature.

There are some weaknesses to this style. While consistency of application is good in many cases, it also implies inflexibility, which automatically eliminates any exceptions to the rules, even if the situation calls for them. The bureaucratic style also tends to bog down in red tape, and it slows the decision-making process, because proposals must move through the hierarchy step by step. Employees tend to view this process as reducing them to a helpless state. The bureaucratic style encourages the success of people who, by their nature, are poor decision makers and lack creativity.

Democratic

This style, sometimes called participative, is characterized by a leader who shares the decision-making responsibility with employees. The leader seeks out input from the group on any situation that interests or affects the group. A vote may be requested to arrive at the decision.

There are many advantages to this style of leadership. Because employees help develop policy, they then accept and fully support it. Also, employees often are the best experts on the situation, and the "democratic" decision based on their opinion is readily acceptable and workable.

The democratic style encourages people to contribute and makes them feel important. This sometimes is useful in developing people to contribute and get used to decision making that is implemented. It creates a friendlier atmosphere because employees are involved.

This style also has some disadvantages. Decisions take much more time. The plethora of suggestions often complicates the decision-making process and may create confusion. Rejected recommendations could cause bad feelings. This style takes some skill on the part of the leader in order for him not to lose control. Some weak leaders may use this style to avoid taking the responsibility for decisions.

Laissez-Faire

This is the free-rein style of leadership. It is characterized by management by exception. The leader who uses this style delegates freely to the employee. Little or no direction is given. Employees are expected to establish their own goals and solve their own problems.

The laissez-faire style is used to best advantage with highly motivated professional groups. It is most useful when the employees are involved in research work where independent thinking is crucial.

The disadvantages of this style include the fact that there is very little control exercised over the work being done. It assumes that the employees are competent enough to come to their own decisions, which introduces a high degree of risk should something go wrong. Confusion can result if it turns out that the employees are incompetent or lack integrity. Not all employees like this degree of freedom; some feel unusual pressure, which may cause them to leave for a more controlled and structured environment.

SELECTION OF LEADERSHIP STYLE

It would be a serious mistake for a supervisor to decide that a particular style is best and therefore to use it to the exclusion of the others. The effective leader will use all four styles, perhaps in combination depending on the circumstances.

However, leadership ability is not something that an individual is born with. It is an art that must be developed. Planning before acting, and considering the consequences of what is said or done, will enable a supervisor to develop the style that works best.

There are certain things that effective leaders will do for best results, no matter what style they are using at the time:

Ensure cooperation. In every case, the effective leader will secure cooperation by letting employees know where they are being led and why. This enables employees to feel a part of a team to achieve goals.

Set goals. Effective leaders set performance criteria to help employees know how they are progressing toward goals. The leader follows up on these standards of performance and lets employees know their progress on the basis of equitable measurements of performance.

Exercise authority. Every leader has authority that goes with the position. The successful leader must exercise this authority when necessary.

The good leader will counsel the worker when standards are not met. If discipline is called for, it must be consistent, fair, and reasonable. Discipline should never be used as punishment but only to bring about corrective action. Authority is useless unless it is effectively exercised.

Delegate. When effective leaders delegate, it is done in such a way that everyone involved understands what tasks are delegated and who has the authority. Employees must know how much authority is delegated. It is also true that delegation is most effective when authority is given to the individual rather than to the group.

Communicate. The good leader is a good communicator. Communication is a two-way proposition. Instructions must be fully understood. The leader must also be a good listener. The supervisor's instructions must be perceived as reasonable and must be acceptable to the employee.

Build and maintain group morale. High group morale generates teamwork, which facilitates the attainment of goals. To achieve this group morale, the leader must view each employee as an individual and regard each person's goal, then help him to see his performance in relation to the performance of the group.

OVERVIEW OF LEADERSHIP

Since it is apparent that any supervisor who is serious about doing a good job must strive to be a good leader, the serious supervisor will want to acquire or improve his or her leadership skills. How does one begin to become a better leader? Some preparatory steps are in order.

Define your own responsibilities. Because many people become supervisors as a result of being the best technician, there may be weakness in the areas of human relations and administrative skills. When the job of supervisor came along, in all likelihood management did not adequately define the responsibilities inherent in the job. This results in the new supervisor "feeling" his way until the job becomes better understood. The unusually good supervisor will probably succeed in this environment. A supervisor who might have been successful with the correct guidance may fail for lack of such guidance. To assume the role of leader, the supervisor will have to define his new responsibilities precisely.

Define your authority. Where responsibilities are not defined, the supervisor can soon learn what they are and begin to meet them. However, the subject of authority is more elusive. If the supervisor does not know what authority he has, he is a supervisor in title only. After defining responsibilities, the supervisor should review these with the boss. At the same time, the authority that goes with the position must be defined and agreed upon by all. Since most managers have probably never had to explicitly define the authority of their supervisors, this will not be an easy task. In the absence of a working definition of the authority one has, supervisors may at times be guilty of overstepping their bounds or not handling a situation that requires action and falls under the scope of their authority.

Be aware of responsibilities to subordinates. Just as supervisors need to be aware of both the responsibilities and the authority that come with the position, so, too, they have a responsibility to subordinates to be definite in assigning jobs to them. Indefiniteness in assignments leads to friction, misunderstanding, and ineffective work.

Set goals. It has been said before, but it bears repeating: good supervisors and good leaders set goals for work that stretch employees to high output. Goal setting is a display of leadership and shows the employees that the supervisor is interested in them and how they perform. It also shows that the department has standards for excellence, which motivate employees to contribute.

Counsel. The effective supervisor also performs the critical task of counseling employees. Good performance must be encouraged and praised. Performance that does not meet the standards set should not be ignored. The supervisor must work with sub-par performers to solve the problem and help employees to improve.

A supervisor who cannot counsel employees is not a leader. This type of supervisor tends to dictate rather than lead. Such a supervisor must question whether he or she is fit for the job and meets the requirements for leadership.

Develop a results orientation. The effective leader is results-oriented. This relates to the goal-setting process. The focus is on solutions to problems, meaningful activity, and properly placed emphasis on the things that matter.

EIGHT STEPS TO BECOMING A BETTER LEADER

There are some positive steps that a supervisor can take to be more effective as a supervisor and leader of the office worker. These steps deal with the substance of the supervisor's job. They help the supervisor get organized by gathering all the essential data about the people, the work, the methods, and the controls in the department.

Step 1: Know Your Personnel

The first thing a supervisor must do is know his or her people. A list should be prepared with the name of each employee under the supervisor. The personnel data should include the name, home address, and telephone number; employment date and history of positions and salary in company, including current salary, dates and amounts of salary increases, and next scheduled increase; and birthdate. It is also helpful to note the names of the employee's spouse and children (if there are any). Another item that is important is the education history and any industry courses the employee has successfully completed. There should be a page for each employee.

The personal data become useful at social functions at the company. It is a nice touch when the boss can remember the spouse's name. Company anniversary date is also important to employees, and the supervisor should recognize the employee on that date for the years of service.

Step 2: Planning

There are some essential ingredients to the planning process. The good leader knows where he wants to go, which means he knows his goals and objectives. In addition, the supervisor must determine how to get there. Setting out for an unknown destination is O.K. for a Sunday afternoon drive in the country, but not for the workplace. The supervisor, as leader, must provide direction, and plan how to get there.

The goals and objectives should be written down. It is a good idea for the supervisor to write each objective on a separate sheet of paper. The objective should be as specific as possible, and quantifiable, such as: "Improve productivity by 20 percent by the end of July." Under that statement of objective should be listed the plans the supervisor has for achieving that objective—for example, "Hold formal training classes one morning each week to review how to do jobs in department."

Each objective and the plan to achieve it should include certain milestones so progress can be checked regularly.

Step 3: Keep and Maintain Records

A supervisor should have at his fingertips the key records being kept in the department—volume counts, key indexes, reports on actual service versus management objectives, and productivity reports. Any well-run department will have some type of volume counts at the very least. Pictorial graphs and charts help spot trends easily.

Step 4: Keep Track of All Assignments

Another key area for which the leader needs data is the assignments that each employee handles routinely. A copy of the job descriptions for each position in the department should be at hand. These descriptions are used for review with candidates for department positions. The supervisor should also review the position descriptions at performance appraisal time. Keeping position descriptions accessible should contribute to keeping them up to date when changes in the work come about.

Step 5: Maintain Procedures Documentation

The supervisor should also have available all the procedures that have been written for the department. These should be on hand to review with new employees, be used as training aids for new employees, and provide a basis for improving methods and procedures.

The procedures manual should include all relevant documentation provided by the methods and procedures department and the work management department and all procedures written by the supervisor.

Step 6: Keep Performance Records

The supervisor should keep records on the work performance of each employee in the department. At least one calendar quarter of performance results should be kept for reference. Most supervisors would want the performance data since the last performance appraisal. These performance results should include quantity of work as well as quality of work.

Step 7: Ensure Flexibility of the Unit

Another key set of facts the supervisor should have at hand is who can do what. The supervisor should know how flexible the unit is, or who would know how to perform key jobs should absenteeism occur unexpectedly. Flexibility should be reviewed frequently (every month) to make sure there is sufficient backup at all times.

Step 8: Keep Records on Employees' Dependability

Since the work will not get out unless there are people present to do it, the supervisor will want to keep detailed attendance records. There should be a sheet for each employee, and it should be set up so that not only the date of the absence but also the day of the week are noted. Each month the supervisor should recap the number of different times the employee is absent (frequency) and the total number of days the employee is absent. For example, is the employee absent once for three days or on three separate days throughout the month? The latter situation indicates "chronic absence." The record should be discussed with the employee each month.

Putting the Concept to Work

The information gathered for each of these eight steps should be organized and placed in a binder which is kept at the supervisor's desk. It may be considered the supervisor's desktop manual, or handbook for operating the department. This manual should be a reference at salary review and performance appraisal times. It can assist in making procedural changes, preparing budgets, and setting goals. The supervisor should review the contents of the manual frequently and use it as a basis for action rather than data collection.

6

Organization Design and Work Restructuring

BEFORE THE INDUSTRIAL REVOLUTION, division of labor was based primarily on the product being made. It was the time of the tradesman, who made the entire product from beginning to end. With the advent of the Industrial Revolution, work became divided by tasks so as to better utilize machines and the people using the machines. This was the beginning of the development of modern organization theory and design.

THE PARADOX OF ORGANIZATION

The division of labor made the economy more productive. It raised our standard of living. However, the very concepts that improved the lot of our forefathers also made life more difficult. It is a paradox of organization that the more successful we are in differentiating work, the more difficult we make our task of coordinating work.

Division of work brings an increasing commitment to subgoals. Eventually, we may fail to see how the subgoals fit into the overall goals of the organization. The organizational subunit becomes bent on maximizing these subgoals, and eventually the subgoals become an end in themselves.

In terms of the effects on people's behavior in the organization, the division of work creates different social systems. Individuals begin to identify with the subgoals of their unit. They begin to adopt norms of social behavior consistent with what is required to get work done in their unit. Often, people have different time spans to make decisions than in other organizational units.

The end result of this development is that people lose sight of the interdependence of their subgoals and the need to cooperate with other subunits. The different time frames of reference and styles of interpersonal behavior make communication difficult, reducing capabilities of the parties to explain what each needs to get done or to arrive at an understanding of why they need to help each other.

This points out the need to design effective communication channels between units so the inherent subdivision economies are not canceled out by people going off in different directions. If the organization is riddled with departments that feel their work is the most important, their people are the best, and the world revolves around them, the warning signals should be evident. Departmental pride is essential, but it cannot be allowed to build barriers to cooperation.

We must design our organizational structures with this problem in mind so that we can avoid it. There are principles of organization design that the supervisor should be aware of. These are discussed in the following section.

THE BASIS FOR ORGANIZATION DESIGN

Although the types of organizational structures appear unlimited, there are some basic concepts that provide the foundation for how work will be divided. Consistency of application of these concepts in any one organization is not necessarily a requirement, but each will be examined as if it were a rule.

Organization by Function

Organization by function groups similar tasks into one unit. These tasks usually are oriented toward a common goal. Some examples of this structure include keypunch departments, word processing centers, check processing departments in banks, and policy change departments in insurance companies.

This structure appears to be the most logical. It takes advantage of similar skills needed by the employees and places them under one supervisor who is knowledgeable about the work. The common goal for each organizational unit under the functional concept should be easily identifiable. In keypunch it is to get information ready for the computer; in word processing it is to get words from dictation or handwritten format to typewritten format; in check processing it is to get the canceled checks filed in such a way that the monthly bank statement can be easily processed; in the policy change unit it is to handle all requests to change the insurance contract between insured and company.

A company that organizes on a functional basis will have a structure similar to that shown in Figure 6-1. In such an organization, management and supervisory

Figure 6-1. Organization on functional basis, First Policy Insurance Company.

personnel must usually have a broad product knowledge, because the full spectrum of the organization's products will pass through the unit for processing. However, these same managers and supervisors can specialize in the operational skills needed to accomplish the job (for example, the word processing supervisor can concentrate on the body of knowledge required to operate such a function).

This organizational structure usually will result in a relatively large number of communication problems, because the work moves back and forth across departmental lines. Since each unit will be committed to its own specific goals without understanding the other units' problems or being concerned about their deadlines, problems can develop.

Organization by Product

Organization on the basis of product lines is usually found in companies with many diversified products. However, it is not limited to just that environment. Sometimes a company will organize functionally except for its new products. In such a case, a separate department will be set up to handle all the functions connected with the special or new product until it is established. Other companies operate strictly on the product basis to utilize special product knowledge that develops in such a structure, or to better establish profit centers.

The advantage of such an organizational structure is that people's attention is focused not on the function being performed but on the product or services being sold. When a company organizes on a strict product basis, there is usually a duplication of some functions. Figure 6-2 depicts an example of such an organization. As we can see, each division has a marketing department, an underwriting department, an accounting department, and a service department in each of its major product divisions.

Organization by Geographic Location

A third major approach to organization is based on geographic location. This type of organization is most commonly found in sales and service departments of companies that market essentially one product. One of the benefits of this organization type is that it puts the sales or service personnel closer to the customer or prospect. This is especially advantageous where the nature of the product is such that personal contact with customers is essential to meet their needs.

Mixed Organization Types

In practice, most organizations have a combination of structures. Marketing may be geographic, the home office may be product-oriented, and some depart-

Figure 6-2. Organization on product basis, Long Lasting Insurance Company.

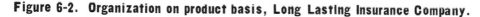

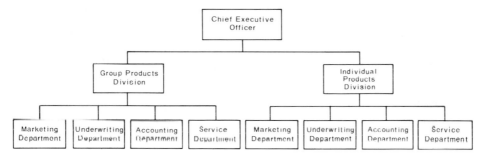

ments may be functional in nature. Because of the inherent benefits of each type of structure, different parts of a company can adopt the structure that maximizes their effectiveness.

CENTRALIZED VERSUS DECENTRALIZED ORGANIZATION

There is no rule of thumb in regard to whether a company should centralize or decentralize its operation. However, it is important to recognize that a fully decentralized company—that is, one that has fully autonomous branches or divisions at separate locations—may still have some centralization in individual units. If we focus strictly on the department, unit, or function, there is much to be gained by centralizing. When skills can be pooled, or management can be better focused on the specialized function, efficiencies are realized. It is also becoming more and more apparent that in today's evolving office with its steadily increasing dependence on electronics to assist in processing the work, more centralization of functions will occur.

Customer Service

Figure 6-3 shows a typical workflow in a service organization of ten years ago. Someone receives a letter requesting service. A clerk requests the customer file and gives it to a service representative. The letter is reviewed, and the requested

Figure 6-3. Typical service organization ten years ago.

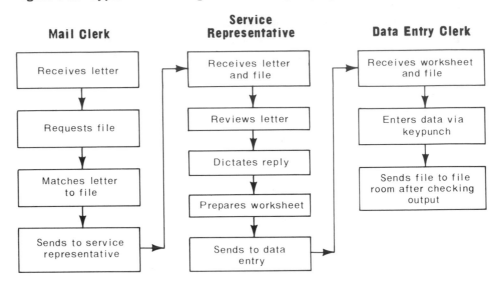

service identified and fulfilled by dictating a letter to the customer and preparing a worksheet to change the computer record. The worksheet goes to a data entry unit for input to the computer.

Figure 6-4 illustrates today's centralized operation. The letter comes in and goes directly to the service representative, who calls up the customer's file through the on-line video terminal, determines what is being requested, and enters the change on the spot. The computer automatically prints a letter to the customer, confirming the completion of the transaction. No files department, no data entry, and no typing department. With the increasing use of WATS (Wide Area Telephone System), where customers use the toll-free 800 telephone numbers, even the mail clerk is bypassed. The customer is able to talk directly to the service representative.

Word Processing

Efficiencies of equipment are also prompting centralization of services such as typing. The concept of "word processing" that uses computers to store and produce the written word is only in its infancy. Where 20 to 30 letters per typist were possible with the standard electric typewriter, 50 to 75 or 100 or more letters per day can be processed by making use of the words already stored on magnetic tape or disk, which can be recalled as needed. Because of both the expense and the capacity of such equipment, good management requires full utilization of the equipment on a daily basis to justify the investment. Centralizing all typing in the word processing unit will result in a better end product, better service, and reduced staff.

Word processing still has its detractors. These are the people who feel that centralizing their typing needs will result in poor quality, because their work will not get the specialized attention and knowledge once given by their personal secretary. The ability to rush over to the secretary and say, "Drop everything and do this now," also is lost by putting typists under a different manager. These apparent problems are easily resolved by good word processing managers and cooperative users. In most cases, the end result is higher productivity at lower cost. It must be recognized, however, that word processing is a threat to an executive's status as personified by the private secretary.

Purchasing

The centralized purchasing function is by no means new to the office scene. However, it illustrates some of the benefits that centralization may bring to a company. The knowledge of a purchasing professional results in many economies to the company. Improved relations with vendors, avoidance of duplication of efforts, savings of user departments' time, and better control of company funds usually result. The purchasing agent can combine similar orders and get quantity discounts. The control that naturally results by verifying all invoices against the authorized purchase order assures that the company receives what it ordered and pays only what it should.

Figure 6-4. Modern-day centralized service operation.

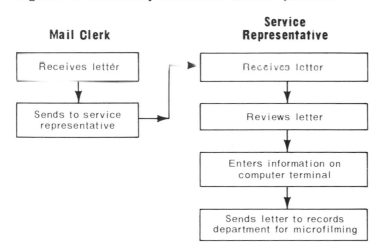

Methods Department

Perhaps the most difficult and as yet unresolved organizational question in many companies involves the methods function. Should it be centralized, thus becoming a "staff" function to assist all managers, or should each user department have its own methods function? Because methods work requires a special body of knowledge and skills, as well as a great deal of independence and objectivity, most companies centralize the function. By its nature, methods work requires continual shifting between projects, which makes effective utilization of human resources more difficult, especially if the activity is decentralized.

However, many companies do decentralize the methods function. Very large corporations with divisional structures that are organized on a product basis will have decentralized methods units. The large size of each division ensures that it will complete plenty of projects and that the analysts will be reasonably independent and objective. Analysts in a decentralized organizational unit become specialists in the product they constantly work with. If they can maintain their objectivity, they will be more effective in the long run than their counterparts in a centralized methods department.

When small or medium-size companies, up to about 1,000 employees, decentralize their methods function, there usually is a loss of effective utilization of resources. To occupy their time, the analysts become trouble-shooters, tracking down unanswered correspondence or errors or researching complex questions from customers. This is not methods work but staff assistant or even supervisory work.

Data Processing

One of the purest examples of how equipment or machinery dictates centralization is the computer department, variously called data processing (DP), electronic data processing (EDP), or computer services. Because equipment is relatively large, extremely expensive, and able to handle great volumes of work, and because it requires special skills and knowledge to run the equipment, centralization became the only way to go. As computers became more and more sophisticated, they had a ripple effect on the organizational structure of other units in the company. The installation of any new data processing system that uses the concepts of data base management, where general information pieces from the entire organization are collected, organized, manipulated, and made available to other subunits that previously had no access to it, will change the organizational structure out of necessity. Management information systems (MISs) that use the data base, integrate the information to be used by the whole company, and process the new information daily, must change the organization. Organizational structures prior to MIS are not adequate for post-MIS. Generally, those older structures had boundaries that defined a narrower scope, encouraged "proprietary information" not known by or shared with other organizational subunits, and had subgoals that sometimes did not mesh with corporate goals.

The integrated management information systems used by today's computers must break down these boundaries and expand interaction of subunits in the organization. It is no longer a matter of reporting figures to the controller once a month or once a quarter; it must be done every day if the controls are to balance and the on-line information is to be current when the department down the hall calls up the file on its cathode ray tube (CRT).

It is the firm belief of the authors that the failure of both computer systems designers and management to recognize and respond to the organizational impact of new computer systems is one of the major reasons some of these systems failed to live up to expectations or experienced large overruns in the development budget. Worse yet, some computer systems were abandoned or are error-prone because the structure of the subunits has never been updated to meet the changing need of the organization's primary goals.

It is obvious that data processing's impact on the organization will change in the future. The pendulum is swinging back the other way. With the advent of the minicomputer or time-sharing systems that connect massive computers to many small users through stand-alone terminals located in the department, each department is able to attend to its special applications without depending on the main computer system. It remains to be seen what impact these increasingly powerful minicomputers will have on the organization. Initial signals are that some data processing functions will be decentralized and the main computer will be utilized more effectively for the centralized management information system.

The Personnel Function

Organizational structures are shaped not only by the forces within companies but also by external forces. A good example is the personnel function. In addition to requiring specialized knowledge of the personnel field itself, the function requires centralization to handle the regulatory aspects. The increasing number of laws that govern how companies deal with applicants to afford everyone an equal employment opportunity require certain records and documentation of activities.

The specialized personnel function keeps watch over the organization and assures that individual managers who are not familiar with the complex laws do not unwittingly violate laws, possibly causing the organization to have disciplinary action brought against it. The centralized personnel function also is in the best position to monitor the use of human resources, including staffing, organizational and individual development through training, and compensation plans to attract and keep good people and reward them in direct proportion to job performance.

Consistency in all these things requires an organization of any significant size (over 100 employees) to have a centralized personnel function.

Customer Service

As we alluded to earlier in this chapter, centralization of functions broadens the concepts of each organizational subunit. Typing units have become word processing, keypunch has become data entry, employment departments have become personnel and now human resources departments. These units are all internal or facilitating units. These same forces are shaping the line or processing departments.

Companies are now centralizing all the functions that are involved with the customer into customer services departments. Address changes, account balances, billing information, and other areas are being organized under the concept of one service department that cares for all the customer's needs. In insurance companies, the departments concerned with underwriting, policy issue, premium accounting, insurance contract changes, and claims are being joined together in the "cradle to the grave" concept. All the customer's needs are handled by one unit from the moment the person becomes a customer. Again, the advent of the computer system puts all the necessary information at the fingertips of the customer service specialists. Rather than going to three different places in a company to have an address changed, change a policy coverage, and pay a premium, it all can be done in one place. This results in better service to the customer and economies to the company. This latter point will be covered in some detail in the "Organization of Work" section later in this chapter.

Profit Centers

A variation of organizational structures is the concept of profit centers. Under this concept, a company may make one organizational structure fully responsible for every activity that is associated with a product or service. A profit center would have its own marketing, financial, and services activities. The head of the profit center is fully responsible for the bottom line of his or her product. Although there is usually a great deal of duplication of organizational functions, there is improved control over the results by the manager.

There are pros and cons for this type of organizational structure. Some experts say that a profit center should never be used in its pure form in service industries such as banks and insurance companies, but that it does work well in heavy industries that are more product-oriented. The duplication of functions in the service environment that is already labor-intensive is considered unnecessary overhead for the benefits returned.[1]

[1]John M. Hamilton, "Decentralized Profit Responsibility for Life Insurance Companies," *Best's Review*, December 1976, p. 76.

PRINCIPLES OF ORGANIZATION

It is important to review again the principles of organization outlined in Chapter 1, as they apply to the organizational structure. These principles apply to the general structure, but as the organizational concepts are discussed and developed, it will be readily seen that they affect the organization of work as well.

Chain of Command

In the organizational structure, the chain of command principle says that each level of the organization is linked to the level above or below it in a superior–subordinate relationship. This link carries through from the lowest level of the organization to the very top. Every person has a superior, every superior has one or more subordinates. No one person in the organization should be an "island" with no superior or subordinate link. Where such a situation does exist, the function being performed by that individual is extraneous, because it does not link to overall organizational goals.

Unity of Command

In order to maintain some order in the organization, it is important that any individual have only one superior. For example, the manager of accounting should have no direct control over an employee in the marketing department. If the accounting manager wants the marketing employee to change the way he or she is doing something, the proper channels of the organization should be followed. For example, the manager of accounting would go to the manager of marketing, who in turn would go to the employee's supervisor, who then would effect the change. For routine matters, the accounting manager could ask the marketing employee to perform a task that has been generally established already and previously agreed upon.

Span of Control

Another issue of organizational structure deals with how many employees any one supervisor can manage effectively. When we think about the supervisor's job as described in Chapters 2, 4, and 5, it becomes readily apparent that the more people any one supervisor must deal with routinely, the less time he can spend with any one subordinate.

The concept of span control says that the span of any one supervisor must be kept to a reasonable scope. The key question is, what is reasonable? Experience proves that the answer depends both on the number of people and the number of different major functions those people perform. A group of 25 people all performing the same function could be controlled by one supervisor, although there is a limit.

Just a few people doing many different major jobs create pressures on the supervisor's time, making the span too great to control. In most offices, a span of seven to ten employees to one supervisor is usually adequate. Supervising fewer employees than that creates a fragmented organization that results in a loss of efficiency and a complication of communications.

ORGANIZATION OF WORK

How the organizational structure is put together affects how work is organized, and vice versa. Keeping in mind the principle of similarity, which says that only one organizational unit should be responsible for work that is essentially the same in nature, it is important to organize the work so that similar skills can be used to process similar work. With that principle in effect, there are still a number of options to how the work is organized within the unit.

Division of Work

All work, whether looked at as a specific task or the work of a whole department, can be segmented into setup, execution, and wrap-up. When the work of the whole department is concerned, work generally does not flow into the department one piece at a time but rather as a batch of work. The setup phase includes looking at the work to determine what is required and who is to handle the work. If there are files to be acquired or information to be gathered within the department, it is usually more efficient to do it at the setup station, often by assigning the task to a mail clerk at a sort station. The execution step is getting the work accomplished by doing what is requested or necessary to move it along to the next step. Once the work is done, it must then be "wrapped up," or readied to be moved to the next department. This may include sorting, updating the file, or refiling materials. Each time work moves between individuals or departments, the setup, execution, and wrap-up steps must be repeated.

In the interest of providing timely service as well as utilizing skills to their fullest, utility clerks are generally used to handle the unskilled portion of the job or the setup and wrap-up phases of the work in each department. This frees skilled labor to apply specialized knowledge on a more or less continuous basis. How should the work be organized, recognizing the three stages of setup, execution, and wrap-up? Here are the possibilities.

Skilled versus Unskilled

The jobs can be organized on the basis of special knowledge needed. Simple jobs like sorting can be handled at the mail desk or some such work station. All work requiring special training or knowledge would be handled by the other employees.

Functional Organization

Work can also be organized by major function. In an accounting department there could be a receivables clerk and a payables clerk, in addition to the mail clerk and a records clerk. There may also be a ledger clerk and an account reconciliation clerk. Each function is assigned to one or more individuals. Naturally, this organizational approach would result in requiring at least one person for each function. Therefore, this structure would be workable only in large departments where each function would make up a full day's job for the person assigned to it.

Task Organization

The work may also be structured on a task-by-task basis. Again, this is best in high-volume situations where each task, such as processing beneficiary change in an insurance company, has a sufficient volume to support such specialization.

Job Design

The structuring of work has job design as an underlying principle. Today's worker wants a meaningful job. It is important that jobs are not fragmented to the point that they become boring and almost meaningless. Naturally, the opposite can be true: jobs can be so complex that one individual cannot comfortably control the end product or be trained in a reasonable period of time, resulting in a loss of productivity.

An example of fragmentation is where someone identifies a problem, a second person investigates the problem, gathers data, and turns all the information over to a third person, who writes the report. A more meaningful job can be designed by merging the problem-investigation and -solution operations with the report-writing operation into one cohesive job.

We will cover job design in more detail in Chapter 7. At this point, we can conclude that the approach to organization of work will affect the amount of staff needed, the services rendered, and the efficiency and effectiveness of the people in the organization.

PART

II

TECHNIQUES
FOR IMPROVING
OFFICE PRODUCTIVITY

7

Work Improvement Techniques

THE EFFECTIVE SUPERVISOR requires three types of skills: leadership skills to get work done through others, job skills to be able to handle problems related to the work, and technical skills to manage the systems and procedures. We have already addressed the leadership skills required. The job skills must be developed prior to assuming a supervisory level. The technical skills are those skills which are most often overlooked.

In some organizations, staff functions such as systems and procedures, planning, and methods provide the technical skills so that supervisory personnel need not make any attempt to learn them. The effective leader, however, should have a working knowledge of the various techniques that are applied by these groups in order to utilize their services productively or, in the absence of staff function, apply those techniques himself.

When we speak of work improvement techniques, we mean techniques for increasing the effectiveness of a procedure with a proportional decrease in cost. The key to understanding the concept of improvement is to consider the value of paperwork in a work environment.

Paperwork is one of the most serious problems facing businesses today. Essentially it is the recording, analysis, transmission, and storage of information in business. The purpose of paperwork should be to help someone do his or her job better. Paperwork improves the performance of work, since it is far more substantial than memory. However, there is a definite cost factor involved; all unnecessary paperwork is a waste of time and dollars. In order to gain management's support for a paperwork simplification program, one must first demonstrate how unnecessary paperwork affects profitability and service.

RESISTANCE TO CHANGE

One barrier that must be overcome when considering any of the work improvement techniques is "resistance to change." Everyone resists change. You don't like to change. I don't like to change. Nobody with a real understanding of the turmoil change can bring about really enjoys it.

Change is work, pure and simple. To change anything, particularly the way we're doing business, is an effort that's easier not to make. But change we must, if we intend to keep up with the rapidly changing world around us.

One-half of what you read today will be obsolete in ten years. One-half of what you should know ten years from now hasn't been thought of yet. Whatever you are doing now, somebody is changing it. You won't be doing what you are doing wrong long, even if you wanted to.

Still, it is basic human nature to resist change, or anything that goes beyond the basic framework or specialty in which we have been trained.

Henry Ford said that if a thing was made the same way for six months, we should check to see if there was a better way; if it was made the same way for two years, he was sure that there must be a better way. If we have not found a better way, maybe our competitors have. This was true of the automobile business. How about our business?

The minute you say a thing cannot be done, you are through with it, and no matter how much you know—even if you are an expert—if you say it can't be done, you are all through. And someone knowing nothing about it, but thinking it can be done, now is a better person for that job than you.

SYSTEMS ANALYSIS

Systems analysis is an organized approach, using established techniques to assist in evaluating a complete operation by breaking it down into manageable segments for detailed analysis and then analyzing the total system. An organized approach is a logical, step-by-step approach to problem recognition, problem identification, problem definition, and problem solution.

Established systems analysis techniques include procedural flowcharting, forms analysis, work distribution charts, flow process charts, and other techniques to organize the data.

Steps Required

The steps required to perform a systems analysis are as follows:

1. *Define the system parameters.* A business system is an orderly arrangement of persons and equipment operating under a set of procedures in order to accomplish specific objectives such as marketing products or services, developing new business, or processing checks. This system definition, though seemingly simple, provides the focus necessary to assure that the analysis is applied to an area of concern to the intended user of the system.

2. *Identify inputs, outputs, and processing steps in the system.* This is one of the most time-consuming steps, but it is critical if the study is to result in a workable system that is responsive to the needs of the user.

3. *Organize the data.* The data collected must be organized into a format suitable for systems analysis purposes. Good organization of data is essential if the analysis is to be complete and successful. Many a systems project stumbles on this step, and the project never moves ahead.

4. *Analyze the system.* The system must be analyzed, and every element must be questioned as to the what, when, where, how, why, and who of the current process. The line between step 3 and step 4 is often very gray. The very organization of the data causes questions to be asked. This step assures that the questioning takes place.

5. *Develop all alternative processing techniques.* This is where the creativity of the analyst is so important—as is the climate of the company. A company that is progressive always comes up with creative systems that solve complex problems in simple ways.

6. *Evaluate alternative solutions.* Each alternative must be critically evaluated and the best alternative selected. The good analyst will be disciplined enough to postpone such evaluation until step 5 is completed. When evaluation gets in the way of developing alternatives, creativity is stifled.

7. *Document the revised workflow.* To assure proper consideration of the proposal, everything must be well documented. This step often reveals missing pieces that require further investigation before a proposal can be considered.

8. *Sell the system.* The revised system must be presented to management in such a way that it will gain approval. The successful analyst is selling all along the way, in the sense of preparing the user to accept change for the better. This step should include no surprises to the user. Rather, it should serve to tie the whole project together into a neat package for consideration and final approval.

9. *Implement the revised procedure.* Great ideas that are accepted but never implemented are a waste of everyone's time and money. Well-designed systems include realistic plans for implementation.

10. *Obtain feedback.* Feedback must be obtained from actual use of the system in line operations. This feedback enables analyst and users to evaluate the system's effectiveness and to assure that the changes have been properly understood and implemented. It is not unusual to do some fine-tuning of the system during this step, which should be ongoing.

There are several advantages of the systems approach. First, it provides an objective and logical procedure for identifying, analyzing, and objectively evaluating a range of solutions. Second, it forces the analyst to develop an organized plan for studying the system and developing and examining alternative solutions. Third, it assists in distinguishing between symptoms and problems in problem identification. For example, the symptom could be a large backlog, whereas the problem may be poor employee training.

WORK SIMPLIFICATION

Work simplification is the organized use of common sense to find easier and better ways of doing work. The term work simplification was coined by Professor Erwin H. Schell of M.I.T. The actual methods improvement approach was developed by Allan H. Mogensen, who used the principles of motion study established by Frank and Lillian Gilbreth in the 1930s. Where systems work crosses departmental boundaries, work simplification usually tends to focus on the desktop methods and procedures as the starting point.

The four fundamental objectives of work simplification are: (1) to eliminate, (2) to simplify, (3) to combine, and (4) to improve. The simplest way of doing work is normally the easiest and most practical. Methods can be simplified by changing the sequence of operations, rearranging the workplace, redesigning the forms, acquiring more up-to-date equipment, and investigating more up-to-date techniques. Everything that is not absolutely essential should be eliminated. If the entire operation cannot be eliminated, then any smaller details that are not required should be eliminated. If you cannot eliminate it, combine it with other steps or operations. Finally, improving means updating by finding a more modern way of doing work.

Steps Required

The steps required in a work simplification study involve a questioning process:

Why? Why is the task being done? Is it really necessary?
What? What is being done? What is the purpose of this detail? What are we trying to accomplish?
How? How is the work being done? Is there an easier or better way? Can it be mechanized? Should it be done manually?

Where? Where else can it be done? Does another department have specialized equipment for this work? Do other areas process similar work?

When? When is the work done? This relates to the time of day or week, as well as to how often a thing is done and in what sequence.

Who? Who does the work? Are they trained to do it? Do they have the skill to do it well? Who should do it?

VALUE ANALYSIS

Value analysis is an organized approach to identifying what is needed from a function and redesigning that function so that it will reliably achieve its objectives with the lowest costs.

Value analysis uses quantitative techniques to arrive at the proper decisions concerning each activity's value to the company. For best results, value analysis should be combined with systems analysis and design, but the key yardstick is "value." It is not so much a tool as it is an attitude that should permeate each newly created and redesigned system. The focus is on why rather than how something is done.

Steps Required

The steps required to perform a value analysis are as follows.

1. *Define objectives.* Determine precisely what you expect to be accomplished by a particular function or system. The disciplined technique of function analysis, which describes everything in a verb/noun format, is essential for an effective value analysis.

2. *Assign rank and weight.* Determine the relative importance of each objective. In every task there is a primary objective, and possibly there are one or more secondary objectives. Using the verb/noun descriptions, each part of the function or system is ranked in relationship to its contribution to the basic objective, and weights are assigned to reflect user satisfaction.

3. *Assign ceiling worth.* Decide what the achievement of each objective is worth. Dollar amounts are allocated on the basis of costs to provide each aspect of the function as described in the function analysis.

4. *Create alternatives.* This is the most powerful of the steps. Creativity, discipline, and imagination of the people suggesting alternatives will affect the end results. No alternative should be rejected, no matter how impractical it appears at the time it is suggested. In fact, the better one becomes at value analysis, the more disciplined one will be at not judging any suggested alternative at the outset.

5. *Evaluate alternatives.* Each alternative should be evaluated on the basis of

whether it can provide reliable achievement of objectives and user satisfaction at the lowest possible cost. Elimination of a function is always an alternative.

6. *Select the one best alternative.* The best alternative will be the one that balances objectives and user needs with the value of doing the function.

Other Factors in Value Analysis

The questions to be asked about a planned information-handling system can be grouped into three areas:

1. *Function.* What will the system do? Is any part of this already being done by some other system? Does this need to be done at all? An example is an accounts receivable system, whose basic function is to "collect money" (note the verb/noun construction).

2. *Design specifications.* Can any part of this system—and the process it carries out—be eliminated or combined with some other one? In the accounts receivable system just mentioned, do all parts contribute to collecting money, or are there some parts that also generate reports on unnecessary data? Can the amount of information collected and retained by this system be reduced? Are daily reports necessary if billing is done at the end of the month? Are the operating-time constraints and other system performance characteristics realistic? How essential is the marketing department report to the collection of money? Is it just nice to have? The reviewing manager should never be reluctant to ask: Does it have to be done this way? Can it be done some other way and still achieve the same results?

3. *Operating environment.* What aspects of the system are critical? What determines their importance? What are the absolutely essential things that must be done to assure that the system produces reliable information when and where managers need it? Meeting these essential information needs in the most effective fashion feasible is far more important than keeping the data processing center staff busy or making the best use of available DP equipment.

The value analysis process is most effective when all possible alternative requirements and courses of action are considered fully and systematically. No possibility should be rejected without some discussion.

Evaluation of these alternatives should seek realistic answers to questions such as: Will implementation of this idea force changes in other parts of the design, or in other systems already in operation? Will use of this idea materially reduce system performance quality or reliability? Can this alternative be combined with any other idea being considered?

The value analysis process is not infallible, but it can provide astute users with better processing and information-handling systems, quickly and with astounding results. Some companies report 35 percent to 50 percent savings as a result of value analysis.

ADVANCED JOB DESIGN

Advanced job design is the meaningful grouping of tasks together while giving to employees the responsibility for performing those tasks.

Most people are familiar with Frederick Herzberg's theories that work environments contain dissatisfiers, or hygiene factors, and motivators. Dissatisfiers include: company policies, company administration, supervision, working conditions, salaries, and benefits.

Dissatisfiers add to turnover problems, rising costs, and lack of employee motivation. Companies have attacked dissatisfiers without total success with programs such as reduced working hours, longer vacations, flexible hours, increased wages, profit sharing, off-hours activities, training, and counseling.

According to Herzberg, the following are motivators: achievements of the employees, recognition based on achievement, opportunity to increase knowledge of the job, and chances for advancement.

Steps Required for Advanced Job Design

- Interview employees to find out:
    What do they do and how do they do it?
    Where is work received from?
    Who is work forwarded to?
    Is work checked?
    What do employees like about job?
    What do employees dislike about job?
- Determine what can be done to eliminate the things employees dislike about their jobs.
- Determine if responsibility for final output, checking, and decision making can be handled by the employee.
- Consolidate responsibility from jobs which precede and follow the job under study.
- Delegate responsibility for routine work to lower level positions to enrich those jobs.
- Develop a relationship between employees and customers.
- Allow employees to work independently when possible.
- Have employees report their achievements.

Advantages

Advanced job design can improve attitudes among employees because it gives them:

A portion or module of activity which is theirs alone.

An opportunity to make decisions affecting their work.

An opportunity to identify with their work.

A chance for achievement.

An opportunity to earn recognition.

An opportunity to grow with the job.

A chance to have a meaningful work experience.

Direct feedback of the results of their actions.

A relationship with "clients" or "customers" inside or outside the organization.

Opportunities to keep learning through the job.

Control over the scheduling of work, allowing them wide discretion so long as they meet deadlines.

An area of expertise uniquely identified with them.

KEY FACTORS FOR SUCCESS

There are three essential steps to getting a work improvement program installed:

1. *Participate.* "We must convince people to work smarter, not harder," declared Allan H. Mogensen, a work improvement pioneer. The employee usually knows the job best and can contribute many ideas for improvement.

2. *Communicate.* Every person at every level must understand what we are trying to accomplish and how they will be affected.

3. *Listen.* One of the most important aspects of a study is the interview. This involves the desk-by-desk visits to find out what the various people do and how they do it, and the collection of forms and work specimens. The analyst must be discreet and be a good listener and a good questioner.

COMMON FACTORS

Each of the techniques or approaches mentioned has a common pattern. Each attempts to find a better way by examining the factors involved in paperwork, namely, procedures, forms, reports, filing, equipment, space, and personnel. The fundamental concern should be to get the most practical result in the shortest time period, with the least amount of effort, and at the lowest cost. The relationship of these fundamentals is illustrated in Figure 7-1.

USE OF GRAPHIC TOOLS

There are six basic tools for providing a graphic representation to be used in conducting a study. They are: organization charts, flowcharts, task lists, work

Figure 7-I. Relationship of fundamentals.

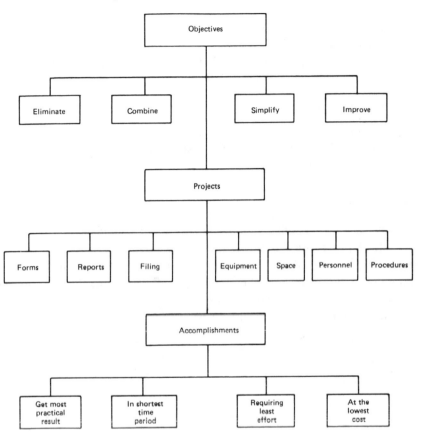

Figure 7-2. Simple organization chart.

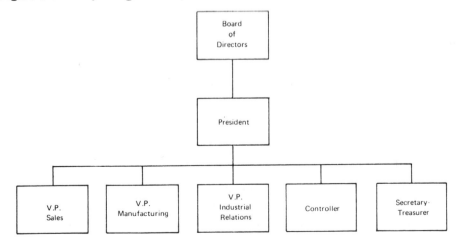

distribution charts, forms distribution charts, and workplace layout. The authors do not recommend the use of each of these tools for every situation, because this could easily lead to becoming preoccupied with the tools and losing sight of the objectives. We will examine each tool and explore its uses.

Organization Charts

An organization chart should show the plan of organization and the lines of authority. Figure 7-2 is a simple example showing officers (and, by implication, departments) and lines of authority.

Flowcharts

A flowchart is a graphic representation of the sequence of all operations, transportations, inspections, delays, and storages during a process or procedure. Frederick Taylor and the Gilbreths are generally given credit for the early development of flowcharting techniques. Figure 7-3 contains the most commonly used flowcharting symbols. Though these symbols may seem somewhat complex, only those few which are important to paperwork analysis need be considered initially:

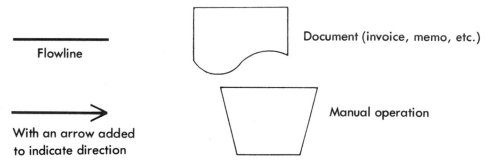

The symbols can be drawn by using a template, which can be obtained from an office supply store or a business machine company such as IBM. In order to facilitate the drawing of flowcharts, one can use chart or graph paper which provides guides for lining up the symbols.

Figure 7-4 is an example of a flowchart that represents the paper flow of an invoicing procedure.

Tasks Lists

A task list includes the names of the tasks performed by an employee. A separate task list is written for each employee or job in the case of a group of employees all performing the same tasks. Figure 7-5 exemplifies a typical task list.

Figure 7-3. Flowchart symbols.

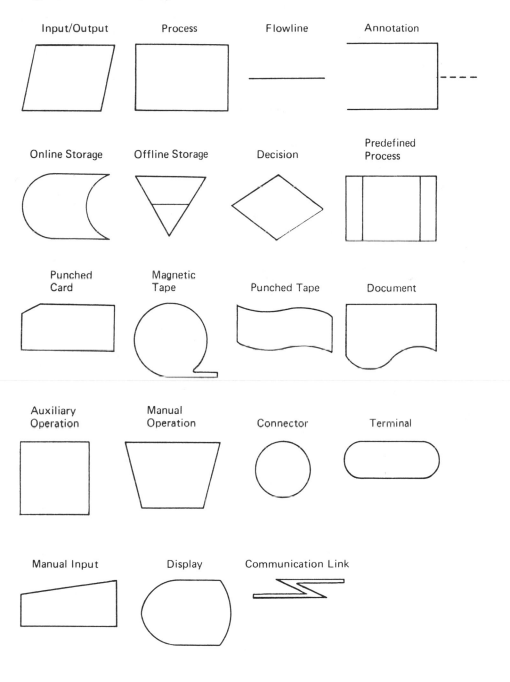

Figure 7-4. Flowchart of an order-invoice procedure.

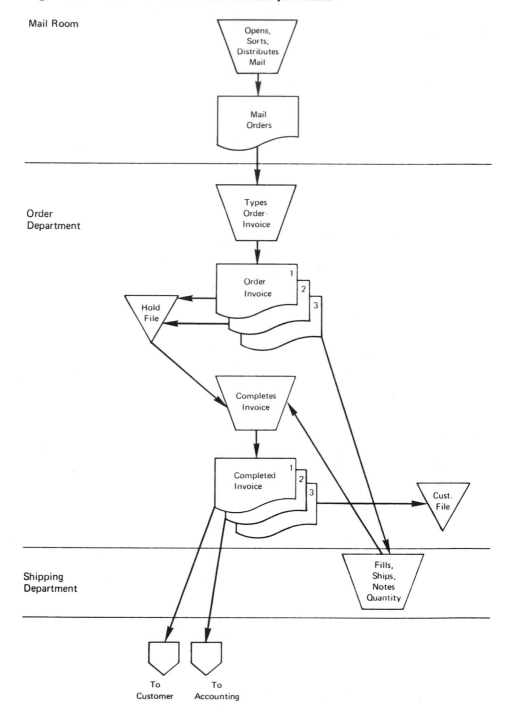

Figure 7-5. Sample task list.

INSTRUCTIONS		
1. Begin each task name with an action verb.	DEPARTMENT ___ Operations ___	
2. Keep task name as short as possible.	UNIT AND/OR SECTION ___ Order Processing ___	
3. List tasks requiring the most time first.	JOB TITLE ___ Senior Order Clerk ___	
4. Quantities and time relate to the frequency.	DATE ___ 11/28/XX ___	
	APPROVED BY ___ Ann Kimball ___	

No.	List of Tasks	Check Frequency*				Est. Quan.	Est. Time %
		D	W	M	Other		
1	Credit Checks — $1,000 & up	X				20	50
2	Type Invoices — New Orders	X				10	30
3	Account Adjustments	X				4	10
4	Order Supplies		X			1	5
5	File Diary Cards		X			30	2

*D = Daily; W = Weekly; M = Monthly

Work Distribution Charts

A work distribution chart summarizes all the tasks performed by the employees in a given department. It provides a basis for verifying that all major tasks have been recorded, examining the balance of the workload, and scheduling work. Figure 7-6 provides a sample format for a work distribution chart.

Figure 7-6. Work distribution chart.

SPECIFIC TASKS OF EMPLOYEES BY HOURS PER ACTIVITY – SOURCE: TASK LISTS

EMPLOYEE NAME / POSITION TITLE	Pilgrim / Sr. Order Clerk	E H	Alden / Order Clerk	E H	Standish / Order Clerk	E H	Miles / Utility Clerk	E H	TOTALS FOR ACTIVITIES HOURS	%
ORDERS	$1000 + Credit Type Invoice	20 12	Check Small Credit Type Invoice	18 13	Check Small Credit Type Invoice	6 4	Make New Files File Invoices Pull Files	4 8 8	93	59
ADJUSTMENTS	Account Adjustments	4	Address Changes	8	Address Change	15	File Changes Pull Changes	5 5	37	24
INVENTORY					Inventory Control	12	Inventory Tickets	6	18	11
MISCELLANEOUS	Order Supplies File Diaries	2 1	Weekly Error Report	1	Weekly Inventory Report	2	Search	3	9	6
WEEKLY TOTAL HOURS PER EMPLOYEE		39		40		39		39	157	100%

PRIMARY ACTIVITIES OF SECTION

EH = estimated hours per month.
Rank employees in orders of responsibility.

Key additional information to reverse side with circled numbers.
Hours are to be rounded off to whole numbers.

Forms Distribution Charts

This type of chart provides one column for each clerk, but no description of the operations performed. This is a good type of chart to use where recording the flow and tying down the copies are more important than recording the exact operations. A common type of forms distribution chart is shown in Figure 7-7.

Workplace Layout

The workplace layout is a floor plan of the department on which the analyst can trace the movement of work throughout the department. Figure 7-8 is an example of a completed layout prior to an improvement program.

INSTALLING A WORK IMPROVEMENT PROGRAM

Where do you start? How can the improvement program be built upon a solid foundation of mutual confidence and understanding? Obviously, it is difficult to generate much enthusiasm at the lower levels if people there have not seen evidence of improvement at the higher levels first. An excellent initial approach to tackling problems of paperwork improvement is to start with top management forms and reports.

The paperwork improvement program must be led by someone who has leadership qualities. The leader of a paperwork improvement program must like people, be firm and just but not overbearing or domineering, be a good listener, and have developed a capacity to analyze situations and people. This individual should have special training in systems and procedures, work analysis, personnel, and training.

If an inside employee is selected to lead the program, the initial thrust should be in a pilot program, where experience can be gained without upsetting "outsiders." Therefore, the program should be started in the project leader's own department, starting with his own desk. No greater lesson in objectivity can be gained than by analyzing one's own performance. Next, the leader should tackle the desk next to his, finally ending up with a project for his own department. However, he should keep the results of his efforts confidential.

If others are to be used in the project, they should be requested to analyze their own and the surrounding desks too, under the guidance of the project leader. Finally, the project-team members should compare their findings and develop a program for their own department.

This practice in individual and team effort will enable the members of the project team to extend the program, in coordinated effort, to other departments.

Figure 7-7. Forms distribution chart.

Form	Typist	Mail Clerk	Bookkeeper	A/R Clerk
Invoice	1 2 3	To Customer	Enters	Posts
Sales Journal			Sales Journal	
A/R Ledger				A/R Ledger

Figure 7-8. Workplace layout.

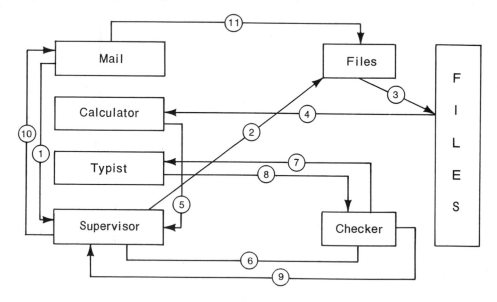

CHAPTER

8

The Need for Standards

WHEN A MANAGER pays an employee an hourly or weekly salary, he expects something in return. The employee, on the other hand, has an idea of what he should do for that salary. What happens in many cases is that both the manager and the employee settle for a "happy medium."

No two supervisors operate in exactly the same style, and this makes it hard to isolate a factor or combination of factors most responsible for successful leadership on the job. One successful supervisor may emphasize certain things, and an equally effective colleague may ignore them while stressing others. Research has shown, however, that certain kinds of action on the part of the supervisor increase his chances of succeeding. And near the top of the list is the setting of high, but attainable, work standards. One leading industrial relations expert says he has never yet studied a highly productive group where the supervisor has not given special attention to maintaining high standards.

Many experiences seem to confirm this idea. Think back to the best teacher you ever had. Did he or she expect much of you or little? We can safely predict the answer. The outstanding teacher extended you to the utmost. And it was not always fun.

People are often capable of much more than they realize. Sports records illustrate this point. The 4-minute mile, the 15-foot pole vault, the 60-foot shot put, and the 7-foot high jump all seemed unattainable—until someone reached each of these marks. Then others came along and surpassed the feat. Tourist parties now scramble to the top of mountains that once seemed unclimbable.

Thomas Edison said, "If we did the things we are capable of doing, we would amaze ourselves." The same thing is true at work. Industrial engineers often find that their greatest problem is to convince a group that a production figure is possible. When people see that the mark is attainable, they often exceed it with comparative ease.

Sometimes in business, however, we encounter the principle working in reverse. Standards may slip to lower and lower levels. Where little has been required of people over a long period, the individuals may become accustomed to a low output, unaware that they are no longer doing a full share. This may become painfully apparent when circumstances change and they are asked once again to carry a full workload.

The supervisor, of course, is not the only force working toward excellence. Nor can we assume that people are always wishing for an easier path. One experiment has shown that workers in the right organizational climate will often set higher standards than their supervisor or an outside analyst. But however the goals are set, the conclusion is inescapable: we can never get high performance without high standards.

Frederick Taylor is generally regarded as the father of scientific management. He defined scientific management as "management based on measurement plus control." It has never been stated more simply or elegantly than this. To elaborate further, you can control only that which you can measure, and the degree of your control is determined by the quality of the measurement system employed.

A MANAGEMENT OBLIGATION

Not long ago, the president of a major Midwestern bank was addressing the senior management group. He started by saying, "You know, there is nothing that grieves me more than to know that there are people who work in this bank who get up in the morning and say to themselves: 'Rats, I have to go to the old salt mines again today.' This is wrong! We, in management, have an obligation to our employees to make this bank a fun and interesting place to work. I want to know what you are doing to prevent this from happening in your area."

This question could easily be asked of any executive in any organization. The authors' experience with attitude surveys taken in a wide variety of offices reveals that one of the most common complaints voiced by employees is, "I am not recognized for the work I do." Many feel that when they work hard, they still get the same salary increase as another employee who gets by doing as little as possible. This, according to David C. Durrill, results in mediocrity in the organization, since "the plodders keep plodding and the achievers begin job-hunting."[1]

[1]"Human Relations Basis for Productivity," *United States Banker*, October 24, 1977, pp. 25–26.

Many management groups feel they have a choice—to use standards or not. We feel that this is not true. Management has an *obligation*, to both employees and supervisors, to set challenging standards. It has an obligation to supervisors, whom it must provide with the tools to get work out accurately, on time, and economically. And it has an obligation to employees to let them know what is expected of them, so that they can be properly evaluated for their contribution to the organization and rewarded for it.

The Concept of PRIDE

A popular name for a performance improvement program is PRIDE. PRIDE is an acronym for *P*erformance *R*ecognition for *I*ndividual *D*evelopment and *E*valuation. These are a lot of words, but they simply mean one thing—giving employees at all levels of the organization an opportunity to take greater pride in their work through recognition of their individual efforts.

HOW PEOPLE VIEW THEIR JOBS

Today's office employee is, on the average, better educated and more interested in the details of his job, his compensation, and the opportunity for the future than his predecessor. If employees perceive that their pay treatment is not fair, then it is going to be difficult, if not impossible, to get through to them on other matters.

Consider what most employees expect from their work. On the basis of considerable academic research and opinion surveys by various consulting firms, we can state that there are five basic expectations that most people have with respect to their work. These are:

Job Security. People want to know that their jobs are reasonably secure. They want to be able to count on the job still being there for them tomorrow—and the day after tomorrow too.

Sense of community. Employees want to identify with their employer, enjoy relationships with fellow employees, and be proud of the organization they work for

Definition of expectations. Employees want to know what is expected of them, including job duties, latitude to make decisions, and performance standards.

Feedback on performance. Employees want to know how they are doing in relation to what is expected of them. (In many organizations there is a considerable gap between the ways individuals view their own performance and the way management views their performance. The reason is that employees are simply not told where they stand.)

Opportunity. They also want to know the possibilities for the future—what promotional opportunities exist, what opportunities there are for pay increases, and what opportunities exist to make more (or bigger) decisions.

THE NEED FOR FACTS

To dramatize the average office supervisor's need for facts about his or her area of responsibility, we can ask supervisors to answer the following questions and to support their answers with facts, not just opinions:

- Do you have the correct number of employees for the workload?
- Is the production of your department getting better or worse?
- Do you know what production results to expect from each worker or from each section?
- Do you have figures to prove which employees (or sections) are doing well and which need help?

It is virtually impossible for the average office supervisor to answer these questions and support his answers with facts unless he uses standards. In the absence of any factual basis to support his evaluation, the tendency is to rate on the high side—to always give the benefit of the doubt.

Imagine a supervisor saying to an employee, "I don't think you are doing a good job." The employee is in a perfectly good position to say, "Prove it," or something to that effect. The supervisor knows it, and the employees know it. Where standards are available, the supervisor is relieved of this burden, because the standards provide a concrete basis to support the evaluation.

WHAT IS A STANDARD?

A standard is defined as any accepted or established rule, model, or criterion against which comparisons are made—that which is set up and established by authority as a rule for the measure of quantity, weight, extent, value, or quality.

Standards are a part of our everyday lives. In the home, we use standards to determine how long to prepare a roast for dinner, how long a TV commercial will last so as to make a trip to the refrigerator, how early to set the alarm in the morning so as to shower, dress, eat breakfast (simultaneously read the morning newspaper), and get to work on time. Additional time may be required if we plan to shine a pair of shoes, drop some clothes off at the cleaners, and do morning exercises. In the office we use such standards as words typed per minute, how long to schedule a meeting, and so on.

A good example of a standard is practiced by many of us when we are out playing golf. Here, par is our standard. Our measurement is the number of strokes taken. By having a form of measurement and a standard to compare against, we can tell how we are progressing by the number of strokes taken. The number of strokes taken compared to par will tell us how we are doing compared with what could be expected. Similarly the use of standards in a business situation tells us how we are doing by comparing the amount of work turned out with what could be expected.

VARIABLES AFFECTING OUTPUT

All work is devoted to one thing: the attainment of output. Output, in turn, is determined by two things, and two things only: the motions we make and the speed at which we make those motions. Figure 8-1 illustrates this point.

Method

The motions we make can also be called the method we use. The better the method, the fewer the motions that are required. Method, however, is influenced by several factors: the workplace, the amount of training given to the individual operator, the physical characteristics of the individual, and any special quality requirements.

The speed with which we make motions is largely determined by the skill and effort the individual is able to put forth, and also the working conditions, such as light, heat, and ventilation. We usually take working conditions for granted in offices, but it is fair to say that if an office is not heated properly, or ventilated properly, it will have an effect on how fast we make motions.

Effort

Effort is largely influenced by our motivation. Industrial psychologists have spent a great deal of time during recent years analyzing the motivational factors that influence the effort people put forth. Certainly, how we feel about our supervisor and other superiors, and the people we work directly with, are factors that affect the effort we put into work.

Motivation can be influenced by many factors. Contrary to what many believe, money has proved to be a motivator when used as an incentive. It is basic human nature to respond to rewards, financial or otherwise.

Attitude also affects the effort we expend. Developing a good attitude among workers is a primary responsibility of supervisors. Robert Ford, in his book *Motivation Through the Work Itself*, put it this way: "It is not a good attitude that brings about good performance, but rather the experience of performing well that brings about a good attitude among workers."

Skill

When we refer to skill, we do not mean the amount of education a person has, or his mental capacity. Skill in this case refers to the ability of the individual to perform the particular task at hand. Generally, skill may be influenced by a number

Figure 8-I. Analysis of output.

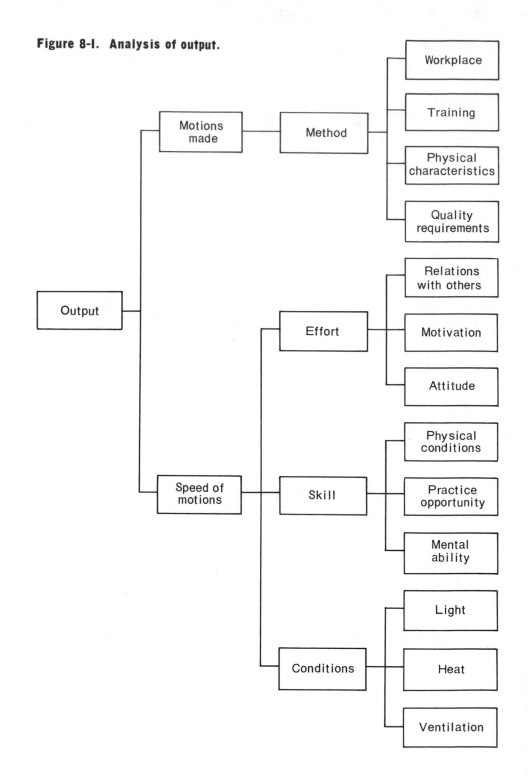

of factors, including physical conditions, health, and well-being, but it usually boils down to how serious the individual is about the work.

We find in work that the frequency with which we do things can greatly influence the skill we develop. This factor is called "practice opportunity." A typist, for example, can never be a skilled typist without a great deal of practice. This holds true for musicians as well as athletes and others.

PARKINSON'S LAW

Many managers feel their people are already producing to their optimum capacity. Are they that good? Probably not! Parkinson's law, named after the noted author, C. Northcote Parkinson, states that "work expands so as to fill the time available for its completion."

Employees quickly learn that being idle is unacceptable behavior in certain offices, particularly where a manager takes pride in running a tight ship. An hour's worth of work can become two hour's worth of work by stretching it out, double-checking things that need not be double-checked, and keeping extra records that they really don't need but now have the time to keep. Unfortunately, what happens when the workload increases is that they continue to keep the extra records and perform the unnecessary checking, and additional employees are added to take care of the added workload.

WORK MEASUREMENT

Work measurement is simply a means of determining what a fair day's work should be. It has two main components: a measure of the volume of work and a measure of the employee time used up. These two factors are expressed in their only common denominator: the amount of time required to produce one unit of work. This is what we call a standard.

Benchmarks of Performance

A standard is equated to a fair day's work pace, or what we can call 100 percent performance. Now, 100 percent is not the maximum; it is not perfection. We define 100 percent as "the work pace at which an average, well-trained employee can work without undue fatigue while producing an acceptable quality of work." This means that a 100 percent performance pace is one that an average, well-trained employee should be expected to maintain all day long. It is a "normal" working pace—not too fast and not too slow.

It is extremely important for people who set standards to have a good understanding of this concept of "normal." Industrial engineers usually spend

Figure 8-2. Accepted benchmarks of performance.

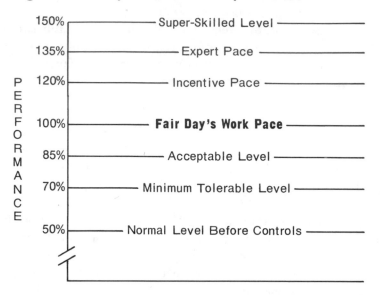

weeks, working with rating films, to understand the concept of normal. Once a clear understanding of "normal" is developed in the mind of the engineer or analyst, he can observe an employee's work pace on any type of operation and rate that individual's performance or pace. If the pace is faster than "normal," the engineer determines (usually to the nearest 5 percent) that the individual is working at a pace over 100 percent—perhaps 105 percent, 110 percent, or 115 percent. Naturally, the method the individual is using, as well as the amount of skill and effort the individual is exerting, is taken into consideration when rating performance.

Figure 8-2 shows the generally accepted benchmarks of performance equated with a concept of a normal, 100 percent engineered level of performance. Some people use 100 percent in a different context. When using a technique called Historical Data, 100 percent performance is used to plot the level of performance today, and all future performance is measured in relation to that reference point. For example, if you are turning out 1,000 units of work today with ten employees, 100 percent performance is 100 units per employee. If three months from now you turn out 1,200 units with ten employees, performance is recorded as 120 percent. When we speak of an engineered standard, we refer to a standard based on good, sound methods and procedures, and corresponding with our definition of 100 percent.

50 percent performance. As a benchmark, 50 percent is considered the average level of performance before formal controls are applied. The range is usually 40 percent to 60 percent. Now, 50 percent performance does not mean that people work for an hour and do nothing the next hour, or work four hours and do nothing the other four hours of the day. What it does mean is that people accomplish about half of what could be accomplished after standards are applied to the work.

70 percent performance. This is generally regarded as the minimum tolerable level of performance. If an employee, after a reasonable training period, cannot perform to 70 percent of standard, it is simply not economical to keep the employee in that position.

Let us say you have an employee who can perform no better than 60 percent of standard. Not only is management getting only $60 worth of work for every $100 of salary, but it is also getting only 60 percent return on fringe benefits, floor space, equipment being used, and so on.

85 percent performance. This level is considered the beginning plateau for an acceptable performance in many offices, particularly when you encounter peak and valley workload situations, critical deadlines, and normal to high turnover. Later, when staffing requirements are discussed, you will learn that 85 percent is a common level of performance at which departments are staffed. For this reason, it is difficult for employers to maintain a higher level of performance, simply because the workload is not there.

100 percent performance. This, of course, is the fair day's work level—the level where a dollar's worth of work presumably is equal to a dollar's worth of pay. This is the goal for all employees, and it is the goal for all supervisors and managers to achieve for their section or department.

An interesting question arises when we speak of 100 percent performance: are all employees who have passed the training stage of their job capable of achieving and maintaining 100 percent performance? For example, in typing, we might equate 100 percent performance with 55 words per minute. Do all people in typing jobs today possess the mental and physical dexterity to achieve and maintain a 55-words-per-minute level or better? Similarly, in coding operations, we might require employees to be able to memorize at least half of the codes to perform at 100 percent performance. Do all people who perform coding operations possess that mental capacity for memorization? Maintaining high levels of performance day in and day out requires a certain amount of concentration and perseverance.

120 percent performance. This level is usually regarded as the incentive pace, because most incentive programs are based on a 20 percent bonus. It also means that people can generally exceed the 100 percent level by 20 percent, on the average, when provided with an incentive or reward. It is not common to find people working at 120 percent or higher without some form of direct reward.

135 percent performance. This level of performance is called the expert level, because it can be achieved and maintained only by expert or extremely skilled workers. There are usually only a handful of employees, even in very large offices, who have the unusual mental and/or physical dexterity to perform at this pace.

SUMMARY

Time and time again the authors have seen the breakdown of the office environment when no standards are in effect. When backlogs grow, more people are added and overtime is instituted. Backlogs and confusion become a way of life. Turnover results, along with poor quality and increasing unit costs. Standards inject order into the office environment. Overtime is reduced and eliminated, backlogs dissipate, and morale improves. In the words of one clerical employee who witnessed the transition from no standards to standards: "Things sure are a lot better around here now!"

9

Informal Techniques

IN THE NINETEENTH and early part of the twentieth century, Taylor, Gantt, the Gilbreths, Emerson, and others worked hard at developing the scientific management concept. Frederick W. Taylor is generally known as the father of scientific management. He was responsible for the first definitive approach to work measurement. Taylor had the firm conviction that high productivity was the only firm foundation for material prosperity.

Taylor followed the time-proven approach of experimenting with new procedures, noting the results, and then drawing conclusions. He developed a simple principle, which underlies the operation of modern industry. It is summarized by him as follows: "The greatest production results when each worker is given a definite task to be performed in a definite time and in a definite manner." This is axiomatic in progressive concerns today.

"Definite task" leads us to the way in which jobs are designed in an office. "Definite manner" refers to the method or proper sequence of motions or functions. These will be covered in later chapters. "Definite time," however, is the crux of the matter when we talk about measurement techniques.

Measurement itself includes two major problems. First, does the work lend itself to measurement? Second, do the measurements correspond to actual performance in the changing fabric of life? Perhaps the major contribution of Taylor and the Gilbreths was a reproducible demonstration that the performance of human beings can be measured.

FACTORS INVOLVED

The authors have always subscribed to the theory that any form of measurement is better than no measurement at all. It also follows that any form of control is better than no control at all. Some techniques provide a very loose form of measurement and, therefore, a minimum amount of control. Other techniques provide a most precise form of measurement, and therefore a high degree of control. The more precise measurement techniques require a great deal of training to apply. Also, as a general rule, it requires more time to establish standards based on these precise techniques. Additional training time and additional time required to set standards increase the cost of measurement.

The Question of Accuracy

If you were to ask the average industrial engineer or office work measurement analyst what is most important in a measurement technique, he or she will respond, "accuracy." Ask, "how accurate?" and the response will usually be, "as accurate as can be." The fact is, accuracy has little to do with measurement. It is an economic, not an engineering, consideration.

The precision of standards, however, can be grouped in three categories: loose, accurate, and tight. Here the term accurate takes on a whole new meaning. Perhaps the best word to equate with accurate is fair. Fair to whom? Fair to the employee in terms of being realistic and attainable, but also fair to management as a fair price to pay for work. It is also called a "fair day's work pace," or "a dollar's worth of work for a dollar's worth of pay."

A "loose" standard is a generous standard and allows more time than is necessary to perform a function. Employees don't object to a loose standard, but it is unfair to management.

A "tight" standard requires a worker to work at a pace that results in undue fatigue or is simply unattainable. To reverse the point made previously, a tight standard may seem entirely fair to management, but it is unfair to the worker. If workers attained tight standards, they would be giving management more labor than management was paying for.

For example, suppose a worker is paid $40 per day to process applications. An accurate or fair standard of 12 minutes per application means the employee should turn out 5 per hour, or 40 in an 8-hour day. This also means a labor cost per application of $1.00. A loose standard would allow more than 12 minutes per application—say, 20 minutes. This would increase the labor cost to $1.67 per application. In contrast, a tight standard of, say, 10 minutes per application would require an employee to turn out 6 applications per hour. In this case the labor cost per application would be $.83.

Workers want to know what is expected of them. If the standards are reasonable, they will produce what is expected. But, if the standards are loose, will they produce more than is expected? Generally not—at least not without some form of additional or special reward or compensation. If standards are tight, they may be ineffective, because people will not even try to meet them.

The conclusions are obvious. From the employer's point of view, the tighter the standard, the lower the cost of labor, the greater is the profit. Let us say that the value of an application is $2.00. If we develop an engineered standard that equates to a labor cost of $1.00 per application, and we can encourage the employees to meet that standard, the profit can be $1.00 per application. On the other hand, if we establish a loose standard that equates to a labor cost of, say, $1.67 per application, the profit would only be $.33 per application.

When setting standards in a casual manner, or in an unscientific way, the tendency is to err on the high side. Whenever rough standards are developed, the standard setter will be sure to inflate the time standard to cover every possible contingency to be certain that the standard can be met.

There are dozens of techniques for measuring work. The three general categories are informal techniques, semiformal techniques, and formal techniques. In the following sections and in subsequent chapters we will examine the strengths and weaknesses of available measurement techniques.

Each measurement technique is a tool. It is wise to know the advantages and limitations of the tools you use. In this way you will not expect more than the tool is capable of providing.

Informal techniques include estimates, short interval scheduling (SIS), and the historical-data method. Whatever time values are derived from these methods cannot be considered "standards" in the true sense of the word but rather benchmarks, reasonable expectancies, or guides.

Semiformal techniques include self-logging or time ladders, work sampling or ratio delay, and unleveled time study. The time values derived from these techniques are usually regarded as rough standards. They are a little more accurate because they are a bit less subjective, but they are still rough.

Formal techniques include leveled time studies and predetermined time data. These are very sophisticated techniques and produce what are known as engineered standards.

In this chapter we will cover the informal techniques. In Chapter 10 we will cover the semiformal techniques, and in Chapters 11 and 12 the formal techniques.

ESTIMATES

An estimate is an approximate judgment of amounts. Everyone is capable of estimating, although some of us are better at it than others. This immediately brings up the questions of accuracy and consistency. As estimate is an attempt to quantify the number of units that can be handled in a minute, hour, day, or week, or simply the amount of time to handle one unit of work. It costs next to nothing to do and requires no special training other than some familiarity with the jobs being estimated. Generally, it is unsupportable. If someone else's estimate differs from yours, or an employee's estimate differs from a supervisor's, there is considerable difficulty proving who is right.

Take the situation where the supervisor estimates that an employee should be able to handle 50 units per hour and a particular employee is handling only 30 units per hour. If the employee says: "I'm doing the best I can," or, "I'm working hard all the time," the supervisor is in a position that is difficult to defend.

Estimates are very loosely based on the method used at the time. There is seldom any documentation of the method, so that changes in method usually go unnoticed.

HISTORICAL DATA

Using historical data, historical records, or past performance records is the simplest form of work measurement. It involves the use of production statistics or records compiled over a period of time—say, a month or a year—to determine how long it has taken in the past to produce one unit of work.

Consider an order-processing unit of ten workers handling an average of 480 orders per day. This is an average of 48 orders per worker per eight-hour day, or six orders per hour. One order is equal to ten minutes. A year later the same unit may have thirteen workers turning out 650 orders per day. This amounts to 50 orders per worker per day, 6.25 per hour per worker, or 9.6 minutes per order.

A comparison shows a 4 percent improvement from one year to the next. In other words, historical data can serve as a benchmark, certainly not a standard, against which future production and performance are compared. It will tell us if we are doing better or worse than previously. Although the historical-data method does not in itself tell us how long a unit of work should take, its value to gauge any increase or decrease cannot be overlooked.

Developing a Base Period

To set up a measurement program using the historical-data technique, select a unit of measure that is representative of the work being done and relatively easy to capture. The unit of measure can be the number of items processed or the number of hours expended for a given function.

In the example in Table 9-1, the historical-data method is used for staffing purposes. The department apparently needs one employee for every 1,250 invoices. The same historical data can be used to measure performance. You can establish 1,250 invoices per employee as equal to 100 percent performance and set

Table 9-1. Invoices per employee.

Year	Number of Invoices Processed	Average Number of Employees	Average Invoices per Employee
1975	17,555	14	1,254
1976	19,680	16	1,230
1977	24,035	19	1,265
1978	26,208	21	1,248
Totals	87,478	70	4,997
Averages	21,869	17.5	1,250
Conclusion: 1 employee per 1,250 invoices			

objectives from that point. For example, if, at the end of 1978, an objective of a 15 percent increase in productivity were established, the year of 1979 might turn out as follows:

Number of Invoices Processed	Average Number of Employees	Average Invoices per Employee	Performance (1,250/empl. = 100%)
30,663	21	1,460	117%

Hours can also be used to display production results in a historical-data mode, as in Table 9-2. This table shows a definite rate of improvement in the number of hours expended to process a claim, namely, a reduction from 6.2 hours to 5.5 hours.

Advantages

The historical-data technique of work measurement, because of its utmost simplicity, offers the following advantages:

Table 9-2. Historical data: hours per claim.

Year	Number of Claims Processed	Number of Man-Hours Paid	Average Hours per Claim
1975	2066	12.809	6.2
1976	2301	13.576	5.9
1977	2550	14.790	5.8
1978	2953	16.242	5.5

1. It is easy to use. All you have to do is gather statistics over a period of time.
2. It requires no maintenance.
3. It requires no formal training. Someone knowledgeable of the work merely determines what should be counted.
4. It is easy to understand. No technical formulas are used.
5. It is economical to use. The time for record keeping and compiling of data is the sole investment.
6. It requires very little record keeping. Usually a week or two of data is all that is needed.
7. It has a very high acceptance rate by employees because of the participation factor—the employees themselves gather the data.

Limitations

The limitations of the historical-data approach must be understood from the start:

1. Standards developed through historical data reflect only what has happened or what is, rather than what should be.
2. The technique does not take into consideration how fast or slow an employee is working at the time the standard, or average, is established.
3. It does not provide any consideration for methods and procedures analysis.
4. Inequities could result when two departments are compared. Department A could be a high-performing group and Department B a very low-performing group. Therefore, if 100 percent performance were equated with their present average items processed, Department B would have a much easier time showing improvement.
5. When there are changes in the way work is performed or the equipment used, there is no provision for updating the standards. New experience must be accumulated before new standards can be developed.
6. Standards developed through the historical-data approach, because they are nothing more than averages, should not be used for payment of incentives.

Summary

This technique provides management with a method for evaluating the production of a unit. The advantages it has over other techniques are that it is simple to administer and quite inexpensive. But, while it is the simplest form of measurement, it is also the least accurate, because it is based on current staff and conditions and does not take into consideration the methods involved. The historical-data approach is a first step to controlling costs. It should not be the last.

SHORT INTERVAL SCHEDULING

Short interval scheduling, usually referred to as SIS, is not so much a technique as it is an approach. However, since it is a separate and distinct method by which work can be measured and controlled, we will include it in the presentation of informal techniques.

Short interval scheduling is defined as the assignment and control of a premeasured, predetermined amount of work with systematic follow-up and problem correction, in planned, predictable short-time intervals throughout the day.

Preparation for a Study

Before establishing SIS in a unit or department, you must know the following:

What are the operations to be performed?
What is the sequence of operations?
What is the time required to perform each operation?
What is the volume of each operation (number of items done at one time)?
How many people are required to perform the operation?
What is the flow of work from one operation to another?

Installation Procedure

An SIS installation can be handled by a trained SIS specialist or work study analyst, or by a supervisor of a department or unit. There are six basic steps involved in installing the program:

1. List all tasks or functions on an activity listing sheet (see Figure 9-1).
2. Determine the items to be counted.
3. Determine a reasonable length of time to process one unit of work. This is referred to as a reasonable expectancy (RE) and can be done with a wristwatch.
4. Obtain current workload figures and multiply volume times RE to determine standard minutes.
5. Calculate manpower required to handle workload.
6. Batch the work in hourly units. (For example, if an RE for processing is two minutes per order, a reasonable batch size would be 30, equal to one hour of work.)

Supervisory Duties

The supervisor plays a key role in an SIS plan. The supervisor batches the work, distributes the work to employees, and notes the amount of work given to an

Figure 9-I. Activity listing sheet.

TITLE *Order Processing*   DEPT. *Processing*

ACTIVITY	Unit of Measure	Freq.	Vol.	Reasonable Expectancy	TIME		
					D.	W.	M.
Sort Mail	*Number of envelopes sorted*	*Daily*	*1,500*	*.5*			
			SUBTOTAL				
			%				
			TOTAL REQUIRED				
			TOTAL AVAILABLE				
			DIFFERENCE				
			% UTILIZATION				

employee as well as the time the work was distributed. If the schedule is missed—that is, if the employee who was given an hour's worth of work is not able to complete the work within an hour, the supervisor fills out a schedule miss report (see Figure 9-2).

Prerequisites for Success

In order for an SIS program to be successful, several key factors must be considered:

1. There must be a relatively continuous supply of work—preferably a continuous backlog. Otherwise, employees will not be kept fully occupied.
2. The time estimates (REs) must be fair and consistent.
3. Batch sizes must be kept between one and three hours. To distribute less than one hour of work increases recordkeeping unnecessarily. To distribute more than three hours of work at one time reduces the supervisor's control over getting the work completed on time.
4. The schedule miss report is an essential follow-up procedure for correcting

Figure 9-2. Schedule miss report.

LOCATION _____

Employee	Time		Man-hrs.		Units		S.A.	Cause of Schedule Miss
	Start	Stop	Actual	Earned	Actual	Planned	%	(corrective action to be taken)

Supervisor _____ Date _____

bottlenecks. The reason that a schedule is missed must be corrected or eliminated.

5. Performance standards must be set. Minimum expected performances must be communicated to employees. Those unable to meet minimum standards must be dealt with.

Advantages

A successful SIS program has numerous advantages. First, the timeliness with which work is processed results in better service—faster turnaround time. Second, productivity is improved. Employees' time is better utilized, and control over their performance is increased. The recorded performance data can be used to develop an incentive plan based on direct relationships between productivity and hours worked.

A well-administered SIS program increases everyone's awareness of how time is spent and gives the supervisor better information for solving problems and handling crisis situations. Finally, SIS can be an effective cost reduction technique and is a valuable tool for forecasting manpower requirements.

Limitations

There are limitations to SIS that potential users should be aware of. The program puts a great deal of pressure on employees and supervisors to meet schedules. Also, the fact that it requires a rather continuous backlog of work may have a detrimental effect on service. Another important limitation to consider is that SIS is not applicable to administration or low-volume work.

WRISTWATCH TIME STUDIES

Although rarely discussed in the literature on work measurement, a common wristwatch can be used to set time standards. Particularly where company policy prohibits the use of a stopwatch, the wristwatch technique can be used effectively as a means of gathering time data.

Essentially, the procedure for setting time standards with a wristwatch is the same as that employed when a stopwatch is used. Because of the similarity in procedure, which is covered in the next chapter, a detailed description of the wristwatch approach would be repetitious. However, two major differences between the wristwatch technique and the stopwatch technique should be noted: (1) the recording of time values in seconds rather than in hundredths of a minute and (2) the omission of performance leveling. In practice, wristwatch studies are infrequently leveled, whereas stopwatch studies are generally leveled.

The continuous time study sheet does not require a detailed enumeration of elements prior to the start of the study. The analyst simply describes and records the elements as the study progresses.

Advantages

The advantages of the wristwatch study include the following:

1. It provides reasonably accurate data.
2. Standards can be developed fairly rapidly.
3. The method is easy to understand and relatively easy to explain.
4. The wristwatch method of setting standards provides fairly good documentation on procedures.
5. The wristwatch approach lends itself to analyzing operating details and provides a stimulus for analyzing and improving procedures and methods.
6. Wristwatch standards can be adjusted easily when work procedures or methods change.
7. The wristwatch approach does not require as much training as the stopwatch approach.
8. No special equipment is required.
9. Wristwatch timing may be less damaging to employee morale than stopwatch timing.

Limitations

As a work measurement technique, the wristwatch study probably suffers from all of the limitations of the stopwatch approach. Moreover, the wristwatch cannot offer great precision. Specifically, some of the limitations of this technique are:

1. Wristwatch time studies may create morale problems. The substitution of a wristwatch for a stopwatch in no way eliminates the need for close observation and timing. While the wristwatch may connote a "soft sell" approach, employees may still resent being studied. As with the stopwatch, employees must be adequately prepared prior to the introduction of a wristwatch in the work center.
2. Because the wristwatch technique requires close observation of the activity under study, it may tend to disrupt the normal work routine.
3. Great precision in standards cannot be obtained, because the timing device is not geared to such precision.
4. Normally, adjustments for workers' speeds are not made with the wristwatch approach; consequently, the standards may tend to be somewhat inaccurate.

5. Wristwatch time studies tend to be useful only for short-cycle, repetitive tasks and cannot be used very well on long-cycle activities.
6. The wristwatch approach is a costly way to measure low-volume activities.
7. The wristwatch technique is not applicable to administrative activities. Its usefulness is generally limited to routine clerical activities.

CHAPTER

10

Semiformal Techniques

THERE IS A DISTINCT DIFFERENCE between the informal techniques described in the previous chapter and the semiformal techniques to be covered in this chapter. The informal techniques measure the average time it currently takes to process work. Particularly with regard to the historical-data approach, that time is usually distorted by absent time, idle time, personal time, and similar nonproductive time. Semiformal techniques, on the other hand, allow us to isolate the time devoted to the specific task.

Another dimension is added when we move from semiformal techniques to formal techniques. Formal techniques not only yield a sharper work pace measure by providing a purer time required factor, they also consider the way the work should be processed (method). Getting back to Taylor's thesis that the greatest productivity results when each worker is given a definite task to be performed in a definite time and in a definite manner, the semiformal techniques take both a definite task and definite time into consideration, while the formal techniques subject all three—task, time, and manner—to great scrutiny.

WORK SAMPLING

Work sampling is also known as random sampling and ratio delay. Ratio delay is the name by which it was originally introduced in the United States in 1940 by Professor Robert Lee Morrow of New York University. There are subtle differences between ratio delay and random sampling that we shall explain. However, a blend of both is incorporated in the work sampling technique.

The Ratio Delay Technique

Ratio delay is a method of finding the causes of delays and the ratio of those delays to total time by random observations. For example, you may wish to find out how much time is spent for a given machine in actual operation, setup, maintenance, and delay. Using the ratio delay method, we can observe the machine a predetermined number of times a day, say, ten times. That does not mean every 48 minutes during an eight-hour day—that would not be "random" sampling. We want ten random samplings during the day that follow no set pattern. We record which element is occurring at the instant of each visit or observation.

At the end of ten days, the record may read as follows:

Function	Observations	Percent of Total
Operation	60	60%
Setup	18	18%
Maintenance	10	10%
Delay	12	12%
	100	100%

The percentage distribution of the various elements, as they occurred during the random observation, tends to equal the exact percentage distribution that would be found by continuous observation. The key to the accuracy of the ratio delay technique is in the number of observations.

The ratio delay technique is based on the law of probability. It works because a smaller number of chance occurrences tends to follow the same distribution pattern that a larger number produces. The simplest way to explain the phenomenon is by reference to tossing a coin or throwing dice.

When you toss a coin, the result is one of two possibilities: heads or tails (standing on edge doesn't count). The law of chance says you should get 50 heads and 50 tails in 100 tosses of a coin. That's the ratio of the average possibility. It doesn't mean it will come out 50-50 on the button every 100 tosses. You may get a score of 60-40, 45-55, or some other ratio. But is has been proved that the law becomes *increasingly accurate as the number of tosses increases*. The percentage of possible error decreases.

Another example of how the law of probability works is dice throwing. It's a little more complex than coin tossing, because one throw of two dice has 36 possible results, instead of two.

Thirty-six throws will tend to produce one 2, two 3s, three 4s, four 5s, five 6s, six 7s, five 8s, and so on. Note that we said *tends* to produce. Each series of 36 throws won't duplicate the pattern exactly. But the results get closer to the pattern (probability curve) as you increase the number of series of 36 throws. The percentage of error decreases.

In both examples (coin tosses and dice throws), the law of probability holds that a small number of chance occurrences tends to follow the distribution pattern produced by a larger number of occurrences. Ratio delay works the same way. A small number of observations, taken at random, tends to follow the same pattern of distribution (ratio) as a larger number (the largest number would be continuous observation).

Random Sampling

Random sampling is a method for getting information by an application of a sampling method to the activity under study. In other words, it is a method of determining from observation of a small portion of an area what occurs in the total area.

The logic of the sampling approach is familiar to most of us. We do not have to drink a whole cup of coffee in order to determine if it is too hot or too cold, if it is sweet enough, if it has enough cream, or if it is strong or weak. A *sample* of the coffee is all we need.

Random sampling is a statistical technique with two main factors: randomness of observations, and degree of desired significance of results.

Like the ratio delay technique, random sampling is based on the probability theory. That is, it operates on the premise that a random sample drawn from a large group will tend to resemble the group from which the sample is drawn. If the proper amount of sampling is done, the characteristics of the sample group will differ little from the characteristics of the large group or universe from which the sample is taken.

For example, let's assume that a large glass bowl contains 1,000 beads—800 white beads and 200 red beads. If we take a random sample of 50 beads, the odds are one to five that the sample will contain ten red beads. If we take several samples of 50 beads (returning the beads to the bowl after each sample and thoroughly mixing the entire bowl of beads to ensure continued randomness), some of the samples drawn will contain more than ten red beads and some will contain less then ten red beads, but the pattern of ten red beads per sample will tend to occur most often. On a cumulative basis, the more samples drawn from the bowl, the more the total sample percentage will approximate the true percentage of red and white beads in the bowl.

Quick Study Example

Let us assume we are to conduct a study of a data entry unit consisting of ten operators. We can categorize the activities that we are likely to see as Punching

Figure 10-1. Sample tally sheet for random work sampling.

Operator	Punching	Handling	Idle	Talking	Away	Total
A	~~////~~ ////	~~////~~ ///	/	/	/	20
B	~~////~~ ~~////~~ //	~~////~~ //			//	21
C	~~////~~ ~~////~~	///	//	//		17
D	~~////~~ ///	~~////~~ //		/	/	17
E	~~////~~ ~~////~~ //	~~////~~ ///	//	//	/	25
F	~~////~~ ~~////~~ //	~~////~~ //		//	///	24
G	~~////~~ ////	~~////~~ //			//	18
H	~~////~~ ~~////~~ /	~~////~~		/	/	18
I	~~////~~ ~~////~~ /	////	/	/	///	20
J	~~////~~ ///	~~////~~ /	//	//	//	20
Totals	102	62	8	12	16	200
Percent	51%	31%	4%	6%	8%	100%

(Keys), Handling (Papers), Idle, Talking, and Away (from Work Station). We decide, for one reason or another, that we want to know how these operators are spending their time.

Throughout the day we would take a number of quick, momentary glimpses or observations of a predesignated operator. For each observation, we immediately record on a tally sheet what we observed the operator to be doing. At the end of the day, our tally sheet shows the pattern of observations in Figure 10-1.

One must be careful when analyzing these results. If we learn that normal break periods are always taken away from the work station, we may accept the 8 percent Away time as acceptable. Four percent Idle and 6 percent Talking can be correctly analyzed as non-productive time, and the 51 percent Punching and 31 percent Handling figures can easily be construed as 82 percent productive time.

Since any knowledgeable data entry analyst knows, from experience, that productive time consists of 95 percent keypunching and 5 percent handling of source documents, the analysis in Table 10-1 would be appropriate.

With 55 percent productive time plus a factor for personal time and normal absent time, we could conclude that seven operators could handle the workload. The proper way to handle it would be not to replace people who terminate

Table 10-1. Analysis of data from Figure 10-1.

Category	Total	Productive	Nonproductive
Punching	51%	51%	0%
Handling	31	4	27
Idle	4	0	4
Talking	6	0	6
Away	8	0	8
	100%	55%	45%

employment. When one leaves, nine will manage to get the work out. When another leaves, eight will manage to get the work out, and so on.

Average well-trained keypunch or data entry operators, like typists, usually have "one" speed while typing or depressing keys. When they wish to appear busy even though not enough work is available, they would find it difficult to type or punch keys at a slower rate. Therefore, they will "shuffle papers" to appear busy. A failure to analyze the results in this way could have led to an erroneous conclusion about the amount of productive time.

Preparation for a Work Sampling Study

There is a fairly well-defined procedure for conducting work sampling studies. However, the preparatory steps are most important.

SELLING THE TECHNIQUE

Although you may think work sampling is simple enough, many managers will need more than a five-minute explanation before they agree. Operators will not buy a brief explanation, either, if you need their participation. The very natural reaction is that you cannot possibly get a true picture if you do not observe the operation continuously.

There is surely no need to explain why it is so important to have the complete understanding and confidence of the people who are concerned with the results of the study. The best way to sell work sampling is to explain how it works and why it works. By all means, bring up the coin, dice, and beads demonstrations. They have proved to be more effective than a long talk in getting the idea across.

Some other examples of situations similar in principle to work sampling are testing anti-freeze in a car radiator, taking blood samples, and trying one package of cigarettes before buying a carton. Since all these samples represent the source from which they came, the opinions formed from the samples would be valid for the source or whole product.

Defining the Problem

What do you want to know? About what? Do you want to know "what's going on down there," or do you have a clear objective like, "I wonder how much time my employees have to spend walking on the job?" You'll never get far until you can define the questions that need answering. If you cannot really define your questions, you do not know where to begin. You cannot decide who or what to observe, or how detailed your observations should be. Ask yourself over and over again: "I know I want information about this activity, but exactly what do I want to know?" Do not move to the next step until you are able to be as specific as possible about your objectives.

Making a Preliminary Study

You have done your thinking and planning. You have some questions now. So, get some information. Find out what is going on. Who are the people involved? What are their jobs? Where do they go? Whom do they have to talk to? Where is the drinking fountain? Get the information you will need in order to conduct the study you want. Get a feel for the area and the activities that you are going to study. Then design your study.

Defining a Reliable Sample

What is a reliable sample? It is one that accurately represents the actual time distribution. More specifically, what characteristics must our sample have to qualify as being reliable? There are three factors to consider: number of observations, randomness of observation, and duration of the study.

1. *Number of observations.* A reliable sample consists of a certain minimum number of observations. Generally speaking, the more observations we make, the more certain we can be that our conclusions are accurate. However, there is a point beyond which additional observations are not justified by the meager increase in certainty they give us. We are fortunate that statistics can tell us how many observations we should make for a given work situation and for the degree of certainty that will satisfy us.

One of the characteristics of a reliable sample is that it consists of a sufficient number of observations—sufficient, that is, to assure obtaining a satisfactory degree of accuracy in our study results. We also said that, thanks to statistical theory, we are able to calculate the number of observations required for various degrees of accuracy.

As a practical matter, however, it is not necessary in planning a work sampling study to wrestle with any mathematical formulas when determining the size of the sample. We can simply consult a table of sample sizes and from it pick the number of observations we should make for the degree of accuracy we want.

Before we illustrate the use of a table of sample sizes, let us ask ourselves what we mean by "degree of accuracy." This phrase refers to *tolerance,* a concept involved in all sampling techniques and found in many other contexts as well. For example, we have all encountered such expressions as "the distance between New York City and Montreal is 400 miles, give or take 20 miles," or, "The flying time between New York City and Miami is four hours, add or subtract 15 minutes," or, "The diameter of these ball bearings is one inch, plus or minus 2/100 inch." In all three statements, the degree of accuracy is expressed in terms of tolerance. We could have expressed these tolerances as percentages: "400 miles plus or minus 5 percent," "four hours plus or minus 6¼ percent," and "one inch plus or minus 2 percent."

Similarly, the degree of accuracy inherent in the results of sampling studies is expressed in terms of a tolerance factor. For example, a conclusion of a consumer preference study might read as follows: "50 percent plus or minus 10 percent (of itself), or between 45 percent and 55 percent, of American married women prefer Brand X over all competing brands." And one of the conclusions of a work sampling study might be: "The clerks spend 20 percent plus or minus 10 percent (of itself), or between 18 percent and 22 percent, of their available time on Activity C."

Table 10-2 is a table of sample sizes. To use the table, we must specify the values of P and T. T stands for the "tolerance factor," or degree of accuracy, we have just discussed. The table provides the number of observations required for each of two different degrees of accuracy: a tolerance factor of 5 percent and one of 10 percent.

Now let us look at P. It is our estimate of the percentage of total available time spent by the workers on the *least* time-consuming activity. This percentage is known as the "estimated critical percentage." Let us assume, for example, we estimate that the workers we are soon to study spend about 50 percent of their time on Activity A, 20 percent on Activity B, another 20 percent on Activity C, and 10 percent on Activity D. We would base these estimates on the best information available to us, for example, workers' and supervisors' opinions, past work measurement study data, or our judgment. Activity D is the least time-consuming activity and thus, in this situation, P is 10 percent.

This factor of the least time-consuming activity is important, because if we have made sufficient observations to obtain the degree of accuracy we require on this activity, we will have obtained an even higher degree of accuracy on the other, more time-consuming activities.

Take a look at Table 10-2. If P is estimated to be 10 percent, we find that if we specify a tolerance factor of 5 percent, we should make 6,080 observations. If a tolerance factor of 10 percent satisfies us, we need make only 1,520 observations. From this simple illustration, and from further examination of Table 10-2, we can

Table 10-2. Sample sizes, computed for 1.3σ (80% reliability).

P	Net Number of Observations* If			
	$T = \pm5\%$	$T = \pm10\%$	$T = \pm15\%$	$T = \pm20\%$
1%	66,920	16,730	7,440	4,180
2	33,120	8,280	3,680	2,070
3	21,860	5,460	2,430	1,370
4	16,220	4,060	1,800	1,010
5	12,840	3,210	1,430	800
6	10,590	2,650	1,180	660
7	8,980	2,250	1,000	560
8	7,770	1,940	860	490
9	6,840	1,710	760	430
10	6,080	1,520	680	380
15	3,830	960	430	240
20	2,700	680	300	170
25	2,030	510	230	130
30	1,580	390	180	100
35	1,260	315	140	80
40	1,020	260	110	60
45	830	210	90	50
50	680	170	80	40

P = estimated critical percentage; T = tolerance factor
*The net number of observations must be multiplied by a factor 1.22, because some observations will occur during the lunch period and some clerks to be observed may be absent. Tolerance factors T are expressed as a percentage of P.

see that the more observations we make, the greater will be the accuracy of our study results. But in planning any work sampling study, we must answer this question: beyond what point does the increased accuracy fail to justify the additional observations and, thus, the time and expense required to make them?

The figures in Table 10-2 represent an 80 percent reliability. For a reliability smaller or greater than 80 percent, see Table 10-3, which lists reliability factors. For example, to find the net number of observations required for $P = .10$, $T = .05$ with a reliability of 95 percent, we would look up the factor for 95 percent from Table 10-3 (2.273), and multiply it by the number of observations (6,080), to get the net number of observations required (13,820).

2. *Randomness*. The observations comprising a reliable sample are made at random. With regard to work sampling, by randomness we mean that each moment of time has an equal chance of being included in the study, and that each person has an equal chance of being observed at that moment. Since this method is based on tables of random numbers, adherence to the observation schedule it provides will assure the randomness our sample requires.

3. *Duration*. A reliable sample is taken over a period of time sufficiently long to include any short-run cyclical conditions which are a normal characteristic of the work situation being studied.

Table 10-3. Reliability factors to be applied to sample sizes in Table 10-2 to provide indicated degrees of reliability.

Reliability	Factor	Reliability	Factor
50%	.269	85%	1.227
55	.337	90	1.601
60	.420	95	2.273
65	.517	96	2.496
70	.637	97	2.786
75	.783	98	3.204
80	1.000	99	3.926

In summary, we can define a reliable sample as one which consists of a sufficiently large number of random observations, taken over a time period that includes the normal conditions of the work situation being studied.

PRELIMINARY MEETING WITH OBSERVER(S)

In the preliminary meeting, we clearly define and discuss each element to be observed and recorded. This step is very important where two or more observers study the same operation. Without it, they may be inconsistent in their interpretation and classification of what they see.

SELECTING WORK SAMPLING CATEGORIES

Each category considered essential to a study must be discrete and must be given a definition that is readily understood by the observer. Failure to define the category specifically and clearly can invalidate the study results.

In addition to the productive categories, work sampling studies will measure the time that employees are not available for work, the time expended on delays, personal/rest time, and idle time. Additional categories may be established as "Other," provided they are nonproductive and do not duplicate a preprinted category already on the work sampling record form.

CODING THE FUNCTIONS

Assign an element code to be used in identifying the work being done using the following system:

Code 10	Personal (if all personal and idle time is to be included in one element).
Code 11	Idle or no work available.
Code 12	Personal walking.

Code 13	Personal talking.
Code 14	Out of the area—personal
Code 15–19	Other personal elements.
Code 20	Unavoidable delay (if all delay is to be included in one element).
Code 21	Official walking.
Code 22	Telephoning.
Code 23	Official talking: supervisor.
Code 24	Official talking: visitor.
Code 25	Official talking: other employees.
Code 26–29	Other unavoidable delay elements.
Code 30–99	Productive work elements.

PREPARING A RANDOM OBSERVATION SCHEDULE

Random numbers can be generated from a random numbers table such as Table 10-4 to determine the items to be sampled. To illustrate, assume that we wish to select a sample of 20 from a lot of 800 items. Each item in the lot is identified by a number from 001 to 800. Therefore, we need to select 20 random three-digit numbers from 001 to 800.

First, we must determine a starting point. Table 10-4 contains 50 rows and 50 columns of digits, grouped in fives. Assume that a pencil point is placed at random in the table and that the first digit of the five-digit number chosen determines the row to be selected. The same procedure is used to determine the starting column. Assume that the 11th row and the 20th column are chosen. We have decided in

ESTABLISHING A WORK-COUNT SYSTEM

Establish a system to record work-count volume on a daily basis. If the activities of the work center preclude compliance with this requirement, record the work count as frequently as the work is completed. If a production report is available, it may be used, but make periodic checks to ensure that it is accurate. The period of the production report must correspond to the study period.

advance that the starting digit chosen will be the first digit of a three-digit number read to the right and that succeeding numbers will be read down the table. With this system, the following numbers are obtained. (Numbers that are not between 001 and 800 must be discarded; these are shown in parentheses. A number that has already occurred must also be discarded; there are no such numbers in the example below.)

626	(903)	352	509	(884)	(830)
274	(894)	620	368	105	(880)
191	119	(946)	236	(926)	091
(909)	(970)	622	795	171	694
247	704	(828)	764	024	746

Table 10-4. Random digits.

57278	28133	04340	19889	27266	77468	02509	27534	00342	30727
97953	43227	41110	86887	19559	64945	54520	90528	18850	43610
07431	45121	73187	80431	57245	77311	44596	23531	63637	47042
20930	54735	95568	86799	49721	89049	01791	81084	03284	24096
78003	86322	23893	19483	18624	78634	31967	06395	34924	67283
48541	02641	89681	97881	69919	24170	85386	25834	75945	90965
52684	87995	43702	10623	95580	75795	59360	87848	83250	41168
44032	67360	54462	31774	01629	03406	81878	92801	27984	89892
40757	07266	13231	93527	51509	19550	24785	11136	35905	44879
42290	21749	34505	46547	03354	83574	17762	07646	66469	61568
37592	08604	53542	99986	26017	84967	96696	19155	88259	03612
32583	59967	64315	84822	74950	80322	10037	19425	96714	97330
75625	48032	05891	58701	91532	81253	87706	42235	44799	58271
91808	34409	59390	38399	09462	07373	19799	04132	31531	16485
19926	91034	26756	37752	47276	70856	94741	55372	50250	48775
78782	17338	68884	04609	03479	59241	39569	13351	64340	34108
54319	43047	73502	30408	94554	18640	91396	16242	96184	64191
34359	78839	55454	08551	19021	56584	84609	26286	31079	89061
52871	79550	40787	87299	70144	45090	45199	80127	21304	88681
69226	39419	66757	59927	04968	56061	66103	59708	36607	79140
07575	50710	92377	67823	52832	36514	56137	11321	62025	09049
91682	48619	15333	05876	20802	39128	75562	10170	72858	07010
62040	64062	70625	57559	46143	46638	37861	12551	58076	87218
80099	81346	54688	70326	22662	08106	82354	94331	29618	38043
77758	41609	69027	03208	28505	06689	61270	67122	45496	30345
20009	11788	77442	46535	09576	24905	46353	63277	36064	58249
52091	84347	27681	24853	68826	04138	83340	96698	89529	46622
19569	02594	04226	93412	36370	16393	05509	43349	01135	92264
48286	19309	39931	61597	95916	59340	30322	56291	45847	85836
44400	82261	21889	89837	64397	05508	31365	36334	08765	89749
19322	99470	86311	96458	84173	06386	39946	49558	80223	69513
21704	81386	35499	57991	05992	47982	01949	50203	45471	18610
59506	33660	80198	19429	26262	42605	64807	29526	50672	49761
69876	11749	18876	54501	71446	40239	42174	14601	51255	24318
47268	55681	53952	54010	24425	21284	90929	05499	37739	88835
80651	73964	85491	79648	30293	31305	96030	25760	85013	03763
91894	81410	81245	09998	80494	86183	01343	82296	80842	58427
40239	16519	23159	32970	91162	40386	81829	16582	45640	07032
88212	51975	93468	83446	94238	48944	63226	05278	32797	27430
55103	14461	92774	26397	46587	51470	41598	29070	26690	69567
15360	93359	86173	53747	03141	75425	69947	37188	30936	99987
70678	38035	89688	64524	08530	87826	82214	05660	04461	28460
23620	33295	98309	16475	26722	92523	62702	02103	38482	28012
71594	59029	79559	67497	56559	05538	38354	61813	04816	66451
63723	62966	40545	65085	77086	03427	62353	77932	81281	32626
24852	88450	99212	80393	72573	59370	75741	05229	43644	29794
80184	48999	76580	84648	04210	76599	43704	23101	06957	66554
46973	78646	73852	44752	50849	07905	65120	48320	23223	96491
18043	96840	23148	89768	10865	45987	55568	08478	73137	03867
84956	48341	26773	23897	70640	75961	04522	09761	81718	63357

Table 10-5. Random sampling: 28 sets of random times.

1	2	3	4	5	6	7	8	9	10	11	12	13	14
0:05	0:20	0:20	0:50	0:10	0:35	0:15	0:25	0:25	0:25	0:10	0:25	0:15	0:20
0:55	1:10	1:20	1:45	0:55	1:00	1:20	1:40	0:45	1:05	0:30	0:40	0:35	0:50
1:20	1:35	1:55	2:00	1:10	1:45	1:55	2:00	1:50	2:10	1:10	1:20	1:00	1:25
2:30	3:05	2:30	2:40	2:00	2:05	2:30	2:50	2:20	2:30	1:30	2:25	1:40	1:50
3:10	3:15	3:10	3:30	2:45	2:50	3:10	3:30	2:35	2:50	2:35	2:24	1:55	2:45
3:25	3:45	3:40	3:50	3:00	3:20	3:45	3:50	3:00	3:10	2:55	3:05	3:05	3:50
3:55	4:10	4:05	4:15	3:30	4:40	4:30	4:40	3:40	3:45	3:15	3:25	4:00	4:25
4:35	4:55	4:20	4:25	4:45	4:55	5:10	5:20	4:30	5:00	3:30	3:40	4:45	5:00
5:00	5:05	4:30	4:35	5:00	5:55	5:30	5:45	5:45	5:50	3:50	4:00	5:10	5:15
5:35	5:55	5:20	5:35	6:00	6:05	5:50	6:15	5:55	6:00	4:15	4:25	6:20	6:25
6:05	6:45	6:15	6:40	6:35	6:40	6:20	6:25	6:35	6:45	4:35	5:40	6:50	6:55
6:50	7:10	6:45	7:10	7:10	7:35	6:50	7:30	7:00	7:45	6:45	6:55	7:15	7:40
7:25		7:35		7:50		7:55		7:55		7:35		7:45	

15	16	17	18	19	20	21	22	23	24	25	26	27	28
0:05	0:20	0:25	0:30	0:05	0:15	0:05	0:15	0:10	0:20	0:10	0:15	0:10	0:15
1:05	1:25	0:40	0:45	0:40	1:30	0:20	0:25	0:30	1:30	1:10	1:25	0:20	0:25
1:30	2:05	1:00	1:10	1:45	2:20	0:55	1:20	1:45	1:50	1:30	1:40	0:50	1:25
2:25	2:40	1:25	1:40	2:25	3:10	1:35	1:55	2:25	2:35	1:45	2:05	1:35	2:10
3:00	3:20	2:15	2:20	3:40	3:50	2:10	2:30	3:05	3:10	2:40	2:45	2:15	2:40
4:25	4:45	2:30	2:40	4:15	4:20	2:45	2:50	3:50	3:55	2:55	3:40	2:55	3:35
4:50	4:55	2:45	3:05	4:30	4:40	2:55	3:00	4:05	4:10	3:45	3:50	3:40	4:35
5:05	5:15	3:30	3:35	4:55	5:00	3:30	3:35	4:50	5:10	4:05	4:25	4:45	5:05
5:50	5:55	4:00	4:15	5:15	5:20	3:45	4:05	5:25	5:30	4:55	5:15	5:10	5:50
6:00	6:10	4:50	5:45	5:25	6:05	5:00	5:40	6:00	6:05	5:45	6:20	6:05	6:20
6:20	6:35	5:50	6:25	6:45	7:15	5:50	6:25	6:15	6:30	6:25	6:30	7:05	7:10
7:10	7:15	6:50	7:05	7:25	7:35	7:20	7:40	6:50	6:55	6:35	7:35	7:20	7:50
7:30		7:30		7:55		7:50		7:25		7:50		7:55	

The selection of the sample is simplified if we rearrange the 20 numbers between 001 and 800 in size order, as follows:

024	191	368	694
091	236	509	704
105	247	620	746
119	274	622	764
171	352	626	795

A table of random sampling times such as Table 10-5 may be used in similar fashion to determine the times of the day for observations. To illustrate, assume that we wish to observe the activities of eight employees. Since the table contains 28 sets of random times, we can arbitrarily select a set of times to observe each employee.

Employee	Use Set
1	11
2	5
3	8
4	2
5	16
6	21
7	9
8	3

For the employee designated as number 1, we will record our observations at the following times:

0:10	3:30
0:30	3:50
1:10	4:15
1:30	4:35
2:35	6:45
2:55	7:35
3:15	

The times represent hours of the working day. Thus if 8:00 AM is the start of the working day, the observations will be taken at 8:10, 8:30, 9:10, and so on.

Conducting the study

The study proper consists of taking the observations and analyzing the data.

TAKING THE OBSERVATIONS

Now that you have completed your preliminaries, you have arrived at the point where the real legwork begins.

There are a few pointers that might help to make your studies easier and more valid.

It is the trips into the area that take the great bulk of your time, not the individual observations you make. So make your trips pay off. Suppose you are interested in the ditto machine utilization in two areas that are fairly near each other. Why not plan your trips so that you take observations in both areas on the same trip? You might make your random time determination indicate the time when you leave your office, for instance, and you could take observations in both areas by extending your walk a bit. Separating the data should present little difficulty. And, even in one area, realize that while you are there on a trip, you might just as well get observations on all the people or machines that you consider worth studying. Get everything you can out of each trip.

Figure 10-2. Daily observation record for work sampling.

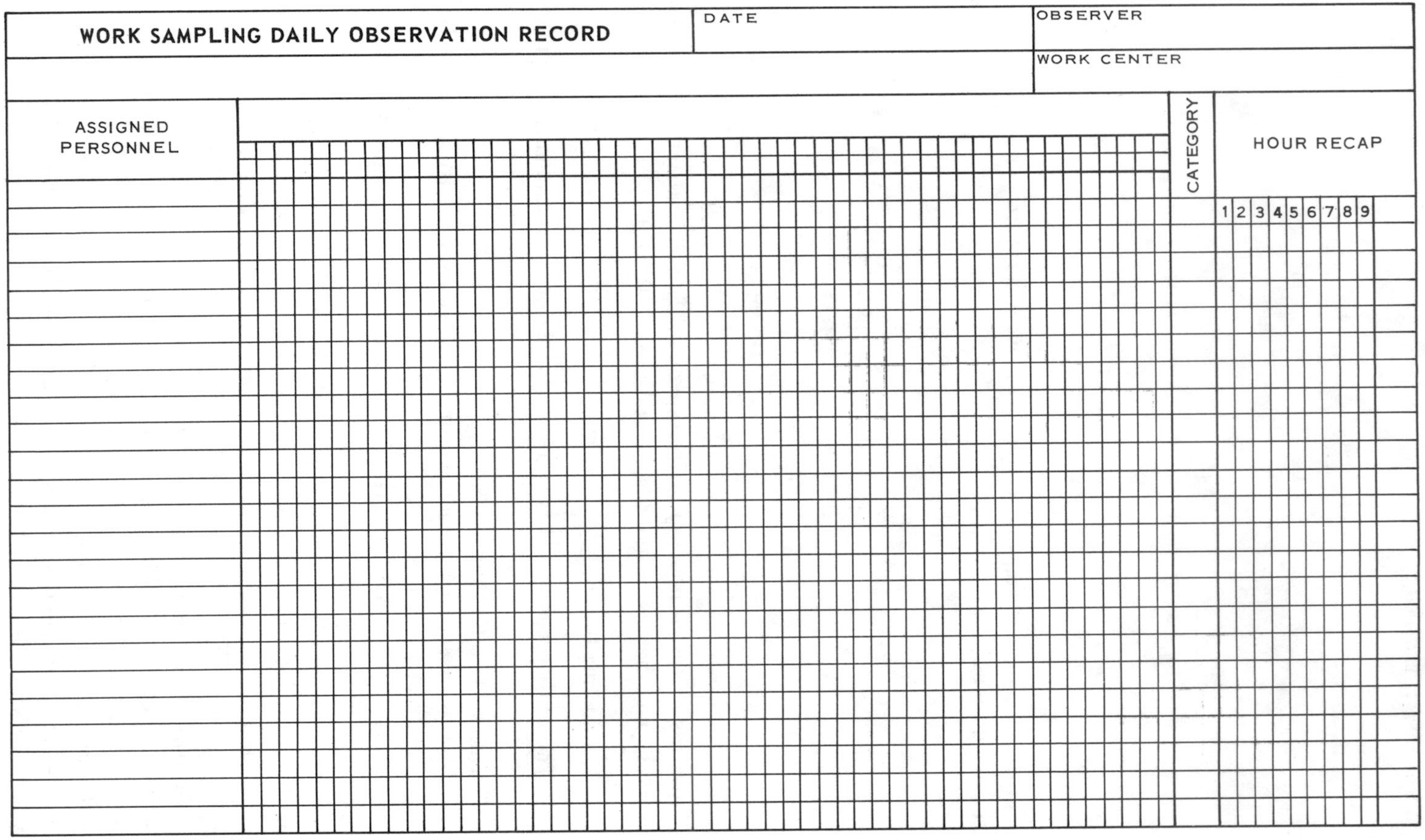

Split up the trips among several observers if you can. Talk it over with them so that you all have the same concept of the method you want to use. In the preliminary study, they should practice the method and acquaint themselves with the situation. Then try to arrange the trips so that each observer contributes in about the same proportion.

This approach has several advantages. First, no one individual has to spend too much time in taking observations. (A schedule of ten trips a day at about ten minutes per trip theoretically should require only two hours of time, but when you begin taking observations, you will realize that the interruptions to your normal work may be a problem far exceeding the actual time lost from your normal work.) Second, this approach will tend to balance the effect of observer bias, since it is a well-known fact that we all see the same situations just a little bit differently. Finally, you will have someone with whom you can discuss the study. You can gain insight into your techniques, categories, and route by discussing the study with others who are interested in exactly the same problems.

Plan your route a little differently each time if you are making a study in an area where your entrance at one point can bias activity at another. This is largely unnecessary if visibility is restricted by machinery and walls, but if you are studying a fairly large open area, you might get some very misleading results by using the same route for each trip.

Don't be too conspicuous about noting your observations. Sure, everyone has a pretty good idea of what you are doing, but it is not natural to like having someone writing notes about you or your work. After a while, you might find people asking, "What did I get?" or offering explanations about their activity which are unnecessary and time-consuming.

Do not carry your accumulated data with you on your trips. If you do, you are just asking for questions, and you may be making misleading information available. Just use a small notebook. Try to develop a code so that your note-taking is speedy but sure.

Learn to take a mental picture of what you see at the exact time designated for your observation, and then, if necessary, watch the activities that follow in order to classify the original observation accurately.

Do not destroy the original data. You may have use for them in the future.

The form in Figure 10-2 is an example of one that can be used to record observations. The daily summaries are posted to an observation summary sheet such as the one in Figure 10-3.

ANALYZING THE DATA

Table 10-6 illustrates the basic procedure for the calculation of time standards based on the work sampling study. The first columns show the categories, number

Figure 10-3. Work sampling observation summary sheet.

WORK CENTER: ______________________ DATE OF STUDY: ______________________ ANALYST: ______________________

	Day 1		Day 2			Day 3			Day 4			Day 5			Day 6			Day 7			Day 8			Day 9			Day 10		
OPERATIONS	OBS	% OBS	OBS	CUM OBS	% OBS	OBS	CUM OBS	% OBS	OBS	CUM OBS	% OBS	OBS	CUM OBS	% OBS	OBS	CUM OBS	% OBS	OBS	CUM OBS	% OBS	OBS	CUM OBS	% OBS	OBS	CUM OBS	% OBS	OBS	CUM OBS	% OBS

of observations, and actual occurrence, in percent, of each activity. The "Actual Man-Hours" column shows the total man-hours worked during the sampling period—2,706 hours. To ascertain the number of hours spent on each category of activity, multiply the total man-hours figure by the percent occurrence of each particular activity (for example, 743 hours were spent on vouchers). Next, the actual man-hours are multiplied by the .95 percent leveling factor to produce leveled hours. Then the leveled time is multiplied by a factor known as a personal and miscellaneous allowance (P and M allowance) to obtain a standard time for each activity (in total hours).

The P and M allowance is usually tailored to each department. The personal allowance covers such things as coffee or rest breaks, trips to the restroom, getting a drink of water, personal conversation, smoking, and cleaning eyeglasses. Personal allowances vary from 5 to 10 percent, although most companies use 10 percent. This means that roughly 48 minutes out of an 8-hour working day, excluding lunch, are usually allowed for personal time.

The miscellaneous portion of the P and M allowance covers such items as questions by the supervisor, getting supplies, loading staplers, sharpening pencils, infrequent phone calls, and unavoidable interruptions. Miscellaneous allowances range up to 10 percent; most companies or departments use 5 percent. This means that roughly 24 minutes out of an 8-hour working day are usually allowed for miscellaneous time. The total P and M allowance is generally 15 percent.

The next step is to divide the total standard time for each activity by the number of units produced, which will result in the unit time standard for each category. The last column shows the unit time standard in minutes.

Uses of Work Sampling

As a measurement device, work sampling provides a means to measure work that is either uneconomical or impractical to measure by time study or predetermined time data. Therefore, work sampling can be used as a stand-alone technique to complement other work measurement techniques. In the latter case, some applications might be:

- To establish standards on difficult-to-measure, nonrepetitive tasks such as business talking, occasional required walking, or telephoning.
- To determine ratios between productive and nonproductive work in a work center.
- To determine distribution of work within a work center.
- To identify factors causing work delays.

Work sampling can also be used to establish work measurement standards. Sampling results can be leveled either in the traditional time study manner or by use of a predetermined time data system.

Table 10-6. Work sampling: calculation of standards.

Activity	Number of Observations	Actual %	Actual Man-Hours	Avg. Perf. Rating	Leveled Time	Delay and Fatigue Allowance*	Std. Time	Number of Units	Unit Std. Time in Hours	Unit Std. Time in Minutes
Statements	4,672	.378	1,047	.95	994.65	1.169	1,162.75	3,890	.2989	17.93
Vouchers	3,989	.323	743	.95	705.85	1.169	825.14	1,642	.5025	30.15
Return Items	533	.043	128	.95	121.50	1.169	142.15	906	.1569	9.41
Registered Items	582	.047	139	.95	132.05	1.169	154.37	5,267	.0293	1.76
Notices	314	.025	73	.95	69.35	1,169	81.07	582	.1393	8.36
Unavoidable Delay	515	.042	136							
Personal, Rest	1,566	.128	398							
Idle	175	.014	42							
Totals	12,346	1.000	2,706							

*Computation of Allowance

Allowance for Personal Needs	=	30 Minutes per Day
Allowance for Rest	=	20 Minutes per Day
Allowance for Delay	=	15 Minutes per Day
Total Allowance	=	65 Minutes per Day
Total Minutes in Work Day	=	450

$\dfrac{65}{450} = 14.44\%$

$1 + \dfrac{14.44}{100.00 - 14.44} = 1.169$ Personal, Rest, and Delay Allowance

Advantages

A summary of the advantages of the work sampling technique follows:

- For the most part, results can be obtained fairly quickly. Estimates range as high as six times faster than continuous observation.
- It does not require observers with special skills or costly training.
- Since it does not involve any special assistance from employees, it does not interfere with the normal work routine.
- It does not require any special equipment.
- It makes it practical to get information you would not otherwise try to collect.
- It can be applied to almost any situation.
- Cost is relatively low.

Limitations

Those contemplating using work sampling should be aware of the limitations and disadvantages it has as a measurement technique:

- It is not readily accepted by employees, because it is difficult to understand.
- It does not lend itself to paperwork simplification or methods and procedures improvement.
- Because of the lack of precise or even specific documentation, it makes maintenance of standards difficult.
- It is easy to have a distortion of results due to inaccurate identification of an activity during observation.
- Employees tend to try to look busy when an observer is present. Precautions taken to mask the observer sometimes cause employees not to trust the study.
- Unless a leveling factor is applied to the observations, an erroneous assumption is often made that while people are working, they are 100 percent effective.
- The standards developed should not be used for incentive purposes.

TIME LADDER STUDIES

The time ladder study, also referred to as self-logging, is a participative approach to work measurement. Employees play a major role in recording, or logging, what they are doing, when they are doing it, and the amount of work they complete during any given time period.

Preparation for a study

The only steps required to prepare for a time ladder study are to prepare a list of the activities being performed in a unit and to explain the study to the people

Table 10.7 Code sheet.

Code	Description	Items Counted
1	Absent Time	Occurrence
2	Personal Time	Occurrence
3	No Work Available	Occurrence
4	Discussion with Supervisor	Occurrence
5	Process Applications	Applications
6	Type Invoices	Invoices
7	File Invoices	Invoices
8	Handle Correspondence	Letters Received
9	Miscellaneous	

involved in it. Since the purpose of a time ladder study is to determine how people spend their time, what activities or tasks they perform, and how much work is processed, a list is developed similar to that in Table 10-7.

SELLING THE TECHNIQUE

It is important that the employees involved have a clear understanding of the purpose of the study. In a work sampling study, an objective outsider or supervisor is recording the data through observations. With a time ladder study, it is the employee who does the recording. The employee should not feel threatened by the results or use of the results of the study. It is important to persuade the employees to report their activities honestly and completely.

Explain that by knowing how they are spending their time and how much work is being accomplished, we can make changes in the work schedule, determine where bottlenecks occur, provide a basis for knowing each individual's contribution to the work effort, and develop time standards for the work.

Distribute a copy of the code list (Table 10-7) and discuss each category, the use of codes, what items to count, when and how to count them, and how to record them on a time log (Figure 10-4).

Conducting the Study

A time ladder study is usually taken over a sufficient period of time so as to accumulate valid data. How long is a sufficient period? It all depends on the normal work cycle. In some work centers, one day is like any other day. Here a two-week period of data accumulation might be sufficient. If there is a weekly cycle, three or four weeks might suffice. If it is a department that involves a number of monthly functions, a two-month period might be required.

Figure 10-4. Time log.

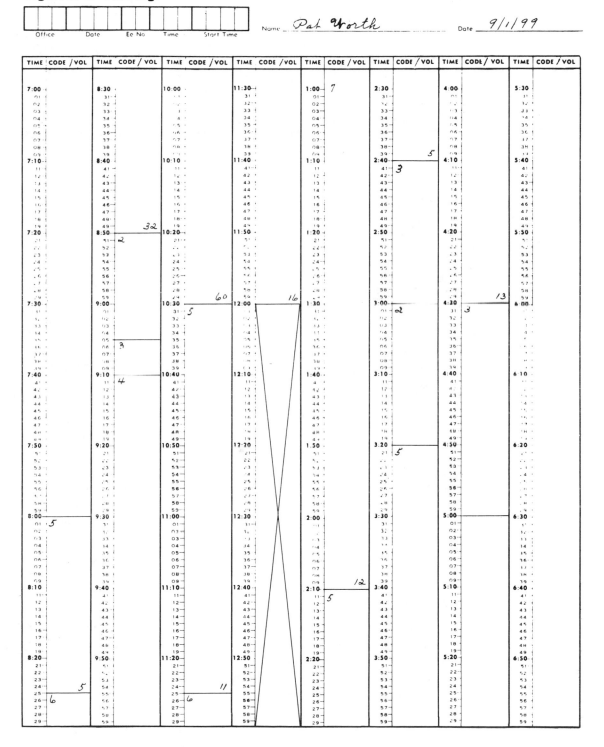

Table 10.8 Summary of one day's activities.

Code	Category	Elapsed Time	Volume	Time per Item	% Time to Total
1	Absent	—	—	—	—
2	Personal	250	—	—	10%
3	No Work	220	—	—	9%
4	Discussion	80	—	—	3%
5	Process Apps.	515	184	2.80	21%
6	Type Inv.	640	128	5.00	27%
7	File Inv.	280	280	1.00	12%
8	Corres.	415	55	7.50	18%
9	Misc.	—	—	—	—
	Totals	2,400	N/A	N/A	100%

The study involves each employee filling out a daily time log. Figure 10-4 is an example of a time log filled out for one day by one employee. It shows that the employee:

- Started work at 8:00 AM, took a one-hour lunch period from 12:00 to 1:00, and left work at 5:00 PM.
- Took a coffee or rest break in the morning (8:50–9:05) and in the afternoon (3:00–3:20).
- Was waiting for work at three different periods of the day (9:05–9:10, 2:40–3:00, and 4:30–5:00).
- Performed a variety of tasks during the remaining periods of the day.

Analyzing the Data

To illustrate the kind of data that can result from a time ladder study, we have prepared Table 10-8, which summarizes one day's activities. As can be seen, the reported absent, personal, and waiting-for-work time has been quantified and isolated from productive time. By knowing how much time has been devoted to each task, and the number of items completed during that period, we can arrive at average time values for each task.

Developing Standards

By taking the time devoted to any given task and the units completed by each employee, we can arrive at reasonable standards. Generally, there are two approaches to developing standards from self-logging data: the array method and the non-array method. The non-array method is by far the simplest and requires considerably less time than the array technique.

Table 10-9. Summary of task (typing invoices).

Employee	Elapsed Time per Item	
Jones	5.10	
Smith	5.95	Eliminate "high" time
Brown	5.05	
Green	4.93	
Long	5.00	
Short	4.92	
Rich	4.15	Eliminate "low" time
Poore	5.13	
Total	40.23	
Minus high and low	10.10	
New total	30.13	
Average	5.02	

With the non-array approach, we simply total all the units of work processed in a category and all the time required to process those units, divide the number of units by the total time, and we have a unit time standard. For example, let us assume that the total number of units produced over a period of time was 23,872 and that the total time for processing these units as reported on the logs was 950 minutes. Dividing the units by the number of minutes results in a unit time standard of .04 minute. The non-array method does not provide any information concerning variations in processing times; it simply gives us an arithmetic mean— the average time taken by the average worker.

The array method of calculating standards provides information on the range of processing time. With this approach, it is necessary to calculate a separate time value for *each occurrence of each activity.* If the study was conducted over a long period of time and included several employees, the number of separate calculations would be quite high, not only for one activity but for all other activities.

Once the separate time values have been calculated, they are arranged in order, from the smallest value to the largest, or vice versa. From this array of time values, standards can be calculated in several ways: (1) we can set a standard based on the median time value, (2) we can set a standard based on the modal value, (3) we can set a standard based on the upper quartile value, or (4) we can set a standard based on a selected average value. Frequently, the selected-average approach is used.

Table 10-9 shows how all the time values for a task (typing invoices) can be summarized. A normal procedure is to eliminate the high and low times in order to get a more representative average. In this case, 5 minutes per invoice will be the standard.

Advantages

The time ladder study, or self-logging, has several advantages:

It is easy to install.
It is economical to install.
It is easy to explain to workers and supervisors.
Employee acceptance is usually high, simply because employees know that the resulting time standards are based on the actual times that they reported.
It is applicable to all types of jobs and functions—simple and complex, repetitive and nonrepetitive.

Limitations

Those contemplating using a time ladder study should be aware of the limitations and/or disadvantages it has as a measurement technique:

- It does not lend itself to paperwork simplification or methods and procedures improvement.
- Because of the lack of precise or even specific documentation, it makes maintenance of standards difficult.
- Because of a lack of direct control over the postings by the employee, the data can contain inaccurate information. The most common errors result from forgetting to post and then trying to reconstruct the day's activities from memory.
- The time values used most likely reflect the time it actually takes to perform work rather than the time it *should* take.
- Data collection over a long period, say two months, can have a disruptive effect on the normal office work routine.
- Unless a computer program is developed to analyze the data (which in itself is costly), the time required to summarize and analyze data can be considerable.
- The standards developed should not be used for incentive purposes.

CHAPTER

Formal Techniques: Time Study

WORK MEASUREMENT HAS BEEN DEFINED as "a management tool based on the use of scientific principles with the aim of ascertaining both the cost of labor in productive situations, and procedures by which that cost might be effectively reduced." This definition implies that engineered standards can be developed only through the use of the techniques we have labeled as "formal techniques."

WORK MEASUREMENT AND TIME STUDY

Work measurement is the result of a great deal of development work extending over many years—as far back as the late 1800s. As we have mentioned previously, the man who is responsible for the introduction of the fundamental principles of work measurement is Frederick W. Taylor. It is mainly through Taylor's efforts that time study withstood the criticisms of both management and labor. The foundation for scientific management was laid by Taylor during the latter part of the nineteenth century and early part of the twentieth century.

Work measurement in its infancy was known as time study. The first measurements were aimed at determining operator performance and production level by relating them to historical data or past performance records. These records, of course, proved to be unreliable. The need for a better and more reliable system of measurement was quite evident. Taylor took the initiative by developing the use of the stopwatch. He developed a technique for standardizing performance times by using the stopwatch to measure a specific method of performing an operation.

A short time after Taylor started his work and had become widely known throughout industry, Frank B. Gilbreth, a former bricklayer, began an intensive study of the motions that workers use in the performance of a given task. He realized that one of the greatest opportunities for cost reduction was in the improvement of production methods. These improvements did not necessarily require the installation of expensive machines and equipment, but often could be secured by analyzing the operation carefully, eliminating unnecessary motions, and installing simple commonsense methods.

The Gilbreth Research Group was responsible for discovering and expressing the 17 laws of motion economy. This group also developed the technique of using the motion picture camera for making detailed laboratory studies. This method of filming operations for the study of motions and methods eventually developed into what is now known as "micromotion study."

The combination of the work done by Taylor and Gilbreth—the two techniques of time study and motion study—came to be known as time and motion study. The system became more formalized during the 1930s and 1940s, but still had certain disadvantages which led others to develop even more effective techniques for the quantification of work.

Definition

Time study is a process of observing an operation while utilizing a timing device, and rating the pace or performance of the individual performing the operation in order to establish a standard for that operation. It involves defining a job or task in terms of its elements and making careful observations—usually using a stopwatch—to establish the time required for the element. The time study analyst—usually someone who has had professional training and experience in this aspect of work measurement—rates the pace of the person performing the operation against the established norm as the study is being conducted. A number of observations consistent with the length of the task, its complexity, and its impact on workload are made to assure statistical accuracy.

Because this method has been used in the factory for many years, it has wide acceptance there and is considered very accurate. Unfortunately, this strength is also its weakness: time study, and the use of a stopwatch, has generally proved psychologically unacceptable to office personnel because of its factory origins.

Using the Stopwatch

The most common type of stopwatch used is one calibrated in decimal minutes. This type of watch registers time on two dials. The outer dial, which is the larger one, is divided into 100 units, each representing .01 minute. The smaller dial records the number of complete revolutions or minutes. The capacity of the smaller dial is usually 30 minutes.

There are two timing techniques that can be used: the continuous timing method and the snap-back method. Continuous timing involves starting the watch at the beginning of an operation, noting the time at the end of each step or after each activity, recording the time in the appropriate column, and stopping the watch at the end of the operation. The ending time of each element is subtracted from the ending time of the preceding element to determine the elapsed time for each function.

The snap-back method involves starting and stopping the watch for each step and recording the time in the appropriate column. Special (and expensive) watches for snap-back timing are available, as are multiple-watch timing boards facilitating the snap-back method. Continuous timing is the preferred choice for longer-cycle tasks, while the snap-back method is most often utilized for shorter-cycle tasks.

Performance Rating

Performance rating, or leveling, involves an evaluation by a trained analyst of the skill, effort, and work pace being applied by an operator under study. The evaluation is based on a comparison with a uniform concept of "normal." This is done to compensate for an employee working faster or slower than "normal" and thus distorting standard accuracy. In industrial engineering terminology, "normal" equates with our definition of 100 percent performance: "the work pace at which an average, well-trained employee can work without undue fatigue while producing acceptable-quality work."

Therefore, while an employee is performing a task or step within a task, and while the stopwatch is recording how long it actually takes to perform the task or step, the analyst rates the pace, in terms of skill and effort being exerted:

- At 100 percent if the analyst feels the employee is performing at a pace which he should be expected to maintain all day long.
- Above 100 percent, normally in increments of 5 (105 percent, 110 percent, and so on), if the analyst feels the employee is performing at a pace greater than can be expected of an average, well-trained employee.
- Below 100 percent (95 percent, 90 percent, and so on) if the analyst feels the employee is performing slower and less skillfully than should be expected of an average, well-trained employee.

There are various rating films available for training analysts to understand and apply the concept of "normal" to office work situations. Some groups have developed this capability to evaluate performance quite accurately. Nonetheless, it is a subjective judgment on the part of the analyst, and has often been referred to as the "weak link" or "tragic flaw" of time study. Analyst objectivity may be influenced by irrelevant factors such as employee personality, appearance, or preconceived ideas of what the standard should be.

Terminology

Here is a list of the more common terms used in time studies.

Task—a process which is placed on one task outline and contains a step, or a series of steps, and which is determined to be a distinct operation.

Step—the process between the logical beginning and ending point of an action performed within a task. A typical task is usually performed in three steps, usually called setup step, "do" step, and wrap-up step. Complex tasks may have many "do" steps.

Item—a single entity that is identified, for a step or a task, as the key indicator that varies in direct proportion to time.

Volume—the total number of items in the sample for a step or job.

Batch—a number of similar items processed together as a group.

Timing—the observation and recording of the amount of time it takes to complete a batch or a portion of a batch of work on the timing pad.

Posting—an entry on one line of the development sheet.

Sample—the total number of postings necessary to obtain consistency in the development of a time standard.

Consistency—the agreement or harmony of parts to one another or to the whole.

Consistency deviation—the percentage difference between one cumulative time or ratio posting and another. (The time can be either on a step basis or on a total task basis.)

Ratio—the relationship between the number of items being handled in any one step and the total number of items counted for the task.

THE TIME STUDY PROCEDURE

There are a wide variety of procedures used to conduct a time study. These vary from highly formalized procedures used by industrial engineers in direct factory labor situations to much less formal methods. We have selected an approach that has proved highly successful in an office situation. This approach can be explained in five phases as follows: (1) selecting the employee(s) to be timed, (2) interviews and data collection, (3) timing the operation or task, (4) rating the performance, and (5) developing the standard.

Selecting the Employee to Be Timed

The customary procedure is to select a qualified employee—one who knows the proper method for performing the task, who is experienced enough to make the necessary decisions or judgments called for in a normal time frame, and who is physically and mentally capable of performing at a normal pace under timed conditions.

To time an employee who is uncertain of the procedures, method, or job requirements would make performance rating extremely difficult. On the other hand, to select a person who has exceptional mental faculties and/or exceptional physical dexterity would also be unfair and unacceptable.

The key word is "normal." The closer we can get to an average, well-trained employee, the better is the chance for developing a reliable standard.

Interviews and Data Collection

If we are to develop an acceptable time standard, there are basic questions that must be answered before the timing can begin.

First, the analyst should interview the supervisor and ask:

- What procedures or steps are involved in performing the task?
- How often is the task performed?
- Are there nonroutine steps that can occur?
- What is the average batch size, and roughly how long does it take? (The answer to this question is critical in terms of establishing a batch size for timing purposes.)
- What is the maximum volume one employee can complete during the work measurement reporting cycle? (The answer to this question is utilized as the basic component for determining an accurate standard.)

Second, the analyst should interview the employee selected to be timed and ask:

- What procedures are involved in the task?
- Are there nonroutine steps that can occur?
- What is the frequency of the task performed?
- What equipment and/or forms are utilized to perform this task?
- What is the average batch size?

Timing the Operation or Task

The analyst should take whatever steps are required to put the employee at ease before starting the timing. This could involve conversation on non-business-related subjects, and an explanation of the stopwatch and how it is used to determine standards. The analyst should explain that the watch can be turned off ("stopped") if the employee would like to explain some of the procedures. Generally, the analyst might suggest that the employee work at her normal pace.

Figure 11-1 is an example of a time study analysis sheet on an actual timing of an employee, J. Abbott, who is performing the task called Sort Index Cards. The task has four steps: step A, get cards and unband (the setup step); step B, sort cards into a sortograph; step C, sort cards into perfect sequence; and step D, deliver sorted cards. The watch reading was started at zero, and the total elapsed time was 12.90 minutes. A total of 135 cards were sorted.

Figure II-I. Time study analysis sheet.

TASK: SORT INDEX CARDS   DATE: 1-6-99

EMPLOYEE: J. Abbott

	WATCH READING	ELAPSED TIME (MIN.)	ACTIVITY		PERF. RATING
	0.00	.30	Get work and return		100%
A:	.30	.25	Unband bundles (3)		
	.55	.55	Sort into sortograph	10	
B:	.80	.25	" " "	10	
	1.20	.40	" " "	10	
	.70	.50	" " "	10	
	2.05	.35	" " "	10	
	.50	.45	" " "	10	
	.75	.25	" " "	10	
	3.05	.30	" " "	10	
	.60	.55	" " "	10	
	.95	.35	" " "	10	
	4.35	.40	" " "	10	
	.80	.45	" " "	10	85%
	5.55	.75	" " "	10	
	.90	.35	" " "	5	
		5.35	Total cards sorted	135	
C:	12.30	6.40	Gather each batch and sort into perfect sequence		90%
D:	12.85	.55	Gather all cards, deliver, and return to own desk		100%
	.90	.05			
		.60			

The analyst starts by filling out the headings, including: Name of Task, Name of Employee, Date, and whether the timing is taking place in the morning or afternoon (AM or PM). Since employees are generally fresher in the morning and less energetic in the afternoon, an equal number of timings should be taken in the morning and afternoon to average out the fatigue element.

The timing can now proceed. During the timing, questions concerning methods, time inconsistency, and/or procedure deviation related to the items being processed are asked at the time of occurrence. The answers may change the method of timing or be used to document the reasons for the deviations if the timing method cannot be changed.

Rating the Performance

During the course of timing a step of a task, the analyst is evaluating the employee's skill, effort, and consistency of work pace. When the step is completed and the employee is about to start a new step, the analyst records the performance rating on the time study analysis sheet.

Developing the Standard

Table 11-1 shows a time study development. It illustrates how four timings, of four different batches performed by four different employees, were summarized to determine a standard time per card for the task of sorting index cards.

Next, an allowance is added to the standard to cover personal and miscellaneous factors involved in the total job for the employee. Since the development of allowances is covered in another chapter, it will suffice to say that an allowance of 15 percent is added to the standard time per card (thus, .0894 minute + 15 percent or .0134 minute = .1028 minute/card).

The final step is to write a *task description*, which contains a narrative

Table 11-1. Time study development (task: sort index cards).

Step	Employee	Date	Items	Actual Minutes Total	Actual Minutes Per Item	Eff. Rating	Adjusted Minutes Total	Adjusted Minutes Per Item
A	J. Abbott	1-6-99	135	.55	.0040	100%	.55	.0040
	K. Bonds	1-6-99	120	.60	.0050	100%	.60	.0050
	L. Cass	1-7-99	90	.55	.0061	100%	.55	.0061
	M. Donner	1-7-99	130	.70	.0053	90%	.63	.0048
			475	2.40	.0050		2.33	.0049
B	J. Abbott	1-6-99	135	5.35	.0396	85%	4.55	.0337
	K. Bonds	1-6-99	120	4.30	.0358	100%	4.30	.0358
	L. Cass	1-7-99	90	4.15	.0461	80%	3.74	.0415
	M. Donner	1-7-99	130	5.80	.0450	70%	4.06	.0312
			475	19.60	.0412		16.65	.0350
C	J. Abbott	1-6-99	135	6.40	.0474	90%	5.76	.0426
	K. Bonds	1-6-99	120	6.00	.0500	90%	5.40	.0450
	L. Cass	1-7-99	90	4.75	.0527	85%	4.04	.0448
	M. Donner	1-7-99	130	5.90	.0453	100%	5.90	.0453
			475	23.05	.0485		21.10	.0444
D	J. Abbott	1-6-99	135	.60	.0044	100%	.60	.0044
	K. Bonds	1-6-99	120	.60	.0050	100%	.60	.0050
	L. Cass	1-7-99	90	.60	.0066	100%	.60	.0066
	M. Donner	1-7-99	130	.60	.0046	100%	.60	.0046
			475	2.40	.0050		2.40	.0050
SUMMARY		Step A	475	2.40	.0050		2.33	.0049
		B	475	19.60	.0412		16.65	.0350
		C	475	23.05	.0485		21.10	.0444
		D	475	2.40	.0050		2.40	.0050
				47.45	.0997		42.48	.0894

description of the task and a summary of the standard developed, such as the summary shown at the end of Table 11-1.

Machine Timing

This section defines machine timing procedures and exception guidelines. First, some definitions:

Handling time is the time before the machine starts its cycle or after the machine has completed its cycle. No handling time is given if the machine is not shut off.

Machine time is the time the machine takes to complete its cycle.

Jam time is the time the machine is unable mechanically to complete its cycle (paper stuck, and the like).

Response time is the time spent by an employee waiting for the machine before adding input (waiting for CRT-terminal output after batch entry, waiting for the machine to warm up, and the like).

Interruptions to the machine cycle include reloading the machine, which requires the machine to be shut off, re-inking, and so on. All interruptions should be verified with supervisory personnel before deciding whether they should be included as part of the job.

MACHINE SPEED AND PERFORMANCE

Special care must be taken when timing multiple-speed machines to ensure proper setup and proper machine speed for the kind of work being done. Generally, there are manufacturer's instruction manuals to ensure proper setup procedures, and supervisory personnel usually know from experience what is the proper machine speed. That speed should be used for timing.

All machines are assumed to be operating at 100 percent performance. No machine should be rated higher or lower than 100 percent, regardless of speed. Machines that can run at variable speed require some experimentation to determine the "best" speed for a given application. The operator risks excessive jams by running the equipment at a greater speed, and his performance is lowered by a slower speed.

MULTIPLE USE OF MACHINES

In some cases a machine does not require 100 percent operator attention. Determine the feasibility of running two or more machines at the same time, taking into account OSHA rules and handling time.

GUIDELINES

The same guidelines should be used for sample size as previously explained, except that "percentage of workload" should refer only to actual handling time.

Additionally, a jam time should be built into a machine standard. Excessive machine jams (in excess of 5 percent of run time) are indications of malfunctioning equipment or an unskilled operator and require further investigation before standards can be established.

ADVANTAGES OF TIME STUDIES

Time study is a technique that has distinct advantages over other techniques:

- Except for pace rating, it is easy to explain and easy to understand.
- Time study standards are accurate when developed by a well-qualified and well-trained analyst.
- Time study standards can be developed fairly rapidly.
- Time study standards can be adjusted fairly easily as changes occur in method, volume, or equipment.
- The documentation in time study provides detailed information concerning the methods and procedures employed and the equipment and materials used, which can be a stimulus for improving methods and procedures.
- Because of the degree of accuracy provided by time study standards, they can be used for incentive purposes.
- The leveling factor, or performance rating, in time study provides for differences in pace among workers.
- Because time study usually involves timing a task a number of times, frequencies and exceptions are usually properly built into the standards.

DISADVANTAGES OF TIME STUDIES

Despite the very worthwhile advantages of time study, the disadvantages can often outweigh the advantages. Here are some of the disadvantages:

- Because people generally associate the stopwatch with factory operations and as the tool of "efficiency experts," its adverse effect on morale cannot be denied.
- Time study usually requires timing a number of employees over extended periods of time, and therefore can put a great deal of pressure on employees and a burden on the analyst.
- Time study requires a great deal of training for analysts to learn to apply it properly, and periodic refresher training to maintain consistent rating skills. The cost of training is higher than with most other techniques.
- The subjective aspect of performance rating can lead to inconsistencies among analysts.
- Time study does not lend itself as easily to measurement of long-cycle or varied tasks as other techniques.

CHAPTER

Formal Techniques: Predetermined Time Systems

A PREDETERMINED TIME SYSTEM, according to Delmar W. Karger and Franklin H. Bayha, is "an organized body of information, procedures, and techniques employed in the study and evaluation of work elements performed by human power." Specifically, these work elements are evaluated "in terms of the method or motions used, their general and specific nature, the conditions under which they occur, and the application of prestandardized or predetermined times which their perform-ance requires."[1]

Predetermined time systems emerged on the scene in the 1930s. At that time, there were three systems: MTA (motion-time analysis), work factor, and MTS (motion-time standards). As one would expect, these techniques were developed for industrial operations. Their emergence on the industrial scene was a result of the misuse of time study and other techniques used by "efficiency experts"—people with little understanding of work measurement who did their "quick and dirty" job of cutting labor costs. It was here that the stopwatch became the symbol of the efficiency experts and fell into disrepute. Predetermined time systems were developed to overcome some of the disadvantages of the stopwatch.

One of the pioneers in the area of predetermined time systems was Asa B. Segur. He was keenly interested in physiology. In the early 1920s he became interested in the time characteristics of thinking, nerve reaction, and muscular reaction. Some of the things he discovered are:

[1]*Engineered Work Measurement*, New York: Industrial Press, 3rd edition, 1977, p. 208.

138

Each action of the body is the result of some chemical reaction that takes place within the body. Since this chemical reaction takes place in a constant temperature—insofar as the chemical reaction is constant—the time for the reaction will also be constant within narrow limits.

The controlling time for human action may be defined as follows:

Average speed of a nerve reaction in the human body is 0.00045 minute per foot of distance traveled. Average number of messages that can be started over any one nerve path in the body is 5,000 per minute. Average time for a single sarcostyle to complete a contraction in response to a nerve impulse is 0.00064 minute. . . . The above times apply to routine thinking, as well as to muscular reaction. These reactions, which are controlled by the brain, are becoming increasingly more important in industry than those which are controlled by the muscles alone.[2]

Segur first experimented with time equations of motion-time analysis in 1924 by analyzing micromotion films taken of experienced operators during World War I. He discovered that:

If the same motion were performed by various operators in exactly the same manner, the time for performing it was constant. This held true regardless of the type of industry in which the operator worked. The announcement was therefore made that "within reasonable limits, the time required of all experts to perform a true fundamental motion is constant.[3]

Segur expanded on Gilbreth's motion studies to prove that as a person works under a well-prescribed method, he gradually becomes an expert. The method was referred to as an engineered motion path. An engineered motion path has a rhythm to it. After sufficient repetition and practice, the nerve system takes over, Segur discovered. He concluded that the time required of all experts to perform a fundamental motion was a constant.

The work done by Segur and others built a foundation for what was to be one of the most widely used predetermined time systems in the world—methods time measurement, or MTM.

According to Karger and Bayha:

The basic key to all predetermined time systems is the fact that variations in the times required to perform the same motion are essentially small for different workers who

---

[2]Harold B. Maynard, *Industrial Engineering Handbook*, New York: McGraw-Hill, 1963, Part 5, p. 108.
[3]Ibid., Part 5, p. 110.

have had adequate practice. Mathematical relationships can therefore be established between motions and times, subject to predictable statistical limits.[4]

The major predetermined time systems include some that are maintained in private industry or developed for internal use within a particular organization:

- Motion-time analysis, or MTA, developed by Asa B. Segur. It is the oldest system and contains well-defined principles. The system is administered and maintained by the A. B. Segur Company.
- Work factor, developed by the Work Factor Company, based on accumulations of stopwatch studies and motion picture and photographic studies done at RCA.
- Systems such as "Get and Place," MTS (motion-time standards) and DMT (dimensional motion times). These systems were developed by General Electric from synthetic data and designed primarily for internal use at General Electric.
- Methods-time measurement, or MTM, which is a system developed in the mid-1940s at Westinghouse Electric Corporation.

While each of these systems has met with wide acceptance for use in factories, one system seems to have the broadest application as a basis for use in offices. That system is MTM.

METHODS-TIME MEASUREMENT

Methods-time measurement (MTM) is the only predetermined time system for which both data and research have been made readily available to the public. It was developed at Methods Engineering Council of Pittsburgh, Pennsylvania, by Harold B. Maynard, Gustave J. Stegemerten, and John L. Schwab after preliminary study at Westinghouse Electric Corporation.

The authors of MTM participated in the development of a nonprofit research and development organization known as the MTM Association for Standards and Research. All of their data and development rights were assigned to this Association. The MTM Association for Standards and Research continues to perform a valuable contribution to the field of scientific management by sponsoring research programs and training programs in this field.

The definition of MTM is the same now as it was in the original work performed by the developers:

[4]Karger and Bayha, op. cit., p. 203.

Methods-Time Measurement is a procedure which analyzes any manual operation or method into the basic motions required to perform it and assigns to each motion a predetermined time standard which is determined by the nature of the motion and the conditions under which it is made."[5]

MTM provides a time value for virtually every motion performed by the human body in a productive or work situation. It was developed by selecting average people (average age, size, and physical characteristics) and placing them under average conditions (average heat, light, and ventilation). The people were requested to perform series of motions, and these work sequences were filmed using a high-speed, constant-speed camera. Using a constant-speed projector, the films were pace-rated by well-qualified industrial engineers until they had validated time values for all of the basic motions performed.

Time Measurement Units

The MTM procedure uses very small increments of time. For example, the time to release an object (MTM symbol RL1) is 0.00002 hour, or 0.0012 minute, or 0.072 second. These are unwieldy figures to work with. Whole numbers are much easier to work with and easier to remember than decimal fractions. This consideration made it advisable to introduce a new unit of measurement, called the time measurement unit (TMU).

The speed of the camera used to develop MTM was 16 frames per second. Therefore, each frame had an elapsed time of 0.0625 second, or 0.00001737 hour. The way to avoid the use of such figures was to recognize that time units are arbitrary by nature. The MTM founders assigned the value of 0.00001 hour as the value of one time measurement unit.

Terminology

Before reviewing each of the MTM motions, a discussion of some of the terms that are used is in order:

Motions—this term covers the motions performed by the human body, such as reach, grasp, move, or release. Each motion is designated by a letter: R for reach, G for grasp, M for move, RL for release, and so on.
Distance—always expressed in inches except in the instance of distances of ¾ of an inch or less, which are expressed as "f," for "fractional."
Case—usually identified by the letters A, B, C, and so on. It indicates the

[5]Harold B. Maynard, Gustave J. Stegemerten, and John L. Schwab, *Methods-Time Measurement*, New York: McGraw-Hill, 1948, pp. 14–15.

destination where the hand or object is being directed, or the degree of difficulty.

Convention—a shorthand expression of an MTM element. For example, RfC is a convention for a reach of a fractional distance to objects which are jumbled with other objects so that search and select occur.

Continuity of motion—this refers to whether or not the motion starts from a rest position and whether or not the motion ends at rest position.

Thought Time in MTM

There are four categories of motions in MTM which indicate the kind of mental or visual control involved in performing the motion:

1. Motions which require no conscious thought or direction and can be performed automatically.
2. Motions which require *either* conscious thought or direction.
3. Motions which require *both* conscious thought and direction.
4. Mental selection.

Mental selection requires different motions. Therefore, if mental or visual control is required to properly execute a motion or combination of motions, it is built into the element or elements. To elaborate, when the time values were developed from films, if a person performed a motion that required moving the eyes (visual control) or concentrating on each precise movement (mental control), the elapsed time would have included the mental and/or visual control time.

Simultaneous Motions

The answer to whether or not two similar or dissimilar motions can be performed simultaneously can be determined from Figure 12-1.* Consideration must be given to whether or not the motions are performed within or outside of the area of normal vision, and to the amount of "practice opportunity" the operator has.

REACH   This motion is defined as follows:

REACH is the basic hand or finger motion employed when the *predominant purpose* is to move the hand or fingers to a destination.
1. Reach is performed only by the fingers or hand. Moving the foot to a trip lever would *not* be classified as a reach.
2. The hand may be carrying an object and the motion still will be classified as a

*Note: The tables in Figure 12-1 through Figure 12-11 are copyrighted by the MTM Association for Standards and Research. No reprint permission without written consent from the MTM Association, 16-01 Broadway, Fair Lawn, N.J. 07410.

Figure 12-1. Simultaneous motions.

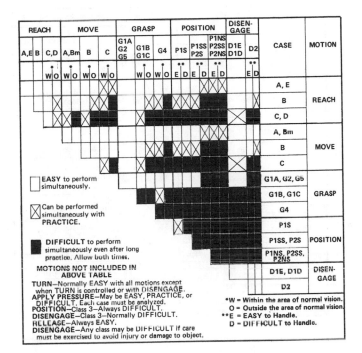

reach provided the predominant purpose is only to move the hand or fingers and not the object. An example would be the 'reach' for an eraser while the performer is still holding chalk in the same hand.

3. Short reaches can be performed by moving only the fingers; longer reaches involve motion of the hand, forearm, and upper arm.[6]

Variables. The variables of REACH are the length of the motion (distance), destination or case, and continuity of motion. For details see Figure 12.2.

Example. An example of REACH is an R14B. This is translated as a reach of 14 inches to a single object that is in a location that may vary slightly from cycle to cycle. It has a value of 14.4 time measurement units.

---

[6]From "MTM Basic Specifications," prepared by the 1957 Training Committee of the MTM Association. The main definition and the numbered subdefinitions are considered integral parts of the complete specification for each motion. These data are derived from Vol. V, No. 4 of the *Journal of Methods-Time Measurement* for November–December 1958 and are used by permission of the MTM Association for Standards and Research. To save repetition of this footnote in subsequent chapters of this text, reference is made to this source and this footnote by the following notation: "From 'MTM Basic Specifications' (see Footnote 6, Chapter 12)."

Figure 12-2. The REACH (R) motion.

Distance Moved Inches	Time TMU				Hand In Motion		CASE AND DESCRIPTION
	A	B	C or D	E	A	B	
3/4 or less	2.0	2.0	2.0	2.0	1.6	1.6	A Reach to object in fixed location, or to object in other hand or on which other hand rests.
1	2.5	2.5	3.6	2.4	2.3	2.3	
2	4.0	4.0	5.9	3.8	3.5	2.7	
3	5.3	5.3	7.3	5.3	4.5	3.6	B Reach to single object in location which may vary slightly from cycle to cycle.
4	6.1	6.4	8.4	6.8	4.9	4.3	
5	6.5	7.8	9.4	7.4	5.3	5.0	
6	7.0	8.6	10.1	8.0	5.7	5.7	
7	7.4	9.3	10.8	8.7	6.1	6.5	C Reach to object jumbled with other objects in a group so that search and select occur.
8	7.9	10.1	11.5	9.3	6.5	7.2	
9	8.3	10.8	12.2	9.9	6.9	7.9	
10	8.7	11.5	12.9	10.5	7.3	8.6	
12	9.6	12.9	14.2	11.8	8.1	10.1	
14	10.5	14.4	15.6	13.0	8.9	11.5	D Reach to a very small object or where accurate grasp is required.
16	11.4	15.8	17.0	14.2	9.7	12.9	
18	12.3	17.2	18.4	15.5	10.5	14.4	
20	13.1	18.6	19.8	16.7	11.3	15.8	
22	14.0	20.1	21.2	18.0	12.1	17.3	E Reach to indefinite location to get hand in position for body balance or next motion or out of way.
24	14.9	21.5	22.5	19.2	12.9	18.8	
26	15.8	22.9	23.9	20.4	13.7	20.2	
28	16.7	24.4	25.3	21.7	14.5	21.7	
30	17.5	25.8	26.7	22.9	15.3	23.2	
Additional	0.4	0.7	0.7	0.6			TMU per inch over 30 inches

MOVE   This motion is defined as follows:

MOVE is the basic hand or finger motion employed when the *predominant purpose* is to transport an object to a destination.
1. Move is performed only by the fingers or hand. Pushing an object with the foot would *not* be classified as a move.
2. The hand must exert control over the object during the motion. In tossing an object aside, for example, the move motion ends when the fingers or hand release the object.
3. The fingers or hand may be pushing the object or sliding it; it is not necessary to carry the object.
4. Using the fingers or hand as a tool is classified as a move. The fingers or the hand itself would be considered as a tool being carried by the hand.[7]

Variables. The variables of MOVE are the length of the motion (distance), destination or case, continuity of motion, and weight. For details see Figure 12-3.

[7]From "MTM Basic Specifications" (see Footnote 6).

Example. An example of MOVE is M10C20/2. This is translated as a move of ten inches of an object to an exact location, where the object weighs 20 pounds and is being transported by two hands. It has a value of 18.9 time measurement units.

GRASP   This motion is defined as follows:

GRASP is the basic finger or hand element employed to secure control of an object.
1. The hand or finger(s) must obtain sufficient control of the object to be able to perform the next basic motion.
2. The object may be a single object or a group of stacked or piled objects which can be handled as though they were a single object.[8]

Figure I2-3. The MOVE (M) motion.

Distance Moved Inches	Time TMU				Wt. Allowance			CASE AND DESCRIPTION
	A	B	C	Hand In Motion B	Wt. (lb.) Up to	Dynamic Factor	Static Constant TMU	
3/4 or less	2.0	2.0	2.0	1.7				
1	2.5	2.9	3.4	2.3	2.5	1.00	0	A Move object to other hand or against stop.
2	3.6	4.6	5.2	2.9				
3	4.9	5.7	6.7	3.6	7.5	1.06	2.2	
4	6.1	6.9	8.0	4.3				
5	7.3	8.0	9.2	5.0	12.5	1.11	3.9	
6	8.1	8.9	10.3	5.7				
7	8.9	9.7	11.1	6.5	17.5	1.17	5.6	B Move object to approximate or indefinite location.
8	9.7	10.6	11.8	7.2				
9	10.5	11.5	12.7	7.9	22.5	1.22	7.4	
10	11.3	12.2	13.5	8.6				
12	12.9	13.4	15.2	10.0	27.5	1.28	9.1	
14	14.4	14.6	16.9	11.4				
16	16.0	15.8	18.7	12.8	32.5	1.33	10.8	
18	17.6	17.0	20.4	14.2				
20	19.2	18.2	22.1	15.6	37.5	1.39	12.5	
22	20.8	19.4	23.8	17.0				C Move object to exact location
24	22.4	20.6	25.5	18.4	42.5	1.44	14.3	
26	24.0	21.8	27.3	19.8				
28	25.5	23.1	29.0	21.2	47.5	1.50	16.0	
30	27.1	24.3	30.7	22.7				
Additional	0.8	0.6	0.85		TMU per inch over 30 inches			

EFFECTIVE NET WEIGHT			
Effective Net Weight (ENW)	No. of Hands	Spatial	Sliding
	1	W	W x F_c
	2	W/2	W/2 x F_c

W = Weight in pounds
F_c = Coefficient of Friction

[8]From "MTM Basic Specifications" (see Footnote 6).

Types. There are five types of GRASP: pick-up, regrasp, transfer, select, and contact. For details see Figure 12-4.

Example. An example of GRASP is G4A. This is translated as a grasp of an object that is larger than $1'' \times 1'' \times 1''$ and that is jumbled with other objects so that search and select occurs. It has a value of 7.3 time measurement units.

Figure 12-4. The GRASP (G) motion.

TYPE OF GRASP	Case	Time TMU	DESCRIPTION	
PICK-UP	1A	2.0	Any size object by itself, easily grasped	
	1B	3.5	Object very small or lying close against a flat surface	
	1C1	7.3	Diameter larger than 1/2''	Interference with Grasp
	1C2	8.7	Diameter 1/4'' to 1/2''	on bottom and one side of
	1C3	10.8	Diameter less than 1/4''	nearly cylindrical object.
REGRASP	2	5.6	Change grasp without relinquishing control	
TRANSFER	3	5.6	Control transferred from one hand to the other.	
SELECT	4A	7.3	Larger than 1'' x 1'' x 1''	Object jumbled with other
	4B	9.1	1/4'' x 1/4'' x 1/8'' to 1'' x 1'' x 1''	objects so that search
	4C	12.9	Smaller than 1/4'' x 1/4'' x 1/8''	and select occur.
CONTACT	5	0	Contact, Sliding, or Hook Grasp.	

RELEASE   This motion is defined as follows:

RELEASE is the basic finger or hand motion employed to relinquish control of an object.

1. Release is performed only by the fingers or the hand.[9]

Figure 12-5. The RELEASE (RL) motion.

Case	Time TMU	DESCRIPTION
1	2.0	Normal release performed by opening fingers as independent motion.
2	0	Contact Release

Types. There are two types of RELEASE: one involving an opening of the fingers and the other involving simply breaking contact with an object (see Figure 12-5).

[9]From "MTM Basic Specifications" (see Footnote 6).

Example. An example of RELEASE is RL1. This is translated as a release of an object simply by opening the fingers. It has a value of 2.0 time measurement units.

TURN   This motion is defined as follows:

TURN is the basic motion employed to rotate the hand about the long axis of the forearm.
1. The hand may be empty or holding an object.
2. Turn cannot be made while holding the wrist firm. Turn involves the bones in the forearm and a pivoting motion at the elbow.[10]

Variables. The variables of TURN are weight and the degrees turned (see Figure 12-6).

Example. An example of TURN is T90°S. This is translated as a 90° turn of an object that weighs two pounds or less. It has a value of 5.4 time measurement units.

Figure l2-6. The TURN (T) motion.

Weight	Time TMU for Degrees Turned										
	30°	45°	60°	75°	90°	105°	120°	135°	150°	165°	180°
Small — 0 to 2 Pounds	2.8	3.5	4.1	4.8	5.4	6.1	6.8	7.4	8.1	8.7	9.4
Medium — 2.1 to 10 Pounds	4.4	5.5	6.5	7.5	8.5	9.6	10.6	11.8	12.7	13.7	14.8
Large — 10.1 to 35 Pounds	8.4	10.5	12.3	14.4	16.2	18.3	20.4	22.2	24.3	26.1	28.2

APPLY PRESSURE   This motion is defined as follows:

APPLY PRESSURE is an application of muscular force during which object resistance is overcome in a controlled manner, accompanied by essentially no motion (¼ inch = 6.4 millimeters or less).

1. Apply Pressure, Alone (APA) is a hesitation or lack of motion having at least a limiting Apply Force component with or without subsequent limiting Dwell and Release Force components. However, the symbol APA is not used unless all three components are present with Dwell at a minimum.
2. Apply Pressure, Bind (APB) is an APA preceded by a Regrasp, or the equivalent, indicated by a setting of the muscles.
3. Apply Pressure may be performed by any body member.[11]

[10]From "MTM Basic Specifications" (see Footnote 6).
[11]From "MTM Basic Specifications" (see Footnote 6).

Types. There are two types of APPLY PRESSURE: one involving a simple tensing of the muscles and the other involving a regrasp to gain better control while applying pressure. For details see Figure 12-7.

Example. An example of APPLY PRESSURE is APB. This is translated as applying pressure such as in tightening a screw. After the head of the screwdriver is applied to the screw, the time value includes regrasping the screwdriver before tightening the screw. It has a time value of 16.2 time measurement units.

Figure 12-7. The APPLY PRESSURE (AP) motion.

FULL CYCLE			COMPONENTS		
SYMBOL	TMU	DESCRIPTION	SYMBOL	TMU	DESCRIPTION
APA	10.6	AF + DM + RLF	AF	3.4	Apply Force
			DM	4.2	Dwell, Minimum
APB	16.2	APA + G2	RLF	3.0	Release Force

POSITION   This motion is defined as follows:

POSITION is the basic finger or hand element employed to align, orient, and engage one object with another to attain a specific relationship.
1. An accurate and predetermined relationship between the objects must be attained.
2. The relationship may be a nesting or mating of the objects, or may be a visual locating of one object to another.
3. Normally, only objects can be positioned; occasionally, the finger or hand may be used as a tool and considered as an object in positioning.
4. Align is to line up the two parts so that they have a common axis.
5. Orient is to rotate the part about the common axis of engagement so that it can be mated with the other part.
6. Engage is to enter one part into the other part.[12]

Variables. The variables of POSITION are Align, Orient, and Engage, which, in turn, are affected by the class of fit, case of symmetry, and ease of handling. For details, see Figure 12-8.

Example. An example of POSITION is P2SSE. This is translated as aligning one part with another where light pressure is required, where the part must be oriented (turned) approximately 45°, and where the part is easy to handle. It has a value of 19.7 time measurement units.

[12]From "MTM Basic Specifications" (see Footnote 6).

Figure 12-8. The POSITION (P) motion.
(Distance moved to engage 1" or less.)

CLASS OF FIT		Symmetry	Easy To Handle	Difficult To Handle
1—Loose	No pressure required	S	5.6	11.2
		SS	9.1	14.7
		NS	10.4	16.0
2—Close	Light pressure required	S	16.2	21.8
		SS	19.7	25.3
		NS	21.0	26.6
3—Exact	Heavy pressure required.	S	43.0	48.6
		SS	46.5	52.1
		NS	47.8	53.4
SUPPLEMENTARY RULE FOR SURFACE ALIGNMENT				
P1SE per alignment: >1/16 ⩽1/4"		P2SE per alignment: ⩽1/16"		

*Distance moved to engage—1" or less.

DISENGAGE   This motion is defined as follows:

DISENGAGE is the basic hand or finger element employed to separate one object from another object where there is a sudden ending of resistance.
1. Friction or recoil must be present. Merely *lifting* one object from the surface of another would *not* be a disengage.
2. There must be a noticeable break in the movement of the hand.[13]

Figure 12-9. The DISENGAGE (D) motion.

CLASS OF FIT	HEIGHT OF RECOIL	EASY TO HANDLE	DIFFICULT TO HANDLE
1—LOOSE—Very slight effort, blends with subsequent move.	Up to 1"	4.0	5.7
2—CLOSE—Normal effort, slight recoil.	Over 1" to 6"	7.5	11.8
3—TIGHT—Considerable effort, hand recoils markedly.	Over 5" to 12"	22.0	34.7
SUPPLEMENTARY			

CLASS OF FIT	CARE IN HANDLING	BINDING
1— LOOSE	Allow Class 2	————
2— CLOSE	Allow Class 3	One G2 per Bind
3— TIGHT	Change Method	One APB per Bind

[13]From "MTM Basic Specifications" (see Footnote 6).

Variables. The variables of DISENGAGE are class of fit, ease of handling, and whether or not binding occurs. For details see Figure 12-9.

Example. An example of DISENGAGE is DID. This is translated as a disengage of an object that is difficult to handle where little recoil is evidenced, such as removing a thumbtack from a bulletin board. It has a value of 5.7 time measurement units.

Eye Travel and Eye Focus

These motions are defined as follows:

EYE TRAVEL is the basic eye motion employed to shift the axis of vision from one location to another.
1. Eye travel is a limiting motion only when the eyes must shift their axis of vision before the next manual motions can be started.

EYE FOCUS is the basic visual and mental element of looking at an object long enough to determine a readily distinguishable characteristic.
1. Eye focus is a hesitation while the eyes are examining some detail and transferring a mental picture to the brain.
2. The line of vision does not shift during the eye focus.
3. Eye focus is a limiting motion only when the eyes must identify the readily distinguishable characteristic before the next manual motion can be started.
4. Eye focus is not the normal control over the reaches, moves, positions, grasps, and other motions; eye control affects the time for these motions, and this time is included as an integral part of the motion.[14]

Figure 12-10.   EYE TRAVEL and EYE FOCUS
(ET and EF).

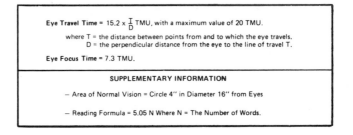

Variables. The variables of EYE TRAVEL are the distance from point to point on the surface, and the vertical distance from the eye to the surface. For details on EYE TRAVEL and EYE FOCUS see Figure 12-10.

Example. An example of an EYE TRAVEL is ET 8/16. This is translated as a move

[14]From "MTM Basic Specifications" (see Footnote 6).

Figure 12-11. BODY, LEG, and FOOT MOTIONS.

TYPE		SYMBOL	TMU	DISTANCE	DESCRIPTION
LEG—FOOT MOTION		FM	8.5	To 4"	Hinged at ankle.
		FMP	19.1	To 4"	With heavy pressure.
		LM__	7.1	To 6"	Hinged at knee or hip in any direction.
			1.2	Ea. add'l inch	
HORIZONTAL MOTION	SIDE STEP	SS__C1	*	<12"	Use Reach or Move time when less than 12". Complete when leading leg contacts floor.
			17.0	12"	
			0.6	Ea. add'l inch	
		SS__C2	34.1	12"	Lagging leg must contact floor before next motion can be made.
			1.1	Ea. add'l inch	
	TURN BODY	TBC1	18.6	———	Complete when leading leg contacts floor.
		TBC2	37.2	———	Lagging leg must contact floor before next motion can be made
	WALK	W__FT	5.3	Per Foot	Unobstructed.
		W__P	15.0	Per Pace	Unobstructed.
		W__PO	17.0	Per Pace	When obstructed or with weight.
VERTICAL MOTION		SIT	34.7	———	From standing position.
		STD	43.4	———	From sitting position.
		B,S,KOK	29.0	———	Bend, Stoop, Kneel on One Knee.
		AB,AS,AKOK	31.9	———	Arise from Bend, Stoop, Kneel on One Knee
		KBK	69.4	———	Kneel on Both Knees.
		AKBK	76.7	———	Arise from Kneel on Both Knees.

or shift of the eyes between two points, eight inches apart, at a perpendicular distance of 16 inches. It has a value of 7.6 (15.2 × 8/16) time measurement units.

Body, Leg, and Foot Motions

BODY, LEG, and FOOT MOTIONS are motions used to locate the body, legs, or feet in order that other elements may be performed.

Variables. The variables of BODY, LEG, and FOOT MOTIONS are, in most cases, distance, case, and, for foot motions, pressure required. See Figure 12-11 for details.

Example. An example of a LEG motion is SS12C2. This is translated as a side step of 12 inches involving the movement, sideways, of both feet. It has a value of 34.1 time measurement units.

TYPES OF MTM PATTERNS

There are four types of MTM motion patterns: consecutive, combined, simultaneous, and compound.

Consecutive Motions

The definition of CONSECUTIVE MOTIONS is:

Figure 12-12. Example of consecutive motions.

OPERATION_____Insert Pen in Holder_____

Description — Left Hand	Class	Time	Class	Description —Right Hand
		12.9	R12B	Reach to pen
		2.0	G1A	Grasp pen
		13.5	M10C	Move pen to holder
		5.6	P1SE	Position/insert pen
		2.0	RL1	Release pen
	Total	36.0		

CONSECUTIVE MOTIONS are individual, complete motions *performed in sequence* by the same or different body members without overlap or pauses between motions.
1. The effects of the motions on objects must be logical and physically reproducible.
2. Each motion in a consecutive series may be connected to the preceding and following motion by constraints in basic motion definitions.[15]

An example is shown in Figure 12-12.

Combined Motions

The definition of COMBINED MOTIONS is:

COMBINED MOTIONS are two or more complete motions *by the same body member* performed during the time required by the limiting motion.
1. The body as a whole, excluding the limbs, may be considered as a single member for such action.
2. Motion assistance often is a factor in combined manual motions.[16]

An example is shown in Figure 12-13.

[15]Karger and Bayha, op. cit., pp. 593–594.
[16]Ibid., p. 596.

Figure 12-13. Example of combined motions.

OPERATION___Deal Cards_____

Description — Left Hand	Class	Time	Class	Description — Right Hand
		7.2	mR8B	Reach to card
		3.5	G1B	Grasp card
		7.2	M8Bm	Move card to pile
		— —	RLT	Release card
	Total	17.9		

Simultaneous Motions

The definition of these motions is:

SIMPLE SIMULTANEOUS MOTIONS are two complete motions *by different body members* performed during the time required by the limiting motion.

1. This definition covers a restricted case of general simultaneous motion.
2. The commonly accepted abbreviation is *simo*, taken from the first two letters each of *si*multaneous *mo*tion.
3. Balancing tendency and interaction time may be factors during simple simo motions.[17]

An example is shown in Figure 12-14.

Compound Motions

The definition of these motions is:

COMPOUND MOTIONS are the simultaneous performance *by different body members* of complete single or combined motions during the time required by one limiting motion in the set.

1. *Single* compound sets include a single motion by one body member and a combined motion by the other body member.
2. *Dual* compound sets include combined motions by both body members.

[17]Ibid., p. 598.

3. *Higher-order* compound sets may include motion overlap or entire sequences by both body members which mesh only at start and finish points.[18]

An example is shown in Figure 12-15.

Figure 12-14. Example of simultaneous motions.

OPERATION____Move Ledger to Work Area_____

Description – Left Hand	Class	Time	Class	Description – Right Hand
Reach to ledger	(R8B)	12.9	R12B	Reach to ledger
Grasp ledger	G1B	3.5	G1B	Grasp ledger
Move ledger to work area	(M10B)	13.4	M12B	Move ledger to work area
Release ledger	RL1	2.0	RL1	Release ledger
	Total	31.8		

Figure 12-15. Example of compound motions.

OPERATION____Place Files in Storage Box_____

Description – Left Hand	Class	Tome	Class	Description – Right Hand
		2.0	G1A	Grasp file
Reach to folder	R12B	12.9	(M10B)	Move file to other hand
		– –	(T90S)	Turn over
Transfer grasp	G3	5.6	G3	Transfer grasp
File to box	M12C	15.2	(R10B)	To next file
Release	RL1	2.0		
	Total	37.7		

[18]Ibid., p. 601.

ADVANTAGES OF MTM

MTM is a methods measurement system that predicts an average performance time for the average operator working with average skill and effort under average conditions. Therefore, and with this brief preface in mind, it offers the following advantages:

It permits and requires fairly precise methods description.

It forces the analyst's attention toward method rather than time.

It eliminates the need for performance rating, since the time values have already been leveled.

It results in more consistent standards between jobs, departments, divisions, and branch offices.

It limits the usage of a stopwatch to process timing.

It allows for methods to be determined and evaluated in advance of their installation.

It is accurate to within plus or minus 5 percent.

It limits disagreements on standards to method rather than performance of an operator.

DISADVANTAGES OF MTM

MTM is not without disadvantages. Here are the main ones:

It requires considerable training of and by qualified personnel.

It still requires the use of the stopwatch to capture machine process time.

It still requires judgment on the part of an analyst to select the best method.

In its basic form, it is still too detailed to be economically practical to apply to office operations.

Office Standard Data

WE HAVE ANALYZED the various techniques available to measure office work. The informal techniques have a definite place in the business world as a first step. The semiformal techniques are helpful in pinpointing problem areas. And the formal techniques can be used to measure performance.

The need to establish standards is easily recognized. Managing with standards is a more responsible, scientific, and professional way to run a business. The fact that there is an unequal degree of motivation among workers in any endeavor makes this approach highly desirable.

How we establish standards is a matter of choice. At this point we should be able to apply a set of criteria to select the best technique for our particular needs.

Table 13-1 shows a comparison of techniques. It illustrates the degree of accuracy, consistency, control, and savings one can expect.

One factor that cannot be ignored is the time it takes to measure office functions. Since the amount of time required to develop standards is in direct proportion to the size and number of work elements with which the analyst must deal, we must take steps to reduce the number of work elements and increase the length of time of these elements. This step is called "developing standard data."

STANDARD DATA

Establishing standard data gives work analysts the opportunity to practice what they preach—to develop the most efficient methods to do their own work. In other

Table 13-1. Comparison of work measurement techniques.

Technique	Accuracy	Consistency	Control	Savings
FORMAL	HIGH Can be validated by other formal techniques	HIGH Properly trained analysts working independently will arrive at same standard ±5%	HIGH Due to factual basis of information	HIGH (20%–45%)
SEMIFORMAL	MODERATE Will not hold up under validation	MODERATE Standards will vary ±10%	MODERATE Due to lack of attention to methods and work pace	MODERATE (10%–12%)
INFORMAL	LOW Accuracy	LOW No consistency at all; could vary 50% or more	LOW Due to reliance on opinion rather than facts	LOW (1%–5%)

words, it is an attempt to reduce the time to set standards without reducing standard accuracy.

The definition of standard time data is found in American Society of Mechanical Engineers Standard 106, entitled "Industrial Engineering Terminology":

> A compilation of all the elements that are used for performing a given class of work with normal elemental time values for each element. The data are used as a basis for determining time standards on work similar to that from which the data were determined without making actual time studies.

To understand standard data, one must understand that work measurement is not an exact science. There is a judgment factor that must be applied by an analyst. In fact, the development of good data requires good analytical thinking on the part of an analyst.

The Building-Block Concept

According to Karger and Bayha,

> Practically all standard data are established with the "building block" concept. This concept is that, with some acceptable loss of accuracy and a tolerable reduction in methods improvement capability, progressively larger time elements are derived for more rapid and less expensive direct rate-setting usage.[1]

[1]Delmar W. Karger and Franklin H. Bayha, *Engineered Work Measurement,* New York: Industrial Press, © 1957, 3rd edition © 1977, p. 690. By permission.

Table 13-2. Standard data—staple sheets.

Description—LH	Symbol	TMU	Symbol	Description—RH
		15.2	M12C	To Stapler
		14.7	P1SSD	Align
Hit	R5Am	5.3		
	G5	0.0		
Depress	mMIA	1.9		
	RL2	0.0		
Hand away	R2E	3.8		
		40.9 TMU		
	or	41 TMU		

elements to determine that it takes 41 time measurement units to fasten sheets of paper together with a table model stapler. To record the same seven elements a second time because a stapling function was required would be to reinvent the wheel.

These building blocks are combinations which always, or very nearly always, occur when a given task is performed. The principle involved is simply that once a standard is developed for a task or portion of a task, it need not be reanalyzed for its standard time each time it occurs.

For example, to staple sheets of paper together may involve the MTM motion pattern in Table 13-2. This requires the analysis and recording of seven MTM

This piece of data and all standard data elements must be developed in such a way as to apply every time the operation is performed. If we could predict how the material, or sheets of paper, will be picked up each and every time prior to stapling, and if we could predict where and how the material will be set down after stapling, and if we knew that the material will be picked up in the same way and set aside the same way every time one staple is affixed to the batch, then we should include these functions in the motion pattern. However, these are not wholly predictable functions. Therefore, the data set developed for stapling items together should have the following parameters:

- START with the items to be stapled in hand.
- INCLUDE moving the items to the stapler, positioning the items to the jaws of the stapler, inserting the items, and stapling the material.
- END with the stapled items in hand.

Types of Data

There are essentially two types of standard data—vertical and horizontal. Vertical data are "based on actual work task elements and are therefore restricted to one kind or class of work." Horizontal data, on the other hand, "are based upon motion sequences common to many kinds and classes of work."[2]

We will explore the development of horizontal standard data because it has the widest possible application. In fact, we intend to show that a set of data can be developed to cover virtually every function involved in a work or productive situation in an office. This system is called Advanced Office Controls.

Coding

A block of data, once developed, is not economical to use until it has been coded. Coding enables it to be cataloged and retrieved from memory or from the computer when it is ready to be used. Some data systems involve such an enormous amount of elements that it becomes faster to develop new data than to try to find the block of data previously developed.

Coding can be alphabetical or numerical. Perhaps the most creative work in this area was done by Richard M. Crossan and Harold W. Nance when they developed an "alpha-mnemonic" coding system. Their thesis was that standard data are no better than the human memory. Or, to put it another way: "You cannot economically use an element if you cannot economically find it."[3]

The alpha-mnemonic coding system is based on three practical rules:

1. No code symbol should be made up of more than three letters of the alphabet.
2. Each code letter must be the first letter in a word which describes all or part of an element.
3. No alpha letter can be used more than once in the first field, or more than once in a subcategory in the second or third field.

Alpha-mnemonic coding simply means that it is an alphabetic coding system that jogs the memory (mnemonic) and thereby simplifies the retrieval of coded data.

Levels of Data

We have identified three levels of horizontal standard data as follows:

- Level 1 comprises basic data such as MTM. It includes time values for all the basic motions performed by the human body—reach, move, and so on.
- Level 2 comprises data developed from basic MTM or similar data systems for functions performed. These can include picking up a sheet of paper, depressing a typewriter key, or writing a digit.
- Level 3 consists of data developed from either Level 1 or Level 2 data for complete office procedures. These can include procedures for opening mail, typing a complete letter, writing a name and address, and so on.

[2]Ibid.
[3]*Master Standard Data*, New York: McGraw-Hill, 1962, pp. 145–164

OFFICE STANDARD DATA SYSTEMS

There are a number of standard data systems developed from basic MTM. For the most part, these are Level 2 data systems and include, not in any special order:

- CSD—Clerical Standard Data.[4] This system was developed in 1960 by, and is available from, Bruce Payne Associates.
- MCD—Master Clerical Data.[5] This system was developed in 1958 by, and is available from, Serge A. Birn Company.
- UOC—Universal Office Controls.[6] This system was developed in the 1950s by H. B. Maynard and Company and is available from that firm.
- MODAPTS—Modular Arrangement of Predetermined Time Standards. This system was developed in the late 1960s by Chris Heyde at Unilever in Australia and is available through Price Waterhouse and Peat, Marwick, & Mitchell.
- MTV—Motion Time Values. This system was developed in the 1960s by Booz Allen and Hamilton and is available from that company.
- MTM-C—Methods-Time Measurement–Clerical. This system was developed in 1978 by a consortium of MTM association members and is available from the MTM Association for Standards & Research.
- AOC—Advanced Office Controls. Developed in 1973, this system is basically a Level 3 data system, but contains enough Level 2 and Level 1 data so as to be able to accurately cover all functions, repetitive and nonrepetitive. It was developed by, and is available from, the Robert E. Nolan Company of Simsbury, Connecticut.

There is also a system developed from motion picture analysis (essentially Level 1 and Level 2 data) known as the Mulligan System. It was developed by, and is available from, Paul B. Mulligan Company.

Many studies have been conducted to compare one system against another. These studies often conclude that one system is vastly superior to another. And, frequently, one system may offer certain advantages, such as greater speed of application, broader range of data, more up-to-date office-equipment data, greater accuracy on short-cycle operations, or less training time required. Often, however, there can be offsetting differences.

On the basis of its acceptance and what we hope is an objective appraisal, it seems that one system does offer more advantages than any other, and we will describe that system in more detail.

[4]Bruce Payne and David D. Swett, *Office Operations Improvement,* New York: AMACOM, 1967.
[5]Serge A. Birn, Richard M. Crossan, and Ralph Eastwood, *Measurement and Control of Office Costs,* New York: McGraw-Hill, 1961.
[6]H. B. Maynard, William M. Aiken, and J. F. Lewis, *Practical Control of Office Costs,* Greenwich, Connecticut: Management Publishing Corporation, 1960.

ADVANCED OFFICE CONTROLS

Advanced Office Controls (AOC) is a proprietary system originally developed by Robert E. Nolan Company in 1973. It is generally regarded as the most advanced system available today, as it contains three levels of data under one coding system.

Cycles of Action

AOC recognizes work in the office not as a series of individual motions but rather as cycles of action. A cycle of action consists of three parts: START, CHANGE, and STOP. Let us look at the Level 2 pattern in Table 13-3.

Table 13-3. Standard data—open envelope.

Description	MTM Convention	Time Units
Move opener to envelope	M8C	11.8
Opener to corner of envelope	P2SD	21.8
Insert opener in envelope	M2B	4.6
Slit open envelope	M8B	10.6
		48.8
	or 49	TMU

The opening of an envelope illustrates the principle of cycles of action. START occurs with the moving of the opener to the envelope; CHANGE with the actual opening; and STOP with the envelope completely open. A single AOC code PEOS records and standardizes this task. The code translates as P (paper handling) for an E (envelope) to O (open) an S (sealed envelope) and has a value of 49 time measurement units.

This same block of Level 2 data, now known as PEOS and requiring 49 time measurement units, can be used to construct a block of Level 3 data as in Table 13-4.

This is a complete mail-opening operation which also involves the cycle-of-action principle: START occurs with the picking up of the envelope and opener; CHANGE with the opening of the envelope, removing the contents, unfolding the

Table 13-4. Standard data—open envelope complete.

Description	AOC Code	Time Units
Get envelope and opener (later aside)	GMG	36
Open envelope	PEOS	49
Remove contents	GLG	49
Unfold papers	PU(2)	64
		198

contents, and setting the material on the desk or table surface; and STOP with the asiding of the envelope. A single AOC code, GRSF, records and standardizes this block of data. The code translates as G (gather), R (receive), S (sealed envelope), F (folded contents) and has a value of 185 time measurement units.

Special Concepts

In order to develop a system that could apply in the broadest possible way, and to get the economy or speed of application, several concepts were developed that require elaboration.

These concepts concerned a method of categorizing data. First, there are three ways in which you can categorize most things: small, medium, or large; easy, average, or difficult; short, average, or long.

On first look, these categories appear to be extremely broad and very subjective. However, when applied to what office workers do in a productive situation, the range narrows dramatically. And when parameters are defined and examples given, the categories become much less subjective.

SMALL / MEDIUM / LARGE

The easiest categories to describe are small / medium / large. Objects that are handled in an office can easily be categorized this way so that:

Small represents paper clips, pins, rubber bands, tacks.
Medium represents any object easily grasped with one hand, such as a sheet of paper, a stapler, a pen or pencil, or a ruler.
Large represents just about everything else. Large objects are usually picked up with both hands, either of necessity because of the weight or to facilitate gaining control.

Assuredly there can be an "Extra Large" or a "Tiny" category, but we do not usually find people in office situations involved with items that would fit in these categories.

EASY / AVERAGE / DIFFICULT

A decision can be easy, average, or difficult to make. As with extra large, a decision can also be impossible to make. However, in office situations where work is usually governed by fairly definite rules, this would involve reverting to a new or different procedure.

An object in a file may be easy to find, average difficult to find, or difficult to find—or impossible to find (if it isn't even there)—depending on how well indexed the files are.

Dictation may be easy, average, or difficult, depending on how creative the situation is. In any case, the respective category can be characterized by fairly free-flowing speech (easy); reflective but controlled speech (average); and deliberate speech, with frequent pauses (difficult). Anything more involved would indicate the speaker lacks preparation.

SHORT/AVERAGE/LONG

Numbers worked with in an office rarely go over nine digits. With this parameter set, we can easily categorize numbers as short (1 to 3 digits), average (4 to 6 digits), and long (7 to 9 digits).

READ/WRITE/COPY

Another special concept involves making a list that covers everything that can be read. Then, whatever one can read one should also be able to write. Our list is contained in Table 13-5.

Coding the Data

AOC employs an alpha-mnemonic coding system. It was felt that a system that is memorizable would be the most economical to use.

Table 13-5. Standard data—read.

First Field	Second Field	Third Field	CODE
Read	Amount		RA
	Complete Name and Address	Complete	RCC
		Name Only	RCN
		Street Address	RCS
		Town, State, Zip	RCT
	Date	Alphabetic	RDA
		Numeric	RDN
	Initials		RI
	Line or Sentence	Average*	RLA
		Difficult†	RLD
	Number	Short	RNS
		Average	RNA
		Long	RNL
	Word	Average	RWA
		Difficult	RWD

*Average refers to average prose in "Read" but to a normal line or sentence in "Write."
†Difficult refers to technical material in "Read" but to composing and writing in "Write."

The first step in coding is to determine the first field or first letter in the code for the broadest possible set of data applied to office functions. This will be the first categorization of the data. It is important to utilize the first field for the major categories of office functions so as to make the best use of the letters of the alphabet.

The system uses 20 letters of the alphabet to categorize the data as follows:

A	Arithmetic	M	Machine Data
B	Body	O	Open and Close
C	Copy	P	Paper Handling
D	Decision	R	Read
E	Extract	S	Sort
F	Fasten	T	Type
G	Gather	U	Unfasten
I	Insert	V	Vocal
K	Keystrokes	W	Write
L	Locate	X	Xtra Data

H, J, N, Q, Y, and Z are not currently used. A brief description of each category follows:

Arithmetic. All elements required to add, subtract, multiply, and divide mentally or with a calculator. Thus, the code AMA represents Arithmetic, Mental, Add; AMS represents Arithmetic, Mental, Subtract; and so on.

Body. All elements required to measure functions such as sitting, standing, or walking.

Copy. All elements required to copy (read and write) information from one source to another.

Decision. All elements required to make decisions or judgments in two subcategories, mental and visual. Mental decisions are decisions that are made after facts are known. They are further subcategorized as easy, average, or difficult. The visual decisions are made during and after reading two sets of information, generally words or numbers, subcategorized as short, average, and long. Therefore, DME is Decision, Mental, Easy, and the time value represents the time required to make a simple yes or no decision.

Extract. All elements required to extract material (to pull material from a file or other source), subcategorized as easy, average, or difficult (to find).

Fasten. All elements required to fasten material with a band, clip, pin, staple, or tape.

Gather. All elements required to pick up and set aside various-size materials, as well as complete mail-opening and mail-dispatching procedures. Pickup and set-aside materials are categorized as small, medium, and large, and locations to which material is asided are categorized as general or specific locations. Decision trees are used in mail-opening and mail-dispatching procedures as to how the material is received or dispatched (in a sealed envelope or opened envelope), and whether the material is folded or unfolded. Therefore, GRSN is translated as Gather, Receive, Sealed Envelope, where the contents are Not Folded.

Insert. All elements required to insert material (to place material in a file or other source), subcategorized as easy, average, or difficult (to find).

Keystrokes. All elements required to operate any kind of keyboard configuration. This includes alphabetic keyboards such as a standard "QWERTY" configuration found on a typewriter, keypunch or data-entry machine, CRT, and the like; numeric keyboards (subcategorized as full keyboard, linear keyboard, or ten keyboard), as well as a variety of functional keys. The keystroke data are Level 2 data that serve as a basis for much of the *machine data* (see that entry).

Locate. All elements required to locate information or material in two subcategories: visually and manually. "Locate Visually" involves the movement of the eyes (aided or unaided by the hand or fingers), and "Locate Manually" involves the manipulation of the fingers through various types of material to search for a specific piece of information. This is further subcategorized by whether the material is easy, average, or difficult to find.

Machine Data. All elements required to operate specific (brand names and models) equipment. This will be covered in greater detail in Chapter 14.

Open and close. All elements required to open and close various objects utilized in an office, such as binders, covers, drawers, handles, lids, prongs, and rings.

Paper Handling. All elements required to handle papers. This includes miscellaneous functions such as counting, folding, jogging, punching, stamping, tearing, and unfolding.

Read. All elements required to read any kind of information so that other elements are possible.

Sort. All elements required to sort material into piles or into perfect alphabetical or numerical sequence.

Unfasten. All elements required to unfasten material, such as removing a band, clip, pen, or staple.

Vocal. All elements covering what can be said aloud, in three main categories: conversation (either telephone conversation or face to face), dictation (either giving or receiving), or read aloud (numbers, words, or sentences).

Write. All elements required to write any kind of information.

Type. All elements required to type information. This includes Level 2 data for all the various functions performed on a typewriter, and Level 3 data for typing a complete letter or memo, or filling in blocks on a form.

Xtra Data. Special license was taken with this non-word to provide a category for special data—a further grouping of elements that is useful for referring to special work situations in a given company.

SELECTING THE RIGHT TECHNIQUE

With the proliferation of techniques for standard setting, it is often difficult to determine which technique is the right one to use. Many companies have decided there is no one best technique. Rather, they use several techniques, the precise choice being dictated by the situation. Sometimes, however, the decision as to what technique is used is a subjective one, based on what the analyst is most familiar with. The authors believe that the selection process should be approached in a more professional manner. We offer the following approach to arriving at this important decision.

Defining Your Objective

No standard-setting technique can be selected until it is decided why the standards are being set in the first place. In other words, what is the objective you want to accomplish?

If the objective is simply to get a general idea about the work being accomplished, then an informal technique, such as estimates or the historical-data approach, is best. Likewise, if the decision to be reached is of the "one-shot" variety, or if time is very short (as in the case of an in-progress meeting requiring an answer on the spot or within hours), estimates or historical data may be adequate. If the decision will have no significant impact on the company's bottom line because it is a small part of a larger decision, then again, an informal technique is most appropriate.

Once the objective advances from these situations to the realm of ongoing management decision making in the areas of costs, performance, methods, equipment, staffing, and profitability, then a formal technique must be selected.

To express the relationship between objectives and technique another way, once it is decided to use the information for important and/or ongoing decision making, or to evaluate organizational or individual performance, the formal technique of either time study or predetermined times must be used. Since the focus of the authors' experience is on that kind of situation, we will continue the discussion on technique selection on the basis of which of the formal techniques to use.

Evaluating Alternative Approaches: Seven Criteria

If consideration of its objectives points an organization toward the formal techniques, the next step is to determine which of the formal techniques should be used. There are certain criteria that can assist in choosing among the many predetermined time systems available. These same criteria can assist in the decision as to whether time study or predetermined times should be used.

The criteria are: *speed* (the time required to measure and establish standards), *training and skills required* (how long it takes to develop analysts), *cost* to develop standards (time and resources needs), *accuracy* (the degree of objectivity), *acceptability* to employees and supervisors, *range of data* (the various levels of jobs, such as clerical, technical, and professional), and *ease of maintenance* (ease of keeping standards up to date). Let's review each of these in some detail.

SPEED

This is a function of how quickly the analyst can develop a good standard. It depends on the size of the elemental times, as noted earlier, which affect how quickly the analyst can apply the technique. Predetermined times are usually much quicker to apply than time study. The time study analyst must observe and time a sufficient volume of each task to be measured. There are no shortcuts in time study. Physical presence over the necessary period of time is required. Then the standard must be developed. With predetermined times, the analyst need only get a firm understanding of the method being used to be able to apply the data elements. If the data elements are large enough, as with a Level 3 system such as Advanced Office Controls, great speed can be developed, limited only by the analyst's skill and speed of comprehension of the job.

To give an example, if the time study analyst must observe 100 occurrences that take the employee an average of three minutes each to complete at an average performance of 90 percent, not counting interruptions and the like, the analyst will have to sit and time for a total of at least 300 minutes, plus about another 45 minutes (15 percent) for personal and miscellaneous time. Judging from experience, it would take at least 240 minutes to develop the final standard. This is a total of 9.75 hours of development and observation time.

Using a predetermined time system with high-level (Level 3) standard data, that same standard could be interviewed for and developed in 4.5 hours (one hour to interview, one hour to document, 2.5 hours to apply data elements and develop the standard). A lower-level standard data system would take more time, depending on the average time values for each element.

TRAINING AND SKILLS REQUIRED

To apply performance ratings in a time study takes someone with specialized training. It generally takes a solid three days of studying loop films and practice rating exercises. Actual on-the-job training for a period of six months to a year also is required to develop these skills to the proper level of technical competence.

Training in predetermined time data also should take no longer than three solid days. If the system is designed in a consistent and logical manner that facilitates lookup and memorization of the data elements, then developing an analyst to full technical competence usually takes from four to six months. With regard to developing usable data, an analyst developing standards with a Level 3 standard data system can develop a usable standard on the first try, pending review by a more experienced and qualified analyst. By contrast, most initial time study standards are scrapped as unusable.

Cost

As noted earlier, this is a function of speed and resources needed. Predetermined time systems are much quicker than time study, generally require less time of the employee, and are therefore less costly. To apply a dollar figure to our example in the earlier speed section, it is apparent that time study is twice as costly as standard data systems. The higher the level of standard data, the less costly is the system.

Accuracy

Assuming equally developed skills, any standard developed by the formal techniques should be of equal accuracy. Saying that is a lot easier than proving it. Time study can be difficult to prove unless there is basic underlying trust and confidence by all concerned. Any predetermined time standard data system should make available the lower-level data elements used in the development of each element to all users of the system. Because of the need for the time study analyst to apply the seemingly subjective factor of performance rating to the data collected, accuracy usually can be questioned.

Acceptability

Acceptance on the part of supervisors and employees becomes most critical. No matter how good the technique, the people who are most affected by it must accept the end result. The degree of their acceptance will be based on how well they can understand how the technique is applied.

The stopwatch starts out behind the proverbial eight ball when it comes to its use in the office. It is attached to the unpopular image of the factory "efficiency expert" that has withstood the passage of time. Because the device is so visible and somewhat ominous, it becomes an emotional issue that has a negative effect on morale. Being timed while one is working is simply unnerving. The outward emphasis is on speed, as far as employees are concerned, no matter what they are told.

Acceptance of the predetermined time system hinges on the ease of understanding by a lay person (employee or supervisor). Since the standard is based on the method used rather than the speed of the employee performing the job, and since no timing device is used, employees are not nervous about doing their work in routine fashion. If the standard data system is coded in such a way that it doesn't look like a lot of technical "mumbo jumbo," employees and supervisors can focus on the method and have confidence that the standard is accurate.

Range of Data

Both time study and predetermined time studies have the range to cover most clerical and technical jobs found in the office. However, certain standard data systems are so detailed that technical jobs become difficult to bring under control. It takes a Level 3 data system to bring these jobs under control. It is difficult to measure these positions using time study, because the job must be observed in sufficient volume and in its entirety. With jobs like underwriters, claims examiners, customer-contact people, and loan officers, this can take a long time. When using predetermined times, it is only necessary that someone can explain how the job should be performed, and the standard can be developed.

Ease of Maintenance

If the technique is going to have long-range benefits, the standards set must be easily maintained. Under time study, when part of a task changes, the analyst must retime the entire job, and in sufficient volume to satisfy the statistical validity. Using predetermined times, it is a simple matter to update the written procedure or task outline and make the actual changes needed in the standard data sheets used in conjunction with the documentation.

Again, the Level 3 standard data system that uses written task outlines and task analysis forms to record the appropriate data elements is much easier to use to keep standards up to date.

Semiformal Techniques

To those with more than a casual interest in the subject of work measurement techniques, it may appear that we have summarily dismissed the semiformal techniques. It is not our intent to do so. Techniques such as self-logging and work sampling have their place. Work sampling that applies a performance rating to attempt to formalize the standards is useful in those situations where the objective is group measurement, and some sacrifice in accuracy is to be tolerated. However, the experience of the authors has been that the semiformal techniques require the same good communications to explain the program, but that their accuracy, ease of understanding, and ease of maintenance leave much to be desired. Although speed of application is good when compared to the formal techniques, we have found that semiformal techniques should be used only when the objective is to gain some control which will be used as a stepping stone to more formal controls. A close eye must be kept on the effects on morale when using techniques such as work sampling.

Standard Data versus Time Study

In addition to the points raised in our discussion of selection criteria, there is an essential difference between these formal techniques. Often, proponents of either technique expound the virtues of the technique with which they are most familiar and downgrade the other. The best source for an explanation of the differences is those who have had formal, certified training in the use of both techniques as well as successful practical application.

The essential difference (other than performance rating) is that the time study analyst takes the raw time observations and, with some additional data gathering for occurrences, proceeds to finalize a standard. The development of frequency of occurrences by nature of time study usually applies only to major steps in the standard. With standard data systems, frequency gathering is usually more detailed and sometimes applied to minor steps within major breakdowns.

Because time study analysts usually take enough sample timings, they do not need to get heavily involved in determining frequency of occurrences of minor elements. It is only after they have been trained in predetermined time systems that they are able to appreciate the value of detailed frequencies.

One time study analyst learning predetermined times expressed his feelings about the situation best when he said, "I've measured that same operation in seven different offices around the country, and everyone did it just a little bit differently. Because I was merely concerned with total time to do the job, there was no way to point out the minor differences in method that actually affected each standard. With predetermined times I can document the differences, compare the time to do each, and recommend the one best way. I feel much better about my standards now."

Controlling
Machine-Based Tasks

IN ORDER FOR A TASK to be considered measurable, normally three factors must be present. First, the task has to be under the control of the person performing the job; second, there must be a relatively continuous supply of work; and third, the work must be covered by fairly definite procedures. When measuring tasks where the employee either operates a piece of equipment or interfaces with a piece of equipment, we must bend these rules somewhat, since the work is to a lesser extent controllable by the employee performing the task.

Normally, in tasks where the employee interfaces with the equipment, such as in typing or data entry, the work is under the control of the employee. In the case of equipment such as duplicating machines, microfilming equipment, and the like, the operator's role, expressed as a percentage of the total task standard, is much less. The argument for establishing standards on these types of tasks is that the high cost of the equipment presupposes a high degree of utilization in order to make it a cost-effective system. The establishment of measures and controls provides a basis for obtaining high utilization.

When an analyst establishes standards for a task where a machine plays a role, he is confronted by some special problems. In the following sections we will address these problems. In particular, we will discuss means to establish machine speeds, determine the limiting motions or tasks, account for machine jams, and determine volume counts.

APPROACHES TO MEASURING EQUIPMENT-CONTROLLED TASKS

There are two basic approaches to the measurement of a task that involves the use of equipment. In the first case, the machine is analyzed and standard data are developed which can be utilized to establish a variety of standards, regardless of the particular application performed. This is the preferred method, since it provides a consistent means of analyzing the equipment and avoids duplication of effort. However, it may be necessary with some types of equipment to establish standards based not on the machine itself but on the application being performed. This second technique is most often used where machines have variable speeds or where there are special problems in handling a special application. To minimize analyst effort, however, every attempt should be made to establish a standard for the equipment itself and not the task performed on the equipment.

DEVELOPING MACHINE DATA

Analysis of Manual Handling

Machine-based tasks are in many respects similar to normal clerical activity. The big difference is that at some period of time during the task the employee must wait for the machine to run its cycle. This waiting time is sometimes called machine "interference" because the employee's action is controlled by the speed of the machine.

Prior to operating the machine, there is a setup step, and at the end of the task there is a wrap-up phase. Additional tasks required include any internal handling necessary to keep the machine operating, and clearing of jams. The setup, wrap-up, and internal-handling tasks can be readily analyzed using the company's primary measurement technique. A predetermined time system such as Advanced Office Controls provides handling standards of high accuracy and allows for the analysis of methods. It may be necessary, in the absence of other data, to use a basic predetermined time system such as MTM (methods-time measurement) for some elements of machine operation.

Anyone who has ever operated an office copier knows that machines do not operate perfectly. In addition to the time required to operate the equipment, we must include time to clear operating jams. The preferred technique for establishing standards for jams or other interruptions is to establish a standard for it. Work sampling or logging of activity can then be used to determine the frequency of occurrence of interruptions, which can then be added to the standard.

At the end of the first phase in the establishment of machine data, there should be standards established for setup, wrap-up, internal handling, and clearing of jams.

Determination of Machine Speeds and Response Times

One of the keys to developing an accurate standard for a piece of equipment is a correct assessment of the time required by the machine to perform a given function. There are a variety of methods to determine machine processing times. The actual method to be employed will depend on the equipment being studied.

One source of machine-function time data is the manufacturer. As part of promotional materials, the manufacturer of a given type of equipment usually publishes data reflecting the time required by its equipment to process a unit of work. Promotional materials should, in the main, not be utilized for the establishment of standards for machine-based tasks. For obvious reasons, productivity figures published reflect the maximum output of the equipment operating under ideal conditions. Virtually all equipment manufacturers publish technical specification manuals for their service representatives that contain machine cycle times. When deciding whether the cost of an equipment purchase is justified, an analyst may find that these manufacturer-supplied machine speeds are the only source of data available to establish standards.

The vast majority of machine operating speeds for office equipment are developed through time study. The analyst must take special care to separate the time when the operator is performing functions and the machine is "limiting"—that is, causing the operator to wait. Man–machine charts (see Figure 14-1) help identify this. The machine causes the periods of idle time noted in the figure. The operator is doing other things while the machine goes through its paces.

For machines that operate at a fixed-cycle rate, such as an office copier, a relatively small sampling will provide standards of the desired accuracy. For machines operating at variable rates, such as a printing press, it will be necessary to determine the maximum effective machine speed. Machines operating at variable speeds are often subject to machine jams induced by the materials being handled. As an example, a given printing press may operate effectively at 6,000 copies per hour; an attempt to operate the same equipment at 7,000 copies an hour may result in an increase in time spent clearing jams that would far outweigh the additional productivity.

In some cases it may be necessary to establish machine standards based on a particular application. As an example, a mailing machine may operate effectively at 4,000 copies per hour when stuffing two items in an envelope, but only be able to operate at 3,200 items per hour when more than two stuffers are used.

Another technique for establishing machine speeds is self-logging. The operator records the starting and ending time of each machine run and the number of items processed. In order to complete the analysis, the operator is also required to record the number and time spent in clearing any jams or any other interruptions

Figure I4-I. Man-machine chart for multilith copying.

	MAN		MACHINE		MAN-MACHINE CHART
	Time	%	Time	%	
Work	25 sec.		10 sec.		Present Method [X]
Idle	10 sec.		15 sec.		Proposed Method [ ] DATE 7/99

ACTIVITY OF MAN NAME: Bonnie Thompson	TIME	ACTIVITY OF MACHINE TYPE OF MACHINE Multilith Copy Machine
Greets requestor Inserts original in plate maker	3:23 60	
Idle	05	} Makes master
	10	
Inserts master in printer Dials # of copies (avg. 5)		
Press start button Inserts second original in plate maker	15	} Prints
Inserts master in printer	20	Makes master #2
Idle	25	
Returns originals to requestor Hands copies to requestor	30	Prints
	35	
	40	
	45	
	50	
	55	
	60	
	3:24	

when the machine was not operating. The problems noted in Chapter 10 on the subject of logging as a means of establishing standards should be considered prior to selection of this technique.

The advent of on-line processing systems has injected a whole new dimension in the establishment of machine times. In many situations when an operator depresses an "enter" key, the computer does not respond instantly. The delay between the time when the key is depressed and the time the information appears on the screen is called *response time*. Response time is a function of a variety of factors, including the actual processing time to handle the transaction, the amount of computer power allocated to the on-line system, the priority of the transaction being performed, and the demands on the system at a given point in time.

Computer response times tend to vary considerably by time of day and by type of application. Time study can be used on a random basis to determine machine response time; however, most on-line systems, as part of the normal processing cycle, maintain an internal clock which records response times. Needless to say, the broader base of information provided by computer-generated information is ideally suited for the establishment of standards. Due to variability of computer response time, it is normal procedure to isolate response times as a separate step in the task so that they may be readily adjusted to meet changing conditions. In extreme situations, separate standards can be established for machine speeds and the average weekly time input to maintain accuracy.

Simultaneous Motions

The employee who operates a piece of equipment may not always be productively occupied. While the machine performs its given function, the operator may observe it at work without any real necessity to be present. Part of the process of establishing standards is to make use of employees' idle time.

Two possibilities exist for improving operator productivity. One, we can restructure the worker's task so that some portions of it are performed while the machine is in process. As an example, the operator of a printing press typically spends two minutes packaging the completed work for shipment and getting the correct type of paper for the next production run. Restructuring of the employee's job would have these functions performed as a completion of the first job of the day while the second job is being done and no operator attention is required. An analysis of average run time, coupled with the frequency and duration of machine jams, will determine the extent of opportunity to utilize machine time to complete internal handling.

A second opportunity to make better use of employee time is through the operation of additional pieces of equipment. It is not uncommon to see one operator operating two or more automatic typewriters generating form letters. Needless to say, careful analysis is required, not only to determine the extent of idle time available for operation of a second piece of equipment, but also to be certain that operation of the second piece of equipment will not require the operator to work at a level of performance exceeding 100 percent.

If the standard for performing a task utilizing a single piece of equipment is two minutes and the operator can run two pieces of equipment simultaneously, the standards should be factored downward to one minute per machine per item, or the volume of output can be divided by two to make the same adjustment. The preferred method would be reduction in standard. It may be necessary, where management cannot provide enough work for an employee to operate two machines continually, to establish standards for both unit operation and simultaneous operation. A complete discussion of the potential and the problems of simultaneous machine operations may be found in *Work Measurement in Machine Accounting* by Morrison, Nolan, and Devlin (New York, Ronald Press, 1963).

SPECIAL PROBLEMS OF KEY-CONTROLLED EQUIPMENT

Data entry equipment such as keypunch, cathode-ray tubes (CRT), and word processing equipment, in addition to the problems discussed earlier, has unique features that should be considered individually.

In the recent past, data entry was performed largely in centralized departments, such as the keypunch department or the typing pool, by specialized employees with strong keying skills. The move toward on-line processing systems has greatly increased the number of employees in a given organization who are responsible for data input. At the same time, high schools and business schools have placed less emphasis on keyboard skills, so that fewer employees are available for these functions.

A continuing controversy rages over whether or not there should be separate sets of standards for employees who are occasionally required to operate key-based equipment and those who operate key-based equipment continually as a relatively small proportion of their overall job. We recommend making no special allowance for the occasional user of key-based equipment. Standards are developed on the time required for the average well-trained employee to produce a unit of acceptable-quality work. Engineered standards—either leveled time study or predetermined time data—in essence measure the work performed by the employee, not the employee who performs it. Establishment of differential standards changes this philosophy to that of employee measurement. Where an employee uses the equipment only occasionally, the overall impact on that employee's performance or the performance of the unit as a whole will be slight even if the employee has low keyboard skills.

As an example, if an employee spends 20 percent of his time keying and performs the keying function at 60 percent of performance, the overall impact on that employee's performance is only 8 percent, assuming that other tasks are performed at 100 percent of performance. Where keying is a larger portion of the task, differential standards should not be established, but the employees performing those tasks should receive keyboard training.

It is not necessary for an employee to key continually to develop good speed and rhythm. Everyone is familiar with newspaper reporters who type nearly as well with two fingers as skilled typists with ten. Another common example, in the airline industry, is the key speed developed by reservationists at the ticket counter working with their on-line reservation systems.

An adjustment of standards made to reflect lack of skills in the keying area might well be eventually utilized by management in other areas as a wedge to provide differential standards for other types of activity, which would tend to erode the overall credibility and accuracy of a standard structure. It is the goal of a work management program to create reports defining what the conditions are, not what management would wish them to be.

A second major problem in dealing with keystroke-oriented tasks is the subject of errors. It is unreasonable to expect that an employee can, on a continuing basis, create errorless work. This becomes especially important where an employee has the opportunity to find his own error and then must go back to correct it. Typically, encoding-machine operators who balance their own work and word processing employees who proof their own work require some additional allowance to compensate for a reasonable number of errors.

A common technique for establishing an error allowance is to establish a standard time for correcting an error on the particular piece of equipment and then, with the consent and guidance of management, establish a reasonable frequency of errors for that area. The authors usually avoid fixed-percentage error allowances where the nature of the work is variable.

Advanced Machine Data

Major companies and consulting firms that have established predetermined time systems normally include in them a library of data that can be used to establish standards on machine-based tasks. Among the advantages of a library of machine data are that it reduces the cost and time required to establish standards and provides a consistent base for standards where machines are involved.

While there are many machine data systems on the market, we will look at Advanced Machine Data as an example of how machine data might be assembled and coded. Advanced Machine Data, at the time of this writing, subdivides office equipment into eight categories as follows:

1. Calculating equipment.
2. Data entry equipment.
3. Encoding and proof equipment.
4. Filing equipment.
5. Mailing equipment.
6. Reproduction and microfilm equipment.
7. Security and money-handling equipment.
8. Word processing equipment.

Within each major category there is a further breakdown by manufacturer.

Advanced Machine Data maintains the alpha-mnemonic coding system of Advanced Office Controls. As an example, a National Cash Register proof machine Model No. 775 is coded:

M   Machine Data
    E   Encoding & Proof
        N   NCR
            04   Model   775   (MEN04)

All data relating to this piece of equipment may be found on a single page similar to Table 14-1.

Table 14-1. Sample coding system.

Operation	AOC Code	TMU	Frequency
Keystrokes			
Digits	KET	5	Digit
Function	KFW	6	Occurrence
Switches	OH	25	Occurrence
Other Functions			
Insert document	GMO	19	Document

The continuing growth in office equipment makes it imperative for economical measurement that an organization subscribe to a service which will provide updated machine data.

VOLUME COLLECTION

Tasks involving machine use invariably produce a high volume of work. In reporting results, the guidelines of ease of reporting and accuracy take on a new meaning.

Most pieces of equipment have internal counters that record the number of items processed. These counters can be read by the employee and reported on a job basis or daily basis, or the readings can be recorded by a supervisor or work distribution employee at the end of the day. Often, when establishing standards for machine-oriented tasks, one standard is established for the actual machine run time, and a second standard for machine setup. This allows making adjustments for varying lengths of machine run. Availability of standards for both setup time and run times can be used to schedule work, too.

The development of on-line processing systems has provided another opportunity to simplify the recording. Many on-line systems have internal volume collection as part of the normal work flow. At the end of a given work period, an employee or his supervisor may request the output count from the computer, which has recorded transactions.

The same general principles which apply to sound standard-setting practice in the clerical area also relate to the establishment of standards for machine-based tasks (see the preceding chapter, where we have examined techniques available to broaden the coverage of standards in an organization and to accurately report the performance of employees whose work is not always under their control).

Measuring Technical Work

UP TO THIS POINT, when discussing the subject of office work management, we have referred mainly to clerical or routine office work. However, with the advent of data processing we are finding more and more of the routine office work being performed by computers, and office workers performing more of the analytical work.

What were once clerical jobs are continually being upgraded because of improved job design as well as improved office technology such as on-line computer video terminal systems. It seems that paper-shuffling tasks are being replaced with decision-making tasks that deal largely with exception processing.

Furthermore, there is a growing segment of the office work force that has thus far eluded objective productivity measurements: the technical or professional employee. Technical jobs such as insurance claims examiner and underwriter, bank loan officer, customer service representative, and systems programmer are increasing rapidly.

Efforts to develop measured standards for these workers have often been hampered by the variety of tasks they perform and by the longer delay between their productive effort and the tangible results of that effort. Where the use of measured standards appeared to be feasible, the potential savings through staff reductions were often outweighed by the cost of establishing and maintaining the necessary work standards.

There is another aspect of the matter of studying technical jobs that puts the problem into better perspective. Experience has shown that no matter how effective an individual is, whether he is a corporate executive or a scientist, part of his time is frequently devoted to activities which are not fully productive or truly creative. Take a systems analyst, for example. The time he or she spends going to and from the computer room and filling out programming sheets is certainly not spent creatively. So, the challenge is there to help an individual use time more effectively to return maximum value for salary dollars expended.

Any task is measurable if you wish to take the time to measure it. Take the United States space program as an example. It is perfectly illustrative of an effort that is creative, scientific, judgmental, varied, and whatever else may be said of technical work. Nevertheless, time spans from launching a rocket or spaceship, to exercises performed on and about the moon and other planets, to touchdown time were predicted within a matter of seconds.

So it is true with the establishing of standards for technical work found in offices. The difficulty lies not so much in setting the standards as in getting people to accept the measurement.

CONTRASTING MANAGEMENT ATTITUDES

The authors conducted a survey, preparatory to developing a work management program, in a property and casualty insurance company in New England. In addition to interviewing the managers of clerical departments, we also interviewed managers of technical units. Underwriting is considered a technical or professional-level job.

The manager of the personal lines underwriting department of 28 employees was skeptical. He said, "I don't believe in operating by numbers. To address my people in terms of units of output or performance would result in a poor quality of work, since the emphasis would be on quantity. I feel if you ask for more output from my underwriters, it will be at the sacrifice of quality. Besides, I can't understand how you can measure the variety of things our people do."

On the other hand, the manager of the commercial lines underwriting department of 22 employees was enthusiastic. He said, "It's about time we took a look at the clerical 'pish-posh' our technical people are doing. I also feel we need to know what our people are doing. For example, I can give an underwriter 30 applications and know that he handled 30. However, he may get ten calls from agents requiring considerable work on his part. He can also receive mail which generates work, and can have other people come for assistance while he's handling the 30 applications I gave him. All I know is that he did 30 applications. How can we, as managers, evaluate our people properly if we don't know what they are doing? We can't, because we don't know. Therefore, I welcome any assistance you can give me with respect to work standards and analysis of what our people are doing."

The situation is fairly clear. The personal lines manager says, "I don't know how you can help me, but if you can convince me that standards can be established and put into effect without sacrificing quality, I'll be the first to go along with it." The commercial lines manager says, "I need help, so let's work together and develop some standards that I can use to evaluate my people." Who would you rather work with?

To develop work standards for technical and professional-level jobs you need four things:

1. A measurement technique that has proved to be successful in measuring work of this nature.
2. Experience in establishing standards for work of this nature.
3. Management support.
4. A spirit of cooperation between the management of the technical unit and the work management team.

The question of whether or not the study is desirable must be resolved before undertaking it, or it will surely fail. A manager who is not convinced cannot win the confidence of the employees who report to him and whose jobs are being studied.

The personal lines underwriting manager in our example may introduce the study to his people in this way: "We are going to have a study of our work to determine if time standards can be developed. Management feels this is desirable." The chances that employees will develop any enthusiasm when presented with the program in this manner are slim at best.

OBJECTIONS TO TECHNICAL MEASUREMENT

Before we can develop a successful productivity measurement program for technical jobs, we must be prepared to address the more common objections. There are four typical objections. Each should be examined very carefully and reconciled.

Objection 1: "My job involves judgment, thought time, and decision making. Since you cannot measure these functions, you cannot measure my job." A closer examination of a typical technical job reveals that the technician does not just sit and stare into space as decisions are "mulled over." Rather, the technician gathers information by reading source documents such as files, correspondence, computer listings, or reports. Decision making for these types of jobs also includes calculating alternatives or "discussing" the subject with the customer through a series of questions. Judgment definitely enters into the decision. However, this judgment factor is more a matter of the knowledge and experience of the technician than of time. Time to make the decision involves the time to read, discuss, calculate, or choose between alternatives, all of which are measurable. The training and experience of the technician influence the quality of the decision and the ease with which the decision can be reached once enough information has been gathered.

Objection 2: "My job does not involve routine matters or repetitive functions. Therefore, you cannot measure it." Yes, there may seem to be limitless possibilities to the number of alternatives a person can take in dealing with a particular matter. Nevertheless, the approach to reaching a decision will have some readily identifiable pattern. One example is a personal loan officer evaluating a loan application. The purpose of the loan, the amount requests, the financial condition of the applicant—all may be unique to that case. However, the analysis and the eventual decision to grant or refuse the loan characteristically follow similar steps or some patterned approach. Lack of a uniform approach to the job is indicative of an opportunity to improve procedures and the training of staff.

Many people feel their job is not repetitive because each item they deal with has peculiarities not found in the others. A claims examiner does not feel his job is repetitive, because, while he may do nothing but process one claim after another, each one is different. In reality, there may be a standard procedure for processing a basic claim; however, as a claim gets more complicated, there are additional steps to be taken. These can be enumerated, measured, and included in the standard on a weighted basis commensurate with their overall importance.

Objection 3: "If I have to account for everything I do, I'll end up spending most of my time keeping records." We quite agree! A cumbersome record-keeping system for technicians must be avoided at all costs. We find that we can usually reduce the number of productivity measurements to two or three key activities. We make every effort to capture these counts from some external source rather than have the individual count the work or make tick marks.

Objection 4: "If you measure my job, I will lose the special status as a professional that I worked so hard to attain." This objection is heard most often when the same measurement program used for clerical employees is used for the technical level. Designing a unique and separate program specifically for technical employees can overcome this objection.

In summary, objections in this vein indicate the need to design a specific program tailored to the nature of the technical job.

Once again, our motive should be to provide a basis on which people can be recognized for their accomplishments. This is not demeaning by any stretch of the imagination.

THE NEED FOR A DIFFERENT APPROACH

First and foremost, it must be recognized that the technical job is different in nature from the clerical position. In addition, the intellectual caliber of the employee is generally higher. Any approach to work management must take these important differences into consideration.

If a company already has a clerical work measurement program, every effort must be made to design the technical program to be different. The difference must be evident in every detail—in the program name, the record-keeping requirements, the documentation, the design, the reporting techniques, the standard-setting approach, and most important, in communications and employee participation.

ESSENTIAL INGREDIENTS

A successful technical measurement program has several essential ingredients. The steps discussed in this section will greatly enhance chances of a successful implementation.

Establish Good Communication

The introduction of the program, as well as communications throughout the implementation, must be carefully designed and executed. While a few short meetings are adequate for explaining most clerical programs, communications for the technicians must be more detailed and more frequent. Here is a pattern used successfully by several companies:

1. *Conduct a feasibility study.* The analyst meets with the manager of the function to explain the objectives of the feasibility study, such as determining the nature of the work, the patterns of work completion, the key output activities, the data base available, and any processing problems. Results of the study are then reported along with the recommendations to management.

2. *Hold an introductory meeting with technicians.* The results of the feasibility study and the objectives of the program should be discussed thoroughly and well in advance of the program's implementation.

3. *Explain how the study is conducted.* To kick off the program with the technical employees, the analyst holds a meeting to review the objectives, explain the approach, and stress the need for employee participation.

4. *Gather and review the task list* (see Figure 15-1). The analyst interviews each technician and develops a task list. Usually, the task list for a technical unit is short. The list must be reviewed with the technicians for their approval.

5. *Write and review the procedures* (see Figure 15-2). Through detailed interviewing of each technician, the analyst documents procedures and has them reviewed for approval. Any changes are to be incorporated at this time. It is not unusual for the technician to make suggestions for simplification at this stage. Changes the analyst is recommending should be discussed at this time.

Figure 15-1. A typical task list.

```
┌─────────────────────────────────────────────────────────────────┐
│                          TASK LIST                                │
│                                                                   │
│  EMPLOYEE NAME  All     DEPARTMENT/UNIT   Health Claims   DATE  9/9/99 │
│                                                                   │
│  JOB TITLE   Claims Examiner                                      │
├─────────────────────────────────────────────────────────────────┤
│                       List of Tasks                               │
├─────────────────────────────────────────────────────────────────┤
│  Review File                                                      │
├─────────────────────────────────────────────────────────────────┤
│  Complete Payment Record                                          │
├─────────────────────────────────────────────────────────────────┤
│  Enter Data on Terminal                                           │
├─────────────────────────────────────────────────────────────────┤
│  Process Pending                                                  │
├─────────────────────────────────────────────────────────────────┤
│  Write Letter                                                     │
├─────────────────────────────────────────────────────────────────┤
│  Make Phone Call                                                  │
├─────────────────────────────────────────────────────────────────┤
│  Receive Phone Call                                               │
├─────────────────────────────────────────────────────────────────┤
│  Research Medical Terms                                           │
├─────────────────────────────────────────────────────────────────┤
│  Prepare Authorization Request                                    │
├─────────────────────────────────────────────────────────────────┤
│  Discuss Case with Supervisor                                     │
├─────────────────────────────────────────────────────────────────┤
│  Prepare Duplicate Coverage Inquiries                             │
├─────────────────────────────────────────────────────────────────┤
│  Prepare Coordination of Benefits                                 │
└─────────────────────────────────────────────────────────────────┘
```

6. *Conduct the frequency study* (see Table 15-1). Each step the technician takes while performing his job must be assigned a relative value, expressed as a percentage of the key activity. These percentages are determined by review of the existing data base or by sampling, or by the technicians through a frequency study kept over a sufficient period of time to be statistically valid and representative of the normal processing cycle time.

7. *Present the standards.* Using the actual procedures agreed upon and

Figure 15-2. Sample procedure.

Procedure: Process Health Claim

Department: Health Claim

Date: 9/9/99

Review File

1. Compare name on mail to file.

2. Review age, coverage, date of illness, diagnosis, type of service, claimant statement.

3. Determine if eligible for coverage, on the basis of date and type of service.

4. Determine if additional information or correspondence is necessary.

5. Review file for duplicate charges and other insurance.

6. Decide if charge must be reviewed to determine whether it is reasonable and customary.

Complete Payment Record

7. Complete form 900 for each group of bills by entering code, date of service, provider, and charge.

8. Total all charges and enter deductible, maximum per illness, and coinsurance amount.

9. Send copy to claimant and file copy in folder.

10. Call up screen HC10.

Enter Data on Terminal

11. Enter data from payment record.

approved by the technicians, explain how the standards were set, in sufficient detail for full understanding and confidence. Table 15-2 shows how the final standards are arrived at by combining the frequency study results with the time to perform each step.

8. *Present the reporting system.* Explain the mechanics of the record-keeping system, how the data are captured, and how the results are displayed. Also, explain the meaning and uses of the data.

Table 15-1. Frequency study for the task list in Figure 15-1.

Task	Occurrence
Review File	150
Complete Payment Record	80
Enter Data on Terminal	100
Process Pending	30
Write Letter	20
Make Phone Call	10
Receive Phone Call	15
Research Medical Terms	7
Prepare Authorization Request	1
Discuss Case with Supervisor	1
Prepare Duplicate Coverage Inquiry	7
Prepare Coordination of Benefits	2
Issue Check	100

Table 15-2. Calculation of final standard.

Task	Frequency* (%)	Time (min.)	Total Time
Review File	1.50	1.2	1.80
Complete Payment Record	.80	.8	.64
Enter Data on Terminal	1.00	1.1	1.10
Process Pending	.30	.5	.15
Write Letter	.20	1.3	.26
Make Phone Call	.10	1.5	.15
Receive Phone Call	.15	2.2	.33
Research Medical Terms	.07	.7	.05
Prepare Authorization Request	.01	2.5	.03
Discuss Case with Supervisor	.01	2.6	.03
Prepare Duplicate Coverage Inquiry	.07	4.1	.29
Prepare Coordination of Benefits	.02	1.3	.03
Issue Check	1.00	1.0	1.00
Total Time			5.86
15% Personal and Miscellaneous			.88
Standard Time			6.74

*As percentage of checks issued.

Get Technical Assistance

As with anything else, you need credibility. We have found that recruiting at least one person who has specific experience in the work to be measured tends to increase the confidence of the technicians. If you are studying health benefits claims examiners, get a senior claims examiner released from normal duties for a period of weeks, train that person as an analyst, and have him assist in the development of standards.

In this way the other employees will feel that the complexities of their jobs are understood and properly evaluated. Because the analyst is familiar with the terminology and the procedures, the length of the study is reduced. The analyst is better able to keep the study in perspective for all concerned, and overall acceptance is usually high.

Emphasize Participation

Each technician is interviewed in detail and assists in building the procedures for the job. Differences in the way things are processed are discussed and resolved. The new procedures are agreed upon by all concerned.

Develop Good Documentation

Technicians look at their jobs as complete procedures rather than fragmented tasks. The documentation should be in the playscript procedure format (see Figure 15-2 for an example) and should include all the routine steps as well as the exceptions to routine.

Simplify the Record Keeping

Nothing will kill a technical measurement program faster than a cumbersome record-keeping system. Since a characteristic of the technical job is that the employee is in control of his own workload, the record keeping must not reduce this freedom to act by keeping track of every minor thing that happens. Volume counts should be limited to one to three key items, preferably one. If at all possible, the clerical support personnel should keep the actual volume counts. Recording of time "off standards" should be kept at a minimum, and should include only absent time, no-work time, and special projects of long duration (over one hour). Meetings and interruptions should be factored into standards so they need not be recorded as off-standard time.

Establish a Meaningful Reporting Period

Since most technical measurement programs will have few units of count and relatively large time standards, the reporting period should be based on the logical cycle of completing a full procedure from start to finish. This usually means a reporting period of two weeks or a month.

Use Results Properly

Considering the weighted basis on which the standards were developed and the long reporting cycle, it is meaningless to pinpoint specific performance results for purposes of remedial action. Goals should be set in terms of units per day or week, and results evaluated in terms of ranges. Percentages should still be calculated, but to record 89 percent for one month versus 86 percent for another month may be rather meaningless—both should probably be viewed as being in the range of 85 percent to 90 percent.

We should develop a good attitude about standards and their use right from the start. The program should never be allowed to degenerate into a numbers game.

A popular misconception about standards, particularly for technical workers, is that a standard tells you how long it should take an average well-trained worker to process an item. The standard for a customer service representative to handle a customer complaint could be 20 minutes. Does this mean the customer service representative should hang up the telephone on a customer with a complaint after 20 minutes? Certainly not! It should be recognized that some complaints can be handled in three or four minutes and some can take an hour or longer. The 20-minute standard is an average. It could mean that a customer service representative should be able to handle 24 complaints per day over an eight-hour period (480 minutes ÷ 20 minutes/complaint = 24 complaints/day), or 120 per week.

BENEFITS OF A TECHNICAL MEASUREMENT PROGRAM

Let's examine some of the benefits that can accrue from a well-conceived and properly executed technical measurement program.

Objective data for goal setting and evaluation. The technical manager is better able to set individual productivity goals for each technician, based on objective standards. The technician gets regular feedback on the achievement of these goals.

Standard costing. Without a technical measurement program, standard costing becomes less than scientific, since the cost of handling a claim or loan or whatever by the technicians must be estimated or included as an overhead cost. With a technical measurement program, these standard costs can be better identified and accurately measured.

Methods and procedures improvements. The documentation and standard-setting phases point out obvious areas for improving the way the work is processed. Alternative methods can be evaluated objectively and the best method selected. The most common change is that of relieving the technicians of clerical work that can be handled by a lower-salaried worker, and thereby obtaining greater use of the technician's skills.

Identification of training needs. Analysis of performance as well as of individual frequency studies will point out the errors in handling and the problems in decision making on the part of the technician. In some cases, specific training may be required.

Quality control. Supervisory audits of completed work for purposes of checking quality are made easier. Supervisors can refer to the documentation to illustrate missing steps and indicate the proper procedure to follow.

Improved service. Improved methods and procedures, better quality, and increased productivity all result in better service for the customer. In today's competitive market, this translates into increased sales.

CHAPTER

Quality Controls

THE SUPERVISOR'S JOB is to get work out accurately, on time, and economically, in that order. It makes no sense to strive to get work out on time at any cost. What good does it do to get work out on time if it is not accurate? The same applies to stressing economy without regard to accuracy and timeliness.

Work measurement standards tell us how long it should take to perform a task "while producing work of acceptable quality," but what assurance do we have that the result will be of an acceptable quality? The answer is that usually we have none. Most office work measurement programs leave quality control up to the supervisor. The supervisor is told to spot-check the work of an employee. If the work is of good quality and error-free, accept it. If it is not, give it back to the employee to rework it until it is acceptable. This is what any good supervisor does—with or without work measurement.

A popular misconception is that people who work under standards work faster and therefore make more errors. The truth of the matter is that "slow but sure" and "haste makes waste" are nothing but tired old sayings that provide dignity to clods. People who work on standards and at acceptable levels of performance actually produce fewer errors and turn out better-quality work than employees not on standards. Furthermore, the higher performer generally turns out better-quality work. You might expect higher-performing employees to make more errors since they are doing more work. However, the opposite is true, because it takes higher concentration to achieve higher performance. If a disproportionate number of

191

errors are made by a high performer, it is usually a result of not following the approved procedures but taking an unauthorized shortcut.

In any case, it makes good sense to get a handle on quality. Should a company ever get into a wage incentive plan, quality control is essential.

Definition

Quality control is a proven method for economically determining, improving, and maintaining a high quality level of products and performance.

Usually the nomenclature a company assigns to this effort reflects the attitude of the personnel. Some of the common terms are quality assurance, quality performance, quality control, quality improvement, statistical quality control, and error prevention. One company, ITT, developed the acronym DRIVE (*Do* it *Right* *I*nitially for *V*alue and *E*ffectiveness) in connection with its zero defects program.

Symptoms

What are some of the signs that a quality control program is necessary? Whenever 100 percent checking of the work of fully trained employees is encountered, we generally feel there is a problem. When employees are spending a great deal of time on rework or correction of errors, it is an obvious sign of wasted time and material. Also, delays in workflow and poor service beg for attention. These factors result in low employee morale and customer complaints.

Objectives

The objectives of a quality control program assuredly depend on the needs of each company. They can be a combination of any of the following:

- To improve the quality of work.
- To reduce costs.
- To provide better customer service or to improve relations with customers.
- To eliminate 100 percent checking and thereby increase employee productivity.
- To provide a continuous record of quality, thus enabling management to determine the quality level for any individual, operation, or department.
- To permit immediate detection and correction of errors and prompt discovery and investigation of troublesome conditions.
- To initiate changes in methods and systems after investigation of poor-quality work.
- To improve employee morale and increase employee interest in producing high-quality work.

Essentially, we would hope to complement a work management program by providing a formal approach for error detection, correction, and elimination. This means that we would concentrate on the elimination of the error cause rather than just on error correction.

Sources of Errors

For the most part, it's people who cause errors. They make errors for a variety of reasons—because they do not know, because they do not think, or because they do not care.

Occasionally, the cause may not be people. Perhaps equipment is not operating properly. Perhaps it is not suited for the job. Or methods and systems can be the source of errors or poor quality. They can be the cause of delays and/or duplication.

For obvious reasons, it is important that the source of errors be pinpointed and corrected. Errors create complaints, increased work activity, and unnecessary expense. Beyond that, employees want to do a good job. They need to feel that they are doing a job that is worthwhile and appreciated.

Acceptance

The effectiveness of a quality control program will be weakened unless management cooperates and understands the principles. A quality control program must incorporate easy-to-comprehend reporting methods, differentiation of types of errors, documentation of the principles, functions, values, and requirements of the quality program, and specific guidelines for each individual unit.

Management, supervisors, and employees must understand that a quality control program is not a fault-finding program. Motivation and attitude are the key words. Management must communicate to all employees its sincere desire to improve quality. This should involve a thorough explanation of the program at the outset and continuous monitoring of progress by all levels of management. The benefits of high-quality performance, such as a sense of pride, personal growth, and personal success, should be stressed. Employee participation is also important. Management should emphasize that each individual's participation is essential and should encourage ideas and suggestions from employees.

Management's Role

Management must realize the need for a program to ensure quality. Once the program is established, management must accept full responsibility for communicating it to employees. Performance expectations must be known from the management level on down. Management is responsible for getting things done through other people. The answers to the major questions must come from management. What are the quality requirements? What errors are being made?

What are the quality factors? What are the causes of errors? What is the action plan for achieving error-free performance?

IMPLEMENTING A QUALITY CONTROL PROGRAM

The quality requirements in each department are different. How errors are caused, what the various errors are, and how errors are detected depend on the type of work that is being done in a department. Despite these differences, quality control programs have a common basic format. Let us review the steps that go into developing a program.

Survey

A survey must be conducted to determine the presence or absence of quality control. It must be determined whether there is evidence of a quality problem. The first step may be to see if there is a concern for quality work. Next, we must identify opportunities to improve quality and provide a mechanism for introducing a quality performance plan.

The normal approach will be to start with the department manager. An interview with the supervisor follows, and finally each employee is interviewed. The questions to be asked are along these lines:

How well is work now being done?
How much checking is being done? By whom? When?
How are errors detected? By whom? When?
How are errors corrected? By whom? When?
What kinds of errors are being made? By whom?
What records of errors are kept?
What edits are run? How often?
What causes errors? What reasons are given?
What are the complaints concerning errors?
What are the employees' criticisms and attitudes toward the work?
Have there been any changes in methods and procedures? Are systems stable?
Are there workflow problems?
Are there personnel problems? Turnover problems? Absenteeism? Need for training?
Are there equipment problems or problems with materials?
Are known causes of errors being corrected?
Is quality performance documented in employee appraisals?

After this type of questioning, the analyst should attempt to verify information collected from the interviews. He should chart the flow of work in the department. He should observe the various working conditions, quality of supervision, employee work habits, control techniques, and communication techniques. He should review the records and reports to determine the common categories of errors, the percentage breakdowns by types of errors, trends and fluctuations, and the relationship to work management results. The study should provide some documentation of the strengths and weaknesses of the present quality control system and should include tentative lists of error causes and recommendations for quality improvement and the elimination of error causes.

The next step is to review the survey with the manager and the supervisor. The analyst should offer assistance in developing a quality control program and in explaining the objectives of quality control. There has to be a sincere desire on the part of the department management to take corrective action. Otherwise, the program would do little more than document errors, create resentment, and provoke deliberate attempts to sabotage the quality control program.

Indoctrination

Communication is essential. The program should be announced to all employees in the department or organization. The employees should be acquainted with the purpose of the program, its scope, and the benefits to be derived. We should invite participation in the development and installation of the quality control program from each and every employee and communicate a strong concern for quality work. Without the full cooperation and confidence of all employees the quality control program can acquire a bad name, and resistance will accompany it. A suggested presentation to employees goes something like this:

> Quality—does it matter? You bet it does. To begin with, every job in this department is important. Each, when performed properly, contributes to the continued success of our company—which means better compensation for each of us who performs well. After all is said and done, quality is really up to each and every one of us.
>
> You can care about the quality of your work, your worth, your professionalism, or you can allow yourself to sink into routine and be content just to get by. But just getting by isn't fun. There's no excitement in it, no possibility.
>
> You have to prove yourself, but not just to others. Sure, it's important that others recognize a job well done. It's essential for security, possible advancement, and all those other very real, very necessary concerns. But it should be equally important that you be proud of your own skills, your sense of making a contribution. Every job you do, every day, is a measure of your capability and responsibility. So it follows that it should be done right, if you are to succeed in any way.
>
> You are the one who can make the difference between ordinary and extraordinary, between better and best. It's really up to you.

Inspection

Work can be inspected by a supervisor, the individual responsible for training employees, or a designated checker. The checker can be someone from within the department or a quality control analyst/checker.

Items to be checked or inspected should be the major work items—the high-volume or most time-consuming items. Also, the critical "money" items should be checked—errors that have no chance of being discovered and that seriously influence profits. We should identify the items that have the greatest risk of being in error and/or have the greatest effect on the overall quality of the product. Naturally, "hot items," those which are current problems or have the interest or concern of management, should be included in this category.

Checkpoints should not interfere with workflow, cause delays, or create additional work. The checkpoints should be close to the work, in both location and time. Errors can then be detected and corrected on the spot, and the corrected items can reenter the normal workflow immediately.

The question of how much checking should take place is a sensitive one. This can take one of three forms: daily random spot-checking, control sample plan sizes, and 100 percent checking.

When using the daily random spot-checking method, the supervisor or designated quality control clerk is responsible for checking a sample of each employee's work or a sample of all types of work. When using control sample plan sizes, there are almost as many types of sampling plans as there are aspects of statistics. The goal of control sampling is to control and reduce the causes of errors, not to ensure the accuracy of acceptance and rejection numbers. The sample size guidelines in Table 16-1 will provide a plan which minimizes the expense of sampling, encourages quality work, identifies quality trends and frequencies, and provides accurate quality performance factors.

The items that require 100 percent checking are usually critical money items or

Table 16-1. Guidelines for sample sizes.

No. of Items Produced per Week	or	% of Total Std. Hrs./Item	Weekly Sample Size
25 and under		1%–3%	—*
26–65		4%–6%	1 of 7
66–180		7%–15%	1 of 10
181–234		16%–20%	1 of 15
235–656		21%–56%	1 of 25
657 and over		57%–100%	1 of 50

*Sample size too small.

work performed by inexperienced employees or an employee with a high error frequency. The purpose of 100 percent checking is to identify the problem and eliminate the need for error correction.

Reporting Techniques

The purpose of reporting techniques is to gather data on quality and provide a tool for communicating expectations on quality to employees. These reports can serve as a basis for recognizing quality output and rewarding those who achieve quality goals. Also, it enables the supervisor to take corrective action where quality is below target levels.

Two methods are generally used to express quality levels:

$$\text{Error ratio} = \frac{\text{items wrong}}{\text{items checked}}$$

$$\text{Quality factor} = \frac{\text{items correct}}{\text{items checked}}$$

The quality-factor method is favored because it expresses values in positive rather than negative terms. It is accepted better by employees when they are advised that their quality factor is 94 percent (94 percent of their work is of a good quality) rather than that their error ratio is 6 percent (6 percent of the work is not acceptable). And, corrective action seems easier, because an improvement in quality from 90 percent to 94 percent seems more readily achievable than a decrease in the error ratio from 10 percent to 6 percent.

Another method of reporting results combines quality factors with quantity measures—performance. This involves assigning a weight to each factor to get a combined index (CI). For example, we could assign a weight of 60 percent to performance and 40 percent to quality. Therefore, an employee with a performance of 85 percent and a quality factor of 98 percent would have a combined index of 90 percent—$(85\% \times 60\%) + (98\% \times 40\%) = 90\%$.

The frequency of reporting is normally monthly for fully trained employees. For trainees and employees with unsatisfactory quality levels, weekly or even daily reporting is advisable.

Communications

Employees should always be informed as to what quality level is expected of them. Feedback to employees should be continuous. Some method of rewarding those employees who achieve or exceed goals should be determined, as well as remedial action steps to be taken when goals are not met.

Remedial action can take several forms. To determine the cause of poor quality, one should look into whether or not the employee is properly trained in all aspects of the task. Determine whether or not an employee follows the known correct procedures. Possibly the employee is simply careless in carrying out his or her assigned responsibilities. Whatever the cause of low performance, the employee should be trained or retrained in the correct procedure. The supervisor should discuss the cost of errors and their impact on the company and the customers' perception. In any case, when an employee produces work of unacceptable quality, the work should be returned to the employee for correction, and the problem should be discussed so as to eliminate the cause.

CONCLUSION

Employees are keenly aware of where management places emphasis within the organization. If the emphasis is just on production (output), employees will strive for quantity. If management also emphasizes quality, employees too will concern themselves with quality. Existence of a quality control program indicates appropriate emphasis on quality.

DESIGNING
AND IMPLEMENTING
THE PROGRAM

CHAPTER

Planning
a Work Management Program

PERHAPS THE MOST IMPORTANT ingredient in a formal work management program is the planning stage. The old adage, "A problem well defined is half solved," seems to apply here as well. Sometimes, what you want to accomplish clashes with the specific needs of the organization. Proper attention to all aspects of the program during the planning stage will assure that needs and objectives are compatible.

THE STEERING COMMITTEE

A typical approach to work management planning is to select a steering committee of three or more persons to investigate the needs of the organization and select the program that best fits those needs. This type of planning takes into consideration what kind of program is needed, what are the objectives, who will be affected, what kind of timetable is involved, what it will cost, what it will save, and a cost-versus-savings breakeven analysis.

The steering committee should be made up of department heads of the largest processing areas, and at the very least include the executive most likely to have day-to-day responsibility for the program. It is not unusual for the steering committee to be made up of all members of senior management.

USING CONSULTANTS

Few companies, if any, can afford to hire the very best person available for every department and for each activity in which the company is involved. This is one reason many companies, large and small, have chosen to retain consultants with proven track records and reputations for building and managing successful businesses of various sizes. The consultant should have the ability to isolate and identify the real problems, not just to treat the symptoms. This comes from experience and exposure to similar business situations.

A consultant specializing in work management usually has developed analysis and measurement techniques that can save a great deal of time, as well as training programs for analysts, supervisors, and managers that have proved to be effective in getting cooperation from all levels. Also, the consultant can design reporting systems that are tailored to the individual needs of a client.

Selecting the right consultant is an important step. The chief executive, and the whole senior executive committee for that matter, must be able to feel comfortable with the consultant. They must be able to communicate easily. The "chemistry" must be right, and there must be mutual respect, or management won't feel safe in following the consultant's advice. The caliber, integrity, and reputation of the individual consultant should be carefully considered before spending any significant amount of time and money with him or her.

Whether you bring in a consultant or try to develop the program with your own people, it requires an experienced professional to determine the needs of a company and to develop a program to fruition.

DOING IT YOURSELF

There are some who take a dim view of consultants. They feel that consultants are expensive. The salesman might be very impressive, these people would say, but the consultant assigned often does not measure up to expectations. Therefore, the company management may decide to develop its own program.

The chance of having someone already on your staff who is experienced enough to develop a program is very remote. Unless you are fortunate in hiring an experienced person, the prospects for success are not bright. There is a long list of companies who have tried to develop their own program and who have failed miserably. The disadvantages of trying to develop an in-house program are numerous. Each failure makes it that much more difficult to later implement a successful program.

PITFALLS OF IN-HOUSE PROGRAMS

The reason work management programs are installed is to achieve results. The ability to achieve results is hampered by an inexperienced program manager without skilled guidance.

Technique

The technique selected to measure work by inexperienced people is usually of the informal or semiformal varieties on a trial-and-error basis. Proprietary techniques cannot be used by such people. Time may be lost to develop an untested system of measurement if higher-level approaches to measurement are utilized. Often, it is quite obvious to employees and supervisors whose jobs are being studied. Using an in-house program may mean that methods analysis is overlooked.

Inexperience

It requires experience to handle the various problems that arise during the development of standards and installation of a program. To allow potential problem situations to fester into serious problems is a high price to pay for using in-house programs.

Credibility

People always question how certain activities they perform can be measured. These questions must be answered with the utmost care. When they are not answered properly, people tend to lose confidence in the individuals with whom they are dealing. In-house staff may lack credibility in this crucial area.

Ability to Cope

A formal program needs someone who can develop management support, overcome a natural resistance to change, and motivate people to use the information that is supplied to them to make potential improvements. An in-house employee does not normally possess the stature, or clout, to carry it off. Even experienced in-house people must concern themselves with the politics of the company, which makes them less effective due to loss of objectivity.

Development Time

In the hands of an inexperienced person, program installation generally takes a great deal of time, because of the foregoing reasons. In-house personnel usually have little experience in applying the measurement techniques, have difficulty in making changes in methods and procedures, lack the experience to handle problems, lack credibility, and have difficulty in rallying the support of management.

Unless a realistic time schedule is developed and maintained for getting the program installed, people begin to lose interest and the program enters into a state of limbo.

ADVANTAGES OF USING CONSULTANTS

Studies conducted by numerous organizations, such as the Life Office Management Association in the life insurance industry, the Bank Administration Institute in the banking industry, and the MTM Association for Standards and Research, have concluded that the chances for success with a productivity improvement program are far greater using a consultant than not. At the risk of being less than objective, let's examine some of the advantages of using consultants.

Experience

Most consultants specialize in a particular field—banking, insurance, health care, publishing, government, public utilities, and so on—and can usually boast a long list of clients within a special field or industry. This usually means that the consultant has studied the type of work performed in a department many times. The consultant has seen variations of good methods and poor methods and is usually able to sort out improved ways of performing the work.

Most important, the consultant is familiar with the problems usually associated with people and the way they perform their jobs. The same problems recur on many assignments—for example, how jobs can be measured; the reasons why a person who has been recognized as one of the better performers in a department is coming up with a low performance under measurement; how to handle situations involving long-service employees who cannot meet minimum standards of performance; how to handle the recalcitrant employee; how to handle the supervisor who feels that he or she does not need this type of control; and how to deal with the employee or supervisor who believes that measurement has an undesirable effect on employees because of the regimentation it implies. There are no pat answers for these problems, but an experienced consultant can deal effectively with them.

Proven and Tested Techniques

Most reputable consulting organizations have developed their own techniques for measuring work. Beware of the consultant who has no proprietary technique to offer. This person may lack the real expertise to design a good program, and is probably just an expensive alternative to hiring an experienced in-house person. Some employ informal techniques while others employ semiformal and formal techniques. A number of consulting firms deal only with proprietary predetermined time data systems. These techniques have usually been developed for a particular segment of offices, and they generally have been tested and validated over a number of studies. Techniques such as Advanced Office Controls have been used to measure clerical work as well as technical work, and the consultant can provide illustrations of how the data have been applied to a wide variety of jobs.

The consulting firm that is in business to provide a service to clients will usually, if using a predetermined time data system, have developed a set of office data for equipment. This means that it also provides as a regular service to clients updated standard data as new equipment is put on the market. This will prove to save clients a great deal of time during the maintenance of the program.

Objectivity

One of the greatest assets that a consultant brings to the task is the ability to be objective. His motivation is to develop standards and conduct studies that are fair to both the employee and to management. His reputation is based on the ability to make valid, objective recommendations.

Lower Installation Costs

Because of the extensive experience in proven and tested techniques that a consultant brings to an assignment, and because of the objectivity of the consultant in dealing with day-to-day problems, the program will be installed at a faster rate, and therefore at a lower cost, than if a client were to attempt to install it himself. Most consultants will develop a master schedule for installing the program over a specified period of time—say six months or twelve months. The program will be scheduled in such a way that progress can be monitored periodically and adjustments in timing can be made as needed. However, the reputable consultant feels that it is important to bring programs in on schedule. Naturally, this should not be done at the risk of sacrificing quality.

CRITERIA FOR SELECTING A CONSULTANT

How does a company go about selecting a consultant to assist with a work management program? The most common way to go about this would be to check with other companies that have successful programs and determine the name of the consulting firms they used. The most common ways a consultant gets business is by his reputation and by referral through satisfied clients. However, there are a number of factors that a company should take into consideration when looking at a consulting firm, and we will examine these factors now.

Reputation

A reputable consultant is more than happy to provide prospective clients with a list of references to check on work done for others within the same industry. A company can check with these references to determine how satisfied they were with the services provided, the senior consultant assigned, the techniques and supporting information provided, results promised, and results achieved. Each company should decide at the outset how many references to contact, or how many companies constitutes good experience within one's own industry.

Techniques Used

A consultant will provide descriptive material concerning the techniques that will be used on an assignment, as well as a demonstration of the applicability and simplicity of the techniques as they would apply to the work in your own company. As pointed out previously, the choice of a measuring technique is important because of the differences in accuracy, consistency, economy, understandability, and simplicity of different techniques. The technique determines the type of documentation that will be provided, as well as the complexity and difficulty of maintaining standards developed with that particular technique.

A company can compare the economy offered by different techniques simply by comparing the amount of time a consultant will take to cover a given number of positions and the number of analysts that will be required to do it. For example, if you are comparing Consultant A with Consultant B, and you find that Consultant A will cover 400 positions in 12 months using four of your people as analysts, and Consultant B proposes to cover 350 positions in 12 months using five client employees as analysts, it would be clear that Consultant A will accomplish more at lower cost. You might find that Consultant A plans to bring under control 50 additional positions that may be considered unmeasurable by Consultant B. This indicates greater measurement capability and overall technique on the part of Consultant A.

In addition to measurement techniques, there are a number of other services a consultant should be capable of providing. These include special orientation and training sessions for supervisors, middle managers, and senior management; reporting systems, both manual and automated; special approaches to the improvement of methods and procedures and/or paperwork simplification techniques; and methods for communicating various aspects of the program to employees, including booklets, brochures, presentations, and written articles that explain the benefits of the program.

All these aspects should come out in the consultant's initial presentation to the prospective client.

Style

One of the key elements in the style of a consultant should be his flexibility, or his ability to adapt to the needs of the client company. As a prospective client, you should evaluate the consultant in terms of his ability to work within your own organization, to implement your type of program, and to adapt to the conditions that prevail within the company. Style also refers to how the consulting firm operates. Will a consultant be assigned to the project for a period of weeks or months, without any supervision, or does the firm intend to supervise the assignment through periodic visits by senior consultants throughout the duration of the assignment?

Style also refers to the approach the consultant takes in maintaining harmonious staff relations. The obvious question to ask is how the employees will be affected by the program. Determine what benefits the employee is likely to perceive when the program is introduced and implemented. Determine how the employee will participate in the program. Some consultants do not involve the employee at all; others feel that the employee is an integral part of the program and involve all employees in the project.

A heavy-handed approach can easily be detected when the consultant emphasizes the need to use the clout of the chief executive officer. This is usually done as a scare tactic to gain submission.

Consulting Personnel

The consulting firm should provide a biographical sketch of the consultant it plans to assign to the project. The sketch should illustrate the previous experience of the consultant, the length of time he has been employed by the consulting organization, and a list of typical assignments performed by the consultant. It is not uncommon for the client company to ask to be able to meet the consultant prior to accepting the proposal. When interviewing the consultant, one should take into consideration his technical abilities, teaching skills, project management skills, communication skills, and ability to handle interpersonal relations.

Results

Results expected from the program can be covered in one of two ways: in a general way in a preliminary presentation before a survey is conducted, or in very specific terms after a survey is completed. Some consultants will not volunteer to conduct a survey. Others will offer to conduct a survey at no cost or obligation to the client in order to get a firm grasp of the situation, to determine what benefits exist, and to develop a cost-benefit analysis. A consultant cannot very well offer to conduct a program with anticipated benefits without a survey.

In any case, a consultant should be able to outline what he expects to achieve, how long he expects it will take to achieve those results, what the client's participation in the program will be, what the consultant's role in the program will be, what the benefits will be, and what the internal and external costs will be to achieve those benefits.

Survey

The consultant should volunteer to spend a couple of days on the client's premises to get a better feel for the company, the style of management, the current condition of methods and procedures, the current automated systems, the caliber of supervisors and managers, and any other factors that would help in evaluating the type of business. The survey involves tours of the office facilities to see the people at work, the housekeeping of the departments, the location or proximity of supervisors to the employees, the tempo or pace at which people are working, the layout of the department, the positioning of various types of office equipment, worktable arrangements, and so forth.

Interviews should be scheduled with key people at each level of management. The purpose of these interviews usually is to discuss style of management, tools presently used, current problems in getting work done, as viewed by the managers concerned, how deadlines are met, workload and backlog, and the type of information each manager would like to have to perform his or her job better. On the basis of the tours of the office and the interviews with people at all levels, the consultant can determine the objectives of the program.

TYPICAL OBJECTIVES OF A WORK MANAGEMENT PROGRAM

There is a wide variety of objectives that can be considered for a work management program. It is important to be very specific when announcing objectives to the staff. On the other hand, too long a list of objectives will cloud the intent of the program. Let us review the typical things that can be accomplished by a program. Then we will look at the type of program that must be designed to meet those particular objectives.

Reducing Costs

Our experience with literally hundreds of programs, and the experience of other consultants in this field, indicates that the average company can realize payroll savings from 20 percent to 40 percent from a well-conceived and intelligently applied work management program. Stated another way, for every 100 positions that can be brought under measurement control, the same amount of work can be done by 20 to 40 fewer people (that is, by 60 to 80 employees). These savings generally come about from three primary sources: discontinued activity, improvement in methods and procedures, and improvement in individual performance. Normally, one-third of the savings comes from each source.

We normally find the average performance before controls are installed, in a department or companywide, to be about 50 percent. The typical range is from 40 percent to 60 percent average performance before controls are installed. This does not mean that people work only half the time. It does not mean, for example, that people work for an hour and do nothing for the next hour, or work for four hours and do nothing the other four hours of the normal work day. What it means is that the amount of effective work turned out over a period of time is about half of what could be done by an average well-trained employee. It also means that people are not always working as effectively as possible and on the right things. The method could be poor, or the employee could be doing an unnecessary amount of checking simply because he or she has had the time in the past to do it. This is a typical way for an employee to fill up the time available when there is not enough work to do. Typically, performance will be improved from the 50 percent level at the start to a level of 85 percent to 90 percent.

Improving Methods and Procedures

A part of the study will involve simplification of paperwork and evaluation of all methods and procedures used to get the work done accurately, on time, and economically. If this is one of the objectives, then one should ensure that the analysts who are conducting the studies are trained to evaluate methods and procedures, and that the measurement technique lends itself to methods and procedures analysis.

Improving Systems

It is normally not desirable to try to improve major systems along with the installation of a work management program, simply because this is a study that should be performed separately or independently from the establishment of work standards. The reason is that to evaluate the impact of a system change on other functions or departments will generally require a great deal of investigation. Normally, the approach is to document recommendations for systems changes as the program is being installed and consider these as a second phase of the program. However, when it is found that the system is badly in need of change, the decision should be made to suspend the work management study until a systems analyst can effect the necessary changes. Analysts still need some systems training, however, so that they will be better able to recognize systems problems and areas for potential improvement.

Improving Supervisory Control

This is commonly one of the primary objectives of a work management program: to provide supervisors with better tools to carry out their responsibilities. This means that the thrust of the program is directed at the supervisor's job. It means that the supervisor should have better information about the performance of each employee under his or her control, and a method for quantifying the amount of work being performed by each employee. To ensure that the supervisor knows what to do with the information, supervisor orientation sessions must be included in the work management plan.

Evaluating Employee Performance

In order to accomplish this objective, it is necessary to measure employee performance on an individual basis. Generally, this involves the use of formal techniques to set accurate, engineered work standards so that performance will be measured accurately and consistently. Employees miss out on a major benefit to them—objective evaluations—if individual performance is not measured.

Improving Service

In an insurance company this objective would more appropriately read, "improve the accuracy and timeliness of service to agents and policyholders." In a banking environment this objective would probably read, "improve service to customers." In any other type of work environment, it would be desirable to state more clearly the type of service one is attempting to improve. If service is poor because of certain factors, these factors must be taken into consideration when designing the work management program so that proper attention is given to them. In a typical work management situation, the turnaround time of documents is measured so that one can determine the current level of service and establish goals, based on the standards developed, for improvement in service.

Improving Morale

While one might expect that morale will improve under a work management program, this is not generally listed as one of the primary objectives of the program. It is usually something one would expect as an indirect benefit. Nevertheless, we believe that people are happier working in an environment where they are told what is expected of them and are given feedback on how well they are performing their jobs in relation to what is expected of them.

Evaluating Equipment

Evaluation of office equipment is normally done when one is studying the methods and procedures in a department. This would be a natural item to include as part of the study, and recommendations for change in the equipment can be made to get work out more smoothly and at a lower cost.

Recognizing the Achievements of Supervisors

Supervisors should be recognized, along with individual employees, for the job they are doing. When supervisors are given an equal opportunity to use the best management tools available to carry out their job, then they can be recognized on the basis of how well they are able to improve performance in their area of responsibility.

Developing Better Budgeting Tools

The information on performance and staffing that is generated from a work management program can be used to create budgets for a company. In all cases the information on staffing in departments should be used as a guide when determining the budget for the coming year. Staffing formulas will help budget for people and equipment, and work standards will help select the right equipment. Staffing needs lead to space needs also. Materials such as forms also can be better budgeted through data provided by work management.

Developing Standard Costs

A very common objective of a work management program is to develop a cost accounting system based on standard costs within an organization. Standards can be applied to various product lines to determine functional costs, and a comparison of these costs with actual costs will indicate the room for improvement within the organization.

Pricing Services

The use of standards is natural for developing prices for services. Service costs in service industries are generally charged back to customers. If one has the ability to determine how much it actually costs to perform a service versus how much it should cost, one can reduce the cost of performing the service to the lowest possible level in order to achieve the highest possible profit. Or, one can reduce service costs and improve the firm's competitive position.

DETERMINING YOUR PRIMARY OBJECTIVES

The primary objectives of a program are usually limited to two to four objectives. These objectives must be clearly stated so that they can be easily remembered by all levels of the organization. As with any objective-setting or goal-setting plan, an action plan should be developed to show how each objective will be accomplished. The proper tools and implementation procedures should be designed to help accomplish the stated primary objectives.

Typical objectives would be stated as follows:

- To help supervisors and managers to be even more effective in meeting their goals and objectives.
- To help employees work smarter, not harder, by improving methods and procedures.
- To improve service to customers.

These objectives are clear. There is something in them for everyone. Supervisors and managers benefit by having better tools to work with. The employee benefits by having an improved job design and better methods and procedures to make it easier to do a better job. And the customer benefits by having improved service. It follows that the attainment of these goals will result in cost reduction.

Ingredients for Success

There are prerequisites or ingredients that are essential to the success of any program. Unless special attention is paid to each in the planning stage, the chances for success are slim.

Management Support

Perhaps another word would be commitment. Mere approval from management is not sufficient. Management support is much more than that. Management support really involves three things: showing an interest, expecting improvement, and having patience.

Management must demonstrate its support by showing a strong interest in the program, and by effectively communicating this interest to all levels of the organization. Management must be visible when announcing the program and continually "talk up" the program before, during, and after its installation. There should be no doubt in anyone's mind that management is interested in seeing the program installed in all areas of the organization.

Management must expect that improvement will come about as a result of the program. That expectation must be communicated to all levels of the organization. Improvement is the name of the game. A manager who feels that there is no room for improvement in his or her area of responsibility is unfit for the title "manager." The feeling that should be conveyed is: "To date we (management) have not given supervisors and managers the best possible tools to carry out their responsibilities properly. However, with the proper tooks, we know that each and every one of us can make improvements. I can. You can. We all can. We expect it."

Finally, management must be patient. You cannot expect results overnight. People and entire departments have been working at a given level of performance for quite some time. Many even believed that was an acceptable or even exceptional level of performance. It will take time to work with the new controls, to develop confidence in the techniques, and to learn how to use the program.

If overstaffing is detected, it usually cannot be remedied on the spot. Take a department with ten employees. Suppose the work management figures indicate that seven employees should be able to handle the current volume of work. How long should it take to get the staff down to seven? The answer is, at a pace that is agreeable to the supervisor. If one employee were to terminate employment, the supervisor may decide not to replace that individual. He will redistribute the work among the remaining nine employees. Later, he could reduce to eight, then seven, when he is convinced that it can be done. Moving at a pace faster than supervisors and managers feel comfortable with will cause frustration, resentment, defensiveness, and, eventually, failure of the program.

Good Communications

Time should be taken at the outset, before the program starts, to ensure that everyone understands the objectives of the program and how he or she will be affected by it. Also, people must be assured that fears concerning job security and unfair treatment of employees are unfounded.

Everyone must understand his responsibilities in achieving results. Supervisors and managers should attend special orientation and training sessions to learn as much as possible about their respective roles in the program.

Proper Selection of Analysts

It is very important that the right people are selected as analysts. The analyst has direct contact with the staff. Generally, how the people feel about the program is in direct proportion to how they feel about the analyst.

Attention to Methods and Procedures

A work measurement program that does not address methods and procedures cannot be effective over the long run. If standards are established on existing methods and procedures, and no attempt is made to find the best possible method, the employees will find shortcuts, thereby distorting the performance results. This will cause inequities and poor employee morale.

Fair Work Standards

The standards must be perceived by all concerned as fair, realistic, and attainable.

Well-Designed Reporting System

The reporting system must not be too time-consuming or require more effort than the results are worth. The supervisors must appreciate the value of the information that comes from employees on work counts and time distribution. Furthermore, employees must perceive this information as useful and valuable for the supervisor. To any employee who asks, "What is the value of my counting these items or filling out these forms?" the supervisor must be able to explain in what way the information helps the supervisor plan, organize, and schedule the work.

The bywords of reporting systems are: keep it simple, and give supervisors and managers only the kind of information they want and need to manage effectively.

Program Maintenance

The program that is not properly maintained will not survive. Office procedures, office technology, and office systems are very dynamic. They respond to

Table 17-1. Comparison of Consultants.

	Consultant A	Consultant B	Consultant C	Consultant D
Technique				
Type	Time Study	Sampling	Predetermined	Predetermined
Accuracy	±5%	±15%	±5%	±5%
Backup Data	N/A	N/A	Manual Prov.	On Request
Machine Data	None	None	Regular Updates	On Request
MTM-Based	No	No	Yes	Yes
Employees to Be Cov.	310	500	500	400
Maintenance	Time Consum.	Must Start Over	½ Time to Install	⅔ Time to Install
Training for Analysts				
Number of Analysts	7	2	5	5
Length of Formal Training	2 wks.	3 days	2 wks.	2 wks.
Future Training Needed	No	No	Yes	No
In-house	No	Yes	Yes	Yes
Future Training by	Consultant	In-house	In-house	Consultant
Instructor's Manual	No	No	Yes	No[a]
Guidance for Analysts				
Continuous	No	No	Yes	Yes
Length	5 days	—	26 wks.	26 wks.
Follow-up	No	To Be Determ.[b]	3 wks.	2 wks.
Supervisor Orientations				
Number of Sessions	None	1	8	1[c]
Length	None	1 hr.	2 hrs.	1 hr.
Follow-up	None	None	Yes	Yes
Management Orientations				
Number of Sessions	None	None	5	To Be Determ.
Consultants				
Size of Firm	250 Consulr.	1	12	25
Supervision	No	No	Yes	Yes
Specialists	No	No	Yes	Yes
Time to Fully Install	2 yrs.	1 yr.	1 yr.	1 yr.
Total Cost of Proposal	$15,000	$4,000	$67,000[d]	$65,800
Breakeven	?	?	11th mo.	?

[a]Says can be passed by word of mouth, but prefers we send analyst to off-site training courses.
[b]As needed.
[c]Will help develop if we feel necessary.
[d]Includes supervisory materials, supervision of consultants, instructor's manual, and visual aids.

various stimuli that cause them to change. As the work changes, so too must the time standards. A staff must be employed to update standards to reflect current operating conditions.

GETTING MANAGEMENT APPROVAL

A proposal or master plan that covers all the necessary details must be prepared for management approval. If a consultant or several consultants are engaged to conduct surveys and prepare proposals, these should be summarized, and one firm selected to assist in the development of the program. The recommended program should contain: survey findings, recommended objectives, proposed outline, number of analysts needed, length of time to install, benefits, and costs.

If you take all the key points that must be addressed when planning a program and compare all the consultants invited to prepare proposals as to how they propose to handle these points, the choice becomes easier to make. See Table 17-1 for a typical approach.

Selecting
the Right Technique

WHAT IS A SUCCESSFUL work management program? There are two criteria: results achieved and the feelings about the program of people at all levels of the organization. A program that achieves very good bottom-line results but alienates employees and supervisors cannot be considered a success. It may seem to succeed, but the results will not be long-lasting. On the other hand, a program that everyone likes but that produces few or no results cannot be considered a success either. Both ingredients are essential.

How important is it to select the right work measurement technique? Perhaps if we analyzed some successful work management programs, we could find a common pattern. We may find, however, that people will not readily attribute the success of the program directly to the technique but to the fact that "they did everything right." If we examine weak programs or programs that have failed, we may have a better opportunity to determine the value of a technique or its advantage over others.

A recent study of work management programs in the life insurance industry[1] indicated that the most common reason for failure of a work measurement program was loss of top management support. This loss of support was attributed to poor planning, poor implementation, and poor selection of a consultant. A number of the companies reporting in the survey mentioned lack of confidence in the standards as a reason for their problems. It seems reasonable that loss of management support, resistance to measurement, suspicion of motives, and the like can result from a lack of confidence in the standards. Standards and the technique utilized for establishing them are the heart of a work management program.

---

[1]Life Office Management Association (LOMA), *Financial Planning and Control Report #41: Survey of Work Measurement Results,* Atlanta, Georgia, 1978.

SELECTING A TECHNIQUE ON THE BASIS OF OBJECTIVES

Once a clearly defined set of objectives has been established, the best measurement technique should be selected to meet those objectives. The "best" technique simply is the one that fits your particular style of management and that will allow you to achieve program objectives.

Cost Reduction

A simple objective may be to reduce operating expenses. Generally speaking, the method that has proved to be most effective over the long haul is a department-by-department review of activities by an in-house staff or team under the direction of an experienced person, usually an outside consultant, and standards that are kept up to date.

Staff reductions should occur through normal attrition—that is, not replacing people who leave the company. When staff is reduced in this manner, and a proper match of staff to workload is achieved, a standard staff level can then be maintained for many years. This is not to say that when one arbitrarily cuts staff by, say, 20 percent, that level of staff cannot be maintained for very long. If you do not add to staff, it will remain constant. However, this method is usually accompanied by a drop in employee morale, a reduction in level of service, an increase in overtime and turnover, decreased productivity, and other problems.

Improvement of Methods

If paperwork simplification is one of your objectives, then the technique you select is especially important. Some techniques lend themselves better to methods analysis than others. Methods and procedures cannot be improved by a measurement technique. Improvement comes about by having an intelligent and creative analyst evaluate what is presently required to accomplish a given task and to decide if, in fact, it needs to be done at all and, if it does, how it can be done better.

To say that one technique lends itself to methods analysis or methods improvement more than another refers, first, to the degree to which one can associate time values with a model of the theoretical "one best method" and, second, to the documentation afforded by the technique. Documentation is a way of illustrating a basis for the standard. Good documentation, from a methods analysis point of view, provides the ability to weigh the value of each step of an operation. This may suggest possible alternatives or improvements. Documentation can also save time in making changes to a standard. If a step is eliminated, we can simply remove the block of time associated with that step and we have a new standard. Similarly, new procedures and time can be added as work is added to the task.

Only the formal techniques of time study and predetermined time data lend themselves to this detailed methods analysis—and the predetermined times approach more so than time study.

A time study analyst can handle methods in one of two ways. First, and most commonly, the analyst judges or rates the performance of a person using a poor method as lower than average to compensate for the longer time the poor method takes. (This can be minimized by selecting a person to be timed who is regarded as a knowledgeable, efficient—though not necessarily fast—worker.) Second, the analyst can review the step-by-step (motion-by-motion, if possible) procedure to be followed, and time the person performing that specific method. Motions and interruptions can still occur within a given process to make this type of study difficult to handle.

The predetermined times approach lends itself to methods analysis in that the analyst must first build a model of the best available method. Once the analyst is convinced the method is good, he applies the time values to that particular method. Then the analyst can analyze where time has been allocated to perform the various functions and make a final judgment as to the relative value of each element (value analysis). Another advantage of using predetermined time data for methods analysis is that the analyst has an opportunity to visualize an alternative method and, by applying the time data, determine which method takes less time to perform.

There is no practical way of controlling methods and procedures with informal or semiformal techniques. When these types of techniques—estimates, historical times, sampling, and time logs—are used, any attempt at methods improvement must be handled as a separate and unrelated study. Since the early stages of a methods study, such as task identification, are performed in much the same way, using informal techniques for measurement creates a duplication of effort on the part of the employees and the analysts, both of whose assets are too valuable to waste on needless activity.

Improvement of Service

Improving service generally refers to both the turnaround times of items to be processed and the quality of service given. The better-engineered standard usually results in a higher level of performance, which reduces processing time. This is so because the engineered standard is the most accurate standard.

Because of their accuracy, standards are usually attainable by any conscientious employee who is properly trained and has the proper amount of work to do. The engineered standard identifies "the proper amount of work" more accurately. When the employee achieves the standards, more output results than when informal or less accurate standards are used. Service quality improves with the attainment of good performance, since attention to the job at hand is a requirement for good productivity and good quality.

Improvement of Supervisory Control

A measurement technique can help provide supervisors with better tools to carry out their responsibilities, but only in proportion to the quality of the standards. The better the standards, the greater the degree of control.

We have said that work management provides facts for the supervisor and eliminates opinions. The more accurate the facts upon which to base decisions, the better the quality of supervision. Anyone in management realizes that one of the toughest parts of decision making is assembling the proper facts with which to work. It is just as simple as that.

Performance Evaluation

Perhaps one of your objectives is to provide a basis for evaluating the performance of employees. Many companies have tried to do this with informal or semiformal techniques and have had serious problems doing so.

Measuring individual employee performance is an extremely sensitive matter. Here we are dealing with the livelihood of people. This places a great deal of responsibility on the shoulders of those charged with establishing standards.

This is one of the prime reasons that standards are usually found to be on the high side when informal or semiformal techniques are used. People using these techniques realize the lack of accuracy of these techniques and will almost always err on the easy side rather than develop a standard that can have a detrimental effect on an employee.

This is also the reason that savings achieved as a result of informal and semiformal techniques are always lower. It is easier to meet the standards. And human nature being what it is, in the absence of some incentives to do otherwise, people will work to achieve standards rather than exceed them, unless the standards are so ridiculously off that minimum effort will give 120 percent to 150 percent performance results.

Individual versus group measurement. The severity of the problem of accurate standards diminishes if the standards will be used to measure only group performance—that is, only the collective performance of all employees, not their individual performance. The necessity for a fine-tuned standard is not as great under these conditions. Where individual remedial action is not possible, results will also be at a lower level.

Program maintenance. Another consideration with regard to technique is whether or not to maintain the standards after they are installed. Some set generally acceptable standards and then pay little, if any, attention to creeping changes that occur. This stance should not be taken when measuring individual employee performance. Once employees perceive that the standards no longer apply to the jobs they are doing, they begin to resent the program. Explaining to them that the standard is not taken at face value is not much help as long as the standards are kept in place and not updated.

Development of Standard Costs

Once again, well-engineered standards provide greater reliability and credibility and thus are more effective for developing standard costs.

Summary

The selection of a work measurement technique has a bearing on how well one can achieve the objectives desired. Table 18-1 provides a summary of the relative value of each technique in relation to the more common objectives.

Table 18-1. Comparison of techniques by objective.

	Informal	Semiformal		Formal	
Objective	Historical Data	Time Ladders	Work Sampling	Leveled Time Study	Predetermined Time Data
Reduce Costs	Fair	Good	Good	Excellent	Excellent
Improve Methods	Poor	Poor	Poor	Fair	Excellent
Improve Service	Poor	Fair	Fair	Excellent	Excellent
Provide Control Tool for Supervisors	Fair	Good	Good	Excellent	Excellent
Evaluate Employee Performance	Poor	Poor	Fair	Excellent	Excellent
Evaluate Department Performance	Fair	Good	Good	Excellent	Excellent
Develop Standard Costs	Poor	Fair	Fair	Good	Excellent

EVALUATING THE TECHNIQUES

One cannot make a decision as to which technique to use solely on the basis of the objectives to be achieved. There are other factors to be considered. Let us examine each of the criteria that should be considered in evaluating techniques.

Economy

Economy of a technique refers to several things. The first is speed of application. How long does it take to set standards? How much is involved in maintaining standards? Another aspect is the caliber of people needed to apply the techniques, and the time required to train the analysts. The more sophisticated the technique, the higher the caliber of person required, and the greater the cost. Training time refers not only to classroom training, if any, but also to the time required on the job to achieve an acceptable level of proficiency.

There are few costs associated with informal techniques. The time values are relatively easy to develop and easy to apply. Semiformal techniques can be applied by clerical-level employees with a minimum amount of training. Large numbers of people performing similar functions can be studied at one time, making these techniques quite economical to apply. Formal techniques require above-average people, heavy classroom training, and a fairly lengthy qualifying period. The time required to set standards is also greater. In the case of predetermined time data, standard-setting time varies in proportion to the level of standard data employed.

Accuracy

Accuracy, ironically enough, is usually not listed as one of the prime requirements of a measuring technique. Consistency is considered more important. If your 12-inch ruler is actually 13 inches, you can build just as good a house, as long as you use the same ruler.

What is accurate in terms of standards? The generally accepted degree of accuracy for engineered standards is plus or minus 5 percent. This means that any two people, properly trained, can independently go about setting a standard on the same operation and develop a standard that deviates no more than 5 percent from the other.

Consistency

As accuracy is a function of consistency, so is consistency a function of accuracy. Without consistency in standards, no reliable judgments about performance can be made. It may be desirable to be able to say that two employees, each performing different functions at the same level of performance—say, 90 percent—are each exerting the same amount of skill and effort required in their job.

Simplicity

Simplicity of a measurement technique refers to the ease with which supervisors, as well as the employees whose work is being measured, understand the standards. Problems in measurement are usually the result of a failure to understand the basis on which standards were developed.

Acceptability

The key to the acceptance of standards is the confidence of both employees and supervisors that the technology used is a reliable method of determining how long it should take to perform a task and, therefore, how well people perform their jobs.

The less formal techniques have been accepted very well because they are easy to understand and because the resulting standards are not very demanding. Engineered standards developed by predetermined time data have been accepted well in areas where the people who administer the program have taken the time to explain the purpose and methodology involved.

The least acceptable technique in the office has been time study. The stopwatch has long been the symbol of the "efficiency expert." The actuation of the watch sends a shock wave up the spine of many a person whose work effort is being timed. In all, its continued association with factory measurement, measurement of machine functions, reducing people to machines, or treating humans as automatons have maintained very negative feelings about the stopwatch.

Applicability

Another measure of the value of a measurement technique is range of work or types of jobs to which it applies. In offices, the categories of work involve maintenance, clerical, technical and professional, and administrative management.

Informal techniques, particularly the historical-data approach, can provide the broadest possible coverage of productivity measurement. Since productivity is the relationship between input and output, one can easily cover the entire company by comparing the relationship between input and output at many points to measure progress.

However, this only measures the actual change that occurs and does not provide a comparison between actual and standard, or what is possible to achieve.

Semiformal techniques, because of their "broad brush" approach, are also applicable to a wide range of work and jobs.

Formal techniques have until recently been limited to the clerical jobs. Lately, however, with higher-level data systems being developed, they are being applied more and more to technical jobs.

Reproducibility

Under a building-block concept, a great deal of time can be saved by building data in blocks of time that can be used over and over again for other situations that require the same motions. Informal and semiformal techniques do not allow this type of flexibility at all.

We have already covered the subject of standard data and their reproducibility in Chapter 13. It is sufficient to say that time study lends itself fairly well to standard data development, and predetermined time data, very well.

Usability

Usability of data or measurement techniques refers to the variety of uses it can be put to—scheduling production, scheduling overtime, balancing workloads, developing learning curves, evaluating performance, and so forth. This factor is in direct proportion to the quality of standards resulting from the technique, an issue we have already covered. The better engineered the standard, the more uses, and more reliable uses, it has.

Interruption of Employees

Informal techniques are least disruptive (in fact, there should be no disruptive factor at all). Semiformal techniques are not consistent in this regard. Work sampling, for instance, requires initial interviews to learn what the various operations are so that the observer can differentiate one activity from another. During the course of the study, however, there is no disruption at all, apart from the presence of the observer over a period of several weeks. After the first day or so, the employees hardly know the observer is there.

Time ladder studies may not be so much disruptive as they are sometimes considered a nuisance by employees. Employees are expected to fill out a form every day, usually for a one- or two-month period, posting the time they start and the time they stop each activity, a code for each activity, and the number of items completed.

The disruption factor with time study is very slight as far as interviewing of employees is concerned. Most time study analysts merely make their observations while the employees perform their tasks. Actually, the reverse of disruption is the net result, since the presence of an analyst in a department often causes employees to turn out more work than usual by avoiding time-consuming and personal interruptions.

Somewhat more of an employee's time is taken up when predetermined time data are used, because the analyst spends more time during the interview to determine what the employee does, why the employee does it, and so on. The extra time is explained by the concern for method. The analyst must understand the purpose of each step in an operation in order to determine the best method for performing the task. With other techniques, this attention to detail is ignored.

Cost

Informal techniques have a negligible cost, since very little training is involved, very few calculations are made, and no employee time is required. The cost gets progressively higher as you advance to the more sophisticated techniques. They require more classroom training for analysts, and more time, on the part of both analysts and employees, to establish standards.

Savings

Here again, the amount of savings achieved (at least as far as the standard-setting technique is concerned) is a reflection of the degree to which a standard is engineered. The better the standard, the greater will be the savings.

Table 18-2. Evaluation of work measurement techniques.

Criteria	Historical Data	Time Ladders	Work Sampling	Leveled Time Study	Predetermined Time Data
Economy	High	Medium	Medium	High	High
Accuracy	±50% Poor	±30% Fair	±20% Fair	±10% Good	±5% Excellent
Consistency	Poor	Poor	Poor	Good	Excellent
Simplicity	Excellent	Good	Good	Fair	Fair
Acceptability	Acceptable	Acceptable	Acceptable	Least acceptable	Acceptable if properly understood
Applicability	Universal	Universal	Universal	Limited	Limited by data base
Reproducibility	Negligible	Negligible	Negligible	Good	Excellent
Usability	Low	Moderate	Moderate	Good	Excellent
Interruption of Employees	None	Some	Little	Some	Fair
Cost	Negligible	Inexpensive	Moderately expensive	Costly	Costly
Savings	5%–8%	8%–10%	8%–10%	15%–30%	15%–35%

A summary of how each technique measures up against the aforementioned criteria can be found in Table 18-2. This should provide a good basis for evaluating each technique and selecting the right technique for your particular needs.

CHAPTER

Introducing the Program

HOW A PRODUCTIVITY IMPROVEMENT or work management program is introduced can have a great impact on the success of the program. As in the old saying, "You only get one chance to make a good first impression," the way the program is first perceived by the staff is critical. There is also a logical sequence of events in announcing a program—in particular, who is exposed to what level of detail first.

Occasionally we encounter firms that want to use a subtle approach and not make any formal announcement. The way the office grapevine works, whether you announce it or not, the news will travel fast. Unfortunately, there may be more said about what has not been said than about what has been said. The key to a successful program is properly planned communications to all levels of the organization. People at all levels have a right to know about a new program that affects their jobs.

We will discuss the announcement of a program in terms of a full-scale work management program. We will assume that the program involves establishing engineered time standards. If a reference to a specific technique is called for, we will use Advanced Office Controls as an example. In this way, if you select a less sophisticated program, you will be able to "modify down" rather than have to extrapolate introductory ideas.

COMBATING COMMON MISCONCEPTIONS

What are the questions and problems that are likely to arise when introducing a work management program? It would be wise to be aware of these and to have answers and solutions before you start.

The Program as a Speedup Device

This question appears in several ways: "Are you just trying to get more work out of fewer people?" Or, "Is this a speedup?" Or, "We're already doing all we can. How can we possibly do any more?"

These questions must be answered in a very positive way. No, this is not a speedup! No, you will not have to work faster, unless, of course, you are very slow. The standards are set for normal people who know their jobs. Even then, the performance required as a minimum is less than what a normal person can do.

So, employees will not have to do more work, unless one considers replacing idle or wasted time with work as making one work harder.

Deteriorating Quality of Work

Questions on the effect of measurement on quality come from supervisors and managers. They are generally concerned that if people will be expected to do more, the emphasis will be on quantity, and quality will suffer.

Ample time is built into the standard to do a job of an acceptable quality. The supervisor should spot-check work periodically to make sure that quality standards are maintained. The supervisor should be on guard when employees seem to be working at higher-than-usual levels of performance, and should make certain that no shortcuts are taken at the expense of quality.

Who Benefits?

Employees may ask, "Will the program benefit me, as well as my supervisor and the company?" The answer is an emphatic "yes!" Here are some of the things the program will do:

- It will result in a reassignment of work so that everyone gets a more equal share.
- Each employee will be recognized for his or her individual performance on the basis of facts, not opinion or guesswork.
- An improvement in methods and procedures will make jobs easier to perform.
- We will be able to make better use of the time and talents of our employees.

We expect it will help the company in many ways. Better methods, fairer treatment of individual employees, ability to forecast the need for additional or fewer employees as business changes, finding individuals who need retraining, reduction of idle time, wasted time, and delays, and better service to our customers are but a few advantages. All these things mean savings to the company. This makes the company healthier and a better place to work and adds greatly to the job security of all employees.

Record Keeping

One question usually asked by the new employee is, "Will I have to keep records?" The answer is yes. How else would the supervisor know how much each employee contributes to the group effort? Of course, the supervisor also needs this information for planning and organizing both the work and the staff.

An employee may well feel that "keeping records will add to my work. Is this really an improvement? Also, will time be provided for me to do this extra work?" The answer is, "yes, it is extra work, and yes, ample time is provided to keep records." Furthermore, we might ask, "Aren't you curious as to how much you did, and don't you want to tell and show your supervisor?" How can a supervisor properly evaluate an employee's performance without knowing how much work the employee does?

Finally, the employee should know that the time to make and record work counts is kept to an absolute minimum. It usually amounts to about two minutes per day per employee, or less.

Unfair Standards

Employees may feel that there is something disconcerting about the fact that someone else is applying the time standards to measure their work. Might it not have an unfavorable effect on employee morale? Interestingly enough, the experience of companies that have installed these programs generally is that morale has noticeably improved as a result of a work management program.

In the first place, the program invites active participation of the employee. Not only is he consulted about changes in his job, he's often the one who suggests them.

Second, the changes are invariably to the employee's benefit, since they level workloads and create more interesting and better-paying jobs. Finally, believe it or not, there is no proper psychological substitute for knowing that you've done a fair day's work—and knowing that your supervisor knows it!

Layoffs

"Will the program result in layoffs if it reveals that there are too many people for the workload?" This is a very common fear among employees. They want to know what the company policy on this issue is.

We can explain that normal transfers, promotions, loaning of people from one department to another, borrowing work, terminations due to pregnancies, health, moving, and so on, and expansion of business and workload are going on all the time. These factors usually reduce a department staff (or increase the workload) within a very short time. In any case, the company policy is that no satisfactory employee will find himself out of a job as a result of the program. In other words, there will be no layoffs.

Unionization

Management-level people may feel that any attempt to get people to produce more work will result in bringing in a labor union. If employees were unfairly treated through any efforts on the part of management, the result could very well be an attempt to join a union. However, this need not be the case.

The use of fair and realistic standards is an advantage to both employees and management, not only where no organized union is in place, but also in a union environment. In fact, if current predictions that labor unions will make significant inroads in offices are correct, having well-defined standards in place prior to an attempt to organize would be highly advantageous, particularly for management.

TECHNIQUES FOR INTRODUCING THE PROGRAM

Once a decision is made to develop a formal work management program and a specific date has been set to get started, there are various techniques and approaches that can be used to announce the program to the various levels of staff within the organization. It is important to anticipate how the program will be perceived by each level of the organization. If we've done our homework so that we are acutely sensitive to the mood of the people, we are ready to explain all aspects.

Preliminary Surveys

There are a number of approaches that can be employed successfully. One is the use of an attitude survey prior to the development of a program.

The survey can be formal or informal. A formal survey should be handled by a professional consultant or, at the very least, someone with previous survey experience. This type of survey can be helpful in addressing key issues on the minds of people at all levels of the organization.

An informal survey can also be very helpful. This is usually done by interviewing people at each level of the organization. The method used by the authors is to first interview each member of senior management, including the president, the chief executive officer, and the chairman, then representative members of middle management and supervisors to give them an opportunity to provide input for the design of the program and the formulation of program objectives.

Introducing the Program Where a Previous Program Failed

If the company had a program previously, we ask each individual what he or she liked and disliked about that program. It won't take long before a clear picture is formed of the useful aspects of the previous program and of the aspects that served more to irritate than to help. For example, positive responses might include:

We had information on performance.

We had a way to determine how many people were needed.

We were able to cut costs.

We had production figures (work counts) that were useful in planning.

The negatives might include:

We didn't have confidence in the standards.

There was too much record keeping.

We did not understand the reports.

The quality of work suffered.

In designing a program with this type of feedback, we would ensure that we accomplish these goals:

- Select a technique that is accurate and consistent and provides good documentation.
- Train a staff of analysts to keep the standards up to date.
- Keep the record keeping to an absolute minimum.
- Provide better orientation and training in what the reports revealed and how this information could be used to make improvements.
- Develop a quality assurance program along with the standards.

The next step would be to communicate to the staff the fact that the previous program was not successful because of the disadvantages noted, and that the new program will overcome these disadvantages.

Introducing the Program Where There Was No Previous Program

If this is to be the first attempt at a productivity improvement program, we try to determine what style of management is currently in use. We ask each individual at the various levels of management and supervision:

"What tools are you presently using to get the job done?"

"Where, in your opinion, is the greatest potential area for cost savings within the company?"

"What would you like to have in the way of better tools to work with?"

"What do you not want to see happen with a new program?"

From these interviews we generally get such comments as:

"I feel that the greatest area for cost savings within this organization is better management of time and people."

"I feel we need to know what is expected of us and our people, and how we or they are doing in relation to what is expected."

"I feel we could improve our methods and procedures."

"I feel we need better training for our supervisors and managers."

"I do not want to see staff reductions forced too quickly."

"I do not want to see too much pressure put on people to improve performance."

Here again, the new program can be perceived by people at all levels of the organization as an honest and reasonable effort on the part of management to improve the effectiveness of the operations of the company. It is management's method of correcting unfavorable situations.

Written Notices

A month or two prior to the official start of a program is a good time to start preparing the staff. An occasional memo on the subject of productivity can be put on the company bulletin boards each week.

Another method would be to have articles on the subject of productivity or the need for improvement in productivity published in company periodicals or publications. These can be effective in shaping attitudes on the subject of productivity improvement.

Introductory Letters and Memos

The normal procedure for announcing a companywide program involves two letters or memos: one addressed to all officers, department heads, and supervisors, and another addressed to all employees.

Here is an example of a memo to all officers, department heads, and supervisors. It covers the purpose of the program, its objectives, how the program works, the benefits to different levels of people, and who is involved in it. This memorandum will be further explained in the introductory meetings held with each level of management.

MEMO TO: All Officers, Department Heads, and Supervisors

In our continuing emphasis on supervisory development and effective management, we will announce a new program next week called project PRIDE.

PRIDE stands for *Performance Recognition*
for *Individual Development and Evaluation*

PRIDE is designed to provide all levels of management with a comprehensive means of evaluating and supervising production. This program is based on studies to be made by our own analysts working with the supervisors and department managers throughout the company. These analysts will be carefully selected from our own staff and will be specially trained by a management consultant from the ABC Company. They are professional consultants in work management with techniques developed particularly for our industry.

Our objectives are:
1. To help supervisors and department managers to be even more effective in meeting goals and objectives.
2. To help employees work smarter—not harder—by improving methods and procedures.
3. To improve the accuracy and timeliness of the service we provide to our customers.
4. To reduce administrative costs wherever feasible.

How it works:
1. Our analysts will be trained by _____of ABC Company in the most advanced methods of analyzing, evaluating, and supervising production.
2. Supervisory and management personnel will also receive classroom instruction in the approach and techniques used to install the program.
3. The analysts will work closely with the supervisors in studying each unit. The analysts will write detailed descriptions of the methods used and review each step with the supervisor.
4. The analysts and the supervisor will make changes in the methods employed which will improve the efficiency of processing the work before establishing new standards.
5. A simple reporting procedure will be developed to provide meaningful management information to supervisors in regard to performance and staffing requirements.

Benefits to supervisors:
1. Provides information to objectively and fairly evaluate the performance of each employee.
2. Determines proper staffing of departments.
3. Helps to better handle peak loads.
4. Aids in job training.
5. Provides an objective means for recognizing the achievements of all supervisors on an equitable basis.

Benefits to employees:
1. Provides a means for fairly recognizing the contribution of each employee.
2. Provides a means for distributing work on an equitable basis.
3. Makes it easier for employees to do a better job.
4. Gives employees a sense of pride in knowing they are doing a good job.

When it will begin:
Our analysts, _____, _____, _____, and _____, will begin training on _____ and will be ready to start work in selected areas on _____.

It is estimated that 80 percent of the jobs in the company can benefit from this type of analysis. Therefore, most departments can expect to participate in the program some time during the next twelve months.

Supervisors and managers in other companies who have participated in this program have found it to be a valuable tool. We firmly believe that you will too. In the coming weeks and months, as your department becomes involved, you will receive much more information on the work management program. If you do have any questions at this time, contact the Personnel Director. Thank you for your cooperation in this important corporate effort.

John J. Jones
President

An example of a memo to all employees follows. It covers the purpose and objectives of the program, and essentially what the program is designed to do and what it is not intended to do. Particularly, it addresses the matter of job security by assuring the staff that no one will lose his or her job as a result of the program. The memo or letter usually carries the signature of the president and is distributed in connection with or after the meetings discussed next.

MEMO TO: All Employees

It is a pleasure for me to announce the beginning of a very important new program at the _____. The program, to be known as PRIDE, will affect you and the way your unit or department operates.

> PRIDE stands for *Performance Recognition*
> for *Individual Development and Evaluation.*

Our greatest asset is our people, and without the energy, ability, and pride you bring to work each day, nothing could be accomplished. We constantly try to provide the best working conditions possible and are continually looking for ways to more effectively serve our customers. We believe this program will help us do that.

We all want to know what is expected of us and how we are performing. One of the goals of project PRIDE is to enable each employee to know how well he or she is doing, and to be recognized for performance on a more objective basis. At the same time, through your help, the program should make it easier for each employee to do a good job. The results should be better service for our customers and more job satisfaction for our employees.

This will be an ongoing _____ program designed for us, to be operated and administered by us. It is expected to take a full year to fully implement the program throughout the company. Four management analysts will be selected from our staff and will be given an intensive training program in the techniques to be used. The training is being conducted by Mr. _____, an experienced consultant from ABC Company, which specializes in programs of this nature.

Following their training, the analysts will be working with you to study the methods in your department and the functions of your job. All supervisors will be thoroughly trained in the concepts underlying the PRIDE program. Once the program is under way, supervisors will attend a series of classroom briefings. Thereafter, an analyst will interview you as to what you do, how you do it, and why you do it. It will be appropriate at that time for you to ask any questions regarding PRIDE that you may have, either of the analyst or of your supervisor.

Also, your suggestions and ideas will be most welcome. The department analyst may recommend to you that your supervisor improve ways of doing things. The analysts will do this only after thorough discussion with you and your supervisor. It is hoped that this detailed attention to the work we do will enable us to do our job in a more productive manner.

Our company is moving forward. We wish to grow in a controlled and orderly fashion. The results of this program hopefully will give us objective criteria for appropriate staffing levels. Should improvements in procedures and efficiency indicate some adjustments in our present staffing, this will be accomplished through the normal process of transfer or promotion, plus the result of normal voluntary terminations of employees. I would like to firmly set your mind at rest should there be any concern on this matter. No one will lose his or her job because of this program.

In the coming weeks and months, you will receive much more information about PRIDE. Meanwhile, I hope that you will give this important program your wholehearted, enthusiastic support and cooperation.

John J. Jones
President

Introductory Meetings

Once the program has been approved, a consultant selected (if one is to be used), a management coordinator appointed, a team of analysts named, and a date set to start the training of analysts, you are ready to formally announce the program to the staff. Occasionally, as stated earlier, we encounter management groups that feel they do not want to make a big deal out of a program and simply want to get started in one or two departments. This approach can very easily lead to problems if the people misunderstand what is being done.

To avoid misunderstandings, and to present the program as clearly and positively as possible, a series of introductory meetings should be held, to coincide with the distribution of written announcement material.

The day designated for announcing the program is usually the first day of the training program for analysts. It's a good idea to meet with the senior management group of the company first thing in the morning. The typical sequence of events covered in this presentation is as follows:

1. The president makes a formal announcement of the program and explains how the company will benefit.
2. The president introduces the person designated as management coordinator for the program, or the principal from the management consulting firm engaged.
3. The management coordinator or the management consultant
   - Explains the various aspects of the program and distributes the memo to officers, department heads, and supervisors.
   - Reads the memo to all employees that will be distributed to the staff that afternoon. If senior management can anticipate any questions that would be difficult to answer, now would be a good time to bring them up.
   - Introduces the analysts who will be a part of the project.
   - Introduces the consultant (if any) who is assigned to the project.
4. The consultant (if one is used) explains his or her role in the program.
5. A question-and-answer period follows.

After this meeting there will be repeat sessions with the middle-management group and, after that, with the supervisors.

At this point in the day, all supervisory management personnel will be apprised of the program and the respective roles played by the participants. The letters or memos to employees can be distributed. If any employee has a question, he or she can ask the supervisor, who should be able to answer it after the orientation session.

Each supervisor may wish to conduct a special meeting with his or her staff of employees and distribute the memo from the president at that time.

There will be other meetings with the employees when an analyst is eventually assigned to a particular department or section. This will be covered in subsequent chapters.

CHAPTER

The AOC
Work Management System

MANY PEOPLE EVALUATE THE SUCCESS of a work management or productivity improvement program by the results achieved. "What is the bottom line?" they will say. But is that really what we are after? Of course, nobody can deny that a program resulting in first-year savings of 30 percent in payroll costs is successful. However, there are other factors involved.

If employees or supervisors do not like the program, it is certain to be short-lived. Although significant results may be achieved early in the program, the gains may be maintained only over the first year or two. On the other hand, if people at all levels like the program, the program will become a permanent part of the company's operations, and the benefits will be realized year after year. For this reason, we must measure success by how the people feel about it. If supervisors and managers like it, they are likely to use it. If they use it, they will achieve results. If employees like the program, it almost certainly is because they see themselves benefiting directly from it. And, if they like it, the program will be long-lasting.

Other factors that have a direct effect on the program are the analysts, how well the supervisors and managers understand the program, and the role played by the employee. Let us examine each of these below.

THE ROLE OF WORK MANAGEMENT ANALYSTS

The analyst must be able to respond to technical training and be well equipped to handle the direct relationships with supervisors and employees. Some say it is a very unusual combination that we look for—the ability to do very detailed work and an outgoing personality that puts people at ease, wins their confidence, and develops their enthusiasm.

Qualifications

The qualifications required depend on the way the job is structured. If the program is designed to improve methods and procedures as well as to develop engineered work standards to measure individual or group performance, the following factors should be taken into consideration:

Personality	Integrity
Education	Analytical ability
Communication skills	Mathematical skills
Imagination	Sense of urgency
Intelligence	

Personality. The analyst must be naturally able to make people feel comfortable and put them at ease. He or she must be enthusiastic about the work and how the program can help people at each level of the organization.

Education. College-trained people are usually selected to launch a new program. Once the program has proved successful, analysts with somewhat lesser skills can maintain the program. Many firms have discovered that training as a work measurement analyst is an ideal stepping stone into managerial positions.

It might also be stated that "college training or equivalent work experience" is required. This means simply that an intelligent high school graduate who has four or more years of valuable work experience can also qualify for a position as an analyst to launch a new program.

Communication skills. The analyst's job requires people who can listen to an explanation of a job and get a mental picture of how it is performed. Conversely, the analyst must be able to explain to employees what the program is about in a way that leaves no room for misunderstandings. The analyst must also be able to communicate effectively with supervisors and managers. We often hear supervisors say, "I told the analyst several times, but he was not listening."

Imagination. Call it creativity or any other name, the analyst must have the type of inquisitive mind to ask the right questions. He or she must have the type of mind that does not accept things at face value. People who do a job day in and day out often can explain it in such a way that it sounds perfectly logical. We must look for people who are imaginative enough to suggest *better* ways of doing things, or at least alternative ways.

Intelligence. Common sense may even be a better term to use. Methods and systems work is something that requires a great deal of common sense.

Integrity. This type of work requires an honest person who can accept the responsibility entrusted to him. The analyst is being trusted to develop fair and realistic standards upon which management can base decisions on such things as how well people perform their jobs and the staffing of departments.

Analytical ability. An analyst must have the ability to see a network of events from verbal descriptions and to readily determine what pieces are missing, or what information is missing so that the proper questions can be asked. This person must be able to analyze information, sort things out, and put things together in a logical and consistent manner.

Mathematical skills. This type of work does not require high-level math. "A feel for figures" would probably describe it better.

Sense of urgency. Work performed by the analysts is scheduled so that commitments can be made to management. A good analyst must be able to work under a schedule and pick up the pace if it falls behind. If a study takes too long to come to a conclusion, people begin to lose interest.

There are various methods of determining whether or not candidates possess these qualifications. A college record of grades achieved and major, minor, and outside or extracurricular activities may form a basis. The individual's own track record since leaving college also helps. Finally, there are the Analyst Selection Test and the interview method.

The Analyst Selection Test

The Robert E. Nolan Company of Simsbury, Connecticut (among others) has developed an analyst selection test for screening analyst candidates. The test covers six parts: Work experience/education, personality, logic, mathematical skills, problem-solving skills, and verbal skills. The tests are scored, and the results are plotted on the analyst selection profile (Figure 20-1). The profile indicates the candidate's likelihood of succeeding.

The numerical scales refer to the number of correct items scored on each section of the test. The bracketed portion of the profile represents the range in which ideal candidates usually fall. Thus an unusually high score is not necessarily indicative of a good candidate; it may be a sign of an overqualified candidate. People who score below the bracketed portion will have difficulty performing the job of analyst.

The Interview

The interview method is usually preceded by a general explanation of the program and the job. This can be done with a group of analyst candidates to save the time of repeating the information to each candidate individually.

The interviewer, usually a consultant, can determine the level of interest,

Figure 20-I. Analyst selection profile.

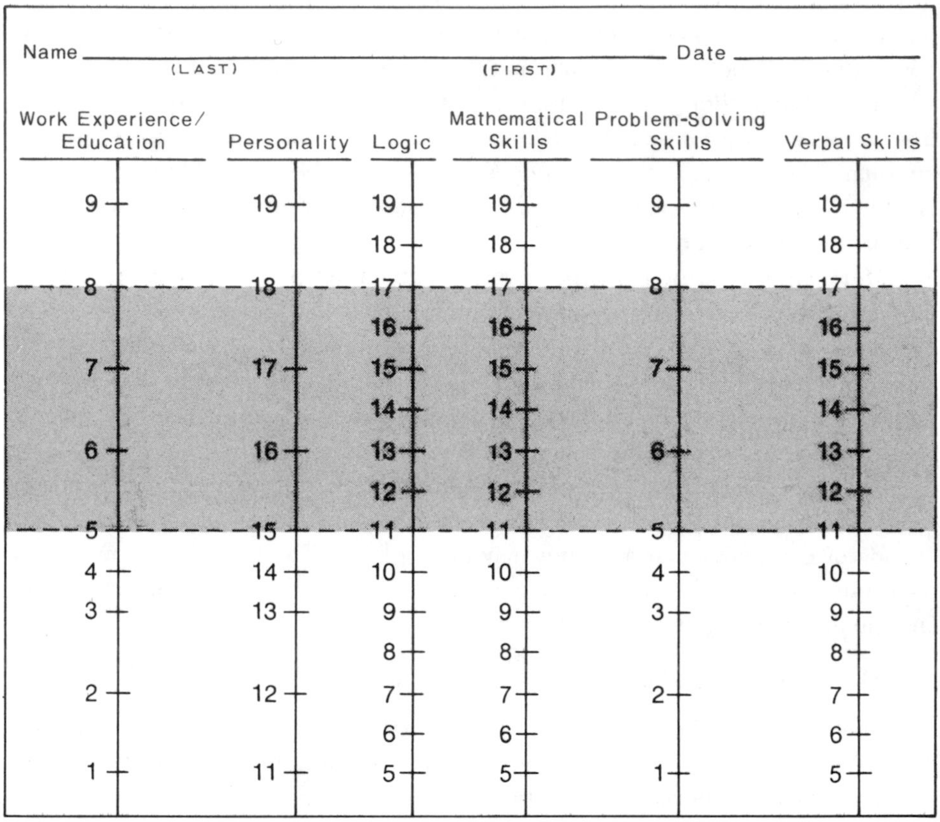

Name _____ Date _____
     (LAST)   (FIRST)

Work Experience/ Education	Personality	Logic	Mathematical Skills	Problem-Solving Skills	Verbal Skills
9	19	19	19	9	19
		18	18		18
8	18	17	17	8	17
		16	16		16
7	17	15	15	7	15
		14	14		14
6	16	13	13	6	13
		12	12		12
5	15	11	11	5	11
4	14	10	10	4	10
3	13	9	9	3	9
		8	8		8
2	12	7	7	2	7
		6	6		6
1	11	5	5	1	5

enthusiasm for the work, personality, how inquisitive the individual is, and how adept the candidate is with figures. Naturally, we are seeking people who can ask questions and get all the facts before they make a decision. Once again, we are looking for people with a good personality who are not hopelessly confused when asked, "If it takes .10 hour to type a form, how many forms should a person type in an hour?" or "What is 33 percent of 225?"

A half-hour interview is usually sufficient to determine how good the candidate is. The normal selection process is to rate all candidates on a scale of 1 (unacceptable) to 10; (outstanding). The final selection must also take into consideration questions of balance and availability. For example, if there are four divisions of a company and we are screening representative candidates from each division, it usually is not desirable to select all candidates from one division, and it is desirable to select one or more candidates from each division.

Figure 20-2. Outline of basic systems and procedures.

SESSION	SUBJECT	DURATION
1	**INTRODUCTION**	1 Day

In this session we establish the ground rules for the course, provide a brief introduction and discuss:
- The feasibility study
- Planning the project
- Scheduling the project
- Announcing the project

| 2 | **FACT GATHERING AND ANALYSIS – I** | 1 Day |

Here we define what facts must be known and explain where to go to get them. We teach solid interviewing techniques, and some basic methods of documentation and analysis, including procedural flow-charting.

| 3 | **FACT GATHERING AND ANALYSIS – II** | 1 Day |

We continue where we left off in Session 2 with additional methods of documentation and analysis, including work distribution and flexibility charts, equipment evaluation, office layout and design, forms analysis, records analysis and organizational charting and analysis.

| 4 | **GAINING APPROVAL FOR AND IMPLEMENTING THE SYSTEM** | 1 Day |

An outstanding project will be ignored if its results are not approved and implemented. We walk the analyst through this process, stressing how to sell ideas to users by using visual aids and other persuasion devices. Then class participants complete a comprehensive case study that ties everything they have learned together in preparation for the final exam.

| 5 | **IMPLEMENTATION AND AUDIT** | 1 Day |

The audit phase of a project is often overlooked, thus reducing the system effectiveness. We teach the analyst how to identify potential problems before they surface, correct them and ensure that they do not develop again. The session ends with an examination.

5 Days

ANALYST TRAINING

The training program for analysts must be tailored to the needs of the work measurement program. The extent of training in manual systems or methods and procedures must take into consideration the backgrounds of the candidates selected as analysts, as well as what the program is designed to achieve.

Generally, the first five days of full-time training are devoted to basic systems and procedures (see Figure 20-2 for an example of a typical five-day-course outline). The work management portion of the training program usually consists of ten days of full-time training (see Figure 20-3) covering the following:

Work management theory. This involves what work management is and how it affects each level of the organization. Case studies are used to convey why supervisors need work management and how they can use work management to carry out their responsibilities. An analyst must understand what standards are and why they are advantageous to everyone concerned.

Work measurement theory. The analyst should be familiar with all the techniques of work measurement and the advantages and disadvantages of each. Naturally, emphasis should be placed on the primary technique selected.

Study procedure. This is the step-by-step procedure for conducting a study. It is covered in detail in Chapter 21.

Figure 20-3. Outline of analyst training course.

SESSION	SUBJECT	DURATION
1	**INTRODUCTION TO OFFICE WORK MANAGEMENT**	1 Day
	This involves what we call the theory of Advanced Office Controls. It provides analysts with a solid appreciation of work management and the impact on all levels of the organization.	
2	**METHODS AND PROCEDURES ANALYSIS**	1 Day
	This is a full day on all aspects of a work study program including Advanced Job Design, work simplification, steps to improving methods, procedures and systems in a dynamic organization.	
3	**METHODS-TIME MEASUREMENT APPRECIATION**	1 Day
	Here we cover all of the basic motions performed by the human body, and provide the analysts with confidence in the original research and training in basic motion pattern construction.	
4	**ADVANCED OFFICE CONTROLS**	1 Day
	This includes an introduction to AOC, and training and practice exercises for the first seven sections of AOC.	
5	**ADVANCED OFFICE CONTROLS**	1 Day
	Here we cover the next seven sections of AOC with appropriate practice exercises.	
6	**ADVANCED OFFICE CONTROLS**	1 Day
	We will cover the last four sections of AOC including the development of time standards for office equipment, the writing of Task Outlines, and proper documentation of standards with AOC.	
7 & 8	**PRACTICE TASKS WITH AOC**	2 Days
	The analysts will have practice, under a controlled situation, in developing time standards with AOC. This includes tasks involving mental decisions and thought process time.	
9	**REPORTING TECHNIQUES AND REMEDIAL ACTION**	1 Day
	Various methods of reporting and how the information is used to make improvements.	
10	**FINAL PREPARATION AND AOC EXAMINATION**	1 Day
	Fundamentals of work management and review. AOC examination and review.	
	TOTAL	10 Days

Reporting techniques. The analysts must be able to see the end product of the management information system they are to design. A variety of approaches to presenting work management data to management should be presented for discussion, ranging from very simple controls to very detailed information.

Remedial action. The analysts are trained to use work management data to make improvements. From this, they can work with supervisors to help them.

SUPERVISOR ORIENTATION

A supervisor orientation program is usually conducted for first-line supervisors whose areas are currently being studied. Typically, eight two-hour sessions are conducted at the rate of one or two sessions per week. The last session is usually conducted during the week prior to putting the unit on standards. To allow for maximum participation, the classes are limited to eight to ten supervisors. See Figure 20-4 for an outline of a typical supervisor orientation program.

The success of the sessions depends on how they are conducted, how the material is presented to the supervisors, how much the supervisors enjoy the sessions, whether they are confident of all aspects of the program, and whether they feel they have learned something of value. That is a tall order. There are three prime factors necessary for this to be achieved.

First, the supervisor must be motivated from the start. This can be achieved by ensuring that the program is announced by the chief executive officer as an important program that will benefit the entire organization. Also, a few well-chosen words from the supervisor's immediate superior concerning the importance of the supervisor orientation program will go a long way toward making supervisors start the course with an open mind.

Second, the material presented must have some substance. The program must be perceived by the supervisor as well-planned, well-organized, and proven to be successful. It should involve participatory role-playing sessions, case studies, practice exercises, practice problems, and the like.

Third, the instructor must possess a certain amount of charisma—call it personality or charm—to address the supervisors on their level and present the material as interestingly and enjoyably as possible. The instructor must be able to set the climate for discussion of all aspects of the program.

The objectives of a supervisor orientation program are to explain the objectives and mechanics of the program, to develop supervisors' confidence in the techniques used, and to show the supervisors how to use the program to carry out their responsibilities.

The eight formal sessions are conducted while the study is taking place. This means that all the knowledge the supervisor gains is before the fact—before any live results are seen. This dramatizes the need for some follow-up supervisory orienta-

Figure 20-4. Outline of supervisor orientation seminar.

SESSION	SUBJECT	DURATION
1	**INTRODUCTION TO OFFICE WORK MANAGEMENT**	2 Hours
	This session lays the groundwork for the program through a discussion of common supervisory problems and the management tools available. We also cover the objectives of a formal work management program, how these objectives are achieved, and the benefits to each level of the organization.	
2	**FACT GATHERING & ANALYSIS**	2 Hours
	Here we explain how a study is conducted from A to Z. We cover the interviews with employees as well as define tasks and basic methods to be employed.	
3	**AOC & OTHER MEASURING TECHNIQUES**	2 Hours
	A look at some of the techniques used to analyze and measure office work, with an appreciation of MTM and the way we set standards with Advanced Office Controls. Our objective is to develop confidence in the standards developed with Advanced Office Controls.	
4	**WORK SIMPLIFICATION**	2 Hours
	An introduction to work simplification in the office. Emphasis is on the practical approach to the simplification process.	
5	**THE REPORTING SYSTEM**	2 Hours
	This includes an analysis of the reporting system, how the information is gathered and summarized, and how it is used to make improvements in the departments.	
6	**REMEDIAL ACTION**	2 Hours
	This session deals with the goal-setting procedure and how the supervisors use the information provided to solve problems, improve performance, and improve the utilization of time and people.	
7	**USING WORK MANAGEMENT DATA FOR EFFECTIVE PLANNING**	2 Hours
	A primer on planning workload and expenses through the use of work management data.	
8	**GUEST SPEAKER FROM MANAGEMENT**	2 Hours
	Reinforcement of the objectives and responsibilities involved, and a discussion of various aspects of the program.	
		16 Hours

tion after standards are installed. The typical approach is to schedule a follow-up session one month after installation and once every three months after that. The purpose of follow-up sessions is to discuss results and how further improvements can be made.

One approach that has resulted in favorable feedback is to have a supervisor as a

Figure 20-5. Outline of management orientation seminar.

SESSION	SUBJECT	DURATION
1	**INTRODUCTION TO THE PROGRAM**	1 Hour
	Explanation of why the use of work management is a more responsible, scientific, and professional way to run a business. We cover program objectives and techniques used to train each level of supervision and management to use the program effectively.	
2	**MEASURING TECHNIQUES**	1 Hour
	Overview to acquaint top management with the paperwork simplification process, and the techniques used to establish time standards.	
3	**REPORTING TECHNIQUES**	1 Hour
	Analysis of the reporting system at each level (employee, supervisor, manager, executive), and how this information is used by supervisors and managers to make improvements. Question-and-answer period.	
4	**MANAGEMENT'S ROLE IN REMEDIAL ACTION**	1 Hour
	Explanation of how improvements are made, and the important role management plays in order to get the maximum benefits. Question-and-answer period.	
5	**ANALYSIS OF RESULTS**	1 Hour
	Discussion and display of actual results. Question-and-answer period.	
		5 Hours

guest speaker. The supervisor selected should be one who has achieved a great deal with the program. The supervisor can share some of the special techniques that he or she uses to get results.

MANAGEMENT ORIENTATION

The management orientation seminar is usually conducted for senior management. This includes the chief executive officer and everybody who reports to him. Typically, the seminar consists of five one-hour sessions at the rate of one session per month. See Figure 20-5 for an example of a typical management orientation program.

The format for each session is usually a half-hour presentation on the main topic, followed by an oral progress report (five minutes). The remainder of the period usually is used for questions and answers and discussion of the current status of the program.

These sessions are extremely important for several reasons. Management support for the program is enhanced as a greater understanding of the objectives and mechanics of the program is gained. Also, management is given an opportunity, as the program is being developed, to discuss how reports are designed, how employees and supervisors are affected, and how various enhancements to the program can be developed. Furthermore, these sessions are designed to update progress and discuss program problems.

REPORTING TECHNIQUES

The various reporting techniques are covered in Chapter 22. Our discussion here will be limited to indicating the importance of designing the reporting system properly and showing how the reporting system fits into the AOC work management system. The reporting system involves four levels:

1. Record keeping at the employee and supervisory levels.
2. A reporting system for supervisors.
3. A reporting system for middle management.
4. A reporting system for top management.

Essentially, what is required is a method of collecting statistics on the amount of work done and how employees spend their time, and comparing this information with standards in order to prepare performance, workload, and staffing reports for supervisors. A summary of this information must be prepared for each department for middle management, and a further summary of all departments for top management.

The main problem is to decide how much information and what kind of information supervisors and managers really need and want. This will determine the amount of record keeping required. At one extreme, management might want to know how well each employee performs on each task. This would involve the recording of detailed work counts as well as a record of how much time each employee devoted to each task—a great deal of record keeping. The opposite end of the spectrum would be for management to want simple controls to determine overall performance by department and the required number of employees for the workload. This would involve a minimum in recording of work counts.

The main issue, however, is not how much or how little record keeping is involved, but rather what information supervisors and managers really want, and how much they are willing to pay, in terms of time required for record keeping, to get this information. The serious problems in attitudes result from requiring people to do work for which they see no value. If you tell a person he needs a great deal of information about his department, but he does not see the value in it, he will resent it if he is required to do a lot of work to gather the statistical information.

The solution is simply to give supervisors and managers a thorough appreciation of work management as a management tool and then get their input as to the level of detail they want. In other words, give them what they want rather than what you think they should have, and there will be no problem.

FULL MANAGEMENT SUPPORT

Full management support is an essential ingredient for a successful program. But mere approval of the program is not sufficient. Rather, active management support is needed.

First, management must show an interest in the program and communicate its interest to all levels of the organization. This is the very least an executive can do when a formal commitment in resources has been made.

Second, management must expect that improvements can be made and will come about, and communicate this expectation to all levels of the organization. No one should feel, "Well, I know I run a good department, so there is no room for improvement here." Everyone can improve. If an executive is not convinced that the program will improve things, he or she has the responsibility to check with other companies to learn of the results achieved by the program and/or to get further details from the individuals recommending the program.

Finally, management support involves patience—not expecting too much too soon. The people who have to do the work—the supervisors and managers—must be convinced that the information they are getting is accurate. They need time to make adjustments in work assignments and work schedules, and they need time to work with low performers. They are quite naturally concerned about increasing flexibility by cross-training and about periods of high absenteeism. Work management frequently involves a change in the style of management. And, as with any type of change, there is always a period of adjustment.

What happens when a program is being installed and management is not showing the required interest? What can be done when management loses confidence in a program and merely tolerates it? Or, what happens if a management group feels that visible high-level support is not necessary? ("Just get the program in and work with the people and it will be successful.")

This type of situation can be very frustrating to someone charged with getting a program installed. There are no easy answers other than to bring to management's attention the necessity for top-level involvement. Recommend periodic management orientation sessions, even after the initial formal management orientation sessions, to bring to management's attention the actual and potential improvement possibilities, and the steps necessary to achieve them.

COMMUNICATIONS

Full, open communications concerning all aspects of the program should be forever ongoing. This can include developing a booklet for employees—especially new employees who were not on board when the program was introduced—that covers the employees' role in the program, rules, benefits, and so on.

A *supervisor's manual* should also be developed so that supervisors have a handy reference when questions arise Frequently this is distributed as part of the training materials during the formal supervisor orientation program. Weekly newsletters or monthly magazines published by the company should include articles on various stages of the program development, special achievements and accomplishments, and the like, to keep interest high.

The above-mentioned methods, together with supervisor and management orientations, follow-up sessions with supervisors and management, and presentations to employees before and after the study, all serve to form an effective communications network.

METHODS AND STANDARDS

There is a formula that goes: the one best method plus accurate work measurement equals accurate standards and effective results. Soundly engineered work standards based on good, sound methods and procedures form a solid basis for an effective work management program.

SUMMARY

We have discussed the AOC work management system. The key ingredients for a successful and long-lasting program are:

> Proper selection and training of in-house analysts.
> Well-designed supervisor orientation sessions.
> Well-designed management orientation sessions.
> Full top-management support.
> Good communications at all levels.
> A carefully designed reporting system.
> Accurate work standards based on good methods and procedures.

If these guidelines are followed, the program will provide lasting results while maintaining harmonious staff relations.

CHAPTER

How to Conduct a Study

THE VARIOUS STEPS INVOLVED in conducting a work management study using a predetermined time system are highly dependent on the objectives of the program. As pointed out in previous chapters, a well-defined set of objectives communicated properly to all levels of the organization will make it clear to all concerned precisely what will be a part of the study and what will not. Readers utilizing other measurement techniques may wish to modify some steps in the procedure discussed here.

There are limitations of the study that are related directly to the skills, experience, and training of the analysts commissioned to install the program. These factors have a definite bearing on how far the analysts can go in improving productivity. For example, light, heat, ventilation, noise, decoration, and color schemes may directly affect productivity. However, many of these factors require special training to evaluate and therefore are not normally a part of a study.

Factors such as job duties and responsibilities of supervisors and managers may well be considered a part of the study. However, these are sensitive matters and must be explained in advance so that everyone involved understands that recommendations for organizational change will be a part of the study. Office layout and office equipment are also important considerations. They have a great impact on workflow and job design and are normally included.

There is a general outline available that allows a great deal of flexibility depending on how a study is desired. This outline is a 13-step approach that has proved highly successful in thousands of applications. Some steps are small and may appear to be relatively unimportant, but they should not be overlooked. Each step is an integral part of the communications network and/or investigatory procedure. Here is the outline:

1. Assign analyst to department.
2. Meet with supervisors.
3. Make presentation to employees.
4. Interview employees
5. Analyze job design.
6. Write task outlines.
7. Obtain supervisor approval.
8. Develop standards.
9. Develop controls.
10. Hold installation meeting with employees.
11. Install controls.
12. Set goals.
13. Use feedback and control information.

Step 1: Assign Analyst to Department

As pointed out previously, the analyst group is a team. As in any team, each member may have different skills and often play very different roles. The instructor who trains the analysts is usually able to consider the profile of each in terms of personality, temperament, attention to detail, and technical knowledge of business functions, so that these factors can be considered when assigning analysts to departments. It is only natural to expect that some analysts have greater ability than others. Some have a more outgoing personality than others. Some have developed greater confidence than others. Some are much more persuasive than others.

The departments or units to be studied also vary quite a bit. Some are very technical, such as underwriting and claims in an insurance company, and some perform work that is quite easy to understand, such as filing and typing. One would naturally try to match the skills of each analyst to the appropriate unit.

Some analysts are more creative than others. If a department appears to have very poor methods and procedures, we would try to assign a more imaginative analyst. The analyst who has not yet achieved a full level of confidence should be assigned the more straightforward units to study.

Another consideration is the personality of the supervisor or manager of the unit to be studied. If the individual has a reputation for being difficult to deal with or being resistant to change, it is logical to assign an analyst with demonstrated persuasive abilities.

A typical company might consist of twenty different departments, sections, or units with an average of four to twelve employees assigned to each. A typical analyst group might consist of four analysts—two males and two females; one extremely creative, two average, and one lacking in creative ability; one with great attention to detail, two average, and one who lacks attention to detail; one with a very outgoing personality, two with average to good personalities, and one who might be considered shy or retiring. Each compensates for his or her weakness by being exceptional in one or more other areas.

Under these hypothetical conditions—four analysts and twenty units to study and bring under control—each analyst will study five units. The skills and temperaments of the analysts must be matched with the complexities and variables found within the departments to produce the best results.

Step 2: Meet with Supervisors

When a department or section has been selected to be studied and the relevant layers of management have agreed to participate in the program, a meeting is held with the highest-level manager, middle-management person, unit or first-level supervisor, the analyst to be assigned, and the consultant or work management program manager. The purpose of the meeting is to introduce the analyst to the user department management, review the purpose and objectives of the program and the study, and arrange for the supervisor to attend the supervisor orientation seminar, the middle-management individual to attend a middle-management orientation seminar, and the senior management individual to attend the senior-management orientation seminar. These orientation seminars on the work management program are started before the analyst actually begins the study so that supervisory management personnel have a preliminary understanding of what the program and study procedures involve.

The consultant or work management program manager will want to arrange a method of keeping each level of line management informed on the progress of the study and to set up a method of getting together periodically to discuss problem situations.

The supervisor and the analyst can meet privately to discuss further details of the unit. The analyst is interested in learning as much as possible about the primary functions of the unit, its secondary and tertiary functions, and the conditions under which work is performed. They will discuss the personnel assigned in terms of tenure, level of training, problem situations, and situations which may require a special amount of tact and diplomacy. The analyst will want to review records pertaining to overtime, borrowed or outside services, open personnel requisitions, available production records, and the current organization charts. They will also discuss how to handle the introduction of the analyst to the department personnel.

Step 3: Make Presentation to Employees

All the employees in the unit to be studied are assembled for a ten- to fifteen-minute introduction to the program and the analyst. The supervisor and/or higher-level line management personnel usually say a few words about the program and the forthcoming study. The supervisor introduces the analyst, who explains the purpose of the study, how the study will be conducted, how the information will be used, and how each level of the organization—particularly the employees—will benefit. The meeting is then opened for a question-and-answer period. An example of a first presentation to employees follows. (It should be emphasized that the presentation should be spontaneous and reflect the personality of the analyst.)

Opening Remarks
Hi, I'm _____. As most of you know I work here at _____ in the _____ department. I've been selected to work on the team which is setting up the _____ program, and more important to you, I've been assigned to work in your department. You've all read the introduction from _____'s letter explaining the program and the need to develop more accurate ways of planning our work so we can better serve our customers.

How I'll Conduct the Study
In order to meet these goals, we will be studying the work that you do, determining what work is required, and the easiest way to do it. The best way to gather this information will be to talk to the people actually doing the work, namely you.

First, I'll want a list of all the jobs you do and how often they're done. Then I'll be talking to you about the forms you use, and how the job is done in general, and I'll probably want to watch you process one or two items of each type. From this information I'll study each job and find the easiest way to do it. I will prepare a task outline, which will document the way I think is best. Your supervisor will review and approve it if it is acceptable. Once I have your supervisor's approval, I will develop a standard for the job. The standard is developed from data specifically designed for clerical work. A standard is a measure of time which tells how long a task should take when performed by an average, well-trained employee.

Following standard development, you will be asked to record the volume of work you do and, in general, how you spend your time.

I'll be discussing the details of the reporting at a later meeting.

What Will Management Do with Reports?
The program objectives are to:
1. Make an analysis of work and establish the easiest way to do it, and to document these procedures.
2. Provide supervisors and managers with a tool to help them to budget effectively, and schedule the department's work so that it may be processed efficiently.
3. Determine the proper staffing of the department on the basis of the work being performed.

What's In It for You, the Employee?
Through use of the reports, your contribution to the organization will be recognized. You and

your supervisor will be evaluated objectively. Work will be more evenly distributed, resulting in better service to the customer, and at a lower cost.

The program is not intended as a speedup, nor will you be overburdened with additional work. This is an honest effort on the part of the company to improve its effectiveness through better planning, elimination of unnecessary work, and improvement of methods.

Conclusion

I want to make it clear that no one will be out of a job as a result of the program. If we find that in some departments there are too many employees for a given work volume, normal turnover or mutually agreeable transfers to equal or better jobs will be used to adjust staff size. Conversely, some departments will be understaffed, and they too will have their staff adjusted to reflect workload. We are striving in all cases to balance staff and workload.

Everyone stands to benefit, including the company, which will mean more growth and greater job opportunities for all of you.

I will be talking to each of you individually, but in the meantime, let me answer any questions you might have.

It is extremely important for the analyst to make a good impression during the presentation. How the employees perceive the program, and the study, from the presentation will be difficult to change. Therefore, a great deal of preparation is required. A rehearsal presentation is usually given by each analyst to a test group and appropriately critiqued.

Step 4: Interview with Employees

There are two types of interviews that the analyst conducts. The first is a general interview to determine *what* tasks are done, how often these tasks are done, how the work flows, and some idea as to the volume of work. The second type is an in-depth interview to learn *how* each task is performed.

The interviews are an opportunity for the analyst to build the confidence of the employees in the program and the analyst. Each interview should start with the supervisor introducing the analyst to the employee. The interview should be a pleasurable experience for both interviewer and interviewee. The analyst usually guides the interview from the social amenities through the fact-gathering stage, ending with eliciting any questions the employee may have. The analyst will avoid listening to gossip or backstabbing comments about the supervisors, other employees, and managers.

The primary tool used by the analyst in the general interview is the task list described in detail in Chapter 7. The analyst interviews each employee in the unit and fills out a task list for each employee, starting with the major tasks or tasks that occupy the most time of the employee. At this stage the analyst is not interested in how the tasks are done but merely what tasks are done.

The general interview should involve a five- to ten-minute session with each employee. Even in situations where a large number of employees perform the same identical function, it is important to interview every employee. If the department is very large and many employees perform the same tasks, it is acceptable to interview employees in small groups of three or four.

Once a task list is developed for each employee, these lists are reviewed with the supervisor in case employees inadvertently omitted tasks or overstated their jobs. The final step is to draw up a work distribution chart (also covered in Chapter 7) and review it with the consultant or the work management program manager. Preliminary recommendations for potential changes in workflow are discussed at this stage.

The analyst now has a list of all the tasks in the unit, in order of importance. The analyst can generally be at this stage within the first couple of days in the department. It is at this point that the analyst and the program leader discuss the schedule and agree on how long the study should take. For example, here is a simple formula for scheduling the analyst's time:

If heavy attention to methods is desired:

$$A + B + \tfrac{1}{2}C = \text{days required}$$

If minimum attention to methods is desired:

$$\frac{A + B + \tfrac{1}{2}C}{2} = \text{days required}$$

where A = number of employees in the unit
B = number of tasks in the unit
C = number of standards to be developed

Using an example of a unit with ten employees performing twenty different tasks, the study would thus require

8 weeks if heavy attention to methods was required, because:

$$A + B + \tfrac{1}{2}C = 40 \text{ days}$$

4 weeks if minimal attention to methods was required, because:

$$\frac{A + B + \tfrac{1}{2}C}{2} = 20 \text{ days}$$

For this sample formula, there should be a provision to add or subtract a week if:

- This is the analyst's first assignment (it may be desirable to add one week or round the number of days *up*).
- The unit is particularly complex or highly technical (it may be desirable to add one week).

- The unit involves high volume and highly repetitive tasks (it may be desirable to subtract one week or round the number of days *down*).

Now the analyst is ready for a closer examination of each task, starting with the major tasks in the unit. The phrase "in-depth interview" can be misleading in that it suggests disruption or a great amount of employee time required. There is normally little interruption in productivity during the interview, since the analyst gathers most of his information by observing employees as they perform their tasks.

For example, the analyst might say to an employee: "You mentioned that one of your tasks was to process applications. I see you have a batch there. Would you please process those as you normally would. I will observe you and take notes so that I can write up a description of the method. If there is anything you do that is not self-explanatory as you are doing it, I will question you, and you can explain it to me."

If there are five employees who perform the task, it is not necessary to interview each one in depth. The analyst usually will avoid interviewing a trainee or a person who is not totally proficient in the job. The analyst usually will interview one employee in depth and merely check the procedure with one or two others. All employees will be solicited for potential methods improvements.

Step 5: Analyze the Job Design

During these interviews the analyst can determine how employees feel about their jobs, without having his questions sound like an attitude survey. (This could lead to a gripe session, which we would want to avoid.) The analyst has an opportunity to explain some of the job enrichment factors, or lack thereof, in the work. The analyst must find out who is responsible for checking the work (or responsible for errors). How are errors made? How are they detected? How are they corrected? What can be done to eliminate errors or improve the quality of work?

The analyst analyzes the job from the standpoint of the possibility of eliminating the complete task, eliminating functions within the task, or simplifying the required work.

Step 6: Write the Task Outline

Once the analyst is convinced that the task is necessary, he writes a task outline (see Figure 21-1 for an example). The upper portion of the task outline contains the name of the task and pertinent data about the task, such as how often it is performed (daily, weekly, monthly), average batch size (average number processed at one time), average daily volume (the average number of items processed by the department per day), and equipment and forms used. The last item serves to determine the specific forms and equipment used at the time the standard was

Figure 21-I. Task outline.

		SYMBOL EC	TASK NO. 001
	PAGE 1 OF 1		
TASK ENTER CORRECTIONS		STANDARD .0054 Hours Per Correction	
REPORTING UNIT Data Entry		ANALYST CCR	EFFECTIVE DATE 12/1/99
EQUIPMENT & FORMS CRT		DAILY VOLUME 112	AVERAGE BATCH 56
Error Listing (ASET Ø10) Batch of Notices (1980-1/98) Usual Desk Supplies		ITEM COUNTED Corrections	APPROVED BY 11/30/99 INIT. DATE

STEP	DESCRIPTION
A	**Set-Up** 1. Get error listing and batch of notices from "in" basket. 2. Unband batch of notices and open error listing. 3. Read notice ID number and locate on error listing record(s) to be corrected for each notice. 4. Get ruler and align with correction on error listing.

B	**Enter Corrections**
	
	1. Key open files commands: ASET OPEN, DATBAS, FILEID=ENTR,ERRS
	
	    ENTER
	    CLEAR
	    ASETE
	
	2. From error listing key identification of record requiring correction and type of correction (Change or New):
	
	    9-digit field, 3-digit field (no spaces), and CHG or NEW
	
	3. From notice key New or Changed information, (Skip fields not changed or new).
	
	4. Key ENTER.
	
	5. Check mark on error listing each record corrected, and date stamp each notice (after new or changed information is entered).

C	**Wrap-Up** 1. Count number of corrections (records check marked) on error listing, and post number on Volume Record. 2. Band batch of notices and deliver to Control Desk. 3. Deliver error listing to supervisor.

established. A different form or different type of equipment detected during an audit a year later would justify a change in standard.

The task name usually consists of two or three words identifying the task. The first is an action verb to describe the work to be done. The second should be a noun to describe the item processed. Examples are "process applications," "type invoices," "file letters," "encode checks," and "film rejects." Where there are different types of drafts to be coded, an adjective is added, as in "code bodily injury" and "code comprehensive drafts," or "process credit card applications" and "process personal loan applications."

The lower portion of the task outline explains the method used. A common approach is to break down the task into three steps: a "setup" step, a "do" step, and a "wrap-up" step. The steps can be described in narrative form as in Figure 21-1 or in outline form with as many hierarchical levels as needed.

The task outline should describe the task rather than the person performing it. Avoid the use of pronouns and articles. Each phrase should start with an action verb.

There is a fine line between too much detail and not enough detail. Here are three examples:

Just the right amount of detail: "Get invoice, post name of purchaser and amount of purchase, fold and insert invoice in envelope, and aside to out basket."

Too much detail: "Pick up invoice from stack, pick up pencil and write on invoice the name of the purchaser and the amount of purchase. Put pencil aside and pick up invoice, fold invoice. . . ."

Not enough detail: "Get invoice, post, fold, insert, and aside."

The task outline is the major documentation for the task. If ever a standard is questioned as to its being too strict or too lax, the first step should be to review the task outline. If the task outline is correct, chances are good that the standard is correct.

Another important use of the task outline is for training new employees. It serves to describe the one best method for performing the task. The outline should be in sufficient detail to accomplish this objective as well as the need of standard setting.

Step 7: Obtain Supervisor Approval

The next step in the procedure is to present the task outline to the supervisor for approval. The supervisor evaluates the task outline to determine whether the analyst has used the proper words to describe the task, whether the method is acceptable, whether anything is missing from the description, and whether any unnecessary operations are being performed.

Figure 2I-2. Task analysis.

			Page 1 of 1	Task No. 001	
Task Enter Corrections		Step All (A, B & C)		Analyst C. C. Robitelle	
				Date 12/1/99	

AOC Code/Step	Description	TMU	Frequency	Total TMU
GLG	Error Listing and Notices	49	1	49
GRF	Notices	85	1	85
OB	Error Listing	56	1	56
RNL	Notice ID Number	27	36	972
LME	Correction on Error Listing	105	36	3,780
LVI	Notice With More Than 1 Correction	33	20	660
GMS	Ruler	44	56	2,464
KA	Open File Commands	5	34	170
KFWO	Open File Commands	6	2	12
KA	Record ID	5	12x56	3,360
RNA	Change or New	20	56	1,120
DME	Decide if Change or New	11	56	616
KA	CHG or NEW	5	12x56	3,360
KFWO	Skip Fields (5) & ENTER (1)	6	6x56	2,016
GMG	Pen	36	56	2,016
WFP	Check Mark	13	56	728
GMG	Date Stamp	36	36	1,296
PS	Stamp Notices	24	36	864
GMO	Notice	19	36	684
PC	Corrections (Records check marked)	13	56	728
GMG	Error Listing - Pages	36	3	108
S-PD	Post & Dispatch (Control Desk & Supervisor)	1,070	1	1,070

SUMMARY:

Total TMU 468	TMU + 15% Pers. & Misc. 538	Subtotal	
.0054 Hr. Per Correction	.32 Min. Per Correction	A – TOTAL TMU............	26,214
		B – AVERAGE PROCESSED ...	56
		C – TMU/ITEM (A ÷ B)........	468

Step 8: Develop Standards

The task outline is used as a basis for developing an engineered time standard with a predetermined time data system such as Advanced Office Controls. The standard is developed on a form called the *task analysis* (see Figure 21-2 for an example).

Step 9: Develop Controls

When all standards have been developed, the next step is to develop a method for collecting work counts and time distributions. The various control systems are described in detail in Chapter 22.

Step 10: Hold Installation Meeting with Employees

At this stage the analyst has been working with the supervisors and employees for a number of weeks to analyze, measure, and develop controls. Hopefully, he has developed a good rapport with everyone concerned and gained everybody's confidence, interest, and support.

Now it is time to assemble the employees to explain the results of the study and how the program will work. For each task, the time standard and the changes made in the method of reporting work counts and time distribution should be discussed. Here is an example of such a presentation:

For the past few weeks we have been working together to accomplish the goals I outlined to you in our first meeting. I am pleased to report that the assignment of determining what work has to be done and the easiest way to perform it has been accomplished. With your help, we have been able to make some changes which will make it easier to perform your assigned tasks. These changes also will benefit the company.

Each of the tasks you perform has been assigned a time value or standard, which represents the time that should be required by an average well-trained worker to complete an item of acceptable-quality work. This standard includes an allowance of 15 percent, which covers your scheduled breaks and personal needs, such as trips to the washroom, personal conversations, and buying a candy bar. It also includes miscellaneous activities which are too insignificant to measure, such as setting up your desk at the beginning of the day, sharpening pencils, answering questions, and other minor interruptions. In an average 7½-hour day, this represents over one full hour.

The record keeping required is divided into two phases. You will be responsible for recording the volume of work you do, and your supervisor will be responsible for recording time spent not processing measured work.

[I would like to pass out a Daily Activity Report and discuss each standard, with particular reference to the item to be recorded and the time allowed for processing one item. It is important that you know the standards against which you are to be measured. I should emphasize that the recording of work is now part of your job and that the time to record volumes is included in each of the standards. It is usually adequate to indicate standards in approximate minutes and seconds; for example, a standard of 1.1 minutes (.018 hour) would be explained as a minute and six seconds. Please be sure to record everything you do as accurately as possible.]

If you are unsure of what is included in a particular standard, your supervisor has a manual with copies of each task outline. Feel free to refer to these at any time.

I would also like to discuss how to record your time. You should "sign off standard" when there is no more standardized work to process, or if you are asked to process nonstandard work which has priority. Simply, the purpose of the time recording process is to advise your supervisor that you have no more work to process so he or she may assign other work or record time as "off standard."

You probably are concerned about earning a good performance. It is never necessary to rush your work or to produce a poor-quality product. The standards allow ample time to produce a quality product and in some cases include time to correct errors or recheck your work.

To earn a good performance, you should work steadily at your various tasks, completing them as soon as your normal pace allows, and then report to your supervisor for more work or to sign off standard. If you attempt to make the work you do last a given length of time, your performance will suffer. As an example, if the work you do requires 5 hours a day to complete and you, by working conscientiously, can complete it in 4½ hours, you will earn an excellent performance of 111 percent. If you try to make it last an additional 2½ hours until quitting time, your performance will only be 67 percent, which is below the minimum acceptable level. In this case your performance has suffered, not because you didn't work hard, but because there wasn't enough to do.

I'm sure that for a day or so things will be a bit confusing, but I will be here to answer any questions about standards, reporting, or procedures. Are there any questions?

Step 11: Install Controls

The first week or two on standards is called a trial period or dry run. The purpose is to allow time to work any bugs out of the reporting system, to give the employees a chance to get accustomed to reporting work counts and time distribution, and to be sure the standards have been established with the proper flexibility. Also, a standard may have been established for processing an item, where the last step of the task is to file the item. We may find during the trial period that filing is frequently done by a different employee from the one who originally processed the item. This means that the task should be analyzed as comprising two distinct phases, with two standards: process items, and file items.

Average batch sizes used during the trial period are checked for accuracy as well, since many standards are dependent on a ratio of setup and wrap-up time for an average number of items in a batch to hold up.

At the conclusion of the trial period, the results are calculated for each week separately, checked for consistency, and prepared for presentation to the supervisor. A consistency check is a way of finding problem areas. For example, if employee performance is about 62 percent each week, it is said to be consistent. An employee whose performance is 62 percent the first week and 66 percent the second week is also considered to be consistent. If, however, an employee's performance is 98 percent the first week and 46 percent the second week, we must look for something to explain the difference. Usually we find there was a misunderstanding about what was supposed to be counted. The problem may lie in the way that the standard was structured or in the frequencies that were used.

After checking out the performance results for the trial period and getting them ready for presentation to the supervisors, if everything appears proper, the standards are typed on the task outlines. The task outlines are reproduced and put in binders, and a copy is given to the supervisor of the unit.

No standard should be installed without the supervisor's approval. At the time the analyst wrote the task outline, the task outline was approved by the supervisor before the standard was developed. The standard was then based on the method described in the task outline.

When the analyst develops a standard, he discusses the time allowed with the supervisor (see the section on "Step 8"). He will present the standard in the simplest of terms. For example, the analyst might say, "The standard for processing orders is .05 hour. This is approximately three minutes and means that an employee should be able to process twenty orders an hour." If the supervisor has a problem accepting the time standard developed, the analyst will review the task outline and, if necessary, the task analysis with the supervisor.

Even if the supervisor has accepted all the standards before or after the trial period, they are never considered to be "carved in stone." Any time a supervisor has reason to doubt the accuracy of a standard, he has a right to call the analyst to discuss it. Again, the basis should be the task outline, because we generally find that if a standard is felt to be too strict, it is probably because something was left out of the task outline. If a standard is felt to be too lax, it usually is fairly simple to find some functions in the task outline that do not belong there.

Step 12: Set Goals

The concept of management by objectives (MBO) permeates this type of program. Performance goals of 85 percent or 90 percent and coverage goals of 85 percent or 90 percent are normally established within a month after the trial period. Also, standard staff—the number of employees required for the current workload—is established about the same time. Therefore, when current performance and coverage are established, goals are normally set. These factors are presented in more detail in Chapter 22.

Step 13: Provide Feedback and Control Information

This is the day-to-day operation of the program where remedial action is taken and performance brought up to and beyond expected levels.

CHAPTER

22

Reporting Techniques

IT HAS BEEN SAID that a productivity improvement program cannot achieve results by itself. Results are obtained only by management using the data generated by the program. The manner in which results are presented is sometimes as important as the material contained in the presentation. In the following sections, we will examine the purpose of various reports and some of the different styles which may be utilized to communicate program results effectively to managers.

USEFUL REPORTS

Everyone is well aware that there is a proliferation of information, some of it useful and some of it not. Those in the field of systems and procedures and work management have the responsibility to design many of the reports the organization sees each day. We should see to it that we do not add useless reports to the pile. To be useful, a report must be timely and accurate, and the cost of compiling it must be commensurate with its impact on the operating environment.

Timeliness. The information contained in a report may be useful in principle, but it must be available when it is needed, or before it is too late to take corrective action. For productivity reports, weekly or monthly issuance usually is most appropriate; with a few exceptions, greater frequency is unnecessary, and less is insufficient. Daily reports tend to become merely information reports rather than generating action. An exception is a critical production process involving high

Figure 22-I. The information pyramid.

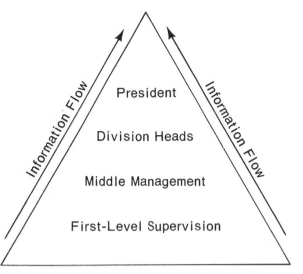

volume and high expense, or certain bank and insurance operations reports that indicate funds available for investment.

Accuracy. This is truly basic. If the report is not correct, it is useless. Whether it is merely an information report or an action-oriented report, if it is not accurate, it is worthless.

Costs versus benefits. Information gathering always has a price tag. Total cost is not the criterion for whether a report should be generated. Rather, the contribution to the bottom line through better decision making is the deciding factor. There is usually some resistance to the time and cost of data gathering for productivity reports. However, the return must be objectively reviewed.

THE INFORMATION PYRAMID

In Chapter 1, we reviewed the layers of management typically found in an organization. In effect, the information pyramid (see Figure 22-1) is a means of communicating facts concerning any aspect of a company's operations through the normal channels of responsibility. Information flows from the broader, lower levels toward the top. This can put a great deal of pressure, in terms of quantity of information, on the top levels unless information is properly managed.

At the lowest level of the organization, individual employees need information about individual transactions and details on how their performance measures up to corporate objectives. At higher levels of the organization, managers need not know the routine details of many transactions but are more concerned with unusual circumstances that may require action at their level.

Since organizations are composed of people, it goes without saying that any management information system, to be truly effective, must not only provide facts but present these facts in such a way that the intended recipient has the right information available, at the right level of detail, to carry out his responsibilities.

A management information system cannot be all things to all people. In every organization you will find "detail nuts" who want every available scrap of information pertaining to their assigned responsibilities, and "generalists" who are interested only in exceptions and overall trends. It is impossible to please all levels of the information pyramid all of the time; however, utilization of data can be greatly enhanced by an understanding of how managers at all levels view their role.

TYPES OF REPORTS

Modern data processing techniques have made it possible to create a virtually unending stream of data at the speed of light. There is so much information available in the typical company that we often lose sight of the reasons that reports are produced. Reports themselves tend to generate additional reports, and it is the rare company that knows which of the many reports produced are used by what people to accomplish which objectives, if any.

To be able to critically evaluate reports, we must first know why reports are produced. A brief examination of the four principal types of reports follows.

Informational Reports

Informational reports provide the highest level of detail. A typical informational report would list all the details of each transaction which passed through the data system. In an insurance company, for example, one type of informational report lists the policy number, the person or entity insured, the amount of insurance, the agent, and so on for each application received during a given day. In banking, a typical informational report might list account number and amount of all checks and deposits processed.

Informational reports of this type are used as a "transaction log" and may be referenced to determine the details of each type of transaction made. Due to their nature, informational reports are most often used by the lowest levels of the organization to monitor the proper acceptance or rejection of the many routine transactions performed.

Action Reports

Action reports, as implied by their title, require the recipient to take some type of action. Typically, an action report is an exception report reducing the many transactions performed to the few requiring action. Typical action reports include error lists of transactions that were not properly entered into the system and out-of-balance conditions in dual-entry bookkeeping systems. Another common type of action report signals when actual conditions exceed pre-established parameters. An example of this would be a report showing all expenses exceeding the monthly budget by more than 10 percent, or a quality control report listing errors, by type, that are present in more than a predetermined percentage of total documents processed.

As we move up through the layers of the organization, reports tend to become more action-oriented than informational, thus reducing the bulk of reports to higher levels of management to more manageable quantities.

Accountability Reports

Accountability reporting is used to monitor how well employees have carried out assigned responsibilities. Accountability reports take many forms and report on a wide variety of functions. Accountability reporting presupposes that responsibility to perform functions in a certain fashion has been placed with the employee, and it monitors how effectively those responsibilities are carried out.

In Chapter 24 we will discuss "responsibility accounting" and project schedules as a means of monitoring the performance of professional workers. Reports on how well schedules are met and how management has utilized financial resources are examples of accountability reports.

At lower levels of the organization, typical accountability reports measure how well employees measure up to work standards or how well the quality of their work compares to overall departmental goals.

Justification Reports

Justification reports are used to report on special circumstances or to take advantage of unforeseen conditions. A justification report, for example, might provide a detailed analysis of the impact of the installation of a work management program on the organization. Justification reports are rarely periodic, for by their nature, they are commissioned or developed because of changing conditions within the organization or the economic sphere in which it operates. There may be some initial confusion between action reports and justification reports. An action report by its nature demands that action be taken, while a justification report points out the consequences of following or not following a recommendation made. It is, for example, imperative that all premium dollars received by an insurance company be properly applied to each insured's accounts. An action report of acceptance or rejection of each transaction would monitor this application. By contrast the acquisition of a new copier may be desirable but not absolutely essential. The facts concerning the consequences of adding the copier would be reported in a justification report.

REPORT FREQUENCY

Report frequency is, in essence, a reflection of the time span before corrective action will be taken. Typical report frequencies are daily, weekly, monthly, quarterly, and annually.

If reports are issued on a daily basis, this signals a short-term, volatile condition where data must be constantly updated. Daily reporting is most often used for informational and action reports where the latest status is an essential part of the day-to-day operations. As an example of daily reporting, in a bank, a report of "stop payment" transactions requested by customers should be made daily so that incoming checks will not be paid. Another common example is a "rejected transaction" list that must be corrected prior to inputting the next live data.

Weekly reports of management information appear to be the most common. Management reports may be either informational or action-oriented. Weekly reporting of work management data allows for the development of reasonably accurate standards and is sufficient to enable supervisors and managers to analyze results and either recognize employees for their good performance or take remedial action.

Monthly cycles appear to be most common for reporting financial data. Here again the cycle is geared to the proper time span for taking remedial action. Typical monthly reports include responsibility accounting, scheduling of major projects, and, in some cases, work management information where the program has been in place for a number of years.

Report cycles of longer than one month are most common for financial and statistical reporting. Various government agencies require periodic financial statements for tax and other purposes, making this cycle the most popular. In any case, the cycle selected for a particular type of report should reflect the ultimate usage. Regular report cycles may be interrupted by special requests for information on a shorter-term basis. As an example, when backlog is a problem in a given area, a daily report of outstanding work will serve to emphasize the importance of reducing that backlog to an acceptable level, although the normal report cycle may be of longer duration.

REPORT FORMATS

Just as there are a variety of types of reports and frequencies of reporting, there are many different methods of presenting data, ranging from ordinary text to complex charts.

Text

Text reporting is most commonly used for justification reports. It may also be used to summarize data from other sources for the review of higher-level management. In the preparation of a text report, one should consider the volume of printed material which flows across an executive's desk during the course of a day. Some successful executives categorically refuse to read any material which is more than one page in length. They feel that if their interest can't be aroused in a page, it is unlikely that a more detailed exploration of the subject would be of any benefit. One executive reports that the shortest memo he ever received was simply, "$7 million." Needless to say, his interest was aroused and he demanded more details.

Trend Reports

Trend reports are used to show progress over a period of time, from a starting point toward a specific goal. Table 22-1 shows a trend report documenting the progress of the correspondence unit in achieving a goal of balancing its actual staff with its standard or required staff. Over the course of the last 13 weeks, actual staff has decreased from 12.2 equivalent full-time employees to 9.2, and the overall goal is in sight. In this particular report, trends in the utilization of employee time are also displayed to support changes in staff size. Note, for example, that during the week of February 5 a drop in supervisory hours signals a reduction of one unneeded supervisor.

Comparison Reports

Comparison reporting is used to evaluate one item against another. In Table 22-2 we are comparing the time required to perform various functions during the current week with the period to date. In this sample report, billing problems required 55.3 percent of the standard hours for the current period, but only 45.4 percent of the standard hours on a year-to-date basis. One might surmise that this trend is a result of end-of-quarter billing problems that might occur in March; however, it might be indicative of an unfavorable trend in improper billing of accounts. The important thing is the ability of such reports to provide a basis for analysis.

Graphs

Graphic representations capitalize on the thought that "a picture is worth a thousand words." Figure 22-2 shows a typical graphic presentation monitoring the progress of the operations department toward its performance goal of 85 percent. Graphic presentations often represent a summary of trend or comparison reporting with the key ingredients reduced to pictorial form.

Table 22-1. Sample trend report for the correspondence unit of a customer service department.

Week Endg.	Staff[a] Base	Staff[a] Actual	Staff[a] Stand.	Distribution of Off-Standard Hours Idle	Holiday/ Vacation	Absent	Train/ Supvr.	Unmeas.	Errors	Total Paid Hrs.	Actual[b] Hrs.	Std.[c] Hrs.	Prod.[d] Hrs.	Perf.[e] %	Cov.[f] %
1/02	14.0	12.2	8.0	39.6	0.0	4.0	79.4	28.1	11.6	475.5	294.8	198.6	322.9	67	91
1/09	14.2	12.4	8.0	37.4	0.0	37.5	76.8	26.4	11.7	465.0	275.2	200.6	301.5	73	91
1/16	13.9	11.7	8.0	38.2	7.5	0.0	81.4	25.2	8.9	438.8	277.6	196.4	203.8	71	92
1/23	14.9	11.0	8.5	35.6	7.5	15.0	80.3	29.7	8.8	412.5	235.5	210.8	265.2	90	89
1/30	13.7	11.5	7.9	34.1	15.0	0.0	82.6	28.5	7.6	431.3	263.5	194.1	292.0	74	90
2/05	15.7	10.5	8.9	30.2	0.0	7.5	45.1	29.6	7.4	393.8	274.0	222.6	303.6	81	90
2/12	13.5	10.8	7.8	28.6	0.0	37.5	44.7	28.0	6.0	405.0	260.2	190.7	288.2	73	90
2/19	13.3	10.7	7.8	24.4	37.5	0.0	47.7	24.1	5.2	401.3	262.4	188.0	286.5	72	92
2/26	14.2	9.7	8.2	11.9	37.5	15.0	44.5	13.6	4.0	363.8	237.3	201.5	288.4	85	95
3/05	14.8	9.9	8.4	10.7	37.5	22.5	43.2	22.8	0.0	371.3	234.6	209.6	294.9	89	92
3/12	15.0	9.6	8.5	8.4	37.5	0.0	43.7	26.4	1.2	360.0	242.8	211.8	306.7	87	91
3/19	14.7	9.4	8.4	6.7	37.5	0.0	43.5	26.8	1.1	352.5	236.9	207.7	301.2	88	91
3/26	15.0	9.2	8.6	.1	39.0	0.0	43.6	27.2	0.0	343.5	233.6	212.5	260.8	91	90
Avg.	14.4	10.7	8.2	23.5	19.7	10.7	58.2	25.9	5.7	399.7	256.0	203.4	281.9	79	91
Total				305.9	265.5	139.0	756.5	336.4	73.5	5,196.3	3,328.4	2,644.9	3,664.7	—	—
% of Paid Hours				5.9	4.9	2.7	14.6	6.5	1.4	—	64.0	—	—	—	—

[a] Equivalent full-time staff.
[b] Paid hours − off-standard hours.
[c] Work units completed, expressed as time required at standard.
[d] Actual hours + unmeasured hours.
[e] Standard hours ÷ actual hours.
[f] Actual hours ÷ productive hours.

Figure 22-2. Typical graphic report — operations department performance.

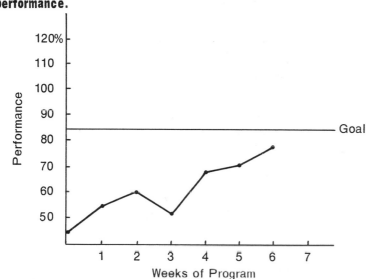

Charts

Various charting techniques are available to assist in a visual display of report data. Figure 22-3 is a pie chart showing the utilization of time in the Atlas Financial Corporation. Another chart style which could be used is the bar chart. The bar chart displays contrasting quantities by a comparison of bars of varying lengths or heights. These bars can be presented either horizontally or vertically. Bar charts offer a variety of styles, including the single-bar chart where, for example, one might compare the total costs of two automobiles on the basis of the length of the bars representing the total of each car. One could also use a relative-component bar chart, where the bar may be broken into several sections representing the base price for the automobile, added accessories, and tax. Another popular bar chart format is the two-directional bar chart, where bars proceed in opposite directions representing attainment of goals or failure to meet goals. If, for example, the goal for performance in a given department is 85 percent, bars below the 85 percent line would indicate the amount by which the department has fallen short of the goal, while bars above that line would represent performance exceeding planned levels.

Pictographs

The pictograph is a means of dramatizing statistical information by pictures which represent the data to be transmitted. In Figure 22-4, each stick figure

Table 22-2. Sample summarized-volumes report.

Std. No.	Standard Task Name	Effect. Date	Hrs./ Item	Current Volume	Current Std. Hrs.	% of Cur. Tot.	Volume To Date	Std. Hrs. To Date	% of Total
101	Billing Problems	06/98	.2400	490	117.6	55.3	4,140	993.6	45.4
100	Customer Inquiry	02/99	.0511	861	44.0	20.9	10,322	527.9	24.1
100	New Accounts	06/98	.0833	371	30.9	14.6	5,106	425.3	19.4
200	Type Correspondence	06/98	.1333	119	15.8	7.4	1,428	190.4	8.7
377	File Correspondence	11/98	.0080	525	4.2	2.0	6,644	53.1	2.4
Unit Total					212.5			2,190.3	

Figure 22-3. Utilization of time, Atlas Financial Corporation.

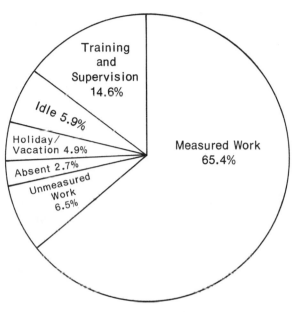

Figure 22-4. Pictograph — comparison of staff at varying levels of performance.

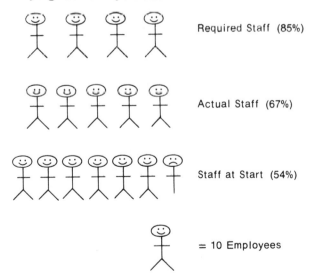

represents ten employees; the pictograph shows that at the start of the work management program there were about 65 employees, that current actual staff is 50 employees, and that the required staff at the goal level of performance is 40 employees.

Pictographs provide an opportunity to exercise a great deal of creativity in the presentation of information; however, if used on a continuing basis, they lose their impact.

GAUGING MANAGEMENT NEEDS

In the final analysis, the report system selected will be a compromise. On the one hand is the need to provide management with current information, thus giving managers a basis for recognizing and rewarding performance. On the other hand, information must be presented in such a form that management will pay attention to it. Endless piles of detail that may be technically perfect will be overlooked by a manager who deals largely with management by exception. Details on methods work performed will be of little value to a financial planner whose major interest is in cost reductions made as a result of these improvements. Before engaging in any reporting of a periodic nature, the potential report format and frequencies should be discussed with the recipients prior to report issue. Preplanning and involving the report recipient in making decisions can avoid false starts which may weaken credibility.

Report Control

Reports tend to proliferate. Management at all levels is continually deluged by different reports. Each new system, each new product, each crisis generates a report or series of reports that are continued long after their usefulness has passed. Controlling the information process is essential if information is to be used to best advantage.

Just as we analyze systems, we should analyze the value of reports. One technique used by a number of firms is to prepare reports according to the usual schedule but not to distribute them until it is determined who wants them and for what purpose. In the case of some reports, no one ever misses them or calls for them. In other cases, a report overdue as little as an hour causes a barrage of phone calls. Each new report's information should be compared with information already available so that duplication of material is held to a minimum. A matrix showing report name and all information contained in the report, similar to that used in forms design, is an effective tool for monitoring report content. When new reports are called for, the first step should be to examine existing reports to determine if the information is already available.

Reporting is an art as much as an exact science, requiring not only analytical skills but, in many cases, artistic accomplishment in order to provide the right information for decision making to the right people on a timely basis.

REPORTING FOR WORK MANAGEMENT

Because of the nature of work management, its reports must adhere to all the principles of good management information reports. They must be timely and accurate, and the cost of gathering the information must be commensurate with its usefulness and impact on the bottom line. However, because of the information pyramid, we must be sure that the reports are designed in such a way that the message comes across loud and clear and provides a basis for action.

Style

When designing the reporting system, the style of management must be considered. It will dictate the level of detail that must be designed into the reporting system. However, a caution is in order here. Since the basic data must be gathered at the employee or supervisor level, even a detail-minded management must exercise constraint in the amount of detail it demands. The authors know of several companies that generate productivity reports for employees on a task-by-task basis. It is not worth the time and cost to develop such reports on a daily or weekly basis. The negative effect on the morale of the employees who had to record such detail is another important consideration.

Nature of Information

Managers need comprehensive reports for total productivity and effectiveness. Therefore, work management reports should address themselves to quantity of work, quality, service, staffing, and backlog.

REPORTING OVERVIEW

There is no one best way to report the results of a work management program. For that matter, there is no one best way to report results within a given organization. It stands to reason that if a supervisor or manager understands the information presented to him and finds it valuable, he will use the data developed to improve productivity and control cost. If a manager is detail-oriented, he will respond best to a system with lots of detail. Senior staff, on the other hand, may want less detail, with only key management indexes reported.

What Information Do Managers Want?

A work management system focuses on three key questions essential to making improvements in a department or company: (1) How much time do people spend working? (2) How well do people perform when they are working? (3) What is the proper staffing of departments?

A Simple Model for Reporting

In the simplest possible report system, we need to answer the questions posed above. Let us first consider the calculation of employee performance. Employee performance is determined by comparing the amount of time that should have been taken to produce the work (standard hours) with the time actually required for its production (actual hours). In formula format, this comparison is expressed as:

$$\text{Performance} = \frac{\text{standard hours}}{\text{actual hours}}$$

To collect data, we need to have standards established for each task and a volume of activity during the report period.

Suppose, for example, that an employee works against a single standard which requires that, in order to earn 100 percent performance, one item be completed every 7 minutes (.12 hour). If the employee completed 40 items during a given day, then it should have taken 4.8 hours (.12 × 40) to perform the work. If the employee actually spent 6½ hours doing the work, then the employee's performance would be 74 percent of standard (4.8 ÷ 6.5). Data required for this calculation can come from many sources. Volume data may be reported by the employee himself or by a supervisor or work distribution clerk counting the work. As a by-product of the completion of the work, many of today's processing systems also keep track of volume of items completed. Figure 22-5 is an example of a volume report completed by an employee.

The time required to complete the work is probably most easily kept by exception. Since in most departments the majority of the work will be covered by standards, it is necessary only to record time spent on work not covered by standards in order to calculate the time actually spent completing the work. In the example above, the employee may have been paid for 7½ hours, but one hour may have been devoted to completing tasks which were not measured, learning new work, or carrying out other unmeasured activity.

We recommend a goal of 100 percent performance for individual employees. This goal is based on the average well-trained employee working at a normal pace. For unit performance, we recommend a goal of 85 percent to 90 percent. The difference between the unit goal and the individual employee goal may be attributed to many factors. Most departments, for example, experience some turnover. Thus at any given point in time all employees in the unit will not be well trained. In other cases, employees may not be capable of performing at 100 percent of standard because of physical or mental handicaps; in other words, they do not

Figure 22-5. Volume report.

DATE
9 / 13 / 99

EMPLOYEE	UNIT	DEPARTMENT
R. M. Martin	Correspondence	Customer Service

TASK NO.	TASK	ITEM COUNTED	VOLUME	TOTAL VOLUME
1	File transfers	Cards	3-2-4	9
2	Type correspondence	Letters	15-21	36
3	Set up new accounts	Accounts	39-9-6-11	65
4	Change address	Changes	9-12-5	26
5	Close accounts	Accounts	2-2-4-1	9

measure up to the concept of average. The 85 percent unit performance goal allows a manager to be measured against an achievable productivity goal.

Refining the System

In the example above, our employee spent one hour not performing the work covered by standards. To make best use of employee time, the supervisor should determine how the other hour was spent. To aid in this analysis, a report system can be designed with several categories of "off standard" activity. Some commonly used off-standard categories include:

Waiting for work—any time when the employee is available to perform measured work but has no work to perform. Examples include malfunctions of office equipment, scheduling delays, and lack of instructions on how work should be processed.

Absence—any time an employee is absent from the department and thus unavailable for work. Examples are illness for an entire work period, late arrival or early departure from work, and personal business.

Holiday/vacation—time authorized by the company when an employee is not expected to work, such as scheduled work holidays and vacation.

Training—time spent learning new work when there is no actual production.

Figure 22-6. Weekly activity report.

				ELAPSED TIME				

WEEK ENDING 9 / 17 / 99

EMPLOYEE: R. M. Martin	UNIT: Correspondence	DEPARTMENT: Customer Service

WEEKLY TIME REPORT

Day	Reason	Time Off	Time On	Waiting For Work	Unavailable	Training Supervision	Unmeasured	Paid Hours
	Scheduled Hours							37.5
M	Train Leyden on close-outs	10:00	12:00			2.0		
T	Special report for Sharp	8:00	2:10				5.2	
T	Overtime	5:00	8:00					3.0
W	Overtime	5:00	8:00					3.0
F	No Work	3:20	4:10	.7				

CONVERSION CHART

MINUTES	DECIMAL HOURS
4-9	.1
10-15	.2
16-21	.3
22-27	.4
28-33	.5
34-39	.6
40-45	.7
46-51	.8
52-57	.9

POST TOTALS IN BLOCKS BELOW

.7 + + 2.0 =

TOTAL

Total Paid Hrs.
43.5
- 2.7
Productive Hrs.
40.8
Enter in (D)
- 5.2
Actual Hours
35.6
Enter in (B) & (C)

PERFORMANCE

(A) 32.7 Standard Hours + (B) 35.6 Actual Hours = 92 %

COVERAGE

(C) 35.6 Actual Hours + (D) 40.8 Productive Hours = 87 %

APPROVALS

Supervisor E. S. Initials   4 /7/99 Date
Analyst RTY Initials   9 / 18 / 99 Date

23-284A (7-74)

Training time might include attending meetings for training purposes and processing practice work.

Supervision—time spent managing the department by planning, staffing, organizing, directing, and controlling its activities.

Unmeasured work—those tasks performed in the department for which standards have not yet been established. This category might include work that is generally reserved for special projects and low-volume periodic work such as the preparation of monthly or quarterly reports. Figure 22-6 is a typical time report showing the logging of off-standard time.

Coverage

It is axiomatic that you can only control what you can measure. It is useful to compare the amount of time spent on measured activity with the total work time of the department. A typical formula for the calculation of coverage is:

$$\text{Coverage} = \frac{\text{measured hours}}{\text{measured hours} + \text{unmeasured hours}}$$

A typical minimum goal for coverage is 90 percent. With a predetermined time system such as Advanced Office Controls, 93 percent or 94 percent coverage is the rule rather than the exception.

Staffing the Department

The best way to assess how well a supervisor is using the resources available to him is to determine whether the department is properly staffed. Since the characteristics of each department vary considerably, there will often be not one staffing formula but many. The factors to be considered in determining what the staff should be are: the amount of measured work (standard hours), time spent on unmeasured work, hours of absence, employees' holidays and vacations, supervision and training required for the department, and the hours of scheduling delays.

The key ingredient, of course, is the work to be performed. We have already indicated that as a reasonable goal 90 percent of all work should be measured and covered by standards. In calculating the staff of the department, we not only need to establish how long it should take to do the work, as defined by the standard hours required; we must also make reasonable allowances for uncontrollable factors such as turnover and company policy. Typically, then, a staffing formula starts with the development of a factor that takes into consideration the characteristics of the department. If the performance goal for an organization is 90 percent, then a factor to convert standard hours expressed as 100 percent of performance to a 90 percent level would be .11 (10 ÷ 90).

There are two ways to account for unmeasured work. In the first case, unmeasured activity as reported by the employees may be factored for the goal level of performance. If the performance goal is 90 percent and 40 hours of unmeasured activity are reported, then it would take 44.4 hours to perform this same work at 90 percent performance. This, of course, presupposes that unmeasured activity is accomplished at the same pace as measured activity. In the second case, we can develop a factor that can be added to standard hours to account for unmeasured activity. If the coverage goal is 92 percent, a .09 factor (8 ÷ 90) should be utilized.

Departmental records and/or company-allowed sick policy can be utilized to determine what the factor for absence from the department should be. If, for example, the company allows 10 days of sick time for the 250 work days in the year, then a 4 percent allowance (10 ÷ 250) is required.

The characteristics of units vary considerable. A 1 or 2 percent factor for scheduling delays is normally adequate. It should be noted here that departments with high volatility in volume or service requirements need to be staffed more flexibly than departments with more static conditions. In banks, for example, matching the correct number of tellers to the customer arrival patterns in a branch office is a key consideration. Staffing of this nature is often carried out on a day-to-day basis and may even include detailed analysis on an hour-by-hour basis.

Figure 22-7 is an example of the staffing of a customer records department. It includes the development of a 26 percent staffing factor, the calculation of standard hours of work, and the conversion of that workload into the staff required to complete it.

The actual staff of the department may be computed by dividing the hours paid for work completed by the scheduled work time for one full-time employee. If 527 hours were worked, the actual staff of the department would be calculated by dividing the 527 paid hours by the scheduled work week of 37½ hours. Actual staffing would be 14.1 equivalent full-time employees.

An executive once asked one of the authors, "What is the one key number I can look at to determine how well a department is operating?" That number is probably the ratio of actual staff to standard or required staff. If the performance of an individual employee is calculated by dividing standard time (how long it should take) by actual time (how long it did take), it would seem that the performance of a supervisor could be calculated by dividing standard staff (that which should be required to complete the work) by actual staff (the staff actually required). In our example, the overall utilization of this department would be 74 percent (required staff 10.5 ÷ actual staff 14.1).

A typical goal for the utilization of staff is 100 percent. Supervisors who can operate at levels that exceed corporate goals will achieve a utilization of over 100 percent and the accompanying recognition. Supervisors who do not effectively utilize employee time can achieve satisfactory productivity levels by a proper

Figure 22-7. Staffing report.

STAFFING CUSTOMER RECORDS DEPARTMENT

Staff Factor

Performance @ 90%	11%
Coverage by standard @ 92%	9
Absent	4
Scheduling delays	2
	26%

Workload

Task	Std. Hrs.	x	Volume	=	Standard Hours
Open new accounts	.12	x	2127	=	255.2
Close accounts	.04	x	406	=	16.2
			Total Standard Hours		271.4

Staff Development

Standard hours x staff factor = management reserve
271.4 x 26% = 70.6

Total standard hours	+	management reserve	=	Paid Hours
271.4	+	70.6	=	342.0
	+	Required supervision		37.5
	+	Vacations		15.0
		Total hours		394.5

Total Hours ÷ Work Week = Required Staff
394.5 ÷ 37.5 = 10.5

---

balance of staff and workload. This means improving the performance of individual employees and either bringing more productive activity into the department or reducing the staff of the department so that it balances both the workload and the customer service requirements. Obviously, a third possibility exists—bringing in additional work and changing staff requirements. The process of achieving results is discussed in Chapter 25. Table 22-3 is a weekly performance summary showing the type of information supervisors have available to achieve results.

Managers normally need less information than supervisors on an ongoing basis to monitor unit effectiveness. Table 22-4 is an example of a report to management displaying productivity of units. Table 22-5 is a typical report summary.

Work management in and of itself cannot achieve productivity gains. Data similar to those discussed must be analyzed by supervisors and managers and

Table 22-3. Performance summary—customer service department.

Employee	Idle	Holiday/Vacation	Absent	Training/Supervision	Unmeas.	Total Paid Hrs.	Actual Hours	Standard Hours	Productive Hours	Performance %	Cov. %
BA Snyder	0.0	0.0	0.0	2.6	0.0	37.5	34.9	42.0	34.9	120	100
LJ Lange	0.0	0.5	0.0	2.9	0.5	37.5	33.6	35.9	34.1	107	99
RM Weber	0.0	0.0	0.0	0.0	1.1	22.5	21.4	19.6	22.5	92	95
DJ Land	0.0	0.5	0.0	4.4	2.2	37.5	30.4	26.8	32.6	88	93
RM Martin	0.0	0.0	0.0	2.0	7.2	43.5	34.3	28.9	41.5	84	83
NT Thomas	0.1	0.0	0.0	0.0	0.3	15.0	14.6	12.1	14.9	83	98
MB Reid	0.0	0.5	0.0	1.7	3.9	37.5	31.4	23.7	35.3	75	89
AV Leyden	0.0	0.0	0.0	0.0	4.5	37.5	33.0	23.5	37.5	71	88
B Sharp	0.0	0.0	0.0	30.0	7.5	37.5	0.0	0.0	7.5	0	0
S Walton	0.0	37.5	0.0	0.0	0.0	37.5					
Unit Total	0.1	39.0	0.0	43.6	27.2	343.5	233.6	212.5	260.8	91	90

STAFF ANALYSIS

At Start 06/98	14.0
Current Actual Staff	9.2
Required Staff at Goal	8.6

SAVINGS SUMMARY

Achieved Savings	$44,080
Potential Savings	$ 4,560
Total Savings	$48,640

WORKLOAD ANALYSIS

Base Standard Hours	198.3
Current Standard Hours	212.5
Change	+7.1%

Table 22-4. Management summary for customer service department.

Unit	Start	Staffing Actual	Staffing Required	Total Paid Hrs.	Actual Hours	Standard Hours	Perf. %
Accounts	11.0	7.8	8.0	293.8	170.3	161.7	95
Correspondence	14.0	9.2	8.6	343.5	233.6	212.5	91
Dept. Total	25.0	17.0	16.6	637.3	403.9	374.2	93

STAFF ANALYSIS

At Start 06/98	25.0
Current Actual Staff	17.0
Standard Staff	16.6

SAVINGS SUMMARY

Achieved Savings	$66,880
Potential Savings	$ 3,040
Total Savings	$69,920

WORKLOAD ANALYSIS

Base Standard Hours	383
Current Standard Hours	374.2
Change	-2%

Table 22-5. Pattern for reporting work management data.

Recipient	Level of Detail	Frequency
President	Division totals and company totals	Monthly
Division heads	Department totals and division totals	Monthly
Department heads	Unit totals and department totals	Weekly
Supervisors	Individual and unit totals	Weekly
Employees	Individual data	Weekly

corrective action must be taken when indicated if productivity is to be improved and the cost of providing services reduced.

Reporting Work Volume

Volumes alone give management only half the picture of the workload in a department or unit. Standards must be applied to those volumes to determine the true workload in hours. Table 22-2, presented earlier, illustrates how this information helps in decision making. It shows workload distribution for the current period, and accumulated year to date. Shifts in workload can be easily spotted. Also, the percent distribution enables managers to allocate expenses between functions.

Service Reports

Every organizational unit should develop service standards as well as productivity or performance standards. There are two approaches to this type of reporting.

When there is a perceived serious service problem or management is attempting to identify or establish service levels, a detailed report similar to Table 22-6 is recommended. Once a week, at the same fixed time each week, an

Table 22-6. Service report for correspondence unit.

Days in Department	Number of Requests as of 4:30 PM			
	8/9	8/16	8/23	8/30
0–6	310	192	58	4
7–13	237	54	—	1
14–21	44	54	4	—
22–28	37	88	6	—
29–35	32	53	1	—
36–56	21	14	—	1
57+	7	—	—	—
Totals	688	455	69	6

"inventory aging" would take place to show how long each service request has been in the department. This type of report helps in planning the next week's work, as well as in spotting bottlenecks or service problems.

A less detailed approach would be to take a sampling, at random times, of the total work completed. These observations are recorded in terms of the number of days from receipt to completion of work. Percentages are then calculated. For example, for a sample size of 100 items we might find the following distribution:

Number of days to Completion	Number of Items	Percent (Cumulative)
1	60	60
2	10	70
3	5	75
4	5	80
5	7	87
6	3	90
7	3	93
8	2	95
9	0	95
10	1	96
15	4	100

Quality Reports

Just like quantity, quality must be controlled. The most effective approach is to report an individual's quality of work along with quantity of work. The two numbers

Table 22-7. Sample weighted quality report.

Employee	Perf. %	Quality %	Combined* Index
B. Snyder	120	99	112
L. Lange	107	97	103
R. Weber	92	97	94
D. Land	88	98	92
R. Martin	84	94	88
N. Thomas	83	96	88
M. Reid	75	92	82
A. Leyden	71	93	80
B. Sharp	70	100	82
S. Walton	0	0	
Unit Total	91	96	93

*Weighting for each category: performance = 60%; quality = 40%.

can then be expressed as a combined index. Table 22-7 illustrates one possible format for this approach to linking quality to quantity.

REPORTING RESULTS TO TOP MANAGEMENT

On a regular basis, at least annually, the work management department should design a special report for top management to report work management progress and results. In preparing this report, the information pyramid depicted in Figure

Figure 22-8. Measurement rate — scheduled versus actual.

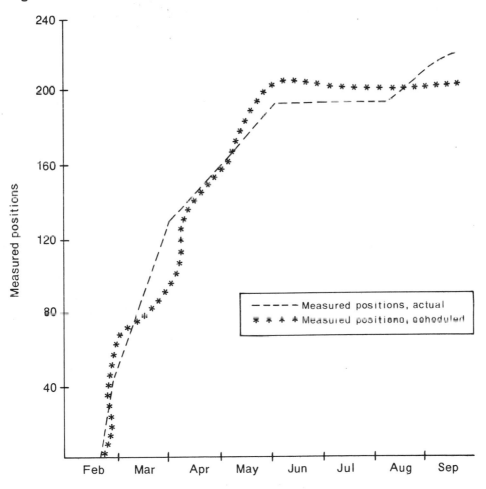

22-1 should be kept in mind. Therefore, the report should be concise, informative, not too costly, and action-oriented. Because of the proliferation of information flowing to the top of the organization, the report should be attractively packaged and the message or points easily identifiable.

To accomplish these objectives, text for top-management reports should be minimized and only essential details should be presented. Also, to facilitate comprehension, trends and comparisons should be presented using charts, graphs, pictographs, pie charts, and other good reporting techniques already discussed. These reporting techniques should be used to highlight progress/activities of the analysts, costs versus savings of the work management program, and overall productivity results. (See Figures 22-8 to 22-10.)

Figure 22-9. Costs versus savings, work management department.

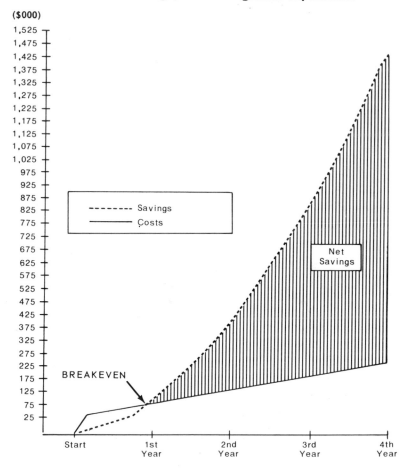

Figure 22-10. Progress report on measured areas for the four week period ending 7-27-99.

REPORTING UNIT	DATE COMPLETED	Performance		Coverage		UTILIZATION			STAFF			IDENTIFIED SAVINGS*		ACTUAL SAVINGS*	
						Was	Is	Change	Was	Is	Req.	Employees	Dollars	Employees	Dollars
Underwriting	04-22-99	95%	93%	88%	85%	60%	70%	+17%	5.0	5.1	3.6	1.4	868	(.1)	(62)
National accounts	05-20-99	102	100	77	81	107	95	−11	22.7*	18.0	17.1	5.6	3,472	4.7	2,914
Premium accounting	06-24-99	80	103	75	83	75	100	+33	9.4	7.4	7.4	2.0	1,240	2.0	1,240
Word processing	07-15-99	76	86	91	96	92	77	−16	2.7	2.0	1.5	1.2	744	.7	434
Claims	08-19-99	79	81	93	88	98	82	−16	14.8*	11.7	9.6	5.2	3,224	3.1	1,922
Treasurer	08-26-99	88	96	67	77	73	90	+23	6.0	6.0	5.4	.6	372	0	0
Purchasing	09-16-99	88	87	78	89	100	105	+5	12.2	13.8	14.5	(2.3)	(1,426)	(1.6)	(992)
Reinstatement	10-28-99	74	80	85	83	70	67	−4	5.0	5.0	3.4	1.6	992	0	0
Policyowner service	12-09-99	72	83	91	85	75	88	−17	7.9	7.1	6.2	1.7	1,054	.8	496
Data processing	12-23-99	92	141	77	70	85	95	+2	4.9	3.2	3.0	1.9	1,178	1.7	1,054
COMPANY TOTAL		86	92	80	84	87	90	+3	90.6	78.3	71.7	18.9	11,718	11.3	7,006
Year to date		87	92	83	84	60	90	+50	113.0	78.3	71.7	41.3	179,242	33.7	146,258
		85% Goal		90% Goal		100% Goal									

*Monthly Savings @ $620.00 for full-time equivalent employee salary and fringe benefits per month.

PART

USING THE DATA

CHAPTER

Maintaining and Improving the System

As we have seen in previous chapters, a properly implemented work management program can achieve immediate short-term results that will readily cover the cost of program installation. These short-term benefits will appear insignificant when compared with the long-range benefits over the life of a program. A successful program, at its inception, is designed with these long-term goals in mind and, as a result, includes provisions for the audit of the system, the maintenance of standards, and the evolution of the program to meet the changing information needs of management.

BUILDING A FIRM FOUNDATION

Regardless of the work measurement technique chosen, the first building block of a firm foundation is an accurate and consistent style of documentation for standards. It would be difficult to discuss in detail documentation styles for each work measurement technique. However, since most programs designed with long-term goals in mind use predetermined times to establish standards, a suggested documentation style for that technique will provide insight into documentation techniques for other standard-setting systems.

A standard represents the amount of time it should take to complete a task under a certain set of conditions. When a standard of three minutes is developed for a particular task, the analyst states in his documentation what conditions and procedures exist. The conditions (forms, equipment, and so on) as well as the technique of standard setting used must be documented. A task outline similar to Figure 21-1 may be used to document the standard.

When an analyst is documenting a standard, he or she must always keep in mind the fact that the documentation may one day be used by another analyst, who may not be nearly as familiar with the task. To save valuable time, the procedure must be complete. Therefore, in addition to describing the method to be used by the employee performing the task, the analyst should also properly record the recognized name of the task, any equipment used, reference materials used, and forms completed. Also, the name of the task outline should reflect what the supervisor and employees know as the task. Most tasks can and should be described in two or three words (for example, Balance Ledger, Input Address Changes, Pre-sort Payments). Long titles are an indication of redundancy, a task that is too small, or an analyst who doesn't understand the task.

It is essential in the standards documentation that the equipment description take into account rapid technological and systems advances. It is not sufficient to record equipment used as "calculator," as this could mean anything from a hand-cranked machine to a programmable calculator. The preferred style is to include not only the class of machine but its model number—for example, Ajax Model 310 Display Calculator. Similarly, forms should be designated not only by nomenclature but by form number and date of last revision.

These precautions are necessary in order to accurately describe the conditions under which work is processed. Office processing techniques are becoming more and more sophisticated, and forms and equipment are regularly updated and changed to reflect current needs. Precise documentation becomes critical to the task outline's usefulness.

Another variable that must be considered in documenting standards is the number of items processed at one time by an employee (usually known as the batch size). The importance of batch size becomes evident when we consider how most standards are formulated. A work standard is most useful when it is expressed as time per item to be processed. However, a typical standard (time per item) is comprised of two key processing elements:

- *Fixed time*—generally, the time used to gather necessary materials into the workplace prior to processing (for example, one minute to set up for a batch of 10, 20, 50, or however many items).
- *Variable time*—the time expended in working on each item in the batch.

In the construction of the standard it is normal, in order to simplify the reporting process, to spread the fixed time, which will be relatively constant regardless of the volume of items processed in any one batch, over the variable time used to process each item of work in the batch. It is important, therefore, to record the batch size, because it will provide an indication of the relationship between fixed and variable time.

The final key ingredient to the documentation of standards is the procedure used to process work. The procedure should be documented in sufficient detail to enable future analysts to determine the procedure that existed at the time the standard was established and, if required, to enable employees and supervisors to utilize the documentation as a means to train new employees. Standards documentation provides important information that can be used for analyzing methods and procedures. As a rule of thumb, although documenting too much detail is time-consuming and serves little purpose, it is better to include some extra detail than to document incompletely conditions which existed at the time the standard was established. The task outline, discussed in Chapter 21, is an example of a documentation style which is suitable for standard maintenance, training of employees, and systems study.

Consistency of style begins with analyst training. A well-trained analyst is essential to the continuing success of a work management program. Regardless of the technique chosen, all analysts should be trained in a uniform manner. Analyst training should not be limited to the technique used to establish standards.

Some of the key topics to be covered in an analyst training program include:

- Historical information on the development of work management at the company.
- Background information on the available tools and techniques of work management programs, including characteristics of successful and unsuccessful programs and the theory of work management.
- Standards establishment techniques to be utilized by the analyst.
- Standards documentation techniques.
- How to conduct the work management study.
- The reporting system.
- Uses of reported data.

Complete discussions of the key elements may be found in other chapters. Topics for an analyst training program will vary by organization and by program goals. To ensure consistency of training and of documentation, it is suggested that one employee in the organization be designated as a trainer of analysts. The trainer should develop a formal training program for analysts that includes a complete discussion of the topics important in the company's work management program. Practice exercises, handouts, and visual aids should also be used to enhance the learning experience. This formal training is essential to maintain consistency in the program.

ESTABLISHING ACCURATE WORK STANDARDS

When accurate work standards are discussed, it is important to keep in mind the definition of accuracy in this context. Accuracy in work standards is a function of two key ingredients: the standards technique chosen, and the intended use of the standards. Analysts, supervisors, and managers at all levels should be aware of the strengths and limitations of the standard-setting technique utilized. In previous chapters we have examined the concept of engineered standards, as opposed to less formal techniques. By way of review: as the technique chosen moves from the informal techniques of estimation and historical data to the formal techniques of predetermined times and leveled stopwatch studies, the accuracy and consistency of standards also increase.

It would be unwise to use informal techniques to attempt to obtain benefits which are possible only with engineered standards. As an example, historical data would be unsuitable for the development of an incentive program to improve the productivity and earnings of data entry personnel. At the opposite end of the spectrum, it would not be an effective use of analyst time to study the work of a manager, or other types of jobs that are end- or project-oriented and have little pattern to them, with predetermined times.

It is essential that work standards be developed in an economical fashion consistent with their intended use. In order to effectively utilize analyst time, every attempt should be made to avoid duplication of analyst effort. Regardless of the technique chosen for measurement, there are, in every organization, numerous repetitive tasks performed throughout the organization. Examples of these tasks would include the receipt and dispatch of inter-office mail, completion of accounting charge tickets, and the photocopying of documents. Once standards have been established for these types of tasks, they should be applied consistently throughout the organization. Obviously, a predetermined time system maximizes the opportunity to develop blocks of data, which can be used by analysts to establish work standards in the most economical way.

THE RETRIEVAL SYSTEM

A work management effort that works with operating departments to assist them to be more effective in filing and retrieving data should, of course, have an effective retrieving system of its own. It goes without saying that if materials cannot be located, they cannot be used for analysis when required. Many an analyst has been embarrassed, and doubt has been cast on a program, when a manager or supervisor asks if a previously accurate standard still applies and the documentation for that standard is nowhere to be found.

The typical work management program filing system is divided into two major categories: (1) standards development material and (2) reports of work management results. It would be impossible to discuss in any detail filing systems for every conceivable type of standard-setting technique and report system; however, the following sections will provide a basis for the development of an effective work management file system.

Standards Development File

Opinions vary on how results of standard-setting activity should be communicated to the management of the operating department and what materials should be retained in the work management department files. In developing a filing system, the factors that must be considered include retrieval, usefulness to analysts and operating departments, and availability to other departments such as data processing, personnel, and purchasing. Decisions must be made concerning how much detail of standards development should be given to the operating departments and what materials should be retained in the work management department files.

For a variety of reasons, the supervisor or manager of the department must have a copy of each of the task outlines for the department. This will inform them of the conditions under which standards were established. Similarly, the work management department should retain, for its use, not only the task outline but the actual standards development material. A typical file system would retain, for each task:

- Task outline—describing the equipment, forms, procedures, and volume of activity of the task at the time the standard was established.
- Task analysis—for each step within the task, an analysis form shows how the standard time for this particular step was derived.
- Task summary—a worksheet which shows the relationship of each step within a task and the development of any allowances for personal and miscellaneous needs or for questions or interruptions.
- Sample forms—to show what information was required to achieve the end result of the task.
- Frequency studies—in complex tasks it may be desirable to maintain copies of frequency studies showing either the relationship of steps within a task or the derivation of internal frequencies used to establish the standard.

Worksheets such as the task analysis and the task summary are usually handwritten, while the task outline should be typed. For the vast majority of work management programs, paper files are adequate for the storage of standards establishment files. In large, multiple-location companies, such as an insurance company with widely scattered branch offices, it may be desirable to use some form of microfilm to retain standards backup at decentralized analyst locations.

If standards are to be economically established and standards common among different areas of the company are to be recognized, it will be incumbent on the analyst team to develop a system of cross-referencing so that the source and existence of previously established data can be determined. The cross-referencing procedure should include the following: (1) a standard data control number, (2) a reference to that unique control number each time the standard data are used in the documentation of subsequent standards, and (3) an index of all subsequent standards that make use of the standard data.

Step three is essential should the basic standard data change. It would require changing all the standards that used the basic standard. The cross-reference saves time by identifying exactly what subsequent standards are affected.

The retrieval system for the retention of input and output documents of the report system will be covered in more detail in subsequent chapters.

The Importance of Standards Maintenance

If a work management program is to be successful over an extended period of time, standards must be maintained to properly reflect current conditions. When these conditions change, the standards must be updated or the data created by the work management program will become useless and/or suspect.

The amount of effort devoted to standards maintenance is largely a function of the number of employees covered by the program and the stability or lack of stability in work processing systems. In the following section we will examine some of the reasons why standards maintenance is an essential part of every work management effort designed with long-term goals in mind.

Impact of Standards Maintenance on Decision Making

Standards and information on the volume of activity are the key data used for decision making. If standards are incorrect, the quality of decision making will be limited. In extreme cases, overzealous use of work management information based on incorrect systems can lead to severe financial loss, because it renders an organization unable to price its products accurately or to provide a level of service that will attract additional customers.

From the employee's point of view, incorrect standards can cause severe morale problems, because a performance rating based on these standards is unlikely to reflect the amount of skill and effort expended. At one end of the scale recognition will go to those who do not deserve it, while at the other end hard work will go unrewarded. Poor morale is likely to result from both situations.

To the employee, incorrect standards indicate that management does not care about the program or its results, and a lack of interest by employees in maintaining accurate performance records and performing well will be the inevitable result.

Techniques for Standards Maintenance

It should be obvious from the preceding discussion that standards maintenance is of the utmost importance for the decision-making process and employee morale. In the following sections we propose ideas for continuing maintenance of work standards.

Placement of Responsibility

The key to a successful standards maintenance program is to allocate responsibility for maintenance to the proper parties. Supervisors and managers in the user departments and the work management program staff share the responsibility for standards maintenance.

The user-department management should have in its possession a task outline describing the contents of the standard. Therefore, when procedures change, the manager or supervisor should review the task outline to compare it to the new procedure and notify the work management department so that a decision can be made as to whether the standard is affected.

It should not be the responsibility of user-department management to decide whether or not a change in procedure will require a change in standard. It is generally preferable to examine a number of minor changes and determine whether they affect standard accuracy than to have user management make these decisions without an adequate basis of knowledge.

Communication Channels

There are several sources of communications that can be used to monitor the progress of standards maintenance.

First, it is desirable for the work management team to keep in touch with the user departments through periodic informal telephone calls and visits. This will afford an opportunity to discuss procedures in use, including any changes made or proposed for the future. The continuing interest of the work management team is extremely important in maintaining supervisors' confidence in the accuracy of information.

Second, formal channels can be established to request standards maintenance. In some organizations a standards maintenance request form similar to that in Figure 23-1 may be utilized to request either changes in existing standards or the development of standards to cover new methods and procedures. Memoranda or phone calls from the user department can also be used for this purpose.

Finally, if the work management program is well integrated into the operations of the company, the work management staff will have continuing access to proposed changes in methods and procedures. The work management staff should be on the review list for forms design changes that are anticipated. Requests to manual or

Figure 23-I. Request for standards maintenance.

TO: WORK MANAGEMENT

FROM:_____Ann Parsons_____   EXTENSION:____2081_____
               SUPERVISOR

      Customer Service_____   DATE:__June 6, 1999_____
               DEPARTMENT

THE FOLLOWING TASKS REQUIRE MAINTENANCE:

	TASK	REASON NEW	REVISED	COMMENTS
1	Address changes	[ ]	[X]	New form
2	File overdue notices	[ ]	[X]	Eliminated
3	Input overdue payments	[X]	[ ]	Now done on CRT
4		[ ]	[ ]	
5		[ ]	[ ]	
6		[ ]	[ ]	
7		[ ]	[ ]	
8		[ ]	[ ]	
9		[ ]	[ ]	
10		[ ]	[ ]	

FOR WORK MANAGEMENT USE ONLY:

ANALYST_____

ASSIGNED_____ ESTIMATED COMPLETION_____

computer systems analysts for revised procedures may also trigger the need for standards maintenance.

Any or all of these techniques should be employed to maintain the integrity of the standards base. It is beneficial, whenever possible, to adjust standards at the time new procedures are developed so that the information from the standard-setting process may be used to assist in procedures development.

Audit

Standards in all operating areas should be audited by work management analysts on a periodic basis. It is usual for a first audit of the program to be conducted six to twelve months after the original standards are set in the unit. This is desirable in order to ensure that changes made in procedures to improve productivity and reduce cost are reflected in the standards structure and that continuing standards maintenance becomes part of management's responsibility. Subsequent audits of standards may be conducted either periodically or when the need is perceived. Generally, the interval between audits should be no longer than 18 to 24 months.

More frequent audits are suggested for those areas of responsibility with high system volatility. Analysts should be on the alert for unexplained changes in the reporting structure, which may require standards maintenance. Among these changes are a marked decrease in coverage by standards and an unexplained increase or decrease in employee performance.

MAINTAINING INTEREST

An examination of work management programs that have been in effect for a number of years indicates that one of the most difficult tasks is to maintain interest in the program by management of the organization at all levels. The key ingredients to maintaining interest are continuing education of system users and ongoing development of the system to meet the changing needs of the organization.

Changing the System

Changing the system can take one of two general forms. Cosmetic changes can be introduced to revise the manner in which data are collected or presented, and functional changes can be instituted to redefine the role of the user and his relationship to the work management function. Instituting changes provides a basis for continuing education of the user, not only to inform him of change but to reinforce the basic principles and concepts of a work management program and the user's role in it.

Education of Users

The education of the user can take many forms. As previously indicated, periodic contact on an informal basis with all users is desirable in order to maintain standards as well as maintain interest in the program. During these sessions, the work management staff may also take the opportunity to discuss forthcoming changes, solicit ideas for improved methods of presenting data, and educate new supervisors and managers as to program objectives and their role in achieving results.

Formal sessions may be held for the same purpose and to discuss how the work management program can better serve the needs of user departments. Care should be exercised that formal sessions to determine program acceptance and status do not become gripe sessions where a series of petty problems or misunderstandings of the system can, through group reinforcement, become major obstacles to success.

As in all successful meetings, an agenda should be distributed in advance outlining new materials to be covered. Time should be allocated for discussion on these topics and other related work management information of general interest. Specific problems regarding standards, staffing, reporting, or the work of individual analysts should be discussed with the appropriate department manager in individual sessions.

Continuing publicity is an important contributor to acceptance of the work management program. Publicity should be two-sided, addressing the achievements of the work management department and user departments equally. Company house organs, bulletin boards, and news releases can be used to communicate achievements. Among newsworthy items are work management analysts successfully completing advanced courses in their field, employees submitting suggestions for improved methods to process work, outstanding employee performance, interesting and unusual uses of data on the part of supervisors and managers, and the impact of the work management program on overall company profitability.

INTEGRATING THE WORK MANAGEMENT FUNCTION

When originally established, a work management program tends to be a free-standing program, surrounded by a great deal of publicity and controversy. As time goes on, the successful program reduces its profile, yet does not decrease its importance in the day-to-day operations of the company. This change in profile is achieved through the integration of work management data into the day-to-day activity of the organization.

Personnel Practices

The first area for integration of work management data usually is that of the personnel practices of the organization. The work management program provides an ideal opportunity for an organization to strengthen its appraisal process for employees at all levels, and also to more scientifically and professionally determine staffing needs in each measured area for any level of workload. It should be stressed that although work management data provide a guideline that can be used for these purposes, they should not be used as a substitute for sound managerial practices.

The typical employee appraisal process, while encompassing a variety of employee attributes, rightly emphasizes the quantity of work produced and the quality of output. These two factors can be objectively and consistently reported by most work management programs. Appraisal forms may be designed to include statements on quantity and quality of work, stated in percentages of performance and correctness factors. Supervisors may use their discretion and deviate from the guidelines in certain situations, provided they support their position with facts.

The key ingredient in integrating work management with personnel practices is to pay for performance. There should be a definite relationship between the employee's performance appraisal and his or her productivity. The reward structure, as codified in the normal personnel process, should be such that employees performing at higher levels will receive larger increases than those performing at lower levels.

The work management program provides a basis for projecting staffing needs for any level of workload. Requisitions for new or replacement employees should be accompanied by factual data from the work management program supporting management's position. It is not uncommon to include statements such as, "This additional part-time employee is required to handle increased work volume of automobile endorsements. Our workload has increased by 100 endorsements daily at a standard of 2.5 minutes each. At current levels of performance, we will require a part-time employee for five hours daily."

The work management function can also be integrated into other areas of the organization. Financial managers appreciate the data that are available for the budgeting of manpower resources and the development of costing and pricing information. These topics will be covered in more detail in subsequent chapters.

In summary, the successful work management program is used by an entire organization to provide a more accurate basis for decision making. Utilization of a predetermined time technique allows for an appraisal of methods, procedures, equipment, and forms prior to acquisition. A systematic analysis utilizing these techniques will provide a basis to select the best alternatives and avoid costly and time-consuming restructuring of procedures after acquisition.

SYSTEM EVOLUTION

The original work management program was designed to meet the needs of the organization at the time the program was implemented. The needs of the organization will change from month to month and year to year. A work management program that is not continuously adjusted to meet the changing needs of the organization will lose its utility and the interest of supervisors and managers at all levels. The work management group should be attuned to the current needs of the organization and develop the system to meet these needs.

A key weakness in work management programs is the failure to redefine objectives on a periodic basis. Initial objectives, once achieved, should be replaced by new and challenging objectives for the use of the system. New objectives will require new means of presenting data and new techniques for the establishment of standards and collection of data.

Work management reporting should be simplified at the earliest possible opportunity consistent with program objectives. The following considerations can help to simplify a work management reporting system.

Tasks should be compressed as much as possible. Too many tasks make it difficult for employees to accurately record their day-to-day activity. Data developed from the past reporting of activity can be utilized to develop a smaller number of more inclusive standards. As a simple example, the original standards structure may include two time standards: one for filling new merchandise orders (Process New Orders), and a separate standard for renewing merchandise orders (Process Renewal Orders). Once employees in the unit are cross-trained to do both tasks, the tasks could be combined into one activity (Process Orders). Naturally, the new standards would be structured to reflect the average order processed, whether new or renewal.

Job enrichment also provides a basis for the compression of tasks. For example, the original processing sequence might include one employee who is responsible for research of customer complaints, and a second employee who communicates the results of the research to the customer. An enriched job of researching and communicating to customers will result in both a decrease in the number of standards and a more satisfying work environment.

Once performance has reached an acceptable level, reporting periods may be extended. We have previously recommended weekly reporting during the early phases of a program. An extension to monthly data simplifies the process in that it reduces the number of reports throughout the year. It should be stressed, however, that an extension of the reporting period also provides fewer opportunities to take corrective action. In all cases, it should be possible for management to monitor the progress of new employees more frequently to speed their development.

New work management programs usually involve individual reporting of employee performance. Consideration may be given to reporting group performance, which provides for some additional simplification of the report structure. However, group data are not normally adequate to assist in appraising individual performance for personnel evaluation purposes. Similarly, the impact of new employees on the group may show up on the group report; however, the progress of each new employee is not known. Should group reporting be utilized, it is recommended that the prior weekly basis for calculating individual performance be made available for supervisors to calculate the performance of new employees.

SUMMARY

In this chapter, we discussed the development of a firm foundation on which decisions can be made, and the means to keep the work management program viable and dynamic. Work management programs that fail do so because the foundation upon which they are built (the standards and the reporting structure) and the uses of data are not in tune with the organization. Work management program managers should not seek techniques for creating more accurate standards and more accurate reports until such time as the programs which they offer are fully utilized in their current form. The development of more advanced techniques will serve no purpose unless the information generated is used to improve productivity and reduce costs.

CHAPTER

Accountability for Professional Functions

EVERY EMPLOYEE AT EVERY LEVEL has the right to know what is expected of him and how he measures up to these expectations. In our first chapter we discussed how every employee in an organization is accountable to someone. In order to assess the impact of an employee's actions, it is essential that each employee have some measure of how well he has carried out his assigned responsibilities. The more objective the measure, the better. As we move further up the organizational pyramid toward the chairman of the board, traditional industrial engineering techniques are less applicable and other techniques for measuring performance should be used. In the following sections, we will introduce some of the measurement techniques which can be used to evaluate how well professional functions are carried out.

THE NEED FOR CONTROLS

Why are controls needed for professional functions? For the same reasons that controls are needed at the clerical level. By way of review, these reasons are:

To establish goals. Everyone in an organization should have goals against which his performance can be evaluated. Goals may be expressed in terms of earnings per share, reduction in operating expenses, percentage of overdue loans collected, sales made, or additional output of work. In essence, overall corporate objectives are translated into these individual goals.

300

To evaluate performance. At the clerical level, where work is more routine, we can measure output and evaluate performance on the basis of work produced. At the higher levels, the evaluation of performance is equally important, but overall evaluations become more subjective as the measures applied are less precise. There should, in any case, be a means to determine how well individuals or groups of individuals have measured up to the goals established for their performance.

To determine and control costs. The cost of doing business, from a labor point of view, may be divided into (1) the direct labor required to produce the product and (2) associated overhead. Professional employee monitoring techniques provide a basis for allocating the expenses of staff departments, management, and technical functions to the products produced in order to determine costs. Obviously, once costs are known, control of these costs becomes possible and overall fiscal accountability improved.

To plan workload. In the absence of a means to measure the effectiveness of professional functions, the planning process becomes more of a guessing game than an exercise in scientific management. It is essential that data development through a program of professional performance measures be used to forecast manpower requirements for these functions.

To assure proper control. Controls tell employees at any level what should be emphasized and what is less important. In the absence of controls the wrong things may get too much attention, causing the organization as a whole to falter from its goals.

Who Is the Professional Worker?

The concept of the professional worker varies a great deal from industry to industry. In the main, there are two major groupings of professional workers. On the one hand, we find technicians with specialty skills and knowledge; on the other hand, we find managerial personnel.

Virtually all firms have a core of professional technicians. Regardless of the industry or the size of the organization, technical skills are devoted to the development of methods and procedures, the development of automated systems, the programming of these systems, accounting, and planning. In specialized industry, technical personnel includes underwriters responsible for selecting risks; we find lending officers, investment officers, and money managers. In the insurance industry, technical personnel includes underwriters responsible for selecting risks: actuaries to determine business profitability and establish insurance and mortality rates; claims examiners; and agency personnel responsible for recruiting and training of agents.

In every organization we find professional workers on the management team at all levels. These range from unit leaders supervising small groups of employees who perform clerical functions, to the chairman of the board, who is accountable to the stockholders.

EVALUATING PROFESSIONAL EMPLOYEES' PERFORMANCE

It would be naive to believe that an in-depth analysis of the many techniques for measuring the productivity of professional work could be presented in a single chapter. It is our intention to give the reader an overview of some of the possible means of measuring professional performance and provide a primary source so that a more in-depth research can be used to develop professional employee monitoring programs within the organization.

The three major types of measurement program are fiscal controls, performance standards, and scheduling techniques.

Fiscal Controls

There are two types of accounting. We can call them statutory accounting and management accounting. Both use numbers. However, whereas statutory accounting involves those numbers used by accountants and other external groups such as regulatory agencies to evaluate a company's performance, management (or responsibility) accounting takes these and other numbers and reworks them for internal use to evaluate managerial performance. We will deal exclusively with managerial or responsibility accounting here.

Responsibility accounting is a technique used primarily to evaluate management's use of resources. In some selected cases, responsibility accounting can be used successfully as a means to control the development and implementation of major systems. As the name suggests, the key ingredient to an effective responsibility accounting program lies in the placement of responsibility. In a typical program, responsibility for the planning of expenses is placed at that point in the organization where management has control over the expenses. As an example, a responsibility accounting program in a bank would place the responsibility for planning and control of expenses in a small branch with the branch manager. In a larger branch office with several diverse functions, including the teller function, the head teller might be responsible for all tellers, while another manager might be responsible for other activities.

Properly implemented, responsibility accounting is a four-step process: (1) goal development, (2) budget development, (3) monitoring results, and (4) remedial action. Elimination of any of the steps severely weakens the system's ability to be used as a means of gauging managerial effectiveness and controlling costs.

DEVELOPMENT OF GOALS

The first step in the process of developing a responsibility accounting program is the establishment of overall corporate goals. Marketing strategy, analysis of past and potential sales performance, and economic conditions are all taken into consideration when developing an overall corporate goal strategy. Overall corporate goals may be expressed in terms of earnings per share, overall gross sales, increases in profitability, or similar measures. Once overall corporate strategies are determined, each of the operating areas of the organization begins the development of a plan for achieving its goals.

DEVELOPMENT OF BUDGETS

Throughout the organization, responsible managers evaluate their resource needs to meet overall corporate strategies. In an insurance company, for example, the overall corporate goal of increasing the amount of life insurance in force by a given amount will be evaluated by the agency manager, who will carefully examine the agent resources and determine whether or not the existing staff is capable of meeting corporate objectives. In the underwriting department, the manager of underwriting will assess the goal for additional insurance in force and relate it to the number of applications which must be reviewed by his underwriting staff. In short, throughout the organization, from the mail room to the president's office, managers will budget the necessary resources to meet overall corporate objectives.

This planning process is not as easy as it may sound. The accounting manager may feel he can handle an influx of new premiums to be collected if there can be modifications made to his data processing system. He must request estimates of the cost of system revision from the data processing department in order to be able to fully evaluate how his resources are to be committed. In turn, the data processing department must develop priorities for use of its resources and must carefully evaluate the overall impact on corporate goals of each project. This evaluation may lead to additional costs in the data processing area, which are underwritten by reduced costs in other operating departments.

The budgets of responsibility managers at the unit, with additions for department staff, become the budget for the department. Similarly, department budgets, with additions for division staff, become the division budget, and the sum of the division budgets becomes the overall company plan.

The other side of the planning process is a similar development of income for the planned level of activity. The overall corporate goal can now be retrieved in terms of its ultimate impact on profitability. If the goal for the organization was expressed in terms of increased earnings per share, the income and expense planning will allow a comparison with this goal. Failure to meet objectives would result in a review of income and expense data. Some low-priority expense items might be deleted to lower expenses while additional resources might be allocated to the generation of new income—say, through increased advertising or additional sales personnel.

Texas Instruments in 1969 developed a program called *zero-base budgeting* (ZBB). ZBB is a powerful tool to assist in the development of the budgeting process for any organization. The basic difference between a ZBB budget and one developed through the techniques previously described is this: in traditional financial budgeting, it is assumed that the activities of the organization are all necessary and that funds should be allocated as part of the overall expense plan to conduct these activities; zero-base budgeting makes the assumption that no function or expense is absolutely required, but all must be justified. The expense of maintaining the chief executive's private aircraft is reviewed in the same way as the addition of a CRT in the accounting department.

In zero-base budgeting, a manager in reality develops a number of budgets for his area of responsibility. These budgets, called "decision packages," represent the expenses required to complete a given function. That function is critically examined in the decision package, and the impact of doing or not doing the function is appraised by the manager. His recommendations accompany the decision package to higher levels of the organization. The decision package not only includes alternative methods of performing the same activity, but also considers the costs and effects of doing only a part of the activity. As an example of this latter course of action, the state of Georgia, using ZBB, decided to reduce the width of the grass strip mowed along highways from 30 feet to 15 feet, thus halving the time required to do highway maintenance of this type.

ZBB is a very formal system. In order for it to be successful, managers must critically and honestly evaluate every aspect of expense when developing their budgets. It is all too easy, for example, to renew a magazine subscription because it represents a minor expense, even though the magazine is not read by members of the staff and no profitable ideas have been developed from it.

MONITORING RESULTS

Once the budget is approved, a reporting mechanism monitors the income and expenses of each budgetary unit (responsibility center). A typical responsibility center report is shown in Table 24-1.

To be effective, budget reports must be accurate and timely. In the sample report, we note that the budget is stated in terms of both the current reporting period (month) and year to date. In general, when analyzing responsibility accounting reports, more weight should be placed on year-to-date data than on data for an individual month. It is often difficult to budget accurately on a month-to-

Table 24-1. Responsibility accounting report for a customer service department.

This Month			Expense/Income Category	Year to Date		
Budget	Actual	Variance		Budget	Actual	Variance
			SALARIES/PERSONNEL			
4,680	4,535	−145	Salary—Full-Time	15,060	15,121	61
—	110	110	Salary—Overtime	310	110	−200
1,404	1,394	−10	Fringe Benefit Expense	4,611	4,569	−42
(9)	(9)	—	Full-Time Employees	(9)	(9)	—
			OTHER EXPENSES			
146	154	8	Postage	525	470	−55
205	160	−45	Forms & Supplies	710	700	−10
317	399	82	Telephone	1,030	1,115	85
500	500	—	Occupancy	1,500	1,500	—
			PURCHASED SERVICES			
1,105	1,370	265	Data Processing	3,580	3,595	15
808	1,455	647	Systems & Procedures	3,055	2,400	−655
100	80	−20	Duplicating	300	230	−70
9,265	10,157	892	Total Expense	30,681	29,810	−871

month basis. As an example, suppose it is anticipated that a new employee will be hired in June, and the appropriate salary budget reflects that assumption. In actuality, the employee is able to begin work a month earlier than anticipated, which causes an unfavorable salary variance for May. Depending on the size of the budget item in relation to total expenses, this type of variation may appear to be a serious variance from plan; however, in light of the total budget it may be insignificant.

REMEDIAL ACTION

Remedial action in the responsibility accounting program can occur both before and after the fact. A manager of a responsibility center may request a variance from budget prior to incurring an expense which is not a budgeted item or which will exceed budgeted amounts. Authorization to proceed with this type of expense can be handled in two fashions. An adjustment can be made to budget, which will allow the additional expense, or the variation from budget can be carried on a continuing basis. In some cases, a manager may bargain for the approval of a current expense by establishing a goal to reduce other expenses by either a commensurate amount or a portion of the extra item.

The keys to an effective responsibility accounting program are the creation of challenging budgets and continual effort on the part of management at all levels to live within these budgets. It should be recognized that any plan may need to be modified during the course of a budgetary period to take advantage of unforeseen opportunities or to react to problems.

Performance Standards

Another possible approach to monitoring professional performance is the development of standards. Because of the nature of professional work, the techniques used to develop standards for professional employees often differ from those used for clerical employees. The following sections introduce some of these techniques.

KEY OUTPUT ANALYSIS

Key output analysis is a simple yet effective tool which can be used to monitor not only the productivity of individuals and groups of individuals but, if properly developed, also the cost of producing goods and services. As the name suggests, key output analysis is a broad-based management index that monitors staff levels, expenses, and the volume of key items. It involves four steps: (1) the index interview, (2) index development, (3) data collection and analysis, and (4) reporting results.

The index interview. The interview is conducted between an analyst and the manager of the responsibility center (in essence, the manager can interview himself). During these discussions, the analyst reviews the nature of the center, the products and services produced, overall department functions, existing records of time, volume, and expense, and the size and makeup of the current staff.

Index development. The second step in the installation process is to develop a workload index, or indexes, representing the effort required to produce one or more key items of work. Key items are those that represent the principal activity of the unit. Normally, historical data are readily available for the items chosen so that it is possible to create "instant trend."

To illustrate the key index concept, in a policy-owners service department in an insurance company, the key item would probably be a request for a policy change, even though there may be some changes in name and address, changes in beneficiary, and changes in mode of payment. In an installment lending department in a bank, the key output item might be loan applications reviewed, even though there may be a mixture of automobile, mobile-home, home-improvement, and other types of loans. In departments with several functions, a "garbage index"—an index based on the processing of unrelated activities performed in the department—can be developed.

A great deal of creativity can go into the determination of the key output item.

Table 24-2. Key output analysis—index development sheet.

Month	Key Volume (A)	Number of Employees (B)	Salary Expense (C)	Other Expense (D)
Jan. 98	87,148	12.2	$7,843	$20,915
Feb. 98	85,451	11.3	7,693	18,806
Mar. 98	86,268	11.8	7,764	25,880
Apr. 98	92,119	11.3	8,291	34,084
May 98	88,307	12.0	7,948	16,778
Jun. 98	90,614	12.5	7,249	15,404
Jul. 98	92,226	12.4	8,300	20,290
Aug. 98	80,793	13.0	7,271	8,079
Sept. 98	93,597	12.3	8,424	15,911
Oct. 98	91,846	12.3	9,185	20,206
Nov. 98	84,043	12.3	8,404	8,404
Dec. 98	70,315	12.5	7,734	11,250
Total	1,042,727	145.9	$96,106	$216,007
Average	8,689	12.2	$ 8,009	$ 18,001

	Actual	Plan	Increase/Decrease
Key Items/Employee (A ÷ B)	7,147	7,647	− 7.0%
Salary Cost/Key Item (C ÷ A = E)	$.092	$.092	—
Other Cost/Key Item (D ÷ A = F)	$.207	$ 186	−11.3%
Total Cost/Key Item (E + F)	$.299	$.278	− 7.6%

If, for example, the principal function of the department is to generate income, the key output item may be expressed in terms of dollars of revenue rather than items of work.

Data collection and analysis. Once the key items are identified, the analyst and/or department manager can begin to collect appropriate historical information so as to analyze past and current trends and develop plans for the future. If no historical information is available, reporting begins immediately, and trends are developed starting with the first reporting period. Overall data collection is quite simple. For a normal reporting cycle, all that would be required is a simple monthly listing of the volume of key items produced, the number of employees utilized to produce those items, and the expense associated with producing them. It is beneficial, when possible, to isolate salary expenses from other expenses in order to be able to develop direct labor costs. Table 24-2 is an example of a typical index development sheet. The development process utilized is primarily that of determining what has been achieved in the past and developing planned levels of productivity and expense.

Reporting results. The report system in a key output analysis program is a model of simplicity. The only data that need to be collected are volume of key items, number of employees utilized during the month, and dollars of expense. These items are compared to plan. Table 24-3 is a typical key output analysis report. Note that in a typical program several months of reporting are shown so that trends may be analyzed. In Table 24-3, three months of reporting (representing first-quarter results) are shown. The longer the period covered by trend information, the more meaningful the data. It should be noted, however, that changes in methods or procedures or product mix may result in extreme distortions of data if the changes made are of significant magnitude. In case of major change, it may be advisable to restate old data in terms of the new procedures. Alternatively, new trend information can be developed from the point of the change forward. Similarly, expense data may be adjusted to reflect the inflationary trends in the economy.

Table 24-3. Key output analysis report.

Month	Volume	Employees	Items/ Employee	% Plan	Salary Cost	Other Cost	Total Cost	% Plan
Plan	—	—	7,647	—	.092	.186	.278	—
Jan. 99	86,138	11.3	6,430	84	.109	.235	.344	124
Feb. 99	84,227	11.0	7,657	100	.093	.187	.280	101
Mar. 99	82,475	10.7	7,708	101	.092	.184	.276	99

Remedial action. Key output analysis does not lend itself readily to specific remedial action. Reported results are indications that there are either favorable or unfavorable trends in employee workload and expense. For example, in income-producing centers, unfavorable results are simply an indication of a failure to achieve sales goals. Key output analysis, however, provides an indication that more accurate data are required to effect corrective action. One of its advantages is its overall simplicity, which makes it readily acceptable to supervisors and managers at all levels.

Analysis from a costing point of view can be undertaken to determine if the unfavorable trends in expense are a result of reduced volume of key items or excess expense. Key output analysis provides a basis for alerting supervisors and managers to the need to review their staffing and budget plans and assess them on a unit-cost and productivity basis.

MANAGEMENT BY OBJECTIVES

Management by objectives (MBO) is a technique of management which has been in use for a number of years. It is not a radically new concept of management but rather a formalization of the way in which an organization establishes objectives, plans to meet these objectives, and measures results.

Webster defines management as "the act, art, or practice of managing; administration," and defines objective as "pertaining to a goal or end." Thus Webster presumably would define MBO as "the art or practice of managing to achieve a goal or end."

Some people maintain that there are as many styles of management as there are organizations and managers. For all practical purposes, however, these management styles can be reduced to a few basic ones. In uncontrolled companies the predominant management style is management by crisis. Management looks neither forward nor back, but reacts to challenges on a day-to-day basis. Managers in these companies are in essence fighting brush fires as they occur, with neither the time nor the inclination to determine why these crisis conditions exist and what means there are to prevent their recurrence.

In a second set of companies, the emphasis of management is on financial considerations. Results are measured in terms of return on investment, earnings per share, actual costs versus the standard costs of producing products and services, and adherence or nonadherence to budgets. Overemphasis on the financial side of business tends to ignore the contributions and needs of people. Managers and supervisors at all levels are swept up with concern for the almighty dollar in their day-to-day operations. Costs frequently become the key consideration, and in some cases, in their zeal to improve return on investment or reduce costs, managers may reduce the quality of goods or service provided or inadequately plan for future growth through a failure to develop individuals and engage in research.

Management by objectives (the term was coined by Peter Drucker in 1954) places the emphasis of management on people within the organization. Managing through people does not mean ignoring financial considerations. On the contrary, in the long run, working through people will provide even better controls over the financial aspect of management.

Management by objectives is successful for a number of reasons. Among those more commonly mentioned are:

MBO requires people to think ahead. Especially at the first-line-supervisor level, the trend in a typical organization is to deal with today's problems. The formal planning process of MBO focuses attention not only on the problem of today but also on the challenges of the future and the means to cope with them.

MBO is a motivator of managers. Professor C. Jackson Greyson of the American Productivity Center identified what he called the three R's of productivity improvement—recognition, responsibility, and reward. The process of management by objectives defines a manager's responsibility, recognizes him for his achievements, and provides a basis for rewarding him for those achievements.

MBO shapes the direction the organization will take. In uncontrolled environments, or where goals are poorly defined, enthusiasm, energy, and resources may be directed to cross-purposes. For example, the forms-control function of an organization may be directing time, money, and other resources to the development of a new coding form to provide statistical data for the data processing system, while the systems department may at the same time be developing an on-line system for direct entry which will eliminate the need for the form.

An MBO program requires that at the beginning of each budgeting period, goals (in essence, a contract) be established between each manager and those who report to him. The second step is a periodic review of individual goals and actual achievements.

The establishment of goals is, in reality, a two-step process. Each manager, in order to identify goals for his subordinates, first needs to identify goals for his area of responsibility. These goals might well be expressed in terms such as profitability of the organization, development of new programs, public-relations responsibilities to be undertaken, recruiting and training of new personnel, or overall productivity. A review of the organization chart is essential so that the goals of the overall organization may be divided among individual managers—in essence, each manager takes on a portion of the responsibilities for the achievement of goals of the organization as a whole. The second step of the goal-setting process involves the agreement between a manager and subordinate that the goals are reasonable and attainable.

Goals established with subordinates will normally fall into four categories: (1) goals for successful completion of the routine responsibilities of the job—that is, processing work accurately, economically, and on time; (2) goals for personal improvement—say, by attending courses for individual development; (3) goals for solving problems that are currently perplexing the organizational unit; and (4) goals for development of creative, novel solutions to old problems.

Goal statements (besides those for routine duties) should include not only a statement of objectives to be achieved and methods of achieving them but also a specific time schedule for implementation, with key checkpoints or milestones identified. Throughout the year, this timetable should be reviewed periodically to determine if a manager is meeting his personal goals. Where possible, goals should be quantified, not only in terms of time on an implementation schedule, but also in terms of implementation costs, volume of activity, product quality, and timeliness of service. These goals should be reviewed on a periodic basis. Where possible, information from other systems such as work measurement, responsibility accounting, or quality control can be utilized to quantify goals and compare achievements with goals.

Reporting results. Reporting of results in MBO is normally an annual process.

As the end of the year draws near, each manager should review his goals and report to his superior on his achievements for the year. Periodic meetings throughout the year serve as a review of targeted timetable goals. The manager, in making the report to his superior on goal achievement, should include not only those goals which have been achieved but also those which have not been met. Where a manager has fallen short of a goal, an analysis of the reason for failure to meet the goal should be made. While it is not the purpose of management by objectives to directly point fingers at unsuccessful efforts, a penetrating analysis by the manager who fails to meet a particular goal, showing the reason for failure, can serve as a basis for discussing past performance and planning for improvement.

Criterion for success. In order to make MBO work, management support is essential. Management support should exist in an organizational structure with clearly defined responsibilities and managers who are given the freedom to manage within the constraints of the good of the organization. It should be understood by all concerned that MBO is not a substitute for excellence in management but rather is a vehicle by which good management may be more effectively practiced. Finally, MBO presupposes free communication within the organization through the normal chain of command.

Problems. Just as there are criteria for success, there are potential problems facing every MBO program. In any results-oriented program, people will tend to promise either more than they can possibly produce or less than they can actually produce. Thus some managers will establish goals that are too challenging to be realistically achieved, and will always fall short of their objectives, while other managers will always appear to achieve a great deal because their goals are not challenging. Good objectives for an MBO program should not only be in writing, but be challenging yet realistically attainable, following the principle that a man's reach should exceed his grasp. Care should be taken to ensure that the employee establishing an objective has control over whether that objective can be met.

Scheduling Techniques

There are numerous scheduling techniques that are useful, not only for monitoring the installation of a project, but also for measuring the performance of professional employees. Scheduling techniques can be used in concert with programs such as MBO, where the goals of the MBO program can be quantified through the schedule.

GANTT CHARTS

These charts were developed during World War I by Henry Gantt. Gantt was one of the pioneers in scientific management. He developed the charting techniques for the planning of production, utilization of equipment, performance of individuals, or project progress. The original work by Gantt, Wallace Clark, and David Porter has been used in a variety of forms effectively. Gantt charts are an ideal project-planning tool, because they monitor not only those activities that have been planned but any activities actually completed.

Figure 24-1 is an example of a Gantt chart for the installation of a work management program in a customer service department. The activities required to install the program are listed at the left side of the chart. The time scale runs from left to right along the top of the chart. The original plan is graphically depicted by a bracket, with the left end indicating the point at which the activity is to begin and the right end, the point when the activity is to be completed. A light line is used for the graphing of the plan. On a periodic basis, usually weekly, the chart is updated to reflect actual progress. In the sample chart, the circled figures at the top of the chart indicate that progress has been posted up through the sixth week of the project. (In the original Gantt system, a V indicated the point to which the chart had been updated.)

Again referring to Figure 24-1, we note that the activities of analyst training and development of task lists have been completed on schedule, while the development of standards is under way. The design of the reporting system is approximately one

Figure 24-1. Gantt chart for a work management program (13-week period).

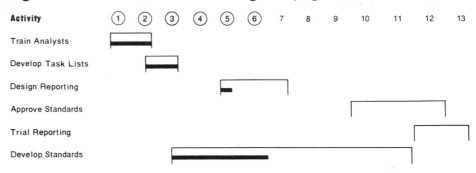

Figure 24-2. Adaptation of Gantt chart for a project plan (8-week period).

	①		②		③		4		5		6		7		8	
	Plan	Actual	Plan	Actual	Plan	Actual	Plan	Actual	Plan	Actual	Plan	Actual	Plan	Actual	Plan	Actual
H. Brown	5	3	5	8	5	6	3		5		2		5		5	
T. Jensen	2	0	2	4	3	1	4		5		5		5		5	
Total for week	7	3	7	12	8	7	7		10		7		10		10	
Cumulative total	7	3	14	15	22	22	29		39		46		56		66	

week behind schedule, and standard approval and trial reporting have not yet begun.

This master chart may be supplemented by individual charts defining each activity in additional detail. Figure 24-2 is a Gantt chart for the standard-setting portion of the project. A review of the chart shows that Brown was scheduled to develop five standards in each of the three weeks of the project. During the first week, three were developed; in the second week, eight; and in the third week, six. Brown's productivity, therefore, exceeds standard, and he is approximately one day ahead of schedule. The other analyst assigned to the project, Jenson, was unable to establish any standards during the first week of the project, when two were required. During the second week of the project, he established four standards, placing him on schedule. During the third week of the project, one standard was established, and Jenson is behind schedule. An overall summary chart monitoring progress shows that, at the end of the third week of the project, 22 standards should have been established, and 22 have actually been completed. The project overall, therefore, is right on schedule.

The discipline of the development of a plan and the periodic updates to the Gantt chart provide a basis for remedial action. Each phase of a project and each employee's contribution can be monitored and corrective action taken where required.

Regardless of the charting techniques used, it is important that a project be treated not as one large undertaking but rather a series of related activities, each one to be completed within a given time. Establishing periodic milestones for completion enables management to take corrective action in time to ensure overall project success rather than determine during the last few weeks of a project that the project is several months behind schedule.

PERT

PERT is an acronym for Program Evaluation and Review Techniques. The PERT concepts were developed by the United States Navy for monitoring the development of the Polaris missile project. These scheduling techniques, which were so successful in the early development of the Polaris missile, have now been applied by numerous firms not only to planning the implementation of projects but to monitoring installation schedules. PERT is not particularly suited to monitoring repetitive work, but it is well suited to developing and monitoring project completion schedules.

A PERT scheduling program goes beyond other scheduling techniques in several respects. First, it provides three estimates of the time required to complete a project, including not only the most likely time required to complete a task, but also the most optimistic as well as the most pessimistic time estimates. Second, it allows for the development of a visual picture of the interrelationship between different functions for the project. Third, it allows for the development of a "critical path" representing those tasks that must be completed before others can be started if the project is to be completed on schedule. Finally, PERT provides a basis for monitoring project progress and establishing new goals and priorities to attempt to meet the projected schedule.

Development of time estimates. PERT deals with "events" and "activities." Events are normally identified on a PERT matrix as circles or squares. They are points in time when a phase of a project has been either begun or completed. Activities are the tasks being performed at the time. As an example, "begin to eat breakfast" is an event that starts at a given point in time. The activities of eating breakfast would include buttering toast, eating cereal, drinking coffee, and so forth.

Once events and activities are defined, time estimates are made for each. In our example of eating breakfast, the analyst establishing the estimated times might interview the person performing the activity and determine that it usually takes about eight minutes to eat breakfast. However, every once in a while I have time only for a cup of coffee, which takes about three minutes, and sometimes I have a full breakfast of bacon and eggs, which requires 15 minutes. The estimates developed for the most optimistic, the most probable, and the most pessimistic times to complete each activity are weighed using the following formula:

$$\text{Estimated time} = \frac{a + 4b + c}{6}$$

In this formula, a represents the most optimistic time schedule, b the most likely, and c the most pessimistic.

Figure 24-3. Fred's PERT chart for getting to work before marriage.

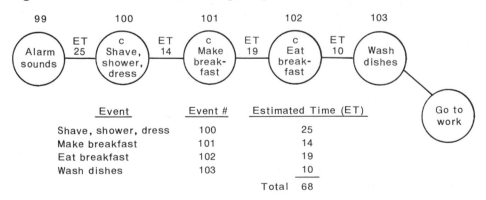

c = complete the task.

PERT matrix. Figure 24-3 is a PERT matrix of a simple series of events with no interdependence among activities other than that they must be completed in sequence. When Fred was single, he was able to arise at 7:00 AM and leave for work 68 minutes later. On the chart, the circles represent the events, and activity lines connecting the circles represent the sequence in which activities are completed. Estimated times (ET) are shown on the flow lines between events, which are numbered.

When Fred married Alice, who had a dog, getting to work become somewhat more complex. In an attempt to determine why it took so much longer to get to work, Fred developed the PERT chart shown in Figure 24-4. He discovered that, since there was only one shower in his apartment, Alice could not begin to shower and dress until he was out of the shower. Since Alice insisted on making breakfast, Fred could not begin to eat breakfast until Alice had completed showering, dressing, and making breakfast. Breakfast took longer, too, since it was accompanied by small talk. Spot, the dog, needed to be fed and walked before Fred could leave for work.

In this simple example, we begin to see the interdependence of activities. Looking at the sums of the elapsed time, we see that Alice's total activities take 139 minutes, whereas Fred's require only 96 minutes. Fred, therefore, is idle for 43 minutes. With the matrix developed, Fred has the opportunity to analyze the project of leaving for work and is able to resequence activities to improve performance.

Figure 24-5 represents the revised procedure. We note that Alice, who takes longer in the shower, showers first, while Fred feeds the dog. Fred begins his shower when Alice has finished her shower, and Alice goes on to make breakfast. Alice has to wait for Fred, since breakfast is completed 8 minutes before Fred is ready to eat it. After breakfast, Fred walks the dog, which takes less time than washing the dishes. As a result, Fred and Alice can leave for work in 97 minutes instead of the 139 originally taken.

This simplistic example points out the importance of plotting activities to make the best use of available time. Additional analysis might suggest the possibility of Fred beginning breakfast after he feeds the dog, which would increase Alice's idle time and perhaps give her time to read the paper. Further improvement in time is probably dependent on more effective methods of showering and dressing or on eating faster. The alternatives, in any case, can be evaluated readily from a PERT matrix.

The more complex the matrix, the more difficult it is to develop the interrelationship of activities. Numerous computer programs have been created by software firms and individual users to allow ready analysis of the slack time in a project and development of the critical path.

Figure 24-4. Fred's PERT chart for getting to work after marriage, before PERT analysis.

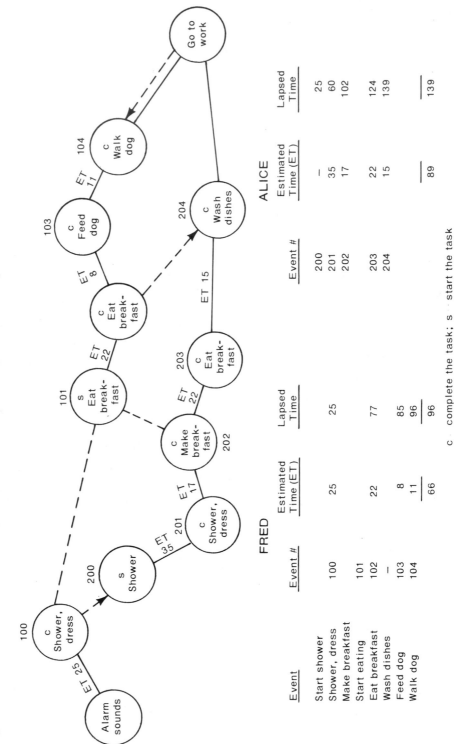

FRED

Event	Event #	Estimated Time (ET)	Lapsed Time
Start shower	100		
Shower, dress		25	25
Make breakfast	101		
Start eating			
Eat breakfast	102	22	77
Wash dishes	–		
Feed dog	103	8	85
Walk dog	104	11	96
		66	96

ALICE

Event	Event #	Estimated Time (ET)	Lapsed Time
Start shower	200	–	25
Shower, dress	201	35	60
Make breakfast	202	17	102
Start eating			
Eat breakfast	203	22	124
Wash dishes	204	15	139
Feed dog			
Walk dog			
		89	139

c - complete the task; s - start the task

Figure 24-5. Fred's PERT chart after PERT analysis.

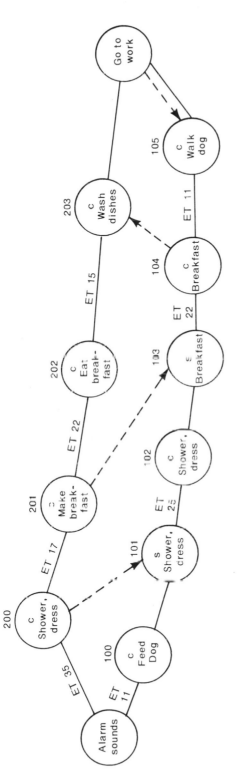

FRED

Event	Event #	Estimated Time (ET)	Lapsed Time
Feed dog	100	8	8
Start shower	101	–	35
Shower	102	25	60
Start breakfast	103	–	60
Eat breakfast	104	22	82
Walk dog	105	11	93
		65	93

ALICE

Event	Event #	Estimated Time (ET)	Lapsed Time
Shower, dress	200	35	35
Make breakfast	201	17	60
Eat breakfast	202	22	82
Wash dishes	203	15	97
		89	97

Conclusion

To monitor the effectiveness of professional workers, a variety of approaches may be used. In addition to those briefly described in this chapter, the reader has the option of creating his own approach, combining some of the best features of the approaches discussed, or researching additional means of controlling the effectiveness of professional workers which we were unable to explore within the limited space of this chapter.

The central themes of any productivity improvement program must be the placement of responsibility, a means to monitor how well responsibilities are carried out, and periodic assessment of the extent to which goals for costs, time, or productivity are met.

CHAPTER

Techniques for Improving Performance

IN ORDER TO IMPROVE PERFORMANCE in anything we do, we must institute some type of change. If we are to improve our golf score, we may need to adjust our grip on the club, change our stance, or simply get more practice in order to improve the fundamentals of the game. In the home, improving our favorite recipe may require a warmer oven, a shorter cooking time, or perhaps more seasoning. Similarly, productivity improvement in the office requires that change be made. Understanding the mechanics of performance and what changes to make and how to make them is part of the supervisor's responsibility to get work out accurately, economically, and on time. The supervisor who says that a work management program has not accomplished anything in his or her department has not used the data provided by the program to institute change.

In the office environment, we really are concerned with two types of productivity: employee performance and unit performance. Employee performance refers to how well individual employees work when they carry out their assigned tasks. Unit performance refers to how well the supervisor or manager uses the resources of his unit to produce the work of the department. While these two types of productivity are related, the techniques required for improving them are different and will be discussed separately.

319

IMPROVING EMPLOYEE PERFORMANCE

To improve employee performance, it is first necessary to gain a complete understanding of the components of performance. You will recall that the formula for calculating performance is:

$$\text{Performance} = \frac{\text{standard hours}}{\text{actual hours}}$$

What this formula says is that performance is equal to the amount of time that *should* be required by an average well-trained employee to do the work, divided by the time the employee actually *did* take. Examination of the formula would indicate that there are only two ways to improve employee performance: either the employee must do more work in the same time (which amounts to increasing the standard hours without changing the actual hours), or the employee must do the work currently assigned in less time (that is, reduce actual hours without changing standard hours).

In the authors' experience, there are very few poor performers. Today's employee is at work, gainfully employed, because he has pride in his abilities and finds satisfaction in earning a living. If there are few poor performers, why then do we frequently see performance of 62 percent, 51 percent, or even 37 percent appear on reports of employee performance? This section will provide some insight into this matter. In addition to examining the reasons why employees do not perform satisfactorily, we will discuss the supervisor's role in moving performance to acceptable levels.

If the intended result of employee efforts is output measured in whatever units are important to the company, it is necessary to trace where this output comes from. In Chapter 8, we covered in detail the factors that affect output of an individual. (See Figure 8-1 to review these important relationships in the output model.) All these factors have some influence on any one employee's performance. The degree of influence depends on the makeup of the individual and the skills of the supervisor. In addition, employee performance is affected by three behavioral factors: (1) communication of expectations for performance; (2) feedback on the results of efforts, and (3) reward or remedial action based on performance.

Communication of Expectations for Performance

Numerous behavioral studies have determined that there is a definite and positive relationship between the expectations for performance that are communicated and the performance actually achieved by a worker. In one well-known study, groups of school children were divided as equitably as possible by age, interest, grade, and behavior into two classes. One teacher was told that she was going to have a difficult year because the class as a whole did not have a great deal of interest in learning and did not measure up to other classes in abilities, and because many of the students had discipline problems that would make control of the class difficult. The second teacher was told that her students were eager to learn, possessed of unusual abilities, and models of proper behavior, and that she would be faced with a continuing challenge in keeping these students interested in their work, since their rate of learning would no doubt outstrip the normal lesson plan.

At the end of the test period, the two groups of students were examined. To no one's particular surprise, the teacher who had been told that she would have a difficult year had indeed been very frustrated by the students. They had become discipline problems, they had only learned a few simple concepts, their attitudes toward school and learning in general were poor, and their progress, when measured against that of other classes, was below par. The students whose teacher had been told that they would be eager and challenging had indeed shown a very positive attitude toward learning, had achieved more than the typical class, and had been models of proper behavior, and the teacher had developed and implemented a number of creative teaching techniques to keep the students challenged and interested.

While one may rightly question the morality of this type of experiment because of its possible impact on the future academic career of the students, it would appear that there is an inescapable conclusion from this test and other similar ones. That conclusion is that where expectations for performance are good (or poor), then performance will also tend to be good or poor.

The first step in improving employee performance, therefore, is to communicate clearly to the employee expectations for performance. Performance expectations should be expressed both in terms of the performance expected on a continuing basis once satisfactory performance is achieved and in terms of increments or milestones so that employees can determine whether or not they are on target toward achieving an overall satisfactory performance level.

Needless to say, performance data from a work management program are one of the best means of communicating expectations of performance on an equitable and consistent basis. Learning curves can be developed for each position in the organization; these curves will provide both a means to communicate how long it should take to reach an acceptable level of performance and a basis for comparing employee performance to the progress of others in the position. Figure 25-1 is an example of a learning curve. Employees, too, will receive satisfaction from seeing the progress they are making compared against norms.

Feedback on Results

If it is important for an employee to know what his performance should be, it is equally important for him to know what his current performance is. Supervisors in some cases may try to shield an employee from reality. If an employee's perform-

Figure 25-I. Typical learning curve for an encoding operator.

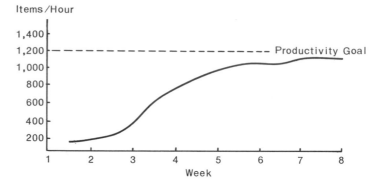

ance is not satisfactory, the supervisor should initiate some form of remedial action to bring performance to an acceptable level. Remedial action will be discussed in some detail later in this chapter.

If there is one single failing of today's supervisor, it is the unwillingness to discuss employee performance, communicate expectations for performance, and take the necessary remedial steps to bring performance to acceptable levels. Too often this results from management's failure to define the role of the supervisor and provide him with the necessary training, tools, and guidance to carry out his responsibilities.

Remedial Action

When counseling and efforts of the individual employee have been unsuccessful in bringing employee performance to acceptable levels, the next steps to be taken are to audit how the employee reports his performance and to reassess the motivation and job skills the employee brings to the workplace. The following subsections will suggest techniques for auditing these important performance factors.

AUDITING OFF-STANDARD TIME

The single greatest cause of apparent poor performance is not the employee's inability as a worker but failure to properly record how time is spent. You will recall from earlier chapters that one of the sources of savings in a work management program is to successfully combat Parkinson's law. Briefly, Parkinson's law states that work expands so as to fill the time available for its completion. In a typical office environment, the low-performing employee usually is not lazy but simply does not have enough work to do. Consciously or unconsciously, the employee therefore paces himself so that the work to be done is completed without any seeming wastage of time. Rather than stretch work out (take longer to do the work than is necessary), some employees will create additional tasks to occupy their time, such as unnecessary additional checking or keeping of records. Since the employee paces himself and always appears to be working, many supervisors and managers feel that there is no room for improvement in their area of responsibility. The following guidelines will provide a basis for auditing off-standard time.

• The employee should know which tasks and which portions of tasks are covered by standards and which are not. In a properly measured area, standards will cover 90 percent to 95 percent of the total workload of the department, so that the majority of an employee's time should be spent "on standard," performing measured tasks. There are cases where employees do not fully understand when they should sign "off standard." Failure to sign off standard after completing work at the normal work pace will result in reduced performance.

• The employee should understand the relationship of productive time to work completed as a means of earning a good performance. A demonstration of the impact of not signing "off standard" will, in all likelihood, improve employee attitude toward signing off standard. As an example, if an employee has four hours of work to do and stretches the work to fill six hours, his performance is 67 percent of standard. If the employee works steadily at his normal work pace and then signs off standard when work is completed, he may be able to complete the work in four hours, earning a performance of 100 percent and the recognition that accompanies good performance.

• It should be stressed to employees that they should sign "off standard" at the time the off-standard activity occurs rather than attempt at the end of the reporting period to reconstruct off-standard time. Most employees—for that matter, most people—have a poor concept of time and will tend to understate off-standard activity rather than overstate it, which will have the apparent effect of lowering their performance.

• Many employees will not report off-standard activity or a lack of work because they are insecure in their jobs. It should be stressed to the employee that reporting off-standard activity provides a basis for scheduling cross-training so that the employee can develop his full potential, and for assigning the employee to special projects which need to be completed, and which may be varied and interesting.

Auditing Volume Reporting

A second significant factor which leads to apparent poor performance is the failure to accurately and completely record the volume of items completed. As we have seen in the concept of standard staff presented in Chapter 22, the volume of activity is the most important factor in properly determining unit staffing. If the employees in the unit do not properly record their volume of work, they not only lower their performance but weaken the data base used for the calculation of the unit's required staff and for other management information.

The importance of recording volume of activity should be stressed from the beginning of a program. Spot checks carried out by the supervisor to monitor the accuracy of reporting will uncover problems of volume recording before they can seriously distort performance and staffing data. The following guidelines will aid in monitoring volume reporting:

• Contrary to popular belief, when employees do not record accurate work counts, the tendency is to record less work than is actually completed. Employees should understand the impact of accurate reporting of volume on their performance and on unit data. The time spent counting and recording work is usually included in employees' performance standards.

• It should be stressed to employees that each task they perform is important. Some employees feel that the operation of an isolated item of work will not have a bearing on their performance. This attitude leads to poor record-keeping habits and, eventually, an ineffective program.

• Employees should understand what item of work is to be counted and recorded. The task outline and, in many cases, the reporting forms utilized will indicate the unit of measure. In some cases, to improve the accuracy of standards and reports or to simplify reporting, this unit of measure may not be a document handled but some finer breakdown. In a typical example, where there is considerable variation in the number of lines coded on a document, the analyst may elect to establish a standard based on number of lines coded rather than number of documents completed. An employee who records the number of documents completed rather than the number of lines coded will not receive proper recognition for the skill and effort put into the job. Similarly, when a standard is based on pounds of mail sorted rather than individual pieces, a mailroom employee will earn a performance out of proportion to effort expended if he records the number of pieces processed.

AUDITING WORK DISTRIBUTION

Employees who are fully capable of achieving a good performance do not do so mainly because there is not enough work assigned to them. The supervisor must always consider this possibility and take the necessary action to assure that each employee has enough work to do to achieve a good performance.

IMPROVE SCHEDULING

Like faulty work distribution, inadequate scheduling prevents capable employees from achieving a good performance because of conditions beyond their control. In the case of poor scheduling, however, there may be enough work to go around, but it just does not flow to each work station in a timely fashion. Since in any workflow, no work station can operate faster than the slowest station in the flow, the supervisor must examine how work flows into the department, in terms of both timing and batch size. Does it flow into the department in large batches, or does it just trickle in throughout the day? If the largest volume of work arrives at 9:30 AM, how were the employees using their time between 8:30 and 9:30? If the work moves in such large batches that the staff on the work station cannot handle the volume within a reasonable time, subsequent work stations may be idle while backlogs are growing in the department. Changes to the flow or the work station assignments will match manpower on the basis of the work standards set and improve service as well as employee performance.

METHODS AND PROCEDURES AUDIT

If the employees properly record off-standard activity and the volume of items completed, and performance is still unsatisfactory, the cause may lie in the failure to use approved correct methods and procedures. The supervisor or designated trainer should observe the employee at work. In many cases, during a work management study, improved methods and procedures are developed and implemented, and the standard is based on the improved way of performing the task. Employees may fail to adopt these revised procedures and, as a result, either perform their tasks in an ineffective manner or perform work that is not required at all.

Another area to observe is how organized the employee is. Effective employees perform their tasks in a systematic fashion and keep an orderly workplace. Less effective employees, while completing all the steps within a task, may perform them in an improper sequence and operate in a cluttered work environment. It is especially important in high-volume tasks, where many items are handled, that the workplace be properly organized. Various types of racks and shelves may be purchased from office-equipment suppliers or created by a company to organize and make effective use of available space.

IMPROVING UNIT PERFORMANCE

Unit performance is calculated in the same fashion as employee performance. It is axiomatic that to improve unit performance requires either doing more work in the same time (an increase of standard hours) or doing the same work in less time (a decrease in hours spent on the job).

The efforts to improve individual employee performance will obviously also improve the performance of the group as a whole. However, these improvements will not lead to a decrease in cost.

At the department or unit level, it is virtually impossible to improve performance by increasing standard hours. Once the unit is operating on a current basis and all backlogs have been eliminated, there will be no other work that can be given to employees to improve either their performance or the performance of the unit. The only method available to improve unit performance is a decrease in the amount of time required to perform available work. There are two means of reducing hours spent: short-term and long-term.

Short-Term Means of Reducing Actual Hours

Short-term means of decreasing actual measured hours will improve unit performance and provide a basis for the development of a more flexible work force that is better suited to operate in a lower-cost environment. Short-term decreases in actual time are created by signing "off standard." Here are some of the available short-term means of utilizing off-standard time and thereby increasing both employee and unit performance:

Training. Once emphasis is placed on improving performance and employees begin to sign off standard when there is no work to be done, the supervisor should first use off-standard time to train and cross-train employees so that they not only fully understand their current responsibilities but learn additional jobs. Acquiring skills with additional tasks has the dual benefit of increasing employee satisfaction while providing essential backup for the temporary or permanent loss of a staff member. There are practical limits to cross-training, however. Not all employees should be expected to be cross-trained, nor is it practical to have them learn all tasks.

Special projects. There are in every organization a number of special projects that can be undertaken productively. The important thing is that projects should be productive, not merely make-work activities such as separating paper clips and rubber bands, repeated and unnecessary checking for misfiled items, arranging supplies, or the like. If they are productive and meaningful, special projects provide a means of rewarding employees who have improved their performance and learned new tasks.

Employee loans. The supervisor should be aware of other operating units within the organization that have a need for temporary employees. Excess staff in one area can be loaned to other areas to assist them with peak workloads and fill in for vacations or other absence to keep work flowing smoothly. Many offices operate an informal talent pool. When time is available, it is reported to a central clearing house, perhaps the personnel department. Similarly, management in need of assistance can request assistance from the pool to meet temporary out-of-balance conditions of staff and workload.

Loaning of employees rarely works well in an uncontrolled environment. Where work management programs are in place, the loaned employees can be recognized for their achievements in the borrowing unit as well as in their assigned unit.

Waiting for work. On a short-term basis, performance can be improved by encouraging employees to sign "off standards" when there is no work to perform. Waiting for work is desirable and can be used as a short-term fringe benefit. In some firms, employees who have finished their assigned tasks are free to leave for the day or are allowed to conduct personal business, as long as it does not interfere with the operations of the department. Needless to say, this type of fringe benefit is of a short-term nature and will disappear when the unit is properly staffed.

Long-Term Means of Reducing Actual Hours

Assuming that workload is relatively fixed, the only way to improve productivity in the department and reduce costs is to decrease the staff in the department. In the preceding section we have discussed artificial means of reducing employee time spent on the job. These do not lead to cost reductions, only to an increase in performance. To reduce cost we must balance the staff and workload of the department by a permanent reduction of actual paid employee hours. The "off standard" procedures discussed previously will provide a basis for proving that fewer employees can do the work in less time than is currently taken.

For an effective work management program, it is important that any reductions in the work force be made in a natural fashion. A good starting point for bringing staff and workload into balance is a decrease in the amount of overtime hours paid. A second step would be a reduction in the hours of part-time personnel on call or elimination of contract help from outside services.

Actual full-time staff reductions may be made through the normal personnel process as employees leave the company, transfer to other departments, or are promoted to higher levels of responsibility. The supervisor should analyze reports of employee and unit performance and consider not replacing employees or substituting part-time employees for full-time employees when staff and workload are out of balance.

A key index for measuring a supervisor's performance is the ratio of required staffing as expressed by a formula based on the work of the department compared to the actual staff in the department. In order to achieve an effectiveness of 100 percent, the department must be staffed in proper relation to its workload. It is the supervisor's goal to bring actual and standard staff into balance as soon as is practical. Because of the nature of the changes involved, it may require as long as four to six months to accomplish this goal without endangering employee morale.

In this chapter we have seen how employee and unit performance can be improved so as to reduce costs. The key ingredients are communication of performance expectations to employees, the development of a skilled and flexible work force, and an informed supervisor who uses performance standards to achieve results.

A work management program by itself cannot accomplish results. Productivity can be improved only by an informed management implementing changes in the light of available data.

26

Management's Role in Remedial Action

IT HAS BEEN OUR EXPERIENCE that the results from a work management program are in direct proportion to management's desire to achieve results. When a work management program does not achieve results projected for it, management often fails to look at how its own efforts (or lack of same) have contributed to program failure. In many cases, technically sound programs do not produce results because of the failure of management to carry out its responsibilities. In this chapter we will discuss the role of management, from the planning of the program through the maintenance phase.

MANAGEMENT'S ROLE IN PLANNING THE PROGRAM

The decision to embark on a work management program is an expression of management's desire to improve the operations of the company. Management involvement in program development begins with the definition of the objectives to be achieved through the program. Managers must objectively evaluate opportunities that exist in their area of responsibility or in the company as a whole and develop from this evaluation objectives that are consistent with the improvement opportunities identified.

During the development of objectives, managers may look to those things that they believe can be improved upon from their own knowledge, but they may also benefit from evaluations made by consultants during a survey or from information on what other firms have achieved. Failure to properly define objectives may make it difficult to evaluate program success accurately later on.

AUTHORIZING INSTALLATION

It is the responsibility of management to authorize program installation. Authorization represents the final approval to proceed with the achievement of program objectives.

Where in-house talent is not available, management should play an active role in either selecting a consulting firm to implement the program or selecting and hiring a trained person to carry out program objectives. The firm or individual selected should not only have the necessary technical skills to implement the proposed program but also, in management's opinion, be able to install the program in a fashion compatible with the management philosophy of the organization. For example, it would generally be unwise for management to select a firm or individual with a hard-nosed approach to work management when its own philosophy is low-key and strongly people-oriented.

Among the better ways to appraise the potential success of the consulting firm or proposed program head is an exhaustive check of references. Management should check references personally to see what other firms have accomplished, to learn of the effectiveness of techniques utilized, and to evaluate the style of the firm or candidate. Delegation of these responsibilities to others may weaken the opportunity to make the best possible selection.

The final authorization process may include the hiring of inside analysts. In previous chapters we discussed the importance of selecting the right analysts. Frequently, those individuals who are best qualified to become analysts currently occupy a key position in the organization where they are considered irreplaceable. They may be managers or supervisors of critical processing areas. Upper-level management should make every attempt to work out a plan by which the best people become available to fill the role of analyst. Sacrifices made to make the best people available are a firm demonstration of management interest in program success.

Hiring analysts from outside the organization is another alternative. However, management must be sure not to hire an analyst whose approach is so caustic and unbending that he will have to be "untrained." It would be better to hire a sharp, recent college or junior college graduate who will be enthusiastic to learn management skills while enjoying working with people.

MANAGEMENT'S ROLE IN INSTALLATION OF THE PROGRAM

The first point at which management's presence and interest is normally felt is during the introduction of the work management program to the company as a whole. The introductory process normally includes distribution of a letter or memorandum to all employees outlining the general conduct of the program and introducing the cast of players who will be directly involved. The introductory letter should reflect management's own particular style and, where possible, link the work management program to an earlier successful and related effort. For example, a major Midwest insurance company, in announcing its PRIDE work management program, described the work management effort as the next logical step to take after a major computer conversion.

In addition to distributing written material concerning the program, management should meet with supervisors and middle managers to "kick off" the program and introduce consultants and analysts. One of the reasons that a program implemented in a Southeastern health insurance company far exceeded the expectations of management was management's presence during a series of meetings that lasted throughout the day. Supervisors and middle managers were aware that senior staff had taken the time and shown the interest to devote an entire day to the process of getting the program started properly, which indicated the degree of importance attached to the project.

Another particularly successful program in the Southwest eschewed the written memorandum. Management chose personal introduction, using the normal organizational lines of communication. As each successive meeting was held (president to senior vice presidents, senior vice presidents to department heads, and so on down to the employee level), the boss's boss appeared at each meeting. More generally, this communication process can be illustrated as follows:

1. Letter to all staff from president outlining objectives of program and stating support.
2. A. President meets with division heads.
   B. Each division head meets with respective managers.
   C. Respective managers (with appropriate division head) meet with supervisors.
   D. Supervisors (with appropriate manager) meet with employees.
3. Feedback from each meeting is provided back up the line, keeping appropriate superior apprised of reactions.

Participation in Orientation Programs

Management plays two roles in participating in orientation for the work management program. On the one hand, managers become students in sessions designed to acquaint them with every aspect of the program. On the other hand, they act as teachers—typically, as guest lecturers for orientation sessions held for first-line supervisors and managers. It is incumbent on management to learn every detail of how the program is to be installed and the progress being made in program implementation and to fully understand its role at each phase of the project. This knowledge can come from formal training sessions or from written or verbal updates on progress from either the consultant or the in-house project manager.

The role of senior managers as teachers is to communicate enthusiasm for the project by demonstrating their interest and commitment to those supervisors and managers in whose departments the project is installed. During the orientation sessions, it is important not only to display enthusiasm for the project but also to outline what it is that first-line management is to do to achieve the program results management expects.

One of the major obstacles to achieving results has been the feeling on the part of first-line managers that they will be criticized for failure to manage effectively prior to the work management program. Supervisors may well be reluctant to agree that improvements are possible, since they feel that making these improvements will be a reflection on their past abilities to carry out their responsibilities. Management should accept the burden of these failures by indicating that prior to the implementation of the program, management did not have the necessary tools to achieve results that have been possible since implementation. Managers may, however, be criticized for not taking corrective action indicated by their new management tool, work management.

Participation in Methods Improvements

During the course of the study, changes will be recommended to improve the way work is processed. Often, these recommendations will be accepted and implemented at the supervisory level without the need for direct management involvement. In other cases, especially where improvements are recommended across department lines or where revisions need to be made in customer service policies, major systems, or equipment acquired, management may well play a role in critically evaluating the impact of suggested changes. In yet other cases, management may be asked to act as an arbitrator when the work management team feels a worthwhile improvement can be made and lower-level management fails to accept it. Developing a climate for change and dealing with methods improvement opportunities in a manner commensurate with their value further demonstrates management's overall interest in program success.

Failure to bring all decisions to a conclusion within a reasonable period is an inadvertent indication to the organization that the program does not have as high a priority as proclaimed. It also seriously hinders analyst effectiveness and delays results.

Progress Reporting

Management should be kept up to date on the progress of program installation. The installation should follow a set schedule that takes into account the areas to be studied, the extent of methods and procedures analysis, and the type of measurement technique utilized. Periodic review of progress should be made by management, not only with the project team, but also with supervisors. Along with the inputs from the installation team, continuing feedback from first-line supervisors and managers can be used to monitor their enthusiasm and project progress. These periodic discussions with management can also be used to recognize the achievements of supervisors and managers who have made improvements in their areas of responsibility. Feedback from the project team will indicate which supervisors have accepted recommendations for improvement, which employees have made suggestions to eliminate unnecessary work, and where recognition can be distributed. Similarly, where there is resistance to the program, knowledge that the installation is behind schedule or that methods require arbitration can be communicated to the first-line supervisor and corrective action can be taken.

Patience

After the planning phases are completed, consultants have been selected or in-house managers hired, and the program has been introduced, there is an apparent slowdown in overall project progress. Although a great deal is happening, there are no tangible results to discuss. During this phase, supervisors and managers are attending orientation sessions and analysts are attending classes and conducting the fact-gathering portion of the project, but management has nothing to show for it.

The pace at which a successful program is installed is most important. If the program is installed too rapidly, first-line supervisors may be resentful. Management should be patient with the progress of the installation as long as it follows the accepted project schedule. It is common that in its eagerness to both demonstrate interest and achieve results, management places too much emphasis on early reported results. Improvements made should be made at a pace that supervisors feel is reasonable. This may mean that some early improvement possibilities, such as not replacing an employee who leaves the job during a study where there is an apparent overstaffed condition, should be bypassed for longer-run gains. (However, supervisors who really dig in from day one will realize this saving at first opportunity.) The staffing of a department prior to a work management program has developed over an extended period of time. It is unreasonable to expect immediate change in the relationships between staff and workload, because it takes time for employees and management alike to adjust to working in a controlled environment.

Rather than attempt to achieve absolute results at this phase, management should stress experimentation. While management may believe that the supervisor can operate a department without filling a requisition for a terminating employee, it may arbitrate the difference with a supervisor who feels the employee should be replaced by urging a period of experimentation. Rather than say, "I'm not going to authorize this replacement," the patient manager will say, "Let's try to get along without a replacement for awhile and see how it works, and if you get behind in your work, we can provide you with some additional support in part-time or borrowed help."

MANAGEMENT'S ROLE IN MAINTAINING THE PROGRAM

Establishing Goals and Communicating Expectations

Once the program is installed and is in the maintenance phase in a given department or section, it is incumbent on management to continue to communicate goals for performance, staffing, work quality, and the like to supervisors. This communication of goals is in effect an extension of the supervisor training that has previously been undertaken by management. While goals can be expressed in terms of absolutes, such as the attainment of an average performance of 85 percent for the department and a proper balance between staff and workload, they should also be expressed in stages so that supervisors have intermediate objectives on which they can focus. These intermediate objectives can be established jointly with management and might call for performance of 65 percent at the end of the first month, 72 percent at the end of the second month, and so forth. Similarly, consistent with departmental turnover, goals can be established to bring staff and workload into balance.

In some cases where jobs are enriched and additional duties added, management must change the complexion of the staff in order to reach the suggested staffing level for a given workload. As an example, in a Northeastern bank, changes in the workflow had the inevitable effect that current employees found it difficult to carry out their assigned responsibilities at an effective level of performance. Management in this area planned to substitute one employee with revised qualifications suitable for the new processing system for each two employees leaving the organization. Obviously, the process of rebuilding an entire staff requires more time to achieve program results. The end product of a smaller, more qualified and better-paid staff is worth the extra time invested.

Naturally, it is not enough for management and supervisors to set goals: concrete plans to achieve these goals must be formulated. A target date is meaningless if plans to achieve the target are not made.

Analyzing Reports

The reporting system designed as part of the work management program provides information for managers to help them better operate their areas of responsibility. As we have seen in Chapter 22, the effective reporting system provides information on department performance and staffing to the first-line supervisor and to higher levels of management. It is a responsibility of management to analyze reports on a periodic basis with three key goals in mind.

1. Supervisors who make improvements identified in the reports should be recognized for their accomplishments. Recognition may be made immediately in the form of praise for a job well done, and in the long run through salary increases and promotion.

2. Where results are not consistent with goals and objectives established, management should question department supervisors to determine why goals were not achieved. In some cases work is under way to achieve goals and additional time may be required, while in other cases little or no progress may be evident. In these latter cases, reinforcement of objectives, volunteering of aid, and, as a last resort, direct action to implement change may be required.

3. Once staff and workload are in balance, a brief analysis of reports will indicate that systems and people are functioning properly. It is at this stage that management frequently loses interest in the program, feeling that all benefits to be achieved have been attained. It is, however, imperative that reporting continue in order that a data base be available to achieve new objectives that may be established or pinpoint problem situations before they can become serious.

When reports reflect the same data from one report period to another for some time, this is an indication to management that not enough attention is being placed on managing the work more effectively. There are always better ways to use resources.

Integrating the Program

Data generated by a work management program have many uses beyond the evaluation of employee performance and determining the proper staffing of departments. Among those we have discussed are the development of more accurate budgets, forecasting of manpower requirements, and the calculation of standard costs. Once the program has been installed in many areas, it is appropriate for management to begin to integrate the work management data base into the overall corporate management information system. In some cases this may mean that more accurate work management data replace subjective information previously used.

Needless to say, the management information system must avoid duplication of effort wherever possible. In some cases, for example, organizations have made direct links between the volume counts developed by processing systems such as on-line teller machines to the work management data base. Similarly, the work management reporting system captures data on employee hours worked, which can be used in place of personnel records to determine hours to be paid. During its installation phases, work management may seem more important than the completion of the work itself. The truly successful program merges into the organization so that while people have the data available for decision making, they are barely conscious of the program's existence.

Continuing Program Development

It is common for management at some point to become disenchanted with its work management program. The program may be technically sound, but the data generated no longer seem to have any real use. An analysis of a typical program at this point would normally find that the original program objectives have been achieved. It is at this stage that the effective program begins to develop new objectives, develops revised and perhaps simplified reporting, and, in general, evolves to meet the changing needs of management. Management should not take it for granted that program management can be responsive to the next phase of the project, and therefore should communicate its needs for information so that evolutionary changes can be made. A program that never changes is in trouble, because it is unresponsive to the needs of the organization.

A work management program has never achieved results on its own. While the program can identify improvement opportunities, it is up to management at all levels to make changes to see that identified opportunities are translated into results. The extent to which these results are achieved is in large measure dictated by the continuing interest of management and how well it communicates this interest to lower-level managers and employees throughout the organization.

CHAPTER

27

Using Work Management Data for Planning

SOME CRITICS OF WORK MANAGEMENT programs note that in a typical work management program, the data generated are based on past productivity. To quote an executive from an Eastern bank, "Those who use work management only to see what has happened are missing the point." It should be obvious that the data made available by a typical work management program are an ideal tool not only for controlling current practice but also for looking into the future and forecasting what should occur under normal circumstances.

In this chapter we will review the planning process and provide examples of typical uses of work management data for forecasting workload, determining staffing, and evaluating alternative methods, procedures, and systems.

OVERVIEW OF A TYPICAL PLANNING PROCESS

In a typical planning process, managers are asked to budget their personnel and other expenses for the coming year. Most financial planning, since it is created from the bottom upward, begins at the lowest level of management. Our typical manager reviews his staffing and expenses for the previous year and for other years for which data are available. He anticipates that, since the company is growing and he has had some difficulty in providing accurate and timely service, additional staff will be required for the coming work period, and he budgets accordingly. The final budget also will include some "fat"—manpower, equipment, and other items that would be nice to have but are not really required for the efficient operation of the department.

337

The budget completed by the first-line manager passes up through the organizational pyramid, with administrative budgets added at each level. The sum of these budgets becomes the initial plan for utilization of corporate resources for the coming year.

Senior staff, in reviewing the initial plan, keeps in mind that this budget may well include low-priority items as well as unnecessary additional expense for personnel. Typically, budgets are returned with an indication that supervisors and managers shall "sharpen their pencils" and reduce their expense budgets by a given amount in order to improve overall corporate productivity. The "fat" included in the original budgets is removed, and the budget is approved.

This type of budgetary process tends to penalize the good manager who has attempted to hold expenses down and operates close to optimum levels of staffing. Arbitrary reductions in personnel and expense that are requested may make it difficult for the good manager to provide good service on a timely basis during the coming period. He may even be criticized for failure to meet goals.

PLANNING VARIABLES

The preceding overview of a typical planning process highlights the problems that exist in organizations without sufficient facts for either short-range or long-range decision making. To better understand the planning process, we should examine the variables involved in determining the proper staffing level for a department.

Workload

In a typical staffing situation, the greatest contributor to staffing requirements is the amount of work that has to be done in order to provide service to that department's customers. Volume counts alone are not enough. Because of the complexities of work processed in today's environments, work must be expressed in a single common denominator: the time required to complete it. In a typical office operation where standards have been established, at least 90 percent of the total work is covered by standards, and work may be readily expressed in terms of the time required to complete it. In the case of other activities, such as special projects, day-to-day work that has not yet been measured, and periodic activity such as annual or quarterly reports, volume needs to be estimated and converted into the time required to complete these tasks.

Productivity

Productivity refers to the rate at which the workload of the department can be accomplished. Standards define the time required to complete the work at 100 percent of performance. Part of the planning process will also require that a department goal for productivity be established and that the actual workload, expressed as 100 percent of performance, be factored by the level of productivity to determine the amount of time required to complete the work.

Management Reserve

It would be an ideal situation if the only staff required were that to handle the workload at a given level of productivity. However, such is not the case. The management reserve which must be accounted for includes time for administration of the department by a supervisor or manager, holidays and vacations that department employees are entitled to take under corporate guidelines, absence from the department for illness or other personal reasons, and various scheduling delays that may be encountered in either workflow or equipment availability.

Service

The final variable to be considered is the timeliness of service to be provided. Where workloads are relatively constant, speed of service is not a major component in the planning process. Where workload varies considerably from day to day or week to week, staffing configurations should be established in order to provide the desired level of service at any given point in time.

THE PLANNING PROCESS AS IT SHOULD BE

Now that we more clearly understand the variables involved in planning, we can establish a plan that will incorporate more accurate projections and eliminate time- and energy-consuming revisions.

The first step of the planning process is to determine what the workload is going to be. Typically, the marketing department will develop forecasts of the volume of activity for the coming year. The volume of activity may be expressed in item counts or in dollars of sales and will be the best projection based on past history, the availability of new products, promotional campaigns to be undertaken, and the like.

With workload projections developed, each manager will translate overall corporate volume activity into a workload projection for his or her department. As an example, in an insurance company, marketing projections may well be based on premium (sales) dollars. The manager of the underwriting department, using other data such as average premiums per policy, can then translate the dollar volume of sales into the number of policies to be underwritten. He may also add from past experience an additional workload for processing policies that are reviewed but not sold. Similarly, the policy service department will project its activity on the basis of the number of new policies to be serviced as well as the amount of time required to service those policies already sold. The volume of activity can be expressed in terms of the time required to complete it, and adjustments can be made, if required, for new technology such as a new computer system and changes in the overall productivity of the department.

The budget again pyramids up through the organization, with administrative expense being added to it. Typically, the budget can be approved with only minor revisions when developed on this basis. The major items to be reviewed would be expenditures for major new systems and equipment. Zero-base budgeting and other techniques previously discussed may well be utilized to evaluate alternative systems for processing the work.

A budget developed in this way will be accepted by all management levels, since it is based on common and well-defined goals. In theory, if a manager is asked to reduce his budget, his first question should be, "What is it that I do today that you do not want me to complete in the future?" Of course, such a statement presupposes that productivity and utilization of time of the department are at satisfactory levels.

Examples of Typical Planning Situations

The following examples illustrate how work management data may be utilized to assist in a variety of different types of planning processes. Examination of the examples will reinforce the understanding of the variables of planning that should be considered prior to undertaking a planning project.

Table 27-1. Department staffing analysis.

Tasks	Std. Hrs.	Volume/Week	Std. Hrs./Week
Catalog Requests	.035	840	29.4
Cash Orders	.097	125	12.1
Credit Orders	.070	1,540	107.8
Correspondence	.163	210	34.2
Total Standard Hours			183.5
+ Productivity Variance (@ 85%)			32.3
Total Hours			215.8
+ Special Projects			25.0
Total Work Hours			240.8
+ Management Reserve (12%)			28.9
Required Supervision			37.5
Total Hours			307.2
Equivalent Full-Time Employees (37.5 Hours/Week)			8.2

Department Staffing

One of the most common purposes of planning is to determine what department staffing should be for any given level of workload. Table 27-1 is a worksheet outlining the steps required to determine the staffing of a given department. A brief summary follows:

1. Determine workload. The departmental workload is developed from overall corporate goals or other pertinent information. For example, corporate goals may suggest a 12 percent increase in volume.

2. Express workload as time. For each task to be performed, multiply the standard hours required to produce a unit of work at 100 percent of performance by the estimated volume for the period. The sum of the standard hours thus derived becomes the total time required to complete the work at 100 percent of performance.

3. Project productivity level. If overall departmental productivity is at a level of performance other than 100 percent, an adjustment should be made to the time required to complete the work. If, for example, the overall departmental performance goal is to be at 85 percent of standard, an allowance of 17.6 percent (15 ÷ 85) is required to reflect the time required at the 85 percent performance level.

4. Calculate total hours. The sum of the standard hours required plus the productivity variance will be the total hours required to complete the measured work of the department at the goal level of performance.

5. Allow for special projects. Estimates of the time required to complete special projects and other unmeasured activities should be added to the total standard hours, which will provide the total working hours of the department required to complete both measured and unmeasured activity.

6. Add management reserve. To the total work hours of the department we add the required management reserve for absence, vacation, and the like and for supervision of the operations of the department. The total hours thus derived can be converted into equivalent full-time employees.

In the example, staffing of 8.2 equivalent full-time employees is required. This staffing might well be made up of seven full-time employees and two part-time employees working the equivalent of the time of 1.2 full-time employees. In the absence of part-time employees, department staffing would require that overtime equivalent to two-tenths of one employee or time borrowed from other units equivalent to two-tenths of one employee be used in order to process the department's workload.

Staffing Customer Service Departments

The departmental staffing allowance discussed in the preceding section presupposes that the work of the department is to be concluded on a weekly basis and that any work not completed during a given work period may be carried over into the next period without the penalty of poor customer service. This carryover of workload is not possible in a customer service department such as the teller lines of banks or telephone sales representatives or walk-in claims adjustors. In essence, our original example ignored the subject of service by allowing workload to be equalized throughout the work period.

Table 27-2 is an example of a very simple teller staffing model. Where workloads vary throughout the day, we need to know at what point in time work is available to be processed. To accomplish this objective, an analysis is made of customer arrival patterns for different time periods throughout the day. In banks, for example, where there is considerable volatility in volume from one day to the next

Table 27-2. Teller staffing.

	Time of Day						
	9–10	10–11	11–12	12–1	1–2	2–3	3–4
Customer Arrivals	116	137	198	258	161	94	141
Time/Customer	.035	.035	.035	.035	.035	.035	.035
Std. Hours This Period	4.1	4.8	6.9	9.0	5.6	3.3	4.9
Required Tellers for Workload	4	5	7	9	6	4	5
Suggested Staffing	5	5	8	8	8	5	5

or one type of day to the next, numerous studies must be made in order to determine customer arrival patterns for different types of days. (In addition, there are special types of days, such as Fridays before holidays, the payday of a major local industry, the day after a major storm, and so forth.) To simplify the analysis in the sample case, the various transaction standards for serving the customer and the number of transactions per customer have been combined to provide an overall time to service any one customer. That time is 0.35 hour (2.1 minutes). This weighting factor can then be applied to the customer arrivals for each work period. The number of standard hours required in each work period and the required teller staffing for the workload can then be determined readily.

The staffing of the customer service function should not ignore the concepts of management reserve and supervision previously discussed; however, for simplicity these considerations have been eliminated from the example.

An even more sophisticated analysis would plot not only customer arrival patterns in a given time period, such as those occurring between ten and eleven o'clock, but also the random customer arrival patterns normally experienced. By random arrival pattern we mean that customers do not enter the bank at precise intervals of .035 hour, but several may appear at a time at an early portion of the hour, and then none may arrive for the next several minutes. Customer arrival patterns have been the subject of numerous texts. Analysts and managers of customer service departments should be aware of the existence of these patterns and refine staffing data as conditions dictate.

Where workloads are volatile, staffing must represent the best compromise between providing good service, providing economical service, and the practicalities of hiring employees in the employment market. In our sample problem, we theoretically should have four tellers between 9 AM and 10 AM, five tellers between 10 AM and 11 AM, seven tellers between 11 AM and 12 AM, and so forth. It would be difficult, indeed, to precisely duplicate this employment pattern during one day or more throughout the week. We simply cannot employ tellers or other employees for such short time periods. The actual staffing represents a base full-time equivalent staff of five tellers, reflecting an overstaffed condition between 9 AM and 10 AM and 2 PM and 3 PM, with additional part-time help on a half-time basis of three employees for the period between 11 AM and 2 PM. We recognize that between 12 AM and 1 PM, our heaviest work period, additional lines will develop behind the tellers, since they will be unable to serve all of the customers. In the following time period, between 1 PM and 2 PM, we will be overstaffed by two persons; however, there will be residual customers to be served from the previous period.

Staffing of customer-service-based departments requires additional skills on the part of management. Not only must the manager cope with the concept of customer service and varying workloads and staffing at given points of the day, but he must also be aware of the proper timing of the personal time required for coffee breaks and lunch periods. Further allowances need to be made for those activities not directly involved with serving the customer but necessary to the continued functioning of the bank, such as balancing and opening new accounts.

Eliminating Backlog

Another common use of work management in a planning mode is for backlog elimination. Table 27-3 addresses the subject of eliminating a backlog of work that may have occurred as a result of increased sales activity from a promotional contest, or problems with systems, or unplanned loss of key personnel. The process of planning for backlog elimination is very similar to determining the overall staffing level of a department. The overall backlog of work in the department is converted to the hours required to complete it at 100 percent performance. We add to this standard time the anticipated productivity of the work group.

Often work groups faced with the need to eliminate backlog will have lower

Table 27-3. Backlog elimination.

Order Backlog	1,552
Standard hours per order	.116
Hours to complete @ 100%	180
Hours at goal (80%)	225
Management reserve (9%)	20.3
Total required hours	245.3
Available employees	7
Overtime per employee	35
Service requirement	10 days
Overtime hours per employee/day	3.5

productivity than their counterparts working on the same activity during the day. This lower productivity may be due to recruiting of less skilled employees to solve the temporary backlog problems. Also, overtime work scheduled to solve backlogs tends to be less effective, because workers have already put in a full day of activity. Management reserve utilized for backlog elimination is normally lower than for day-to-day activity and is mostly a hedge against unforeseen absence on the part of the workers. Management reserve added to the time required to complete the work at a given level of productivity provides total required hours for the project.

The number of hours required may then be factored by the available number of employees to calculate an overtime schedule for each employee. The final consideration would be for service, in this case the length of time in which the backlog must be eliminated. Where service is the prime consideration, we may well calculate overtime requirements on a daily basis and then develop an employee work schedule from that base.

EQUIPMENT ANALYSIS

In the last few years there has been tremendous emphasis on improving the technology in the office. Improved office technology, which will be discussed in detail in Chapter 31, has put considerable pressure on purchasing agents and equipment analysts to determine the best piece of equipment for a given application.

The analysis is complicated by the fact that there are, for any given type of equipment, a variety of quality products available with relatively equal costs, strong product reputation, and sound product service.

Table 27-4 outlines how two possible copiers might be analyzed to determine the most suitable configuration for a given department. Since in this example 8,000

Table 27-4. Equipment analysis.

	Copier A	Copier B
Copies per hour	1,000	600
Hours to produce 8,000 copies	8	13.3
Machines required	1	2
Monthly rental	$800	$460
Rental per month	$800	$920
Annual rental	$9,600	$11,040
Copies per year	2,000,000	2,000,000
Cost per copy	$.025	$.020
Total copy costs	$50,000	$40,000
Operator cost		
@ $7,500 machine	$7,500	$15,000
Total annual cost	$67,100	$66,040
Total cost per copy	$.0336	$.0330

copies are required, our configuration begins with the selection of two models of Copier B versus one of Copier A. We have added to this the monthly rental and service charges to develop an annual rental cost. At this point, Copier A seems to have a distinct advantage over Copier B's requirement for two machines. However, the cost per copy of Copier A is higher, and considering that 2 million copies are to be run per year, Copier B's lower price takes effect. Even when we add in the cost of a single operator for Copier A and two operators for Copier B, we find a very slight price advantage to selecting Copier B. While this single advantage of .06¢ (6/100ths of one cent) per copy does not seem significant, one should also take into consideration the fact that a breakdown of Copier A will eliminate 100 percent of production, while a breakdown of one of the Copier B machines will result in a loss of only half of that production. Currently, Copier A will be fully utilized to perform the work now required, with no room for expansion. Copier B, on the other hand, can absorb a 20 percent increase in workload without adding to machine rental costs or operator costs.

This very basic example of the use of work management data presupposes that standards are available to determine the effective machine rate in copies per hour. It shows how alternative configurations can be compared, assuming other factors are equal.

OTHER USES OF WORK MANAGEMENT FOR PLANNING

It has been said that the uses of work management data to assist in the operations of a company or a department are limited largely by the imagination of the user. The authors believe that the truly successful work management program goes beyond the development of performance and staffing data and becomes an integral part of the overall corporate management information system for budgeting and planning of various types. Here are some of the other uses that might be considered for work management data:

Comparison of alternative methods. When new methodology is about to be introduced, the company which is fortunate enough to have a predetermined time system to establish standards will be able to review both the current and proposed procedures. Time standards for comparing the proposed procedure against one already in use can then be established. In the development of a new system, we may well find that there are two or more apparently equal processing techniques. However, work management analysis will identify the most time-effective method without unreliable and costly trial-and-error techniques.

Work distribution. When a new department is to be organized, when there are staffing changes in an existing organization, or when new functions are added to a department, the distribution of work among individual employees will require revision. The use of work management data will allow us to calculate a fair day's work for each employee, based on a mix of the types of functions which they are able to perform. This analysis also pinpoints potential problem areas of flexibility where only one employee may know how to perform a given function. The process for this analysis again requires that the volume of activity be translated into the time required to perform it.

Development of learning curves. Learning curves can be developed from historical data that plot the progress of satisfactory employees toward full competence at a particular job function. These curves can then be used to project when new employees should be hired to begin training so that when workload increases, the staff will be able to provide accurate service on a timely basis. Needless to say, these learning curves may also be used to speed the training process, because the improving productivity of new employees can be plotted against the curve and those employees with lower-than-normal development may receive additional guidance and counseling in order to bring productivity to acceptable levels as rapidly as possible.

MODELING AND SIMULATION

One of the highest-order activities that can be performed using work management data is the modeling or simulation of overall corporate activity. Simulation models most commonly are generated through computer analysis because of their complexity and the number of variables involved. Computer modeling attempts to answer the question, "What if?" The *what if* could be the addition of a new product line, the discontinuance of an existing product line, the addition of a new system with its attendant costs, the opening of a new office, and the like. In simulation modeling, a computer model of the overall corporate structure's workload, staffing, expenses, profits, and income is developed, and changes are made to the model which then impact on a predetermined variable.

As an example, an insurance company may wish to determine the impact on overall corporate profitability of discontinuing a particular line of insurance. The model would allow for the deletion of income and expenses from the balance sheet and for a recalculation of overall corporate profitability. Work management facilitates this type of analysis by providing a basis for determining which expenses for personnel are associated with a given product or service. Today's complex office environment uses simulations for all major changes in corporate procedures and policies.

We have only scratched the surface in our examination of how work management data can be used to look into the future rather than solely as a vehicle for reporting on the results of the past. The possibilities are limited only by the knowledge and imagination of the planners. The authors have seen companies using work management data to price products, determine needs for major capital expenditures such as new buildings and computers, and even support recommendations for major rate changes in highly regulated industries. The availability of stand-alone computer systems for work management departments, operations research departments, and cost-accounting departments will provide more accurate, up-to-date, and detailed data for decision making that will be required for the company of tomorrow.

Wage Incentive Plans

TODAY'S OFFICE EMPLOYEE MAKES three contributions to his employer: he brings to the workplace his time, his effort, and his ideas. An employee appraisal system, whether based on work measurement techniques or on more subjective judgments, provides a means of rewarding employees in proportion to their value to the organization. As Herzberg has shown, money by itself is not a motivator; however, as part of a program that addresses psychological and social needs of the employee as well as the need for increased efficiency, financial reward can have a significant positive impact.

We know of no long-lasting successful work management program that does not in some way share with the employee a portion of the benefits resulting from improvements made. In this chapter we will discuss the strengths and weaknesses of various types of incentive plans, outline various techniques that may be used to reward employees, and point out the requirements of a successful program.

Simply stated, an incentive system compensates an employee in proportion to his output. The most common type of incentive plan is a merit pay program where an employee's performance is periodically appraised and his salary level adjusted to reflect his output. True incentive plans, however, greatly shorten the usual six- to twelve-month period between output and reward. It is these types of plans which will be the subject of this chapter.

ADVANTAGES OF INCENTIVES

Proponents of wage incentive programs typically cite some or all of the following as reasons why incentive plans should be installed:

Higher output. As we have seen in previous chapters, a work measurement program, if skillfully designed and implemented, will increase performance and the output of work. When a direct form of reward is added to a measurement program, output per man-hour will further increase. The extent of increase will depend on the type of plan, the pre-incentive performance, and overall worker attitude.

Cost. A skillfully designed incentive program, since it improves performance, will produce work at lower cost. Care should be exercised in program design to minimize administrative costs that would eat into the available incentive pay workers may earn.

Higher earnings. A wage incentive program provides a basis for workers to earn more salary than employees performing comparable work in non-incentive environments.

Reduced supervisory effort. The job of the supervisor, as we have previously seen, is to get work out accurately, economically, and on time by using departmental resources. Key among these resources is employee time. In the absence of a work management program, supervisors lack objective data to use these resources wisely. Varying degrees of productivity improvement are possible through a work management program if the supervisor can motivate the workers to use their time more effectively. In a well-designed incentive plan, employees will more readily seek additional work, since the completion of that work will add to their paychecks. Further, the recognition of being a top performer and thus a top earner promotes a higher level of activity. In some respects workers on incentives are self-supervising, though, as we will see later, the supervisor's role in any incentive plan is crucial.

Pay for performance. To some employees, working is a little bit like paying taxes. We don't really like to do it, but, by the same token, the burden is less if we know that we are contributing our fair share. Today's worker may well feel the same way about his job and will less mind working if he knows that his compensation is in proportion to his output. Only through an incentive program can this very direct link between effort and earnings be made.

Reduced absence and turnover. Absenteeism and turnover are frequently reduced in a company or department with an incentive plan. Absence from the job reduces the employee's incentive earnings, which soon become an expected portion of the paycheck. Lower turnover further reduces cost, as the associated costs of recruiting and training are brought down to more manageable levels. Employees in an incentive environment will usually have lower turnover levels as other jobs become less attractive since they cannot compete with the current incentive wages.

Better resource utilization. A department operating at peak performance allows management to staff at the lowest possible level. In a bank or an insurance company, where salaries represent one of the highest controllable expenses, overall costs are reduced through more effective utilization of employee time.

DISADVANTAGES

Before entering into an incentive plan, it is equally important to understand the disadvantages of such a program.

Cost of administration. Unless the incentive program is properly designed, administrative costs can be high. Administrative costs include the time required to collect data, ensure their accuracy, establish and audit standards, settle grievances, and provide payroll information. It goes without saying that the more complex the program, the higher the administration costs. One of the key ingredients to a successful program is simplicity, which can promote understanding at all levels of the organization and minimize these costs.

Quality of work and service. Quality controls are even more important in a department using incentives than in one without incentives. In the absence of these controls, some workers may strive to maximize output and earnings with little, if any, consideration for the quality of service provided. The effective incentive program includes penalties for errors made, which will both improve quality and reduce incentive payments. Service, too, can be a problem. In an office where customer contact is part of the job, some employees may deal brusquely with customers to maximize earnings. In one unsuccessful program, the president received a call from a justifiably irate customer indicating that an employee answering a request had hung up, explaining he was allowed only 2.3 minutes to complete the call and the customer's time was up. In the service industries, where service is one of the few competitive advantages one firm may enjoy over another, monitoring the quality of service as to accuracy, timeliness, and courteousness is essential.

Wage inequities. Wage incentives can create inequities in pay. Employees performing at a high level with an incentive added may well be earning more than other employees in higher job classifications who are not covered by the program. Similarly, a bright, new, high-producing employee may well earn more than a longer-service employee with a lower level of performance. It should be recognized that some inequities in salary structure are a normal result of the installation of incentives. Proper program design and attendant public-relations efforts will minimize morale problems in the staff.

Resistance to change. Installation of incentives may well create resistance to change. Employees who become accustomed to performing a defined task at a defined level of productivity so as to earn incentives may well not wish to use new methods, procedures, or technology in the fear that their earnings will suffer. If standards are adjusted to equitably reflect changes made, the employees will continue to have the opportunity to earn an incentive at the same level as with the old method. There will, of course, initially be a somewhat lower incentive as employees learn the new methods. It is difficult to sell an employee on a new method that may require additional output of items to earn the same incentive wage.

Decreased teamwork. Incentives promote competition between employees. This competition, unless properly controlled, can have an adverse affect on the team spirit that should exist in a group of workers. This lack of team spirit can manifest itself in employees' fighting for "gravy" jobs and group pressures brought to bear on high performers. Attempts to control decreased teamwork due to infighting may result in an overly complex standards structure, which will create difficulties in reporting and maintenance.

Loss of flexibility. Supervisors and managers normally think twice before assigning employees who are covered by an incentive program to a task where incentive earnings are not possible. This hesitation may result in an overall loss of flexibility within the department. Further, employees may not wish to perform work with which they are less familiar, since this would tend to lower their performance and compensation. From the outset, management should promote the philosophy that incentives are available to the worker at the discretion of management and are not guaranteed. Loss of incentives in reality, then, is not a loss but a failure to gain.

Earnings fluctuations. Earnings fluctuations are caused by two factors. Employees may perform at a lower pace and thus earn a smaller incentive, or management may not have work available for the employee that is covered by standards and the incentive compensation plan. In the short term, these fluctuations are inevitable. Techniques can be developed to provide an average incentive as a substitute for incentive earnings should there be a long-run situation where incentives cannot be paid, such as the conversion to a major new system.

Resentment in non-incentive areas. If a company is not completely covered by the incentive plan, there may be some resentment between workers in incentive areas and in non-incentive areas. However, large companies with only a portion of their work force covered by standards and incentives have found that this resentment is of a minor nature. Employees in non-incentive areas usually convince themselves that there are additional pressures of working in the incentive environment that are not worth the additional compensation. On the other side of the coin, employees in incentive areas boast of higher earnings.

Promotions/transfers. It may be difficult to convince employees working under incentives to accept a higher-level position or a transfer to another department where incentives are not offered. Some companies soften the blow by adding, in addition to any normal promotional increase, a "bonus" representing a portion of the incentive wage as an inducement to take such a position. Here again, the experience of most companies is that this problem is of a minor nature. Up and coming employees view the loss of an incentive as a temporary situation, and they recognize that their new position would give them greater exposure, greater opportunity to succeed, and, eventually, the salary recognition that accompanies the higher-level position.

REQUIREMENTS FOR A SUCCESSFUL PROGRAM

The requirements for a successful incentive program are similar in some respects to those of a work management program. Careful consideration of the requirements for success will minimize the chance of failure.

Written policy. Employees' understanding of the program of incentives is essential if it is to be effective. The program should be easy to understand, fair to both company and employee, and well documented. The Aetna Life & Casualty Insurance Company of Hartford, Connecticut, as an example, publishes a booklet for all employees, originally titled "In Business for Yourself," which outlines every detail of its incentive program. (This program, incidentally, dates back to the 1920s.) Changes in policy should also be documented so that there will be no misunderstandings between company and employee as to the rights and responsibilities of the worker in the incentive program.

Management support. Management support at all levels is critical to the success of a program. Management initially designs or approves the program and throughout its life acts as an arbitrator between the employee and the plan. Management must expect the plan to succeed, and must communicate this expectation for success to employees at all levels and take the steps required to ensure that the program benefits employees and management alike.

Accurate standards. Standards are the cornerstone on which all incentive pay programs are based. It is imperative that standards be as accurate and as consistent as possible. In the absence of a companywide standard-setting technique, standards accuracy and consistency within units is absolutely essential. Standards should accurately reflect current operating procedures and equipment. Supervisors must recognize that standards maintenance is critical in order that each employee be fairly compensated for work performed and receive full benefit from incentive payments made. It is strongly recommended that a periodic audit be made of all standards in an incentive area. To maintain the required standards accuracy, this audit should be conducted at least annually. Needless to say, a predetermined time system provides the most accurate and consistent standards and is ideally suited for incentive plans.

Standards should be guaranteed against change as long as there is no change in the procedure employed, the forms and equipment used, and the size of batches of work processed.

Accurate reporting. Accurate reporting is the second key requirement for determining how much compensation each employee is to receive. Spot checks should be instituted to make certain that the volume of items reported by each employee is as accurate as is practical. Supervisors, if they do not already do so, should be required to maintain records of off-standard time for all employees. Many firms consider falsification of time and production records to be of the same gravity as falsification of payroll records, and offenders are treated with a degree of severity commensurate with company policies. The support of management and periodic audits of records and standards will minimize record falsification.

A bonus worth earning. The incentive paid must be worth earning. Few, if any, employees will respond with enthusiasm and improved productivity to an incentive program that asks them to produce a great deal with little reward. There should be no ceiling on an employee's incentive earnings. If standards and reports are correct and the program is properly designed, management will reap a benefit far greater than the incentive payment made, regardless of the amount of incentive earned by an individual employee. Placing a ceiling on potential incentive earnings can stifle productivity and weaken the program.

Quality control. As we have seen in earlier chapters, quality control is an essential part of each department's management program. In incentive installations, in addition to maintaining records of errors made and of overall work quality, it is important to apply penalties to those workers who produce a lower-quality product.

Two avenues appear open to reduce employee incentive earnings if a poor-quality product is produced. The first, and simplest solution is to return incorrect work to the employee for correction. Work is corrected by that employee while he is working "on standard;" however, no additional volume count is taken. This procedure, in essence, reduces performance to 50 percent of standard on those items where rework is required, which will lower earnings.

The second quality-control technique that may be used is a direct charge for errors. This direct charge is usually levied only against incentive earnings, so that an employee's basic pay remains intact regardless of work quality. It is common for allowances to be made for a normal number of errors by establishing either a relationship of free errors to hours on standard or a fixed level of daily errors. In the first case, the ratio might be expressed as one error for every four hours on standard; in the second case, management might allow two nonchargeable errors for each day worked. Needless to say, unsatisfactory quality of work on a continuing basis requires more attention on the part of the supervisor than merely levying the appropriate error charges.

Exposure. Incentive earnings must be visible. Visibility can come from a separate paycheck or pay envelope for incentive earnings, or incentive earnings detailed in a separate block on the stub of the paycheck. Two schools of thought appear prevalent in paying incentives: one feels that it is important to make the payment as soon as possible after the productive period when the incentive was earned; the second school of thought advocates withholding incentive payment until such time as a relatively large sum has been accumulated. Regardless of the method chosen, employees should be informed of what they have earned at the earliest possible date. One company, after records are processed (usually the Wednesday following the work period), provides each employee with a statement showing his or her performance against standard, gross incentive earnings, dollar amount of error penalties, and bonus earned.

Good attitude. The potential problems of installing an incentive pay program will be considerably reduced if the program is installed when overall employee attitudes are good. Incentives should never be installed as a last-ditch attempt to improve morale.

REWARD TECHNIQUES

An employee's salary and the associated fringe benefits compensate an employee for the time he puts into his work, assuming that he produces at the normal level. As we have seen earlier, a merit pay program tends to provide some differentiation in base pay from worker to worker, based on how well each worker performs his tasks. It is the province of an incentive program to reward employees for their efforts and for their ideas. Rewards for ideas are normally the province of a suggestion plan. Ideas submitted by employees are evaluated, and reward distributed, on the basis of their importance to the organization. It is common to base the award for an idea on a proportion of the first-year savings realized from implementation of the idea, after deducting implementation costs.

One unusual suggestion submitted to an Eastern insurance company recommended that the submitter of the suggestion be dismissed, as his job was not necessary. The suggestion earned a 10 percent salary bonus and a promotion to a more meaningful job.

Work incentive techniques include both monetary and nonmonetary rewards. Regardless of the type of reward employed, the beginning point for incentive payments is performance at, or exceeding, a predefined level of activity, which makes the employee eligible for reward. There are a number of currently popular means for distributing incentive rewards:

Piece work. Piece work pay programs are most commonly associated with the factory. A worker's total pay may be dependent on how many pieces of work he produces. In accordance with established standards, the employee earns compensation at the rate of so many cents or dollars per acceptable item produced. The employee's wage is dependent solely on the number of items he can produce in a given time. Due to workload fluctuations which make it difficult to provide any consistency in pay, programs of this nature are generally not employed in the office. It is common for trainees to be covered by a learning curve that provides an opportunity to earn a reasonable wage until skill and speed are developed.

Standard hour. The employee who works under a standard-hour incentive plan is paid for the time he saves his employer. If, for example, standards call for work to be completed in 35 hours and the employee completes the work in 30 hours, he is paid as if he had worked for five additional hours.

Halsey method. This is a variation of the standard-hour plan. In the Halsey method, the company and the employee divide, in some proportion, the savings resulting from improved productivity. Taking the preceding example, where under the direct standard-hour plan an employee might be rewarded for five hours saved, in the Halsey method 50 percent of the saving (or two and a half hours of pay) might be distributed to the employee and the remaining 50 percent retained by the company. The Halsey method has the advantage of promoting teamwork between the employee and the company. However, the distribution formula should be chosen in such a way as to ensure that sufficient incentive is available to the employee to expend additional effort.

The Halsey method is currently used by Aetna Life & Casualty Insurance. Aetna's program pays a one-half share of performance over 50 percent to the employee whose performance exceeds 70 percent. In effect, a 100 percent performance earns a 25 percent bonus.

Gantt plan. Under the Gantt plan, an employee has the opportunity to earn an incentive after he has exceeded standard by a given amount. As an example, if the incentive level is at 120 percent of standard, an employee performing at 125 percent earns a bonus equivalent to a 5 percent productivity increase. Gantt-plan incentive programs are most often found in industry.

Scanlon plan. This is a group incentive program, with reward distributed equally among the workers in the group. In the Scanlon plan, a company determines what its wage and salary level is as a percentage of total expenses or revenue, and employees in a group that is able to produce at a lower expense level pocket the difference.

Sentry plan. The Sentry plan, developed at Sentry Life Insurance Company of Stevens Point, Wisconsin, is a means for an employee to boost his base pay more rapidly than through the normal annual appraisal process. In the Sentry plan, as employee performance increases, it passes through several steps. Attainment of an average performance against standard within a given step qualifies the employee for a percentage increase of his base pay. Once an employee achieves his normal level of performance, additional incentives are based on annual merit, although an employee may at any time boost his performance into the next range and be eligible for a performance increase. Provision is made to reduce earnings when average performance falls below the requirements of the range.

With the exception of the Sentry plan, incentives place overall compensation almost directly in the hands of the employee, on a week-to-week or month-to-month basis. This feeling of control can be important in promoting satisfaction with the job.

In addition to monetary incentives, a company may offer nonmonetary incentives, either on a specialized basis or as part of a continuing program. Examples of nonmonetary incentives include the ability to earn extra days of vacation; tickets to sporting or cultural events; dinners; use of company facilities normally reserved for senior staff; and free lunches in the cafeteria.

Trophies to departments with the highest productivity, pictures in corporate magazines, and visits from the president can also be used to recognize good performance. One Midwestern insurance company has an annual drawing for a Hawaiian vacation and other prizes. Each time an employee's performance exceeds 100 percent, his name goes in the hat. The greater the number of weeks of good performance, the greater the chance to win.

Summary

Today's workers want to do a good job and be recognized for their achievements. Too often the recognition process is too widely separated from the productive period to have any meaningful impact. A soundly engineered incentive program provides the opportunity for recognizing and rewarding employee performance at the time that performance merits reward. Incentive programs that provide a little incentive at almost every level of productivity will stimulate even higher levels of performance from the participants.

Companies that are interested in incentive programs are urged to thoroughly research existing plans and the criteria for success. The expense in payments for which there is no benefit, administrative expense, and poor employee morale can be considerable in a poorly conceived and administered program.

CHAPTER

Standard Cost Accounting

In COMPARISON WITH THE 400-year history of financial accounting, standard cost accounting is a mere baby. Although the roots of cost accounting may be traced to the eighteenth century and Josiah Wedgewood & Sons Ltd., the famous English china manufacturer, it has only recently been brought to its current refined state and prominence.

The development of standard cost accounting can be almost directly traced to the complexities of modern corporations of all types. While financial accounting tells you whether or not money is made or lost overall, it has become increasingly important to know which products or services are contributing to profit or loss and to what extent.

It was fairly easy for the early artisan who purchased leather, twine, and nails to determine, after he had sold a pair of boots, whether or not he had made a profit. In today's complex environment, where thousands of different raw materials and services enter into the production of a single product, management can no longer readily determine each product's contribution to profit or loss. Thus standard cost accounting was developed and refined to enable management to answer these most important questions.

CONTRASTS WITH FINANCIAL ACCOUNTING

To gain a better understanding of the cost accounting principles, it is useful to analyze the difference between cost accounting and financial accounting. There are five key differences between the two accounting practices:

1. *Multiple-purpose nature of cost accounting.* Financial accounting is designed primarily to furnish outsiders with data on how well management has performed. Those outside the organization who are interested in the performance of managers include government agencies, stockholders, and investors. On the other hand, management accounting, of which standard cost accounting is one facet, provides data primarily for internal analysis. Managers at all levels within the organization are concerned with having data available to develop costs and prices for their products, analyze alternative courses of action, evaluate progress toward objectives, and formulate realistic plans.

2. *Adherence to the principles of accounting.* Financial accounting data must conform to a set of ground rules as laid out by the governing bodies of the accounting practice. This degree of uniformity is necessary to ensure that the diverse users of financial accounting information can understand and readily compare the performance and operating characteristics of different corporations. Since management accounting is designed for internal use, it is not subject to these same regulations. In reality, the only principle to which management accounting must adhere is that the information developed must be useful.

3. *Optional nature of management accounting.* Financial accounting must be done to satisfy legal requirements. State, local, and federal governments must have information available for the taxation of profits and property; stockholders need information on profit, loss, and earnings per share; and investors require an analysis of assets, liabilities, and overall financial strengths.

Management accounting is optional. Soundly organized companies routinely prepare reports to management to aid in decision making. Other firms take the more simplistic approach of our early artisan and are concerned only with overall profit and loss. The well-managed firm has, in addition to its financial accounting structure, management information of a financial nature for budgeting, costing, and pricing as an aid to decision making.

4. *Scope.* Financial accounting relates to the business as a whole. All sales, all income, and all expenses are routinely accounted for. By way of contrast, management accounting focuses on particular segments of the company, such as the operations of a given department or the production of a product or service. Many companies further specialize their management accounting system to provide input, not on the company as a whole or various departments or products, but on particular problem areas. As an example, if data processing expense is of concern to the organization, a management accounting program may be established to accurately allocate data processing expense to the user departments or even to individual goods and services. That same firm may well not choose to provide similar allocations for executive overhead.

5. *Precision.* Financial accounting is quite precise and often worked out to the

very last penny. The accountants' recurring nightmare is that their books will be $1,000,000 out on the debit side of the ledger and $999,999.99 out on the credit side of the ledger instead of merely being one penny short. On the other hand, management accounting addresses immediate needs. Managers at all levels in the organization must react to changing conditions with the best available tools for decision making. The need for speed in the preparation of management accounting sometimes compromises the accuracy that can be realistically provided. It is of little use to management to receive precise data five months after expenses are incurred. Delays in receiving data make it difficult for a manager to recall why variances exist and to take corrective action.

PRODUCT COSTING METHODS

There are many different types of management accounting programs. In Chapter 24 we discussed the concept of responsibility accounting as a means of controlling professional functions. A second major management accounting technique is product or service cost accounting, where data are accumulated by service or groups of services. Costs collected in this fashion are ideal for pricing and making decisions on profitability and utilization of resources.

The cost of any product or service is the sum of three key components: (1) the direct labor cost associated with the production of the good or service, (2) materials costs required to produce the service, and (3) the proportionate share of indirect costs allocated to the product, including overhead, management, and the use of facilities. The two major costing methods in use are job costing and process costing.

Job Costing

Job costing is most often applied in a factory situation. In this environment, an accounting method is established to collect all costs for a given product. Generally, the accounting system consists of a series of job tickets that are completed by workers at each step in the manufacturing process. These job tickets include not only materials drawn from supply but also the amount of labor effort expended in each department and any tools and expendable items required. The sum of the charged cost as developed by the job costing system becomes the direct cost of producing the product. Required overhead may then be added to determine total costs.

Process Costing

The costing technique that is most suitable in the office environment is process costing. In process costing, all production costs are accumulated, a determination is made of what units are produced, and unit costs are developed by allocating costs over units produced. In the following section we will examine the process costing technique in greater detail. The reader should recognize that since management accounting is created in essence to meet the needs of a given organization, there are many variations possible. It would be beyond the scope of this chapter to provide complete details of all the available systems.

ESTABLISHING COSTS

Just as work management involves analysis, measurement, and control of work, the process of cost accounting involves the analysis, measurement, and control of costs. The development of a costing system is an eight-step process ranging from the determination of what is to be costed through remedial action that may be taken to improve the profit picture.

Determining Services to Be Costed

When our firm undertook a recent cost accounting project, we asked the management of the organization what products or services it wished costed. The answer was "everything." While it may appear that costing everything is a good idea, as it well may be, one of the most difficult tasks in the development of a cost accounting system is to determine what items should be costed. A good starting point for the development of such a list of products or services is an examination of the company's fee structure. In reality, every expense of the organization is in part borne by those services for which a charge is made. In some organizations this charge may be direct, such as a $2 charge for a catalog, or a $17 premium for $1,000 of life insurance, or a $5 charge for a check returned for insufficient funds. In other cases the charge may be indirect, such as a charge made against the profitability of an account by a bank for services performed.

Once the list of services to be costed is assembled, it should be analyzed to determine if the fee structure makes sense. In some cases industry practice dictates for what services an organization may charge, while in other cases the individual organization has the option of charging for services on the basis of its analysis of the market. In some cases the charge structures are complex, requiring complex costing techniques, while in other cases simplistic pricing structures create similarly simple accounting practices. As an example, when purchasing an automobile made in the United States, it is common to be charged a relatively low base price for the automobile, with each of countless hundreds of options for the vehicle charged separately. By way of contrast, manufacturers of imported cars tend to make virtually all available equipment standard, with a limited number of options. Needless to say, Henry Ford's philosophy— "They can have any color they want, as long as it's black"—required a less sophisticated costing system than current charges for the standard paint job, metallic paint, vinyl tops, and multiple-color paint schemes and stripes.

Developing Product Standards

The accuracy of costs is to a great extent dependent on the accuracy of standards. In an environment where work standards are developed through informal measurement techniques, costs will be less accurate than where the more formal technique of predetermined times is used. It is common in a work management environment to develop standards that are suitable for reporting how well individual employees measure up to standard and how well a department or section operates. In the main, these standards are not suitable for cost accounting. For example, some work management standards (such as standards for opening and sorting of mail) cover many different products, whereas other standards apply directly to one particular product (examples would be standards for making an address change or receiving a loan payment). A third possibility is to divide a work management standard into two parts so as to deal with the fixed time required to handle a batch of work and the variable standards for each item within the process. For example, a standard may consist of a fixed time for the typing and mailing of an insurance policy, with a separate standard for each endorsement typed.

Wherever there is not a direct one-for-one relationship between work management standards and products to be costed, it will be necessary to analyze each standard and allocate it in the proper proportion to the products to be costed. In complex situations, a flowchart will often be required to trace the path of a given product through a responsibility center or the company. Incidentally, a flowchart of this nature may well uncover more effective means of processing the work, which should be instituted prior to the development of costs.

Table 29-1 is an example of the development of product standards in a customer service department. The products to be costed are catalog requests, address changes, and orders. Note that in developing the product standard for orders, management has adjusted the standards to reflect the time to process an order, rather than using the work management standard based on number of lines within the order.

Developing the Workload

The next step in the costing process is to determine what the department's workload is going to be. Historical data or other projection techniques may be used to determine the number of items to be processed in each product category. Actual costing would use data based on work actually completed. Once projected volumes are available and product standards developed, it will be possible to determine the required staffing for the department.

Table 29-1. Product standard development for a customer service department.

Product	Task	Standard Minutes	Freq.	Weighted Standard
Catalog requests	Open Mail (CS-1)	.180	1	.180
	Type Form Letter (CS-2)	.869	1	.869
		Time per Request:	Minutes	1.049
			Hours	.018
Address changes	Open Mail (CS-1)	.180	1	.180
	Pull or File Customer Files (CS-7)	.240	2	.480
	Type Address Change (CS-8)	.649	1	.649
		Time per Change:	Minutes	1.309
			Hours	.022
Orders	Open Mail (CS-1)	.180	1	.180
	Pull or File Customer Files (CS-7)	.240	1.9	.456
	Type Orders (CS-11)	1.460	1	1.460
	Type Order Lines (CS-12)	.149	3.3	.492
		Time per Order:	Minutes	2.588
			Hours	.043

Table 29-2 shows the workload development for the customer service department. For each product, the standard hours required to complete one product item are multiplied by the projected volume to determine the planned standard hours or workload. At this stage, a staffing factor may be applied to adjust the workload to include the planned level of performance, absenteeism, and any unavoidable delays and training.

Any special work contemplated for the department but not directly allocatable to these products should be added in, along with required supervision. The total paid hours thus developed, when divided by the work time of one equivalent full-time employee, will produce the staff required for the anticipated workload at the goal level of performance.

The first analysis that can be made of the overall relationship between standard costs and price involves comparing the current staff with required staff. In the example in Table 29-2, at goal levels of performance the anticipated workload can be completed by 8.8 employees, whereas 10.1 employees are currently employed. This means that either the price of the product must be adjusted to reflect inefficiency or remedial action must be taken to remove the inefficiency in order that the product may be offered at the lowest possible price.

Table 29-2. Workload development for the customer service department.

Product	Standard Hours	+	Projected Volume	=	Projected Standard Hours
Catalog Requests	.018		65,260		1,175
Address Changes	.022		44,200		972
Orders	.043		194,800		8,376

Planned standard hours:	10,523
Staffing factor:	134%
Adjusted standard hours:	14,100
Special work:	1,200
Supervision:	1,950
Total paid hours:	17,250
Required equivalent full-time employees (@ 1,950 hours/employee):	8.8
Actual equivalent full-time employees:	10.1

Table 29-3. Expense analysis for the customer service department.

Expense Category	Amount
SALARY EXPENSE	
Salary—Full-Time	$ 63,000
Salary—Part-Time	4,095
Overtime	293
Fringe Benefits	16,847
Total salary expense	$ 84,235
OTHER DIRECT EXPENSE	
Occupancy	9,600
Depreciation	600
Repairs and Maintenance	400
Telephone	255
Postage	7,233
Supply	14,074
Total other direct expense	$ 32,162
PURCHASED SERVICES	
Computer	$ 1,200
Keypunch	57,348
Duplication	600
Total purchased services	$ 59,148
TOTAL EXPENSE	$175,545

Expense Collection

The costing process presupposes that financial data are available. In the absence of a management accounting system such as responsibility accounting, which reports on a given department's or section's expenses by type, an analysis must be made of financial accounting data and the required information must be extracted.

Table 29-3 is an example of expense analysis divided into three common categories: salary expense, other direct expense, and purchased services. Purchased services are normally those which are distributed throughout an organization, such as charges made for use of the data processing department or of duplication facilities.

Analyzing Expense Categories

Individual expense categories must now be analyzed to determine if particular expenses may be allocated directly to one product or service. Some examples of allocated expenses would be postage costs to mail a particular item; maintenance and depreciation for a piece of equipment that is used solely for the production of a given service; the cost of supplies such as catalogs or forms; the cost of special reports or telegrams.

Table 29-4. Expense analysis worksheet.

	Unit		Total		
EXPENSE CLASS: POSTAGE				Total Expense	$7,233
Product	Cost	Volume	Cost		
Catalog Requests	$.11	65,260	$7,179		
			Total Analyzed		7,179
			Unanalyzed Expense		$ 54
EXPENSE CLASS: SUPPLY				Total Expense	$14,074
Product	Cost	Volume	Cost		
Catalog Requests	$.21	65,620	$13,780		
			Total Analyzed		13,780
			Unanalyzed Expense		$ 294
EXPENSE CLASS: KEY PUNCH				Total Expense	$57,159
Product	Cost	Volume	Cost		
Catalog Requests	$.120	65,260	$ 7,831		
Address Changes	.120	44,200	5,304		
Orders	.226	194,800	44,024		
			$57,159		
			Total Analyzed		$57,159
			Unanalyzed Expense		$ 0

Table 29-5. Rate development for the customer service department.

Expense Class	Amount	Total Standard Hours	Hourly Rate
SALARY EXPENSE			
Salary—Full-Time	$63,000	10,523	$5.987
Salary—Part-Time	4,095		.389
Overtime	293		.028
Fringe Benefits	16,847		1.601
Total			$8.005
OTHER DIRECT EXPENSE			
Occupancy	$9,600	10,523	$ .912
Depreciation	600		.057
Repairs and Maintenance	400		.038
Telephone	255		.024
Postage	55		.005
Supply	370		.035
Total			$1.071
PURCHASED SERVICES			
Computer	$1,200	10,523	$ .114
Keypunch	—		—
Duplication	600		.057
Total			$ .171
TOTAL HOURLY RATE			$9.247

The purpose of this analysis is to separate significant expenses that may be attributed to one product from expenses that are to be distributed over all products.

Table 29-4 is an example of how the significant costs associated with the production of a given service can be removed from the general expenses of the customer service department.

Rate Development

To complete the costing picture, we need to allocate remaining expenses to the various products or services produced. One of the most common methods used to perform this analysis is to develop the cost of operating the department on an hourly basis and then use this hourly rate to charge to each service a fair share of the costs, on a basis proportionate to time expended.

Table 29-5 shows the development of an hourly rate of $9.247 for the operation of the customer service department. To provide a basis for variance analysis, identifiable expenses should individually be divided by standard hours to provide the cost of that expense category for each hour of work produced.

Figure 29-I. Cost development for the customer service department.

PRODUCT: CATALOG REQUESTS

Analyzed Expenses

Postage	$ .110
Supply	.210
Keypunch	.120
Total Analyzed	$ .440

Allocated Expense

Hourly Rate		Standard Hours	
$9.247	x	.018	$ .166
		Total Cost	$ .606

PRODUCT: ADDRESS CHANGES

Analyzed Expenses

Postage	$ —
Supply	—
Keypunch	.120
Total Analyzed	$ .120

Allocated Expense

Hourly Rate		Standard Hours	
$9.247	x	.022	$ .203
		Total Cost	$ .323

PRODUCT: ORDERS

Analyzed Expenses

Postage	$ —
Supply	—
Keypunch	$ .226
Total Analyzed	$ .226

Allocated Expense

Standard Hourly Rate		Standard Hours	
$9.247	x	.043	$ .398
		Total Cost	$ .624

Cost Development

The final step in the development of product costs is to add the analyzed expenses and the expenses allocated by standard hours. The direct analyzed expenses are added to allocated expenses to complete one item of service.

In Figure 29-1, analyzed and allocated expenses for each of the products of the customer service department are totaled to determine the cost of providing that service. The accuracy of the costing process may be checked by multiplying the unit cost for each product or service by the volume. The sum of each service's cost should approximate the total cost of operating the unit, although some small distortions due to rounding errors are common.

Overhead

The process shown has accounted for all the costs of operating the customer service department; however, there are additional overhead items that should be allocated to each product. Typical examples of overhead expense are the cost of the personnel department, executive costs, and building maintenance.

These expenses can be allocated in numerous ways. The cost of operating the personnel department or the cafeteria can be allocated on the basis of the number of employees assigned to a department. Executive costs can be distributed on the basis of estimates by the executives or a sampling of how much of their time they spend on a given department or service. In some organizations, all expenses not accounted for are expressed as a percentage of total expense and added to the cost of producing each product or service.

To simplify the example provided, overhead expenses have been eliminated from the calculation.

VARIANCE ANALYSIS

Once the cost of producing a good or service is known, it is possible to calculate a variety of variances to explain why performance either exceeds or falls short of planned levels. Here are some typical examples of analysis of this type:

- Computation of cost variances due to volume activity falling short or exceeding planned levels.
- Computation of expense variance based on performance variance of employees against standard.
- Cost variances due to the cost of materials or services.
- Compensation variables due to a changed mix in the labor force.
- Analysis of variance in the costs and prices for given services.

As an example of the type of analysis which is possible, you will recall that in the development of staffing as calculated in Table 29-2, the customer service depart-ment appears to be 1.3 employees overstaffed. The current average employee salary is $8,340 per year, which means that overall salary costs in the department are $10,000 too high. The effect of the performance variance is to overstate the required costs of departmental salary expense by somewhat over $1 per standard hour. Following through on the development of cost, this same performance variance adds an additional 1.8¢ to the cost of each catalog request.

Variance analysis, based on some of the possibilities listed above, is limited only by the imagination of the user.

SUMMARY

Any management accounting system must return fair value to management. To put it differently, it must recover the costs of its development and maintenance. This benefit can only be achieved if an enlightened management analyzes available data and takes corrective action to boost productivity, control costs, and more effectively operate its areas of responsibility. These requirements make it incumbent on those developing the cost accounting system to ensure that information will be available on a timely basis and in a simple form that is readily understood. Many cost accounting programs for which there was great hope fail because the data generated are not timely and are accurate at the price of disproportionate complexity.

Work Management and the Personnel Function

IN THE PRECEDING CHAPTERS the point has been made that a successful work management program becomes completely interwoven into the fabric of the company's operating mechanism. It becomes one of the many effective management tools that is used in the day-to-day decision-making process.

In their most popular and meaningful form, work management systems provide data on individual employee performance. It is obvious, then, that we are dealing not just with work but with people. Therefore, a key department that must coordinate its own activities with the work management effort is the personnel department. Work management and personnel departments are partners in the productivity improvement objective.

The personnel function, just like the other functions of the company, is experiencing an evolution. This is creating a new focus. Originally, personnel departments were nothing more than application-taking agencies that saw to it that there were sufficient warm bodies to interview. Then, with the advent of the emphasis on human relations, personnel managers saw themselves as the ombudsmen of the worker, whose job it was to protect the employee from the excesses of production-oriented managers. Today, the government has taken up the role of protecting employees and would-be employees from the excesses of employers.

Equal Employment Opportunity Commission (EEOC) and affirmative action plans can marry a company to an employee for as long as the employee wishes. If the company wants to end the marriage, there must be as much objective data as possible to support the company's position.

369

With the government taking over the role of protector of the employee, the personnel role has shifted again. The function is now looked upon as a contributor to company profitability. Where personnel administrators were once opposed to work measurement programs because of the apparent demands these programs placed on the worker, there now is the attitude that work management can help the personnel people to do their jobs even more effectively and protect the rights of both the company and the employee.

In this chapter, we will explore some of the practical relationships between the personnel and work management departments. We will also give practical examples of how to implement actual programs to use the data from work management in the personnel system.

FUNCTIONS OF THE PERSONNEL OR HUMAN RESOURCES DEPARTMENT

The more familiar term "personnel department" is being replaced by "human resources department." The latter term makes more sense. To maximize profits, a manager must plan, organize, motivate, and control all the available resources. In addition to money, machines, materials, and methods, the essential ingredient of manpower must also be managed. The emphasis on the proper management of people as a human resource ties together all the functions of personnel into a unified system. All the pieces of the system must interact and facilitate one another.

Work management is the best system for managing the work that people do. Since the skill and effort of employees, their personal motivation, the skill of the supervisor, and compensation all affect how well the job gets done, there is a natural tie-in of the human resources or personnel function and work management.

Before discussing the specifics of how the work management and personnel functions should interact, an overview of the potential areas of interaction, and the reasons for interaction, is in order.

Recruitment

Personnel should see to it that competent and qualified people are found to fill openings in the company. Naturally, the line manager wants people who will be productive as well as possess the other qualifications to do a good job. This is a key area for interaction. If you can recruit good people with the right qualifications, the battle for high productivity is half won.

Employee Training

It is rare that any individual would be able to sit down at any office job of substance and be productive immediately. Personnel should see to it that all new employees receive the proper training that gives them the skills to do a good job.

Supervisor Development

We said half the battle to good productivity is hiring good people. The other half is good supervision. Personnel should see to it that those people who have direct control over the human resources of the firm have the skills and leadership to perform the job properly.

Job Evaluation

To assure the ability of the company to attract and retain good people, the jobs in the organization must be ranked comparatively—in terms of complexity, skill required, and salary paid—with other jobs in the company, community, and industry. A solid job evaluation program based on facts will help attract the necessary qualified human resources.

Salary Administration

Every company must have a program to distribute salary dollars on an equitable basis. This is necessary because the salary dollar pot is not bottomless. Personnel sets the guidelines by publishing salary increase percentages which take into consideration where an employee stands in the salary range. Usually an employee below the midpoint of a range will receive a larger percentage increase than an employee above the midpoint of the range. Frequency of increases also must be determined. The primary objective of the salary administration program should be equity in employee remuneration.

In those organizations where the salary administration program is not tied to performance evaluation, the administration becomes easy. The only variables to consider are length of service and job classification. This approach is usually found in government or in quasi-government industries (teaching, the military, utilities, and the like).

Where salary increases are tied to performances, however, it is important to supervisors and employees to have a program that fairly identifies who should get what and how much. Usually, the personnel function will keep a close watch over how supervisors administer the salary program to be sure that all employees are being treated fairly.

Performance Evaluation

There are as many performance evaluation programs as there are companies. At least, there should be as many—maybe even more, because of the nature of different jobs within a company. However, all performance evaluation systems will eventually include the area of quantity of work.

Generally speaking, employees are not hired to be loyal, trustworthy, and clean, but rather to work. "To work" involves being present to process work and producing that work correctly. If shortcomings in loyalty, attitude, personal hygiene, cooperativeness, and so on hinder the productivity of the worker or those around him or her, then these factors are a subject for evaluation.

The personnel staff must see to it that evaluations are objective, consistent, and fair throughout the company. Therefore, the personnel manager will review the evaluations before filing them in employee folders. Personnel should also keep statistics to get a profile of performance evaluations throughout the company and within departments. The statistical profile will identify areas that are staffed with people who are in need of additional training, improved supervision, or a fairer evaluator.

Staffing

In service industries, personnel managers usually have some say about staff needs. From their position they evaluate staff requests and usually have the authority to question needs or ask for additional information to back up a request. This authority, as well as the responsibility, is exercised with a light hand in some companies and a much heavier hand in others. However, if the personnel manager is not attuned to the results of the work management program, then the effectiveness of work management for staff control is either seriously weakened or completely eliminated. If work management data indicate the potential for reduction but at the same time the personnel department is evaluating requests for replacements or additions to staff without consulting the factual data available from the work management program, then both the personnel function and work management program are weakened.

INTEGRATING THE TWO

How does a company go about integrating the work management activities with the personnel function? Before we answer this question it is important to eliminate any possible misunderstanding by a reader who may infer that we advocate an organizational integration.

Many companies do place the work management function in the personnel department. Because of the natural tie-in, this organizational structure often works very well. However, unless the personnel manager is also aware of the methods and procedures skills the work management staff must apply, it is better to associate work management with the methods and procedures function or the financial control function rather than with personnel. Experience shows that functionally, coordination is better when work management is organizationally aligned with the methods and procedures department and coordinates its activities with the personnel department in areas of overlap.

Cross-Orientation

Keeping in mind the preceding points on organization, the first step in coordinating the two functions is to cross-orient the staffs. The work management staff should receive training and orientation in the skills of supervision as well as the activities of the personnel staff. They must thoroughly understand the hiring process, the training techniques, the employee evaluation procedures, the job evaluation and salary administration policies and program, and the disciplinary procedures.

On the other hand, the personnel staff must have a solid understanding and appreciation of the work management system, including the program objectives, the benefits and accuracy of the program, the record-keeping system, the reports and how to interpret them, and the responsibilities of the supervisor under the program.

This cross-orientation will result in work management analysts being more understanding and aware of the problems of supervision and the supervisor. It will also encourage the personnel staff to recognize where the work management system can assist them by providing objective facts.

Recruitment Activities

The current concept of a human resources department advocates the definition of needs and development of skills for each job in the company. By matching the needs of the job with prospective candidates for the job, the chances for success in terms of hiring a qualified employee are greatly enhanced.

The work management program provides detailed documentation of how each task of a job should be performed. An analysis of this documentation by the personnel recruiter will identify precisely what skills and abilities will be required of candidates. This factual knowledge of job content will enable the recruiter to answer general questions about the job and assist the candidate in evaluating whether this job is one he or she would be interested in performing. It could save the valuable time of everyone to be precise at this stage of the recruiting process.

In addition, it is during the recruitment phase that a job candidate should learn about the work management program. Job candidates should be told something to this effect: "Our company believes that each employee's contribution should be fairly evaluated. We have a formal work management program, from which each supervisor determines how much work should be accomplished by each employee versus how much is actually accomplished. Good performance is recognized, and situations where additional training or other improvements must take place are identified. Should you be hired for this job, you will be given more details about this important program."

Employee Training

Assuming that there is sufficient work to be done, the knowledge and ability of the employee to perform that work will affect his productivity. Again, the documentation of the method required to perform the job will identify the skills needed. In addition, the actual performance data for each employee will help identify who needs more training and in what areas.

If the job involves spending a large percentage of time operating office equipment, the ability to operate that equipment will determine that employee's performance. All too often we find employees who lack the skills to do a good job. How many accounting clerks who use an electronic calculator have had any formal training in the proper use of the ten-key keyboard? The authors have seen far too many employees left on their own to learn how to use valuable equipment, with perhaps the help of a business equipment salesman who runs through the functions and features of the machine.

Fifteen years ago, it was a sign of high status for a clerical employee to have a telephone on the desk. Today, virtually everyone has a telephone on the desk. It is fairly safe to say that 75 percent or more of these people have had no formal instruction on the proper use of that telephone. These examples could continue. The operation of computer terminals, customer service techniques, and, most important, the proper understanding of the computer system that an employee uses daily are essential. (By computer system, we mean the particular system the employee must use, such as the "premium billing system" in insurance companies, or the "customer information file" in banks.)

Work management program information will also point out the areas where more broad-based training is needed. It is up to the personnel function to design and conduct these training programs and up to the supervisor to support and participate in them.

Learning curves, which will enable the supervisor to predict how long it will take a new employee to become properly trained, are an invaluable aid in monitoring a new employee's progress. Although there are some very technical approaches to developing learning curves, each supervisor can develop his or her own curves on the basis of actual experience with new employees by plotting their performance each week to monitor progress, summarizing those results, and making adjustments to compensate for unusual skills of trainees or abnormal workflows.

Supervisor Training

The personnel department must also be aware of those supervisors who need further training and development of interpersonal skills. This training is most effective when the work management program is tied into each of the areas discussed. Subjects such as motivation, counseling, group behavior, work structuring, time management, and planning and controlling work all relate to productivity and work management. The topics of job evaluation, performance appraisal, hiring, disciplining, and termination procedures also should make use of data from the work management program.

One of the most effective approaches to tie these subjects together with work management is for the personnel staff to discuss the supervisory function and for a work management representative to discuss the practical tie-in to the program.

Job Evaluation

The key to a successful job evaluation program is to ensure that employees and supervisors perceive it as being fair and equitable. In an effort to gain input from all areas of the company, job evaluation committees are usually composed of managers representing a cross-section of the company. Although this tends to interject a larger degree of objectivity into the evaluation process, it sometimes causes problems when committee members are basically unfamiliar with the job being reviewed.

The authors have also observed that even those committee members who have first-hand knowledge of the positions being evaluated are influenced by their personal impressions of the person(s) or results of the job. This colors their knowledge of the true nature of the job.

To combat these situations and maintain credibility, many firms have found it effective to use the information contained in the task outlines prepared by the work management analysts. The task outlines should be used as detailed documents supporting the more general job description or job outline. Since any one job outline could have several task outlines to cover the same job, the job evaluation committee can acquire a much better understanding of exactly what the position in question involves.

One of the best approaches to integrating these functions is to have a knowledgeable representative from the work management function be a voting member of the job evaluation committee. As a job comes up for review, the job analyst prepares the outline or description. The work management representative would gather the proper task outlines that apply to the job. In addition, the distribution of hours required to perform each task over a period of a week or month would be calculated to demonstrate the relative importance of each task performed. These times will serve as an aid in evaluating true job complexity and will prevent infrequently occurring complex or simple tasks from biasing judgment of job responsibility. This information would be made available to the other members of the committee. Then, as the committee reviews such statements in the job outline as "Knowledge of job required—must be thoroughly knowledgeable in accounting principles and practices," the task outlines can be consulted, which may reveal that the employee "makes entries into account 995 on a daily basis via computer terminal." The two statements can now be reconciled and the proper evaluation made.

Data from the work management program can also show where most of the time is spent. Job titles such as "administrative assistant" can be further defined as to how much time is actually spent on what duties. Often, what is intended for a position is not necessarily what it turns out to be. Employees reshape jobs, and the boss's plans do not always work out as intended. The work management information reflects what is truly happening.

Performance Evaluation

Most supervisors agree that the toughest part of their job is to pass judgment on an employee's performance. With a work management program, the supervisor has more facts available about the quantity and quality of work. It becomes a major advantage to both employees and the supervisor when a supervisor can use these facts in the performance evaluation process.

Although production is not the only criterion for judging overall performance, it is one of the major areas to be considered. A typical "Quantity of Work" section of an employee evaluation form provides for evaluation in terms of four rough categories, such as "very good," "acceptable," "below acceptable," and "unsatisfactory." Unfortunately these terms have very little meaning without some additional, objective criteria. Once objective criteria are available through work management, it is best to eliminate these terms and enter the actual employee performance on the form, as illustrated in Figure 30-1.

An employee's performance should be evaluated over a period of time to identify trends. Although it is informative to keep performance data for a year, for performance evaluation purposes, the emphasis should be on the direction of the trend, as well as on the latest three to four months. One way to relate the time frame to the performances attained is to plot monthly performances on a graph. Figure 30-2 is an example of a graph of employee performance.

Figure 30-I. A suggested ''Quantity of Work'' section of an employee evaluation form.

Quantity of Work								
150% 125%		120% 105%		90%		75%	70% 60% 50%	
Excellent		Very Good	Good		Fair		Minimum	Unacceptable
Indicate performance average over last 13 weeks by checking appropriate area.								

Figure 30-2. Performance graph.

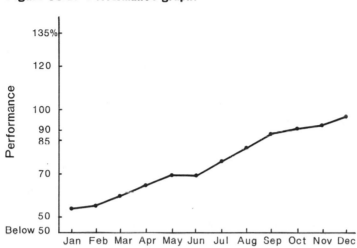

Such a graph introduces the time dimension that enables the supervisor to consider trends rather than just one unrelated performance statistic. These graphs can also serve as the basis for the development of learning curves as previously discussed. One Eastern bank has these graphs maintained by individual employees so there will be no surprises at the time of annual or interim performance appraisal.

There also should be some relationship between the overall evaluation and the performance level of the employee. Figure 30-3 shows one way to build some

Figure 30-3. Sample of "Overall Performance" section an employee evaluation form.

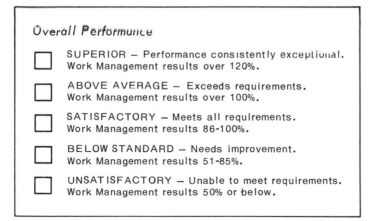

relationship between an employee's quantity-of-work performance and the overall evaluation.

Again, it should be pointed out that work management data are not the sole criteria for a performance evaluation. If a supervisor feels that an employee who is performing at 85 percent should be given an overall rating of "superior," as long as that rating is supported by facts, management should accept it. This works in the reverse also. A consistently excellent 120 percent performer should receive a "superior" overall evaluation unless there are facts to the contrary.

Salary Administration

Since salary administration is intended to reward employees in proportion to their contribution, again the objective data of the work management program should influence the process. Top performers in the department should generally receive a larger part of the salary increase budget than less effective employees. Performance data should be reviewed to determine whether the planned amount of salary increase for a specific employee is still appropriate, or whether it should be higher or lower. An employee who does not receive the proper salary treatment will, not surprisingly, become unhappy with the job.

Naturally, the most dramatic tie-in of work management data to salary administration is the various wage incentive plans covered in Chapter 28. Whether it be a direct incentive payment under one of the plans described, or a better relationship of performance to merit increases, the reward feature of salary must be handled properly. Work management helps the supervisor do just that.

Staffing

Staffing is one of the more obvious areas where work management and personnel functions work together. To be successful, however, the relationship should be a formal one, and should involve the requesting line department as well. The relationship should include providing data for the need to replace employees who are vacating jobs or to add employees to the current complement. The other major area of collaboration is in projecting staff needs of the organization in the future, known as "manpower planning."

The whole subject of staffing is very sensitive to supervisors and managers. Inherent in their positions is control over how many people they need to get the job done. Any intrusion into this area by a staff department is looked upon by line managers as reducing their responsibility and control. Therefore, the best approach in this key area is to enable supervisors to calculate their own staffing needs using the staffing formulas approved by management. Any involvement by the staff areas of personnel or work management should be on the basis of recommendations rather than edicts.

Figure 30-4. Sample Request for Personnel form.

REQUEST FOR PERSONNEL	DATE NEEDED

DEPARTMENT	UNIT	POSITION

☐ Replacement for_____
EMPLOYEE'S NAME

Reason for Termination: ☐ Promotion   ☐ Transfer   ☐ Left Co.

☐ Addition   ☐ New Position   ☐ Current Position

STAFFING DATA:

CURRENT STAFF	WORK MANAGEMENT STAFF REC.	OVER/UNDER

APPROVALS:

_____   _____
DEPARTMENT HEAD   SUPERVISOR

_____   _____
DIVISION HEAD   DATE OF REQUISITION
(If staff data show overstaffing)

FOR PERSONNEL USE

☐ Approved_____   Assigned To: _____
                    DATE   EMPLOYEE

☐ Not Approved

Remarks:

INSTRUCTIONS:
1. Complete all data, including staffing data prior to sending request to Personnel Department.
2. If staffing data indicate overstaffing situation, signature of Division Head is required before sending to Personnel Department.

To facilitate the use of staffing data from the work management program for handling personnel requests, the form used for this purpose should include staffing data. Figure 30-4 is an example of how these data could be incorporated into a typical request for personnel.

Many supervisors will consult with the work management department before

Figure 30-5. Manpower planning—forecast for one year, XYZ Insurance Company.

Marketing Projection: To increase policy count by 24% next year.

Current Volume: 25,000 policies/year.   *Projected Volume Increase:* 6,000 policies/year.

Activities Affected	Projected Volume Increase/Month	Work Standard in Hours	Additional Standard Hours	Additional Staff Required*
Mail Service	750	.003 Hrs.	2.25	.02
Underwriting	520	1.200 Hrs.	624.00	5.17
Issue	508	.050 Hrs.	25.40	.21
Data Input	525	.062 Hrs.	32.55	.28
Premium Accounting	500	.053 Hrs.	26.50	.22
Records	508	.013 Hrs.	6.60	.06
Customer Services	333	.117 Hrs.	38.96	.32
Billing Services	2000	.016 Hrs.	32.00	.27
Total monthly standard hours:			788.26	6.55
Total additional staff required:				or
				6.6
				positions

*Staffing projections based on the addition of a 35% management reserve required for training, supervision, work not covered by standards, and absenteeism. Full-time equivalent employees calculated at 160 hours/month.

completing the staffing data on the Request for Personnel form. The work management analyst can develop objective staffing data that may confirm or contradict apparent needs. Suggestions for alternative methods to process or redistribute work can take place at this point.

A word is in order concerning the concept of "authorized staff." Many companies establish authorized staff levels for each department, based on whatever data are available. Then, when someone leaves the department, management in that department automatically issues a request for personnel. The personnel department will fill the request routinely if this returns the department to the authorized staff level. Any company that has a work management program should abandon the static "authorized staff" concept and use the "standard staff" concept explained in Chapter 22. Standard staff is more dynamic. It reflects personnel needs based on current workload trends. Each personnel request should be evaluated in light of current and projected workload on its own merits, and not filled merely because years ago an authorized staff level seemed appropriate.

Because work management bases its data on standards for each major task to be completed, it is an invaluable tool for manpower planning. As the marketing department sets its long-range goals, the projected sales can be translated into the actual effects on current workload. Standards can then be applied to the projected increase in volume and easily be converted into manpower needs. The results should be matched to present staffing needs and any major systems changes anticipated before the increase in volume is to be realized. The end result is a factually based manpower projection for which the company can budget, recruit, and train in anticipation of needs. Figure 30-5 is a simplified calculation of future manpower planning in the XYZ Insurance Company.

Summary

We have presented some of the important and more obvious areas where the personnel department and the work management department can coordinate their activities to make each be even more effective in assisting the organization to be more productive and make optimum use of its human resources. If this coordination is missing, the work management department cannot be as effective a force in the company. It also means that both the personnel department and line management are not using all the facts at their disposal to make important decisions. This will affect profit, customer service, and costs.

CHAPTER

The Office of the Future

AN OLD SAYING GOES, "Today is the tomorrow you worried about yesterday." If there is anything that is certain about the office of the future, it is that in many ways it will little resemble the office of the past. Advancing technology, the changing lifestyle of the worker, and the development of new products and services are only a few of the changes that will have impact on the office of tomorrow.

Work management programs have often been accused of being short-sighted. They report accurately on what has happened in the past, with little, if any, attempt to address what should be happening in the future. An understanding of what tomorrow's office may look like will provide a basis not only for planning an orderly transition from the office of today but also for adapting a work management program to the needs of the future.

THE PACE OF TECHNOLOGY

Not only has technology made great strides in the last hundred years, but advances are coming at an ever-increasing rate. One only has to look at the development of the typewriter to get a clear illustration of the pace of technology.

The first practical typewriter was developed by Christopher Sholes. Manufactured typewriters were first introduced by the Remington Arms Company in 1873. Sixty years later, in 1933, International Business Machines (IBM) introduced its Model 01 electric typewriter. The electric typewriter provided inventors with a means of solving the problem of repetitive typing, and in the late 1930s, automatic typing systems using punched paper tape similar to player piano rolls were developed.

In the 1960s IBM coined the term "word processing" with the invention of the magnetic-tape Selectric typewriter (MT/ST). That same decade the magnetic-card Selectric typewriter (MC/ST) was introduced. In a sense, the MC/ST created a magnetic document, the card, which could be readily stored, revised, and transmitted to other locations. The development of practical microprocessors and chip technology made text processing systems of the 1970s practical. The majority of these systems function with a cathode-ray tube (CRT), which severs dependence on paper for output. The "text processor" (formerly called a typist) could now create the written word in a form that could be readily converted, if necessary, into hard copy.

Once text was stored in magnetic medium, hard copy could be created by a variety of printers, or the text could be transmitted to another magnetic medium by wire or microwave or even to intelligent copiers or printing presses for reproduction.

The next leap forward will be to eliminate the text processor. This will become possible when a full vocabulary of the spoken language can be reproduced in machine-readable form on magnetic media without human intervention. Limited vocabulary is available in the 1980s.

In the field of computers, we have come a long way from the room-filling vacuum-tube computers of the past to the high-speed solid-state computers of today. Impact printers are being replaced by lasers. Comptometers and rotary mechanical calculators have been replaced by smaller, more reliable equipment available at a much lower cost. The rotary calculator, which cost $1,000 in the 1960s, compares unfavorably to a modern pocket calculator with a memory—and the latter may be obtained as reasonably as a free gift for renting an automobile.

The list of technological office improvements is extensive. The idle thoughts of just a few short years ago are now operating reality in the office of today. Technology exists in the 1980s to significantly change the office of the future. The development of that office will require planning skills and organizational skills far beyond those required up to the present time.

A LOOK AT THE FUTURE

A look at the office of the future may reveal that there is no office at all. The early beginnings of industry and manufacturing were handled on a decentralized basis. Early cottage industry was based on the premise that a representative would deliver raw materials to the home and later collect finished goods. Wool was spun into yarn and yarn knit into sweaters. In reality, the technology exists today to perform all essential office functions and yet virtually eliminate the office. Employees can have in their homes computer terminals linked directly to a centralized office. These terminals could have the capability to reproduce hard-copy materials if needed, access any files, and transmit completed work back to the central processor.

The impact of the non-office is staggering. Employers would not be required to maintain large headquarter buildings; there would be a commensurate decrease in the use of energy for heat and light; there would be less need for parking spaces, employee recreation areas, cafeterias, and the like. From an energy consumption point of view, such an office would have a significant impact on oil consumption and air pollution, and it would of course virtually eliminate rush-hour traffic.

While the office of the future may be no office at all, the sociological impact of such a drastic change in lifestyle may make the ultimate non-office practically unfeasible in the immediate future.

Let us assume, then, that the office itself will survive. What will this office look like? What types of people will work there? What will they do? How will they do it? Perhaps the best way to examine our office of the future is to look at one day in the life of a typical manager.

Our manager arrives at the office at a time which he basically determines. Although he is required to be present during certain hours in order to respond directly to the needs of his superiors and customers, his schedule is his own. A prominent feature of our manager's office is an array of electronic equipment. Almost totally absent are the files, pencils, forms, and other reference materials so common today. Our manager arrives at his desk without the briefcase which today's manager finds so indispensable to carry materials to and from work. This does not mean that our typical future manager works only in the office. When after-hours work is required, our manager of tomorrow, through a computer located in his home, can have all the information available at his fingertips to access any required files and to transmit completed work back to the office.

Upon reaching the office, the future manager might first review his mail. Unlike the mail most commonly used today, the manager of the future will read electronic mail. Mail will be accessed from a CRT display screen and will consist of internal files and correspondence transmitted to him electronically as well as images of mail which has arrived through normal postal channels.

The first piece of mail requires a response. Our manager accesses the correct files with his computer terminal and determines a course of action. The response to, say, a request for explanation of a budget variance is dictated to a central word processing department. Later in the morning, a flashing light indicates that his dictated memorandum has been completed. He reviews the draft of the memo on the display screen, making any required corrections. Once corrections are made, he authorizes distribution through electronic channels to those who are to receive the memorandum.

After lunch, our manager attends a conference with branch office managers throughout the company. By today's standards the conference may not be a successful one, since there are no hands to shake or cigar smoke to fill the air. The future manager's conference is held by television conference room connected to other similar conference rooms throughout the branch system. The pictures of our manager and his spoken words are transmitted by telephone lines or microwave or, in the case of a nationwide branch structure, are beamed from communication satellites hovering in geosynchronous orbits. If some manager attending the "meeting" displays graphs or charts depicting sales, work backlogs, or expenses, our manager can receive either an electronic or a hard copy of the exhibits with the press of a button.

The conference over, our manager returns to his office to dictate a memorandum to a far-flung sales staff. His dictation flows from his office to the word processing center, and once it is completed and approved, the word processing center electronically sends the message to the reprographics department, where an intelligent copier receives the electronic image and produces the required number of copies.

We could go on describing our manager's day in some detail. However, other aspects of the office of the future are even more exciting.

OFFICE ORGANIZATION

Today we are still accustomed to an office that is organized along product or functional responsibilities. A typical insurance organization includes an underwriting department where risks are selected or rejected, a data entry department where information is transformed into machine-readable language through key entry, and an accounting function where the policyholder is billed for his insurance. Similarly, in banks, one department collects credit information, a credit investigation department reviews the applicant's ability to pay, and a third department records payments made. In some larger organizations these responsibilities exist for separate products or services as a complete entity. In a multiple-line insurance company there might be one complete organizational structure for life insurance policies and a separate complete structure for casualty. Across the street in the large bank, individual lending and commercial lending might have their own organizational structures.

In the office of the future, as a result of improved communications and on-the-spot data entry, the organizations as we know them today will not function effectively. There will be too much overlap between functions to effectively process work without duplication of effort. The organization of the future will, in all likelihood, comprise fewer layers of management, and many functional units as we know them today will be eliminated.

As an example, with many people in the organization processing work by using CRTs, the need for centralized data entry will be greatly diminished and perhaps eliminated. Underwriters approving cases will, through sophisticated programming, transmit their approval via CRT in such a fashion that policy issue and billing are automatically authorized. In many organizations, a massive systems department will be required to keep track of the interrelationships of all operating functions and to produce the necessary programs to make them work effectively. The company that does not revise its organizational structure to meet changing methods of processing work will end up with confusion, duplication of effort, and the resultant higher cost.

The Employee of the Future

In the past several decades the role of the "clerk" has changed considerably. We ask the clerical employee of today to perform functions which a few years ago were considered the responsibility of technical employees. In the future we will make even more demands on our clerical employees, and the work they do will become even more complex as more and more work is produced through computer technology. Training curves, which at one time were a matter of days or weeks and in the 1970s stretched to months, may become even longer as work becomes more complex.

After World War II, almost everyone learned to type. While few became proficient at it, high school students, college students, and business students alike learned keyboard skills. In the 1960s it was less fashionable to admit that one knew how to type. One of the major problems of the 1960s and the 1970s was to recruit sufficient office employees with keyboard skills to handle the needs of word processing and data entry. We project that in the 1980s we will have come full circle and that keyboard skills will become a necessity for modern life. One only has to look at available home computer options for such household tasks as recipe storage, checkbook balancing, income tax accounting, and recreation to realize that more and more people will be using keyboards in the future. Modern young Americans are receiving early keyboard training in the classroom as they operate computerized self-learning aids.

Management has an upcoming obligation in the office of tomorrow to revise its thinking on keyboard skills. The current low-creativity entry-level positions of encoding machine operator, policywriter, or word processing specialist have provided management with the idea that employees who operate a key-driven piece of equipment need not be paid very much. Careful, unbiased evaluation of the new types of keyboard entry jobs that will be part of the office of the future will be required to create a salary structure where employees will be rewarded in proportion to the skill and effort they put into their jobs.

The Role of Work Management in the Future

As we have seen, the office of the future will be significantly different from the office of today. What will the role of work management be in the office of the future?

It should be obvious from our scenario of the office of the future that in the coming years, management will be spending millions upon millions of dollars on improving the technology of the office. The costs of the necessary hardware and of the programming support required to develop the systems of the future will be staggering. Part of the funds necessary for these conversions to automated systems will come from improved productivity of the employees of today, as monitored by productivity improvement programs similar to those we have discussed. Further, the extensive investment in hardware will require management to be even more precise in developing cost/benefit analyses for suggested hardware and software improvements. Work management data will play a vital role in this type of analysis.

Work management data for reporting the volume of work completed and the time required to complete it will be collected automatically. Internal monitoring systems in the software of tomorrow will record transaction counts and time required from internal clocks as employees go about their daily work. Employee performance data will become a by-product of processing runs, with time and volume data flowing directly to an automated performance reporting system for calculation of employee productivity and staffing.

There are already systems being developed or in use to do this. In the future, these will be the rule rather than the exception. Employees like to know where they stand in terms of expectations for performance and how well they measure up to these expectations. It will be possible for employees at the end of a work period to receive their current performance data, past performance history, and other pertinent data regarding work quality by requesting them at their own CRT.

Just as we have discussed the possibility of electronic mail in the future, electronic reporting is also viable. Managers will be able to review the performance of individual employees and the group as a whole for analysis and remedial action.

If the ultimate office of the future—the un-office—becomes a reality, work management's role will become increasingly important. The emphasis we now place on being in attendance at the workplace will considerably diminish. Employees will increasingly operate out of their homes and, in essence, be paid a piece-work wage. It will become difficult, in the un-office of the future, to monitor how much time an employee spends working and how much time cleaning the home or tending children. Employee compensation, therefore, will have to be based on the volume of work completed. Office standards will provide the basis for establishing wages in this type of environment. When this occurs, we will have returned to the piece-work wage structure common at the turn of the century.

The office of the future will require more sophisticated measurement techniques. In the late 1970s, third-generation predetermined time systems similar to Advanced Office Controls became computerized. Procedure writing became a by-product of the creation of standards. As the office work force changes, measurement techniques themselves will change to reflect new job complexities. Emphasis and research on decision times and analysis will lead us to a fourth-generation time system that will make it even easier to measure technical activity. Ultimately, the creation of software for job processing may automatically establish performance standards through use of an advanced form of predetermined times.

A soundly developed, properly maintained work management system will become, as we have seen, an essential part of the office of the future. Making the transition to that office will be a challenge for managers, systems specialists, and the developers of hardware. An orderly transition will be possible only through the use of a sound data base from a work management program as an aid to decision making and proper staffing of functions.

Responsible management has an obligation to employees and stockholders to plan this transition smoothly in order to fully assess the impact of change and to pave the way for massive expenditures required to move to the office of the future. The company that is slow to change its office structure will be overwhelmed by those quick to seize the initiative. A poorly organized and inefficient office today will preclude taking maximum advantage of the new technology. The manager of tomorrow will be an initiator, a planner, a decision maker, an organizer. The more flexibility the future computer gives us, the more these skills will be required.

Even as we complete the manuscript for this book, the day's headlines tell us the already amazing microprocessor chip has been improved to handle six times more capacity. If it does not hit the market soon, it will be outmoded by technology under development. Doing the best job possible today with wise use of available resources will assure our presence tomorrow when all these great things will become routine.

Index